P9-CAD-596

HAMMOND®

NATURE ATLAS OF AMERICA

Photographers:

Erwin A. Bauer

Bill Browning

Bruce Coleman

Steve Collins

Ed Cooper

Thase Daniel

Harry Engels

Richard B. Fischer

John H. Gerard

Shelly Grossman

Walter J. Kenner

Leonard Lee Rue III

Jack Wilburn

Joseph Van Wormer

Josephine von Miklos

Robert Zappalorti

and others

Contributing Authors:

Gerard A. Bertrand—**Fishes**

Donald J. Borror—**Insects**

George Porter—**Reptiles & Amphibians**

HAMMOND

NATURE ATLAS

Rocks & Minerals Trees Wildflowers Birds Insects

Fishes Mammals Reptiles & Amphibians

by Roland C. Clement

OF AMERICA

A RIDGE PRESS BOOK | HAMMOND INCORPORATED, MAPLEWOOD, NEW JERSEY

Editor-in-Chief: **Jerry Mason**
Editor: **Adolph Suehsdorf**
Art Director: **Albert Squillace**
Associate Editor: **Moira Duggan**
Associate Editor: **Barbara Hoffbeck**
Associate Editor: **Jean Walker**
Art Associate: **David Namias**
Art Associate: **Mark Liebergall**
Art Production: **Doris Mullane**

Maps prepared by Hammond Incorporated
Special Projects Editor: **Ernest Dupuy**

Copyright 1973 in all countries of the International Copyright Union
by The Ridge Press, Inc. and Hammond Incorporated.
All rights reserved. No part of this book may be reproduced
or utilized in any form or by any means, electronic or mechanical,
including photocopying, recording or by any information storage or retrieval
system without permission in writing from the Publisher.
Prepared and produced by The Ridge Press, Inc.

Library of Congress Cataloging in Publication Data
Clement, Roland C
Nature atlas of America.
"A Ridge Press book."
1. Natural history—North America. I. Title.
QH102.C57 500.9'7 73-7524
ISBN 0-8437-3511-2
Printed and bound in Italy by Mondadori Editore, Verona

Acknowledgements

The section on Reptiles & Amphibians was prepared by George Porter, author of *The World of Frogs and Toads*, an expert nature photographer, and controller of the National Audubon Society.

The section on Fishes was prepared by Dr. Gerard A. Bertrand, marine biologist and currently Assistant Senior Scientist with the Council on Environmental Quality, Washington, D.C.

The section on Insects was prepared by Dr. Donald J. Borror, professor of entomology at Ohio State University. He is the author of several important textbooks, co-author of *A Field Guide to the Insects*, and an expert in the study of bird song by electronic recording devices.

To these gentlemen I acknowledge a great debt for sharing their knowledge and insights and speeding my task.

R. C. C.

CONTENTS

MAPS

1. OUR AM

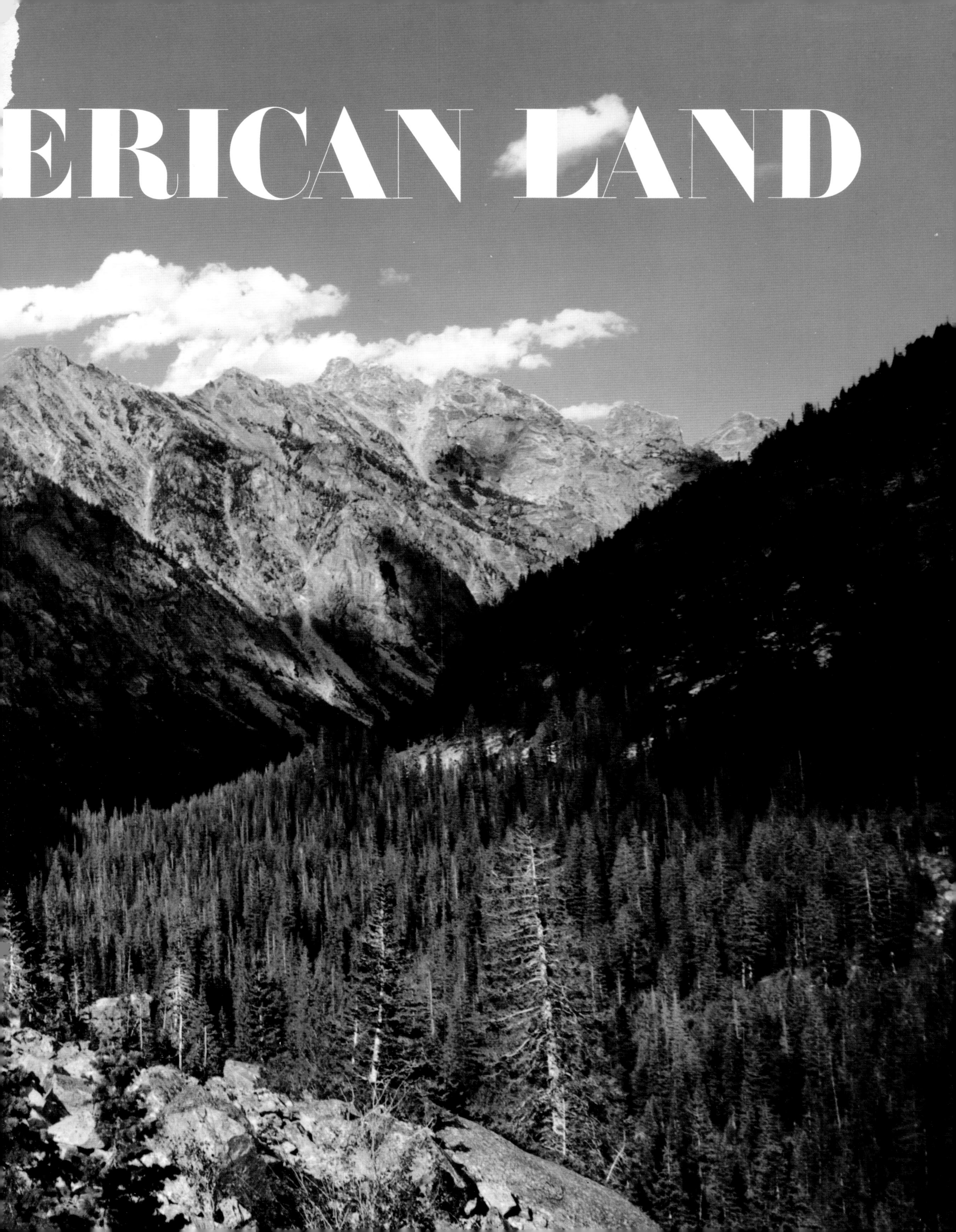
ERICAN LAND

9. COLUMBIA ICEFIELD
BANFF NAT PK
Calgary
8. LAST MOUNTAIN LAKE
Regina
B.C.
WATERTON LAKES NAT PK
ALTA.
SASK.
MAN
54. NORTH CASCADES NAT PK
Seattle
55. OLYMPIC NAT PK
56. MT RAINIER NAT PK
53. GLACIER NAT PK
Great Falls
WA
Portland
57. COLUMBIA RIVER GORGE
58. HELLS CANYON
60. CRATER LAKE NAT PK
59. MALHEUR NAT WR
52. YELLOWSTONE NAT PK
MT
ND
Cody
40. DEVILS TOWER NAT MON
39. BLACK HILLS
Rapid City
Medford
Idaho Falls
61. REDWOOD NAT PK
Eureka
OR
51. GRAND TETON NAT PK
38. BADLANDS NAT MON
SD
ID
50. BEAR RIVER NAT WR
WY
49. GREAT SALT LAKE
Salt Lake City
37. PLATTE RIVER BOTTOMS
48. DINOSAUR NAT MON
41. PAWNEE NAT GRASSLAND
San Francisco
Denver
62. YOSEMITE NAT PK
Merced
Monterey
42. BLACK CANYON OF THE GUNNISON
63. DEATH VALLEY NAT MON
47. ZION NAT PK
64. BIG SUR COAST
Kanab
UT
Durango
65. SEQUOIA NAT PK
NV
43. MESA VERDE NAT PK
CO
Las Vegas
46. GRAND CANYON NAT PK
66. LOS PADRES NAT FOREST
Los Angeles
Flagstaff
Oklahoma City
36. WICHITA MTS NAT WR
CA
Roswell
45. SAGUARO NAT MON
Tucson
44. CARLSBAD CAVERNS NAT PK
NM
AZ
Marathon
35. BIG BEND NAT PK
67. SCAMMON LAGOON
34. ARANSAS NAT WR
Corpus Christi
MEX.

A NATURALIST'S AMERICA

A NATURALIST'S AMERICA

The preceding map and the following keyed descriptions of outstanding natural areas provide an index to favorite American environments accessible by automobile. Many other areas could compete successfully for a place in such a list, but those listed here represent an impressive cross section of the natural diversity of the United States and adjacent Canada.

1. Bonaventure Island, near the little town of Percé at the tip of the Gaspé Peninsula, Quebec, is an impressive whaleback island of red sandstone and conglomerate hardly a mile offshore. It has one of the finest Gannet colonies of North America, plus other nesting sea birds.

2. Gaspésie Provincial Park, Quebec, has miles of spruce-fir forest, and two notable peaks, Mt. Albert (a botanist's mecca) and Mt. Jacques Cartier. It also has the only caribou south of the St. Lawrence River, and one of the best populations of Wood Warblers in North America.

3. Saguenay River, which connects Lake St. John with the north shore of the St. Lawrence River, near Tadoussac, Quebec, is a fine fjord cut by glacial ice.

4. Fundy National Park, near Alma, New Brunswick, at the head of the Bay of Fundy, has spectacular tides. On a rising tide the water comes in so fast over the flats that a prominent wave of water, a tidal bore, sweeps up the bay.

5. Algonquin Provincial Park, in central Ontario, is fine North Woods canoe water and still has a few wolves.

6. Point Pelee National Park, in southwest Ontario, near Windsor and Detroit, has a spectacular autumn migration of small birds and hawks, especially when northwest winds blow in September and October.

7. Quetico–Superior Boundary Waters Canoe Area is astride the international boundary between Ontario and Minnesota. Heavily used by youth groups in summer, it still has a few wolves.

8. Last Mountain Lake, north of Regina, Saskatchewan, has, especially at the north end, spectacular gatherings of Sandhill Cranes every autumn, the peak of their flight being in late September.

9. Columbia Icefield, on the boundary between Banff and Jasper National Parks on the Alberta–British Columbia boundary, is the largest area of glacial ice south of the Arctic Circle. It is currently melting back at about 50 feet per summer.

10. Mount Katahdin, in Baxter State Park, Maine, is an attractive flat-topped monadnock 5268 feet high, and is the northern terminus of the 2000-mile long Appalachian Trail, which extends southward to Springer Mountain, Georgia.

11. Acadia National Park, centering on Bar Harbor, Maine, is small as National Parks go, but picturesque. It combines glacially-polished granite mountains, a good sample of the rocky seacoast of Maine, with attractive tide pools and spruce woodland.

12. Mount Washington, elevation 6280 feet, is the highest peak in the Northeast. The Alpine Gardens on the easterly flank, accessible by hiking trail or carriage road from Pinkham Notch House, are the most accessible arctic-alpine flower habitats in the East. The mountain is noted for its violent weather.

13. Cape Cod National Seashore, near Chatham, Massachusetts, preserves fine dune country and extensive tidal flats that are important shore-bird feeding and resting grounds. The Massachusetts Audubon Society's Ludlow Griscom Sanctuary in North Eastham offers guided tours of the flats from mid–July to mid–September, when migration is at its peak.

14. Block Island Ferry Route, between Point Judith and Block Island, is a pleasant ten-mile ride offering good sea-birdwatching opportunities (petrels, shearwaters, jaegers, and gannets) between June and October. After northeast winds in September and October, Block Island swarms with small birds. The Audubon Society of Rhode Island conducts an annual weekend field trip there in mid–October.

15. Jamaica Bay Bird Sanctuary, on Cross Bay Boulevard, Queens, is a surprising area to see bird life winter or summer. On a clear day the skyscrapers of Manhattan are on one horizon and the jets of Kennedy International Airport take off on the other. A city-managed area, it is accessible by auto or by subway train.

16. Hudson River Gorge, from West Point southward, has spectacular western walls of columnar basalt. It continues as a submarine canyon to the edge of the continental shelf.

17. Adirondack Forest Preserve, larger than the East's National Parks, is a bit of the North Woods within a day's drive of New York City, with a myriad of lakes and peaks and attendant northern wildlife. Geologically, it is part of the ancient Canadian Shield.

18. Watkins Glen is one of several fine, narrow gorges cut through alternating beds of sandstone and shale that are preserved as State Parks in the beautiful Finger Lakes country of central New York.

19. Genesee River Gorge, in Letchworth State Park, is perhaps the finest gorge in the East, cut in limestone and sandstone.

20. Hawk Mountain Bird Sanctuary, a private sanctuary in the Kittatinny Ridge, near Orwigsburg, Pennsylvania, is famous for the autumnal flights of migrating hawks and eagles—best from late August through October.

21. Brigantine National Wildlife Refuge, on the New Jersey coast just north of Atlantic City, is a mecca for the birdwatchers of the metropolitan regions of Philadelphia and New York. Nesting herons, migrating shore birds, and wintering waterfowl, including most of the wintering population of Brant, are present in numbers.

22. Cape May, New Jersey, like Point Pelee in Ontario, is a funnel for migrating birds of many kinds—including hawks—that are pushed eastward by northwest winds in September and October, and follow the coast southward to Cape May before crossing Delaware Bay.

23. Cape Hatteras National Seashore protects 75 miles of barrier beach and lagoon noted for wintering waterfowl and migrating shore birds.

24. Cape Romain National Wildlife Refuge has, on Bulls Island, South Carolina, one of the most pleasant of the wooded barrier islands of the Southeast, as well as interesting wildlife year-round.

25. Okefenokee National Wildlife Refuge is the largest cypress swamp region left in the deep South, over 500 square miles in extent.

26. John Pennekamp Coral Reef State Park, off Key Largo at the base of the Florida Keys, provides access to the wonders of snorkling on a coral reef among colorful fish and other life.

27. Everglades National Park's unique, tropical habitat includes the southern end of the "river of grass," which was the original everglades, wooded hammocks, and extensive mangrove swamp. Its future, and that of its remarkable wildlife, is threatened by conflicts over water.

28. Corkscrew Swamp Sanctuary, reached via Naples or Immokalee, has a mile-long boardwalk through an impressive cypress swamp, with alligators, otter, and the largest nesting colony of Wood Storks in the United States. The National Audubon Society charges a fee for admission.

29. Great Smoky Mountains National Park is the finest forest region in the East, backed by fine national forests, but under threat of excessive road-building. The Black Bear is common here. Cade's Cove at the western end is a touching cultural relict of the past.

30. Mammoth Cave National Park's 150 miles of caverns 300 feet below ground, all cut into limestone, are one of the natural wonders of the world. The year-round temperature in the caves is 54°F.

31. Mississippi Delta and the great meandering loops of the river above it are among the most dynamic geological features in the country. A National Wildlife Refuge at the tip of the delta is especially interesting in spring.

32. Atchafalaya Swamp is an old distributary of the Mississippi River, an unusual wildlife area, and now under study as a national recreation area.

33. Louisiana Marshes, extending from the Texas border to the Mississippi Delta, are a great wildlife area, and the winter home of most of America's Lesser Snow and Blue Geese. Several Federal, state, and private wildlife refuges are scattered throughout.

34. Aransas National Wildlife Refuge is the

Pages 8-9: Grand Teton National Park, Wyoming

winter home of the stately Whooping Crane and an outstanding refuge in its own right.

35. Big Bend National Park will hopefully be an international park some day because the incised meanders of the Rio Grande river that form part of the boundary with Mexico—the magnificent Santa Elena and Boquillas Canyons—and other geological-wildlife features of this rugged area are all deserving of protection.

36. Wichita Mountains National Wildlife Refuge, with its herds of bison, elk, antelope, and Texas Longhorn Cattle, is one of the showplaces of the National Wildlife Refuge System.

37. Platte River Bottoms, especially between Lexington and Grand Island, Nebraska, are the staging grounds for some 200,000 Sandhill Cranes during March, along with White-fronted Geese and many other waterfowl, constituting one of the great wildlife spectacles of America.

38. Badlands National Monument includes 400 square miles of colorful, spectacularly eroded features in soft sedimentary rock located in a semiarid climate where cloudbursts are the principal precipitation.

39. Black Hills, rising out of the prairie, include two attractive parks—Custer State Park and Wind Cave National Park—with bison, antelope, and prairie dogs, plus interesting limestone caves.

40. Devils Tower National Monument is an impressive plug of fluted or columnar basalt, each column ten feet or so in diameter, rising 865 feet above the Wyoming prairie. It has one of the northernmost Prairie Dog towns, and the cottonwood groves of the nearby Belle Fourche River must have been a favorite, winter camping ground of Indians of the Great Plains.

41. Pawnee National Grassland, northeast of Fort Collins, Colorado, is an intensively studied remnant of short-grass prairie, delightful in June, when the prairie flowers are in bloom and its birds sing on the wing.

42. Black Canyon of the Gunnison, a National Monument near Montrose, Colorado, is one of the most impressive geological areas of its size in the country. The narrow gorge cuts 2000 feet and more through some of the oldest rock on the continent.

43. Mesa Verde National Park's stone pueblos built into great sandstone ledges offer a penetrating look back into the past of America's first people, a reminder that man and nature have always been one, though many.

44. Carlsbad Caverns National Park not only is a magnificent example of geological and crystalline processes in limestone, but also the summer roost of a large population of Mexican Free-tailed Bats who leave their caves in a smoky stream every evening near sunset. After feeding on the wing all night long, they plummet back into their caves at dawn.

45. Saguaro National Monument, in two sections, is an extraordinary landscape and an intriguing example of nature's adaptive ways, in this case with large tree cacti called saguaro. One of the "musts" for anyone interested in plants.

46. Grand Canyon National Park is generally conceded to be the most impressive inanimate feature of the continent. Many people prefer the lookouts of its North Rim.

47. Zion National Park has some of the most colorful, most massive sandstone and limestone cliffs and canyons on the continent, and its tree-lined Virgin River bottoms are delightful botanizing and birding areas.

48. Dinosaur National Monument protects over 300 square miles of spectacular canyon country and a quarry that displays dinosaur skeletons *in situ*, the later probably being the nation's finest interpretive display.

49. Great Salt Lake, though now much imposed upon by a burgeoning metropolitan center, is a natural wonder every U.S. traveler should know and swim in. The perched beach terraces of old glacial Lake Bonneville that surround Great Salt Lake tell a fascinating story.

50. Bear River National Wildlife Refuge, protected from the salt of Great Salt Lake by a network of dikes, is one of the great, migratory waterfowl crossroads of America, especially worth seeing during the late autumn migration peak.

51. Grand Teton National Park lifts great, gray, fault-block mountains to the western sky and challenges mountain climbers. Moose live in the marshy hollows and elk work up and down the slopes with the seasons.

52. Yellowstone National Park was the first and is still the largest park, famous for geysers and hot springs, Black Bears and Grizzly Bears (though the latter have recently been thinned and scattered by better refuse management), moose, elk, and bison.

53. Glacier National Park, in its combination of geologic, scenic, and biotic features, is the favorite of many American park connoisseurs. The sedimentary mountains of its eastern front are the most impressive of the northern Rockies. With Waterton Lakes National Park in Alberta, it forms a marvelous international park.

54. North Cascades National Park, because of its active sculpturing by glaciers, is the most spectacular alpine scenery in the United States.

55. Olympic National Park, on the Olympic Peninsula, has more rain than any other area in the country (140″) and, having a mild climate, has therefore the lushest vegetation north of the American tropics—forests hung with mosses, ferns, etc.

56. Mount Rainier National Park centers on a dormant volcano made all the more impressive because its 14,410-foot massif rises directly from the Pacific Coast lowlands. Its glaciers are among the most impressive, and its alpine flowers the most colorful, anywhere in the continental United States.

57. Columbia River Gorge, between Portland and The Dalles, Oregon, is a worthy western counterpart of the East's Hudson River Gorge.

58. Hells Canyon is where northeastern Oregon juts farthest east and is separated from Idaho by the northward-flowing Snake River. The river cuts a spectacular canyon along the eastern edge of the great Columbia River Basalt outflow.

59. Malheur National Wildlife Refuge, though now much constricted by agriculture's insatiable demands for cheap irrigation water, is still a semi-desert wildlife paradise, both during the nesting season and during fall migration.

60. Crater Lake National Park is a gem whose Crater Lake, deep in the throat of collapsed volcanic Mount Mazama (a caldera), has the bluest water imaginable. The subalpine trees of the crater rim make a circumferential hike among the greatest pleasures of America's outdoors.

61. Redwood National Park is a stripling park for the nation to commit to the preservation of the most impressive living things on Earth. The way to savor it is to walk its trails at dawn before truck traffic shatters the quiet and mystery of cathedral-like aisles whose columns rise straight up 200 to 300 feet.

62. Yosemite National Park, as its fame suggests, has some of the finest scenery in the country, including sheer faces of shining granite, waterfalls, and mountain meadows. It has been badly abused by excessive visitation and incongruous activity, however, and is the first park to which it will be necessary to limit access.

63. Death Valley National Monument includes the lowest place on the continent, 282 feet below sea level, some of the most colorful desert scenery in the country, volcanic formations, and interesting flora and fauna.

64. Big Sur Coast presents some of the most attractive seascapes in the world, extensive kelp beds with Sea Otter, Sea Lions, and fascinating seasonal migrations of Gray Whales and birds. Northern California and Oregon also have similarly attractive coasts.

65. Sequoia National Park, on the western slope of the Sierra Nevada, harbors the Big Trees, a species of sequoia different from the Coast Redwood. Individually, these are as impressive as the Coast Redwoods, but their groves are more open, so the impact of their community is very different.

66. Los Padres National Forest, interesting in its own right, is famous as the principal home range of the remaining population of California Condors, comprising a mere 50 or so birds.

67. Scammon Lagoon National Park, in Baja California Sur, protects part of the spawning grounds of the Gray Whale. Most of the calving is done in February, after which the whales migrate north to the Arctic seas for the summer.

OUR AMERICAN LAND

This new *Nature Atlas of America* is a primer on American nature for the automobile age in which we live. A primer is a first orientation to its field. It is designed to satisfy initial curiosity and to arouse interest in delving more deeply. In an age of overspecialization such as ours, it is particularly helpful to begin with an overview. This is what this primer attempts. A choice of examples is always difficult. To present only 50 or so examples of the hundreds or even thousands in each group from which they were selected is to run the risk of being superficial and slighting each subject. But if the user of this atlas will be patient and try at least to learn all of the things presented here, he or she will have acquired a background that even specialists often lack. This will take a little time, since the examples are scattered widely over the country, but the trick is to learn something on each trip and to keep reviewing and adding from trip to trip.

That we are tied to the automobile in our use of the American land is of course evident, not only from the number of cars on the road, but from the fact that in 1972 Americans made 211,621,100 visits to their National Parks.

There are about 5 million sleep-in vehicles in the United States, and in 1972 the National Parks accommodated 4,731,361 overnight stays by people using these vehicles. This book is thus very appropriately designed to add substance and interest to this new nomadism.

It is important to recall that North America was probably the richest lode of natural resources ever assembled on one continent. Our forebears were an energetic and innovative lot, but they were also very lucky. The land was largely temperate in climate and rich in minerals. It had the richest black prairie soils on the planet—and still does. The eastern deciduous forest was the finest of all the forests on Earth. There were two of the largest animal populations in the world—the American Bison and the Passenger Pigeon. There were, and still are, great stretches of coniferous forest, including the greatest evergreen trees of all: the two redwoods, the Douglasfir, and several superlative pines.

We have used this treasure profligately—with a cowboy's philosophy of "use, discard, and move on." The land is still rich but the bloom has decidedly been rubbed off. It is highly probable that our human population is already overextended, especially when we consider its heavy demand for natural resources. There are, in short, already too many of us for a quality existence to be maintained into the future. And a quality existence means one which provides adequate opportunities for all inhabitants to interact between the natural world and the world man has built himself within that original world—between the country and the city, where 75 percent of us now live.

Fortunately, life is lived one generation at a time, and we are now witness to a generational awakening to the importance of nature, now conceptualized as ecology. There has always been a voice in the wilderness — a Francis of Assisi, a Thoreau, a Muir, a Schweitzer, an Aldo Leopold, or a Rachel Carson. But today, thanks to the perhaps common insecurity created by our use of the atom and by the awareness of world events and of space created by television, a whole generation has been sensitized as never before to its dependence on the total environment, natural and man-made.

We are also realizing that material production is no longer a priority activity for us; that we need to strike a better balance. Production is basic, but no longer dominant as it was earlier and as it remains for much of the world. We are the first generation to be freed from the need to sweat for our bread, and the new interest in the natural world we are witnessing is both an escape from our overcrowded cities and a discovery made possible by the productivity of our socioeconomic system.

What is now needed is a little more sophistication in the rediscovery of America we are engaged in to make us aware that we need to zone our uses of the land in order to protect its diversity and its productivity.

For example, some habitats, which are at first glance not unique or very significant in themselves, turn out to be crucial to the survival of several migratory populations of mammals, birds, insects, and perhaps others. Monarch butterflies moving up and down both coasts of the United States are dependent on certain traditional wooded stopping places en route. Black Brant, small geese that move up and down the Pacific Coast annually, stop to rest only at a few quiet points of land where they can come ashore safely instead of being tumbled into the surf and drowned. Few of these places have as yet been reserved for them.

It is for such reasons that the oasis-like river bottoms of the American Southwest must no longer be converted to irrigation ditches, as has been the policy of the Bureau of Reclamation, the Corps of Engineers, the Soil Conservation Service, and many private landowners in search of more water. The cottonwood stands of the river bottoms are essential resting places for large numbers of small birds that breed in the northern United States and Canada and winter in Central and South America. Although these birds sometimes fly hundreds of miles at a time during their migrations, the extent of the arid and semiarid lands of the Southwest is a serious hazard unless it is broken by the ribbons of vegetation that grow in the river bottoms.

Our attitude toward the environment depends upon our understanding of both its interactions and how they affect us. Unfortunately, many of our attitudes are improperly founded on old science and other mistaken views of these realities. Paul Shepard, who wrote *Man In The Landscape*, and Kenneth Clark, who wrote *Landscape Into Art*, agree that many of us see only the surface of particular environments, a sort of picture-postcard view. Indeed, it was artists, beginning in the Middle Ages and especially during the eighteenth and nineteenth centuries, who taught us to see the landscape. But they abstracted from it, distorted it, and froze it for us.

Now we need to learn to see the landscape as a dynamic process involving physical, chemical, and biological systems—in short, as an ecosystem. It is much more important to be aware of the system than to know a lot about a few of its parts. And yet we become aware of the system by studying how the parts interact with one another. The trick is not to let details overwhelm us. This is what happens when one can not see the forest for the trees.

CYCLES AND PROCESSES

Our planet is fit to live on because it is almost the right distance from the sun, its source of energy. Its daily rotation on its own axis brings day and night because it is a process of turning away from and turning toward the sun. This prevents both overheating and freezing. The planet's long, elliptical circling of the sun yields the seasons because, mostly, it changes the inclination of the sun's rays. Direct rays warm quickly, and burn. But inclined rays warm much less.

The changing seasons and especially the daily rotation of our planet create the climates because currents are set in motion in both the oceans and the atmosphere by these changes—currents that tend to be pushed toward the poles. The air currents, which we feel as wind, push on the ocean surface and create waves and accelerate the ocean currents. The Gulf Stream is a result of this planetary system and so are the regular cyclonic storms, hurricanes, tornados, and thunderstorms we all know. The violent phenomena just mentioned are of course complicated by the physics of air and moisture when their temperature changes. A thunderstorm, generated by heat but often producing hail, is one of the planet's most extraordinary phenomena.

Scientists have computed that if all moisture in the atmosphere were precipitated uniformly over the Earth's surface at one time, the result would be a mere two inches of water. And yet the average annual precipitation of the planet is more than two feet of water. We see, then, that rainfall is very unevenly distributed — New York City receives about 45 inches and Los Angeles less than 20 inches annually—but, more importantly, that the Earth's supply is constantly replenished. Since it does not come from outside, it must be recycled.

This is what the hydrologic cycle is all about. Water is evaporated from the surface of the sea and lakes by the sun's heat. It enters the atmosphere as water vapor. This vapor is later condensed back to water when the air that carries it is cooled enough; and the resulting water droplets are then precipitated out of the atmosphere when the air is cooled further, enough to "wring" it out. This process will go on so long as the sun shines on our planet. It cools the air, scrubs it clean every time it rains or snows, and it nourishes plant and animal life. The map on pages 74–75 shows the distribution of rainfall in the United States and has superimposed upon it lines that summarize our experience with growing seasons, the latter a result of both available moisture and temperature. The map on pages 198–199 shows the effect of topography, climate, and vegetation in converting rainfall to runoff into river basins.

Because the life process is dependent on water, oxygen, and a score of so of mineral elements—chiefly carbon, hydrogen, nitrogen, phosphorus — the cycling of materials is vital to life itself. The minerals are our nutrients even though we get most of them secondhand, after they have been built into edible units by plants.

Most of the minerals are tied up in rock, except for nitrogen which is mostly in the atmosphere. Erosion of rock which has been uplifted into some land mass is our chief source of nutrient minerals, except, again, for nitrogen which bacteria and chemists have learned to take from the air. Any mineral loosened from rock by erosion is rather quickly washed back to the sea again to complete the cycle. But this makes it unavailable to us once more. The trick, then, is to recycle that which is temporarily available. This is what happens in complex ecosystems, with layer upon layer of plants and animals—mostly small—taking up nutrients, holding them against the wasting processes for a short lifetime, then ceding them to other organisms who pass them back into the food chain.

For example, a molecule of carbon which has just been loosened from a piece of limestone after spending a hundred million years tied up in rock is taken up by a plant root which absorbs it in solution with ground water. Much depends upon what kind of plant this is. If it is an annual grass the molecule will be recycled again

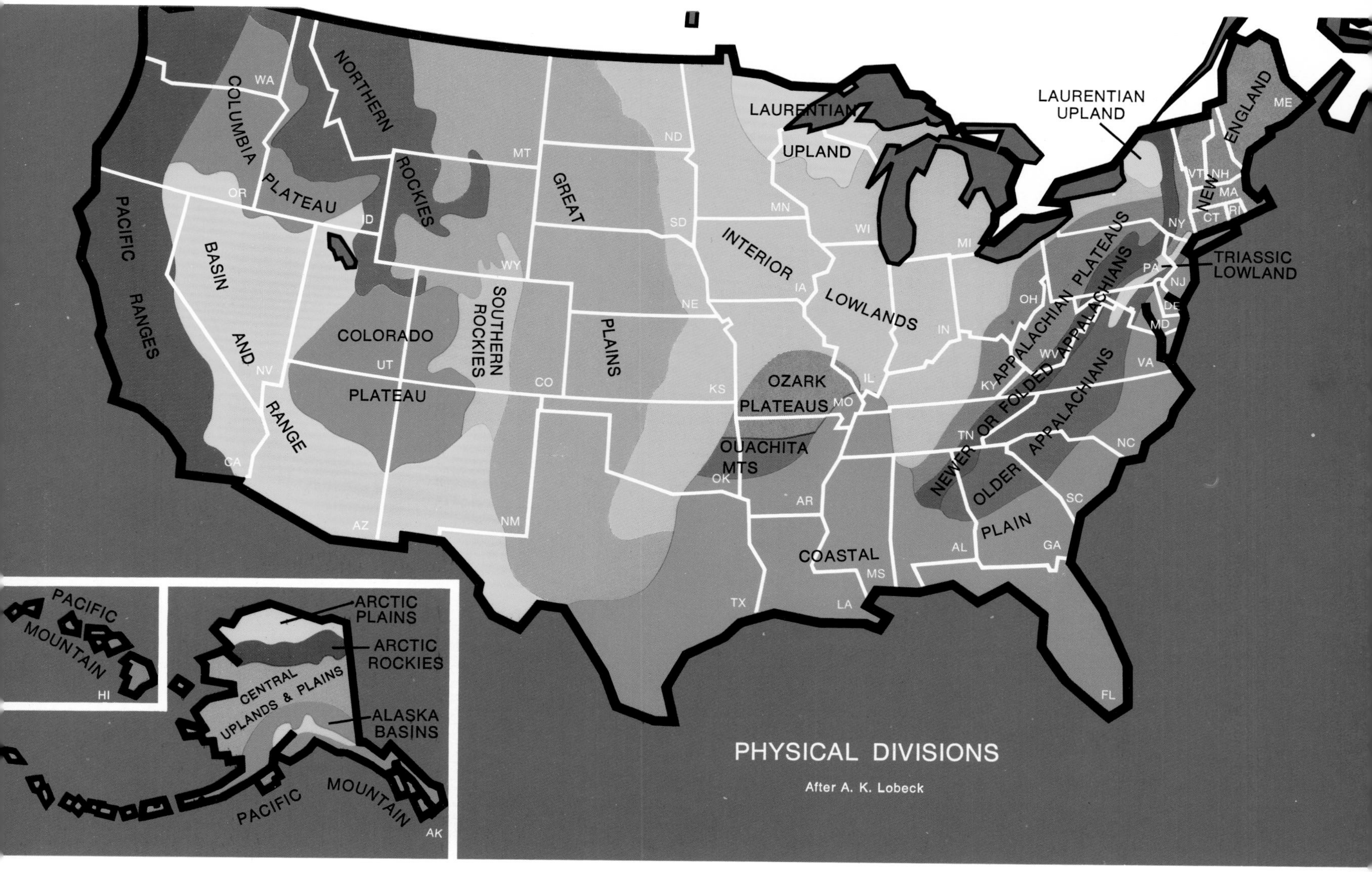
PACIFIC RANGES
COLUMBIA PLATEAU
NORTHERN ROCKIES
BASIN AND RANGE
COLORADO PLATEAU
SOUTHERN ROCKIES
GREAT PLAINS
LAURENTIAN UPLAND
INTERIOR LOWLANDS
OZARK PLATEAUS
OUACHITA MTS
COASTAL PLAIN
LAURENTIAN UPLAND
NEW ENGLAND
TRIASSIC LOWLAND
APPALACHIAN PLATEAUS
NEWER OR FOLDED APPALACHIANS
OLDER APPALACHIANS
WA
OR
CA
ID
NV
MT
WY
UT
AZ
CO
NM
ND
SD
NE
KS
OK
TX
MN
IA
MO
AR
LA
WI
IL
MS
MI
IN
KY
TN
AL
OH
WV
VA
NC
SC
GA
FL
PA
NY
NJ
DE
MD
VT
NH
ME
MA
CT
RI
PACIFIC MOUNTAIN
HI
ARCTIC PLAINS
ARCTIC ROCKIES
CENTRAL UPLANDS & PLAINS
ALASKA BASINS
PACIFIC MOUNTAIN
AK
PHYSICAL DIVISIONS
After A. K. Lobeck

in a few months. But if the plant happens to be a young oak, it has a longer stay in store for it. Of course, if the carbon finds its way to a new bud not too far from the ground, a deer may come along and snip off the bud and build the carbon into its own tissue. In really wild country, a mountain lion may take that deer some months later, and the molecule we are following may be built into the lion for a while.

If the molecule could keep track of all these changes, it might consider it delightful to take part in so many organic systems. Certainly, it would see that life is a process that borrows chemical elements and does something new with them each time. Suppose the deer were shot by a hunter, and he ate the deer meat, and the carbon molecule it contained became part of the hunter for fifty years or so. Whether it was more ennobling to be part of a mountain lion or part of a man would certainly depend on the kind of man. Lions are all rather dependably lion-like; but men vary much more among themselves. Suppose, originally, the molecule had been taken up by a Redwood tree or a Bristlecone Pine, either of which may live two thousand years. Molecules do not tire easily, so a couple of millennia in one place would not induce boredom, certainly not after having survived being locked up in a block of limestone for a hundred million years.

The cycling we have been discussing is nature's way. Unfortunately, clever man has abandoned this strategy, thinking he can make life easier for himself by locating sources of minerals concentrated in one place and by using them to speed the economic processes he favors. For a while this seems to pay. But by tapping rich deposits of minerals and energy sources, like petroleum, man is needlessly scattering the Earth's resources, many of them to the atmosphere or the ocean depths again where they will be inaccessible for "all time," so far as man's short generations are involved. Worse, much of mankind's wastes from this hasty system of exploitation are polluting and destroying the natural mechanisms that help recycle scarce resources. For example, petroleum is much too valuable as a source of chemicals that can be manufactured into various kinds of plastics to be used as fuel. Our present careless uses of petroleum are a serious source of pollution. We should save our diminishing petroleum resources and use our still abundant coal supplies for fuel while we learn to harness the sun's energy more directly, since it is an "inexhaustible" source of energy. Nothing on Earth is inexhaustible, so we need to recycle whatever we use.

OUR SCHEME

The Atlas starts with the planet itself because Earth is our home, and the only one we will ever have. It is childish to think we will run away to another planet after we have overpopulated and abused the Earth. Even if it becomes technologically possible for a few people to colonize another planet, most of us will be left behind, and the planetary colonists, if they survive, will have to adapt to such different environments that they will evolve into new types none of the rest of us would consider human. This book is designed to interest you in Earth, so that you may join in convincing others that whoever abuses the Earth abuses mankind also.

The section Rocks & Minerals is very brief. Rock hounds will already know more than is presented here. Perhaps though, we will help you see familiar things in a new way, as part of larger systems. Most of what we know that is of greatest interest about our planet has been discovered very recently. Geologists—those specialists who study the Earth, and its rocks and processes —have only recently accepted the notion that the crust of the Earth is composed of seven large blocks of rock that rotate against one another. The landform map on page 17 is part of this geological story, and so is the map on pages 24–25, but for more details see the section Rocks & Minerals.

Once we know a little about the planet we walk on, we need to become aware of the plants that clothe the hills and plains. Taken together these plants are called vegetation. There are many, very different groups of plants, but we have selected only two: trees, which dominate the landscape with their large, interesting forms; and wildflowers, which are colorful, sometimes aromatic, and pleasant even for those who know nothing more about them.

The animals had to wait until the plants had worked out the chemical tricks of combining molecules with the energy from the sun to make sugars (carbohydrates) which are a basic food for both plants and animals. Animals cannot make their own food, not even man. This is why the animals come last in our book. However, we have reversed the usual order and placed the most recent and most highly evolved organisms first: these are the Mammals. Birds, Reptiles & Amphibians, Fishes, and Insects represent an evolutionary sequence, and this is the way we treat them.

ON BEING A NATURALIST

Artists, poets, philosophers, and scientists are all involved in the same search. They are trying to understand nature and man. Each may use a different method and often has special limited objectives. Artists and philosophers, for example, have not had much to say about the central questions of man-nature relationships for some while. But ultimately they will return to these questions because they are basic to our existence. The great psychologist Carl Jung went so far as to say, "People who know nothing about nature are of course neurotic, for they are not adapted to reality." And it was Jung who reminded us that when we discover the natural world for ourselves we are engaging in a second creation.

This is so because the world of our senses adds a new dimension to everything that existed before we paid attention to it. Warmth, color, odor, melody, compassion, love—these are all very special human contributions to the original creation that preceded us. So, in studying nature one not only learns to feel at home on the planet—but also to accept responsibility for the creation.

HOW TO USE THIS BOOK

Remember that the photographs are not to scale. The dictates of design may sometimes juxtapose small and large animals or plants without consideration of their respective sizes and may sometimes even reverse their size relationships in illustration. Since this is not a field guide, we trust this drawback will seldom prove deceptive. The reader should focus, instead, on the proportions of each organism separately.

Also, wherever the small range maps show a range abruptly cut off at the United States border with Mexico or Canada, remember that the species probably ranges into those neighboring countries also.

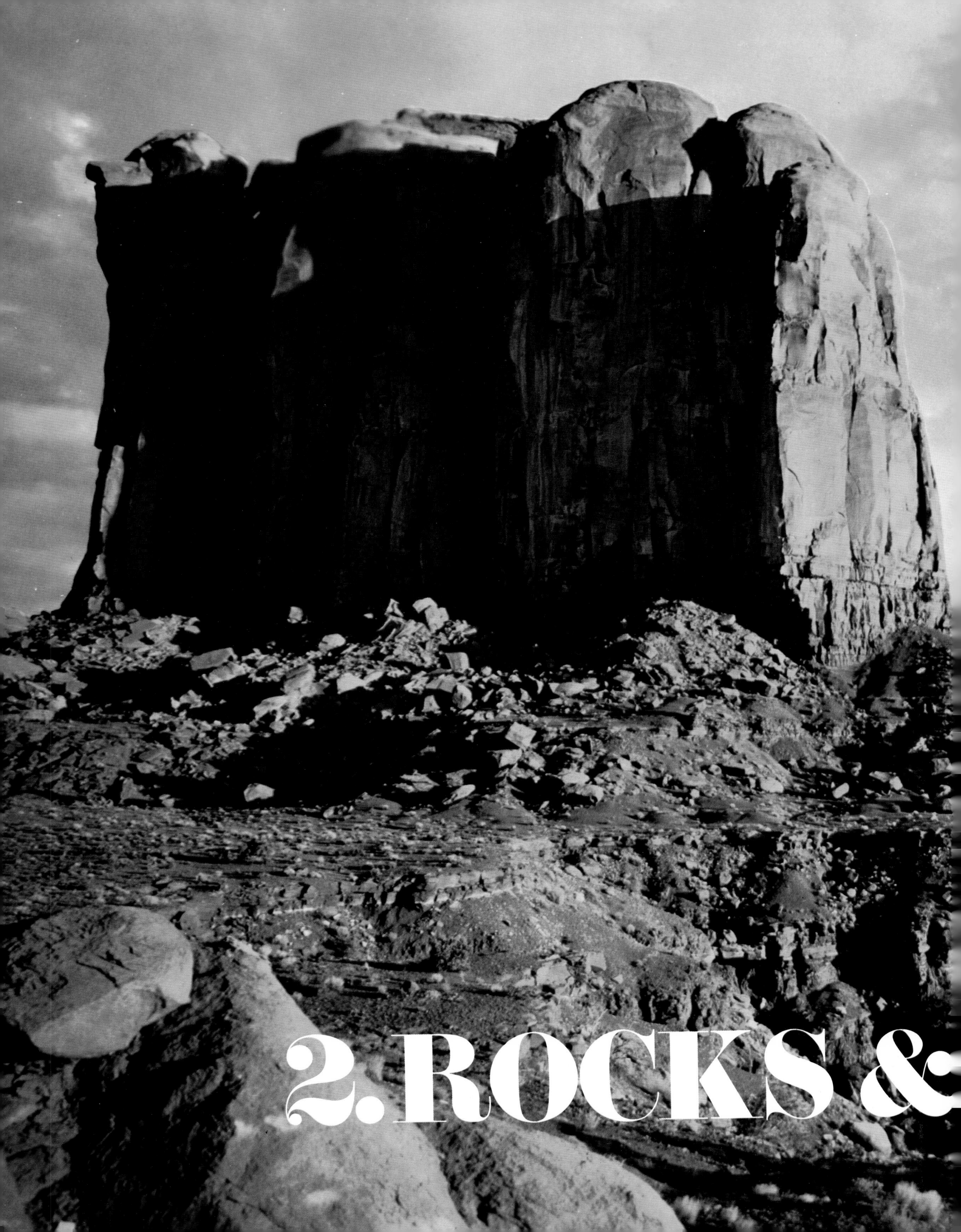

2. ROCKS &

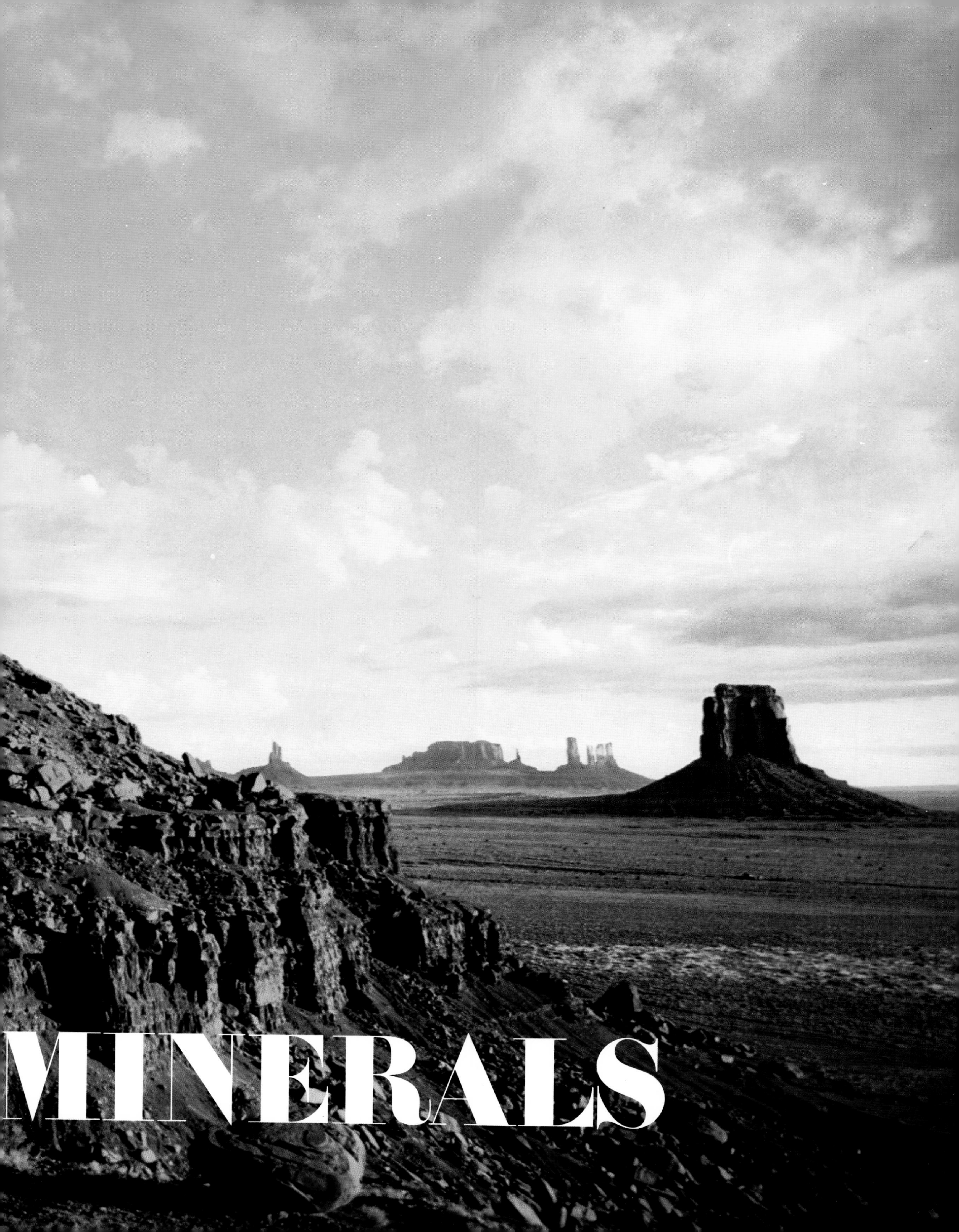

MINERALS

ROCKS & MINERALS

Good science is disciplined thinking about nature. The study of rocks and their constituent minerals, and of the processes that shape and alter both of these, and mold the face of the Earth as well, is geology. Geology is thus Earth science.

It is fortunately not necessary to become a scientist to understand the broad outlines of scientific knowledge about our planet because scientists, in studying the details, have clarified and simplified much of what is happening. Consequently, each of us can easily learn the principles involved in the Earth-shaping processes. It is true that the geologist learns more and more as he pursues his studies, and that the amount of knowledge to learn is sometimes overwhelming. But this is so only for the geologist. The generalization that for the novice the big picture is more meaningful and more easily understood than a vast amount of scientific data remains true. It is sometimes necessary to be patient, however, about the growth of our understanding because only a few scientists are also good teachers.

The United States, along with southern Canada and northern Mexico, is an extraordinarily varied and picturesque land. Almost all the processes that have shaped the surface of the planet are here, many close to home, none of them more than a week's drive by automobile or a half day's flight by jet aircraft. One can easily see volcanos; great earth fractures called faults; uplifted plateaus and sunken valley basins; glaciers and all the landscape features these leave behind as evidence of their work; broad or steep-walled river-eroded valleys; sharply-sculptured young mountain ranges, and gently-rounded older ones; dunes and scores of other shore features. The map on page 248 provides a simplified picture of the distribution of U.S. geological features.

Two things are particularly interesting about the study of our planet. The first is that the more we learn about the Earth, the older it turns out to be. Thanks to a variety of new dating techniques that corroborate one another, for example, we have every reason to believe that the planet is well over four billion years old. Secondly, most of our information about the origin and shaping of the Earth is very recent. This makes geology an exciting science because many of its advances are just beginning.

We actually know little about the origin of our planet, which should not be surprising, given its age. The evolution of molecules from atoms, of crystals from molecular combinations, and the chemistry involved in the joining of various crystals to form the many rock combinations must have taken considerable time. Once the pattern had been established, however, it was used again and again. So far as we know, creative innovation now takes place on Earth only through life processes.

A recent scientific breakthrough is the discovery that the continents actually drift across the planet's surface. This concept, which accommodates all sorts of heretofore puzzling facts about the crust of the Earth, is an outgrowth of the recent accumulation of abundant data on Earth's magnetic field and similarly plentiful, systematically-collected information on earthquakes and their shock waves measured by a global network of monitoring stations.

The essential idea — called plate tectonics — that emerged from a careful study of the interrelationships in these new data, is that the surface of the Earth is composed of seven large, rigid, curved plates that rotate relative to one another. It is as though an orange had its peel removed, was cut up unevenly, and the sections loosely replaced. Since the plates of the Earth are very uneven in outline, and especially since they are curved,

Preceding pages: Eroded Sandstone, Monument Valley, Utah

the movement of any one of them sets all the others in motion according to a complex geometry. The principal contact lines between major plates are also zones of major earthquake and volcanic activity.

The sea floor has ridges made by the upwelling of new rock, and therefore spreads away on either side of these ridges, expanding itself and pressing on the tectonic plates. Where deep ocean trenches have long been known but not understood, it is beginning to be clear that old crust is being buckled under and "consumed," i.e., returned to the Earth's interior where it is reincorporated into molten parent magma, from which sea mounts and volcanos are formed.

Current studies suggest that there has been little dramatic continental drift in the last 12 million years or so. And our present continental outlines seem to have existed in nearly their present form for some 75 million years. But great shifts have occurred over much longer periods of Earth's history. It is now believed that the seeming fit between the bulge of South America and the bight of Africa is indeed a result of the drifting apart of land masses that were once united. This idea was first proposed by the German geologist Alfred Wegener in 1912, but little credence was accorded it until the last decade or so.

LANDFORMS

Fascinating as the Earth-forming processes may be, Earth-shaping processes are equally interesting and of more significance to individual non-scientists. Their study is called geomorphology.

Rocks that form the crust of the Earth come under attack by the elements as soon as they are exposed. Differential heating and cooling of the several different minerals that make up rock lead to its loosening and gradual wearing away. This is the beginning of erosion. Water dissolves certain minerals from rock, and when it carries carbonic acid from dead plants it interacts more actively and speeds rock breakdown. The highest mountains are fated to be reduced to dust or clay by this process. The hills seem eternal only because our lifespans are short, and because the full implications of the seemingly-slow processes of erosion have not been realized until rather recently in the history of man.

Gravity, of course, also causes the downward creep of eroded rock materials, but movement through the agency of water is much the most effective Earth-shaping process on our planet. Its universality makes it so. Rainfall not only helps break down rock but it causes slow, persistent, and very significant sheet erosion. Rainfall that accumulates in rivulets, brooks, and rivers becomes a more powerful agent that moves rock debris and soil to the sea, carving and shaping the landscape in the process. Precipitation that accumulates as snow and becomes flowing ice, or a glacier, is an even more powerful erosional process where it occurs. And in dry climates wind-blown sand not only blasts rock smooth but gradually wears it away.

There are several phases to the erosional process. What is cut away from bedrock accumulates in deposits which are themselves significant landscape features. The rock debris that accumulates at the foot of mountains, forming talus slopes or pediments depending upon the kind of rock and the climate, is evidence of this complex process. As material is transported down valleys, and eventually to the sea, it is redeposited again and again, forming new and fascinating features each time. And, finally, the constant shifting of ocean beaches and dunes illustrates what a restless, endless process is involved in the shaping of the face of the Earth.

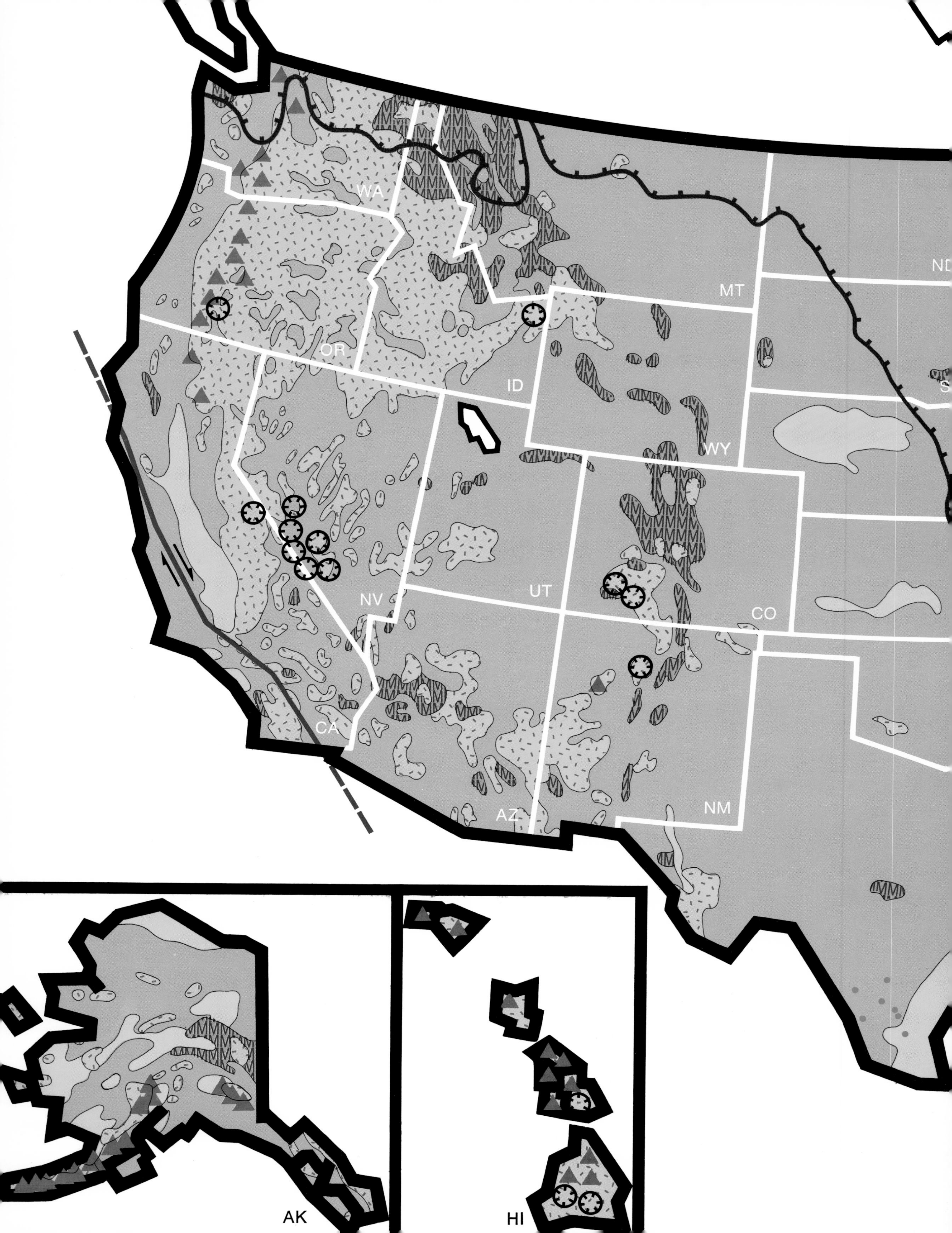
WA
OR
ID
MT
ND
WY
NV
UT
CO
CA
AZ
NM
AK
HI

GEOLOGY & TECTONICS

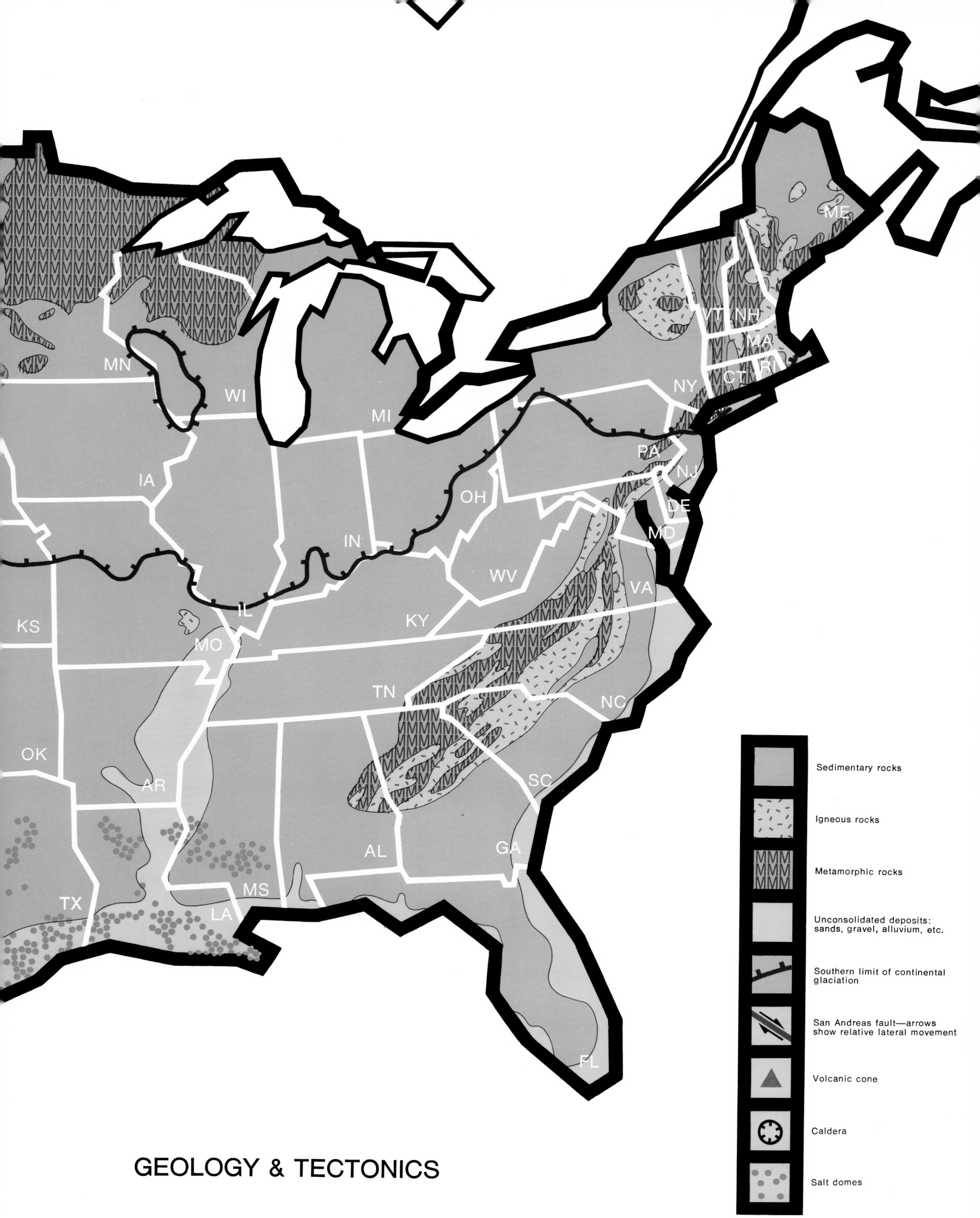

Range Maps of Rocks & Minerals

Basalt

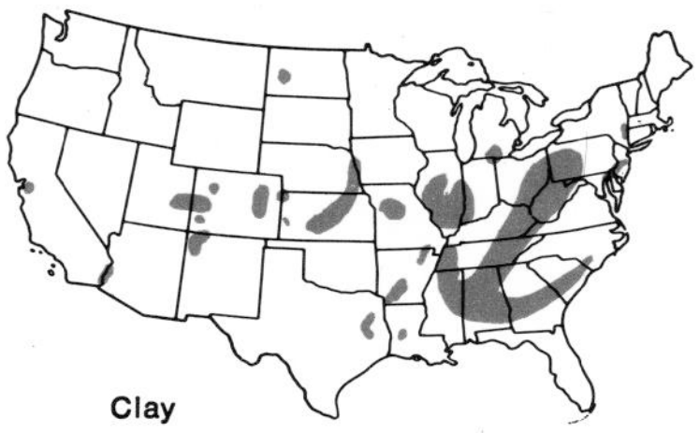
Clay

Gneiss

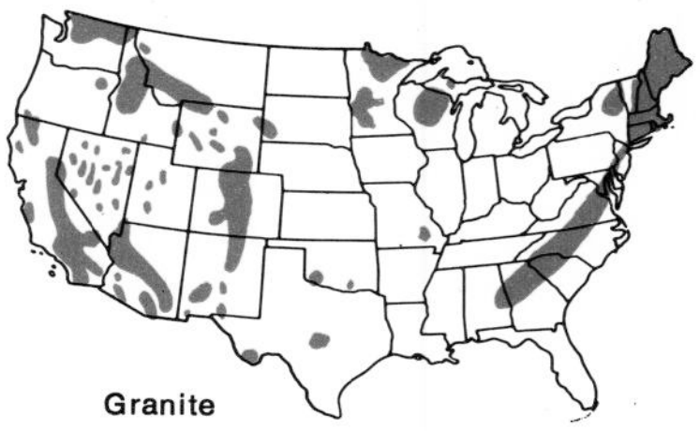
Granite

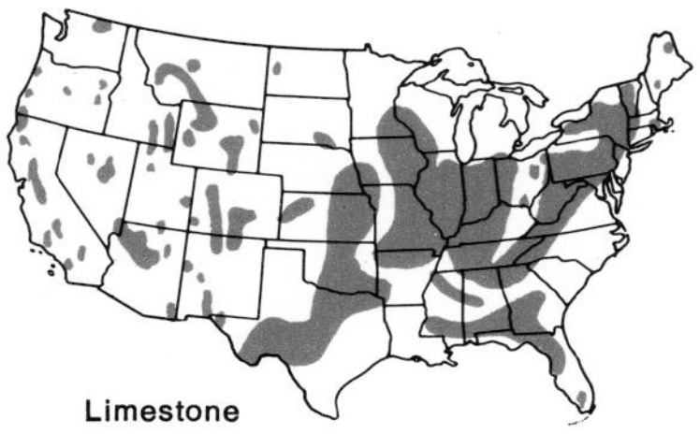
Limestone

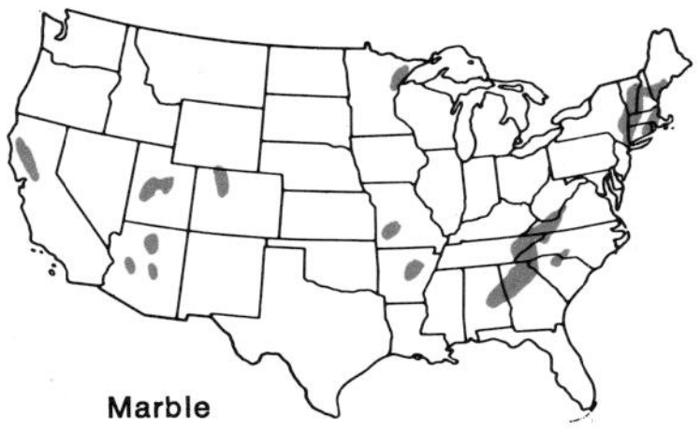
Marble

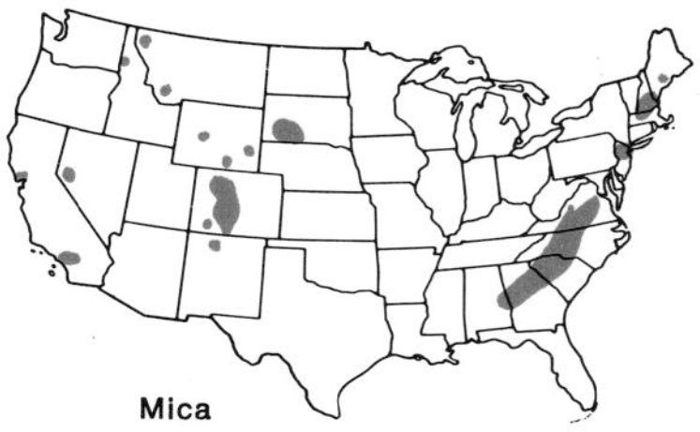
Mica

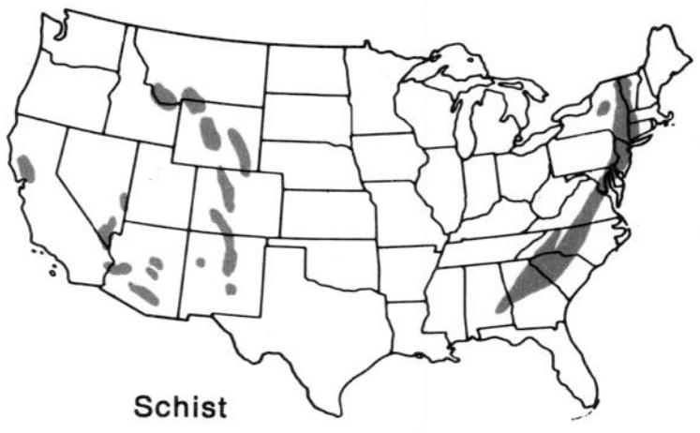
Schist

Slate

Range Maps of Landscape Features

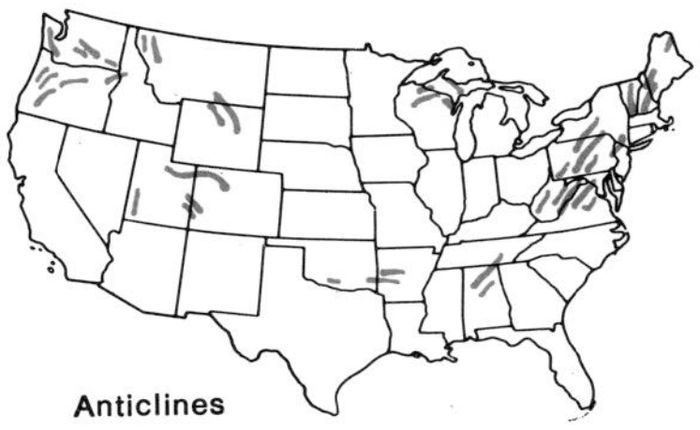
Anticlines

Deltaic deposits

Eskers

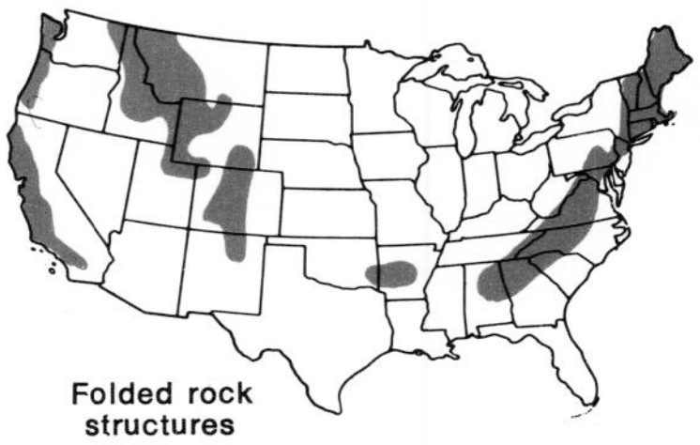
Folded rock structures

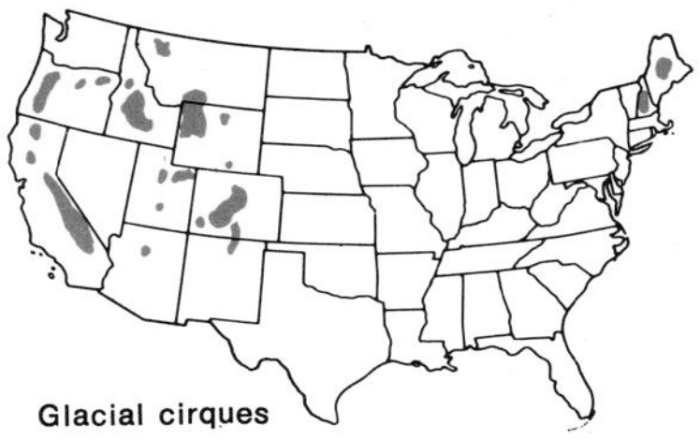
Glacial cirques

Glacial striations

Glacial valleys

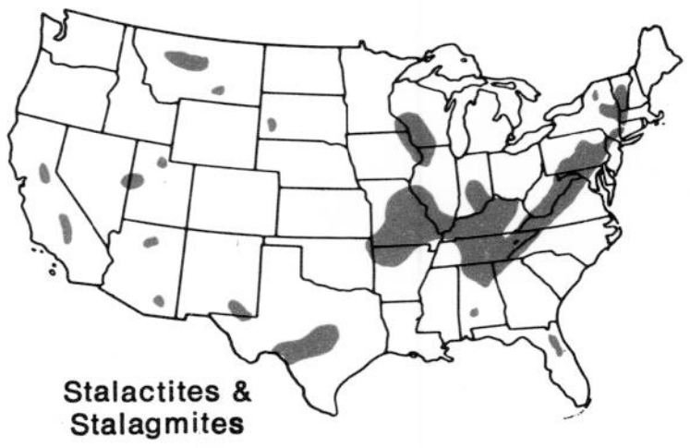
Stalactites & Stalagmites

Overthrust faults

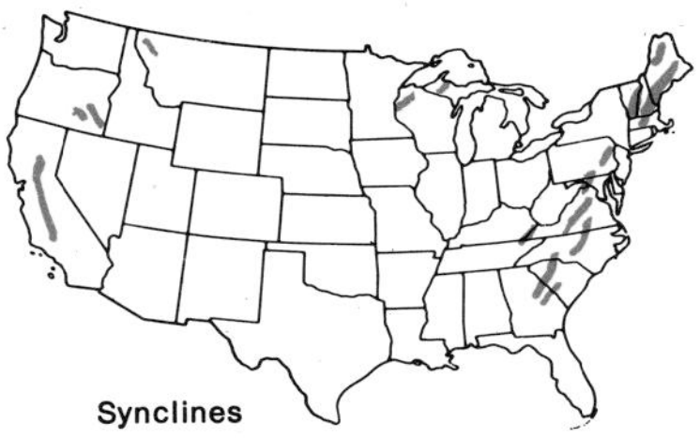
Synclines

Dunes of Quartz Sand

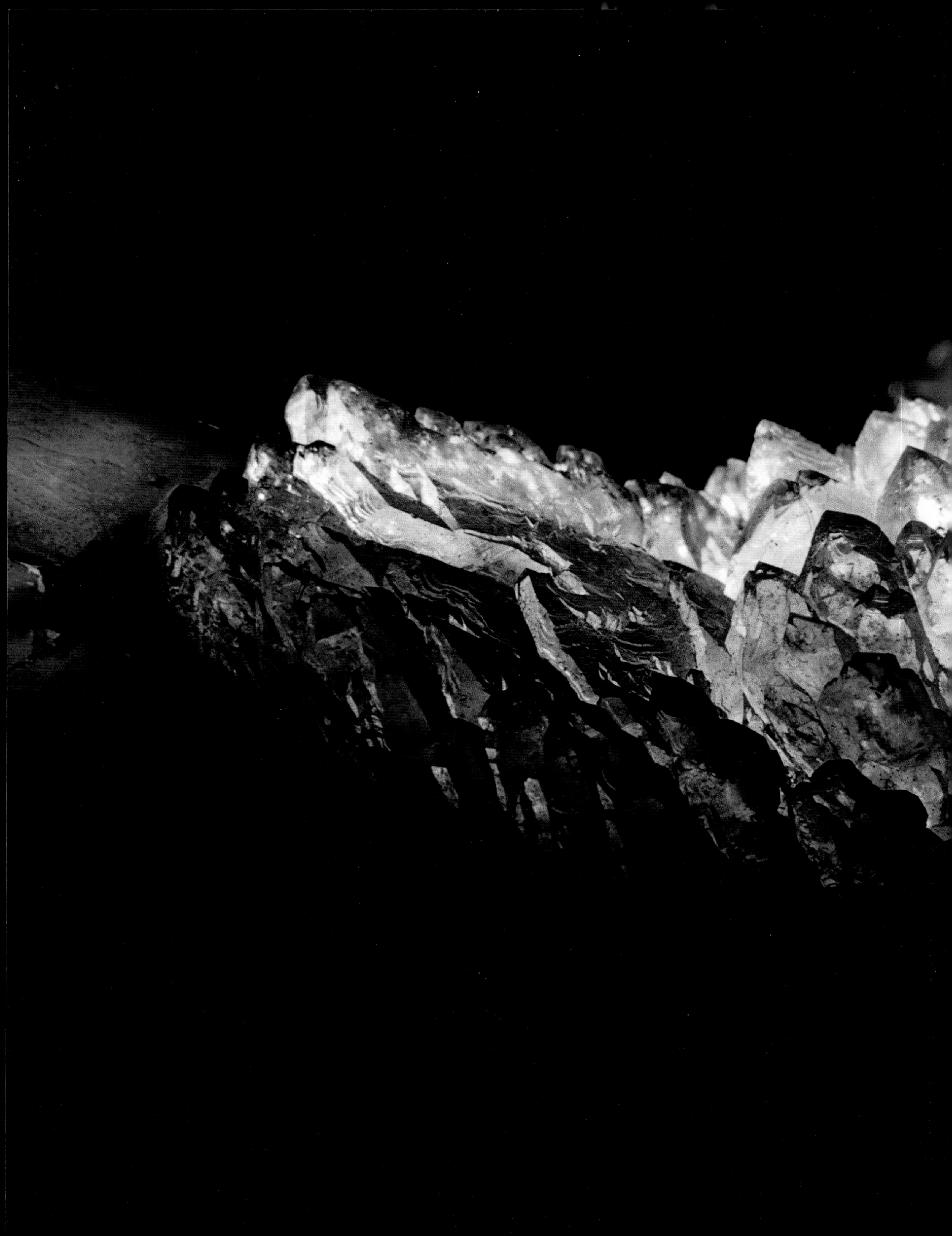

Feldspar

QUARTZ

The crystals of quartz are the most widely dispersed mineral on the face of the Earth. Clear as glass, milky, frosted, small to medium-sized, they are so hard and so resistant to chemical corrosion that they have persisted for millions of years as sand grains or, cemented together, as sandstones. Combined with feldspars, they form the abundant granite rocks of the continents. Hardness and persistence makes sand grains ideal carriers of historical evidence. For example, quartz grains that have been ground against other hard rock after becoming imbedded in the flowing ice of glaciers show smooth breakage plates called conchoidal fractures—like the scalloping of Jello broken into by a spoon. Sand grains bounced in a stream bed or alongshore currents show V-shaped check marks; sands blown by wind are frosted and have rounded corners.

FELDSPAR

As is quartz, feldspar is common and prominent in many rocks, particularly the granite rocks that form a large part of the continents. It is pale, varying from clear to pink, and often flesh-colored. It cannot be scratched by glass or a knife and its fracture faces (cleavages) make a 90° angle. Particularly large crystals of feldspar form when the original molten rock (magma) cools slowly. The resulting coarse-grained granites (usually in dikes or veins) are called pegmatites and are quarried for use in porcelain making. Feldspars exposed to rain and carbon dioxide (from the air or from decomposing plants, usually as carbonic acid) decompose to clay. One kind of feldspar has potassium, another kind calcium, and these two chemicals are basic plant foods. So the decomposition of feldspars by weather is a principal soil-forming activity.

Rose Quartz

MICA

This is another abundant constituent of the original (igneous) rocks of our planet and normally occurs as small crystals. Where conditions are just right during its formation, it may form in large sheets, however, a few inches to several feet across. The perfect cleavage of mica allows it to be split into thin, transparent or translucent sheets, once used as isinglass for stove windows but now used in many forms, from insulators to lubricants, by industry. Mica comes in two forms, both widely distributed in rocks: biotite or black mica, which may be brown, green, or black, and is of little commercial value; and muscovite, a white mica, which is the commercially-valuable transparent and almost colorless form. All micas are soft enough to be scratched by a fingernail, and individual sheets have a surprising degree of flexibility.

White Mica

GARNET

Whether tiny or large, these crystals have a distinctive form: either 12-faced dodecahedrons (oblique parallelograms) or 24-faced trapezoids (none of the four sides of the face parallel). They come in several combinations of chemical elements, however, and a corresponding variety of colors. The best known color is, of course, the garnet-red one finds in the hard, medium-sized crystals that make fine, inexpensive gems when polished. Because they are common, they are often the favorite of beginning collectors. Garnets are of wide occurrence, usually in metamorphic rocks that have been deformed by heat and pressure. In fact, so abundant are they in some rocks—in the Adirondacks of New York and in the Appalachians of New Hampshire and North Carolina — that they are mined, separated, and used as abrasives, including "red sandpaper."

Garnet Crystals

Granite

GRANITE

This light-colored rock that forms the structural mass of all the continents was intruded, as magma, from below into the crust of the Earth, often in massive batholiths. It then cooled slowly beneath a deep cover of older, surface rocks, and is thus exposed only by erosion of the overlying rock. The Sierra Nevada mountains and the Coast Range are just such massive granitic batholiths. Only 14 states lack granite exposures. Because it cooled slowly, granite has conspicuous crystals, mostly of feldspar (60%), quartz (30%), and black mica (10%), all roughly equal in size and tightly interlocked. There are several varieties of granite, depending on the proportion of minerals and crystal sizes. Colors vary from silvery gray to bright pink. When of uniform grain, granite makes excellent building stone and is carved and polished into monuments.

Columnar Basalt Columns

BASALT

Basalt is the dominant, igneous rock (from molten magma) formed at the Earth's surface. It was magma extruded as lava, occurring more often as flows from fissures than from volcanos. Gabbro and dolerite are special forms, roughly similar chemically, but physically distinguished by grain or texture. All basaltic rock is dark, heavy, and so fine-grained that its crystals are hardly visible, though this fine-grained groundmass may include other, visible crystals. Between the northern Rockies and the Cascade Range in Oregon, Washington, and Idaho is the Columbia plateau, one of the world's great basaltic flows, 200,000 square miles in extent and nearly 4000 feet thick. Basalts often show columnar jointing, as in the Hudson River Palisades, Devils Postpile in California, and Devils Tower in Wyoming. Often called traprock, it is used in road-building.

Shale

Sandstone

SHALE
When the feldspar minerals of granite are eroded from rock by chemical action and water, they form clay particles. These are washed into streams, and when the streams reach lakes or oceans, their clay burden is slowly deposited as a bluish-gray mud sediment. Admixtures of other minerals and plant-remains may color some clays red or black. Clay particles are really microscopically-small flakes of aluminum silicates (from feldspars) and mica flakes. These small flakes hold a film of water around themselves which acts as a lubricant and makes clay plastic, so that when one molds it into a special shape it holds its form even after drying. When compressed by heavy burdens of new sediments, these muds and clays are compacted into mudstone or shale, a soft rock that splits somewhat parallel to its bed and feels almost slippery.

SANDSTONE
When granite is eroded it forms clay which may then be compressed to shale, a sedimentary rock. The quartz in the original granite is then loosened and accumulates as sand. This is moved downhill by flowing water and deposited in lakes or the sea. But the sand is so hard that its deposits are not compressible. Mineral solutions, however, often permeate into them, and solidify, gel, or cement the deposits to sandstone, another sedimentary rock almost as common as shale. Because they were deposited in layers, sandstones are stratified. Some strata are coarse, others fine. They are often of different colors. The colors come from bits of organic matter or iron oxides included in the original deposits. The world's most spectacular cross section of sedimentary rocks, many of them sandstones, are in the 4000-foot cut of the Grand Canyon of the Colorado in Arizona.

Stream-polished Sandstone

Slate

SLATE

Compaction, plus cementation, turns such loose sediments as sand, clay, and shells into rock. This sedimentary rock may then be uplifted by an arching of the Earth's crust, thus exposing it to erosion and reinitiating the sedimentary process. Uplift often involves great pressure, heat, and the injection of steam. The heat and pressure alter the original rock, changing it into new chemicals and new rock. Geologists call this process metamorphism, and the rocks thus produced are the third and final great class of rocks. The other two classes are igneous and sedimentary rocks. The simplest metamorphic rock is slate. Muds and clays that have become shale are changed to fine-grained slate, typically a clean, almost lustrous, gray (though some are red, green, or black), and easily spilt into smooth slabs for such things as flagstones and roof tiles.

Limestone (above) and Marble (below)

Faulted and Uptilted Limestone Formation

LIMESTONE

Every year, thanks to rainfall and the chemical weathering of rock, 70 tons of dissolved minerals, mostly calcium carbonate and silica, are washed into the sea from every square mile—on the average—of the Earth's land surface. Although many of these minerals remain in solution as salts, most are either precipitated by new chemical reactions, or withdrawn by tiny marine plants and animals for their own use. These uses are short-lived, however, and the skeletons of billions of mostly microscopic organisms rain steadily down through the oceans to accumulate on the bottom. These deposits are eventually cemented together to form limestones, a third large class of sedimentary rock. Chalk, coquina, and dolomite are merely special varieties. Each of them will fizz if a drop of dilute hydrochloric acid is touched to a fresh surface.

MARBLE

This is metamorphosed limestone. The almost-microscopic grains of original limestone are transformed to visible crystals and the resulting marble is hard and heavy, and polishes to a beautiful finish. Marble is thus the ideal stone for sculptors and architects. Many marbles contain the fossilized remains of larger shelled animals, such as the trilobites that lived in shallow seas 200 million years ago, which add extra interest and beauty to this marvelous rock. As you have by now suspected, rocks and minerals are the products of a continuing process of Earth deformation. Shales blend into gneiss, sandstones become quartzites, and limestones may be marbelized into gneiss. Indeed, the processes are reversible to some extent, gneiss being degraded to schist. It is these processes that add so much interest to reading the landscape and attest to the Earth's age.

Schist

Preceding pages: Cross Section of Limestone and Sandstone Formations, Grand Canyon of the Colorado

Stalactites (upper) and Stalagmites (lower)

SCHIST

When shales with a high content of mica are subjected to metamorphism, a remarkable transformation takes place. The mica flakes are recombined, and the resulting schist is a spangled mass of shiny, mica plates and other minerals, including garnets, mostly obvious to the unaided eye. This is in contrast to the original shale, where the minerals were jumbled together, lusterless, and barely distinguishable. It is also in contrast to slate, whose minerals are too small to see except under magnification, and in contrast to gneiss—the next grade of metamorphism—whose crystals are submerged in a more massive background. Like slate, schist splits easily, but its larger minerals cause it to splinter unevenly rather than smoothly as slate does. Because it may be derived from most other kinds of rock, schist is common but usually local.

Gneiss

GNEISS

Gneiss (pronounced nice) is a banded, coarse-grained metamorphic rock whose several minerals became plastic and flowed together under heat and pressure. Some of this banding is beautifully sinuous, and other folds on itself. Where different layers of sedimentary rock were transformed to gneiss, the results are striking. Gneissic rocks are abundant, especially along the borders of igneous rock masses, because the igneous intrusion, being a hot magma, caused contact metamorphism, partially recrystallizing and distorting the border rock it intruded into. The transition from one rock to another is obvious under such conditions and helped early geologists unravel the secrets of the rocks. The process is, of course, more complex than can be described here, but one can soon learn to interpret the results. Gneiss, more massive than schist, will not split.

Ice Tongues of Worthington Glacier, Alaska

Ice-polished Granite and Glacial Striations, Sierra Nevada Mountains, California

GLACIERS

Wherever snowfall accumulates faster than it melts, the weight of the snow may recrystallize snow crystals into ice crystals. Ice under heavy pressure is plastic—it flows. The lower ice zone of the snow mass flows downhill and its surface is then fractured by parallel crevasses (from the French word for crevices, used first to describe them systematically). This is the origin of glaciers. In North America today glaciers form or maintain themselves only at high elevations, where average annual temperatures are low enough to foster accumulation. Glaciers that flow down river valleys enlarge them by scouring. The tongues of Worthington Glacier, near Valdez, Alaska, illustrate this process. Similar but smaller glaciers occur in the northern Rocky Mountains, the Coast Range, and the North Cascades, most of them melting back.

GLACIAL LAKES

Everywhere today glaciers are melting back at their lower ends faster than they are nourished from above. The lower left photograph looks down a valley recently abandoned by ice to a chain of small glacial lakes called tarns. Tarns are formed by melt-water in the depressions of the valley floor scoured out by advancing ice in an earlier glacial phase. The dam-like separations between lakes are moraines—deposits of sand and gravel dropped where the flowing ice front was exactly balanced by the melting ice. Notice that the upper moraine has already been breeched by lake overflow. Eventually all these moraines will be eroded away. The upper tarn is emerald because of suspended clay and fine silt (glacial flour) from the glacier. The blue tarn below is cleaner, and reflects the sky better because the clay and silt were precipitated out.

GLACIAL POLISH

Hard rocks overriden by moving glacial ice—whether in a valley glacier or a continental ice sheet—often receive a high polish. Because granite is such a hard rock and because it is relatively abundant, it frequently shows signs of having been polished by the glacial ice that overrode the northern third of North America in the last million or so years. Continental ice melted back only about 15,000 years ago, and the valley glaciers on northern mountain ranges are vestiges of that geological epoch, called the Pleistocene—The Ice Age. Wherever the moving ice carried hard pebbles along, they often became cutting tools, and evidence of their passage is seen today in the long, straight scratches (striae) they inflicted on the underlying bedrock. Ice polish of this kind and striations are abundantly clear in the silvery-pink granite rocks of the higher Sierra Nevada mountains.

Glacial Tarns and Moraines, Big Horn Mountains, Wyoming

3. TREES

TREES

Looked at from space, the United States has three great, north-south bands of forest cover. These are the Pacific Coast band of conifers, including the forests of the Coast Range; the great conifer belt of the Rocky Mountains which is separated from the Pacific Coast belt by desert and semi-desert; and the great block of deciduous forest of the East, roughly from the Mississippi River to the Atlantic Ocean, with conifers at its northern and southern ends. This last band is separated from the Rocky Mountain forest belt by the Great Plains grassland, as the map on pages 44-45 shows well.

There were originally over a billion acres of woodland in the United States, and a good deal more than that in Canada. Mexico, however, has woodland, which extends south to a humid tropical forest belt, only on its central uplands.

The U.S. forest is one of the richest temperate-zone forests of all, with over 700 species of trees. About a hundred tree species are of commercial value. When one compares this with the fact that Europe has only a dozen or so commercially valuable species, one can see what a tremendous economic advantage Americans have had. Unfortunately, we have greatly abused the richly diversified forests by clear-cutting and burning, being in too much of a hurry to extract resources. As a result, our forests are much less productive than they once were. There is so much acreage of young woodland, however, that it can be said that the forest is growing faster than ever. This is a deceptive use of facts because thousands of acres in saplings will not be of much use to anyone for a generation or two or three, depending upon the use to which the maturing trees are put.

Trees grow wherever the rainfall during the growing season exceeds evaporation, providing the temperature during that growing season exceeds 50°F. a good part of the time. Since trees have a large evaporating surface composed of leaves or needles, they need more water than grass or shrubs during their growing season. This usually means that trees are found where there is an excess of 20 inches of annual rainfall; elsewhere grasslands and semi-desert scrub prevail. In cool climates, whether due to altitude or latitude, less rainfall may suffice because evaporation decreases as temperature declines; but in warmer regions, more rainfall is needed to maintain forest.

This occurs most dramatically in the western half of the United States where several parallel mountain ranges intercept moisture from the Pacific Ocean at different elevations. Since the western slope of the Coast Range faces the ocean it has the most moisture, is coolest, and has the heaviest forest. However, air which passes over has its moisture wrung out of it, and the eastern slope has much less rainfall. The country to the east of the Coast Range lies in a rain shadow created by the mountains. The next range to the east gets little rain on the lower hills of the western slope, but does receive considerable rainfall on the hills that extend beyond the elevation of the Coast Range. This is why the Great Central Valley of California is a grassland and why one must start climbing the Sierra Nevada massif before trees grow again. An exception is, of course, the trees that grow along rivers, because there water is supplied through soil rather than by rainfall. The rivers bring the water from high areas with abundant rainfall.

Since Death Valley lies in the rain shadow of the Sierra Nevada mountains and also is in a high-temperature region, it is among the driest places on the continent. The Basin and Range region to the east of the Sierra Nevada mountains is also a desert, and trees do not grow again on the mountains until one comes to the Wasatch Range, east of Salt Lake City, Utah.

The high western slopes of the Rocky Mountains receive some moisture from the Pacific Ocean, but the eastern slopes, on the Denver, Colorado, side, get theirs from the Atlantic Ocean. Here, however, in addition to tapping the moisture of moving air masses, the mountains create their own weather in the form of thunderstorms that reach up another 20,000 feet and more. The diagram on the following page illustrates this phenomenon. The rain shadow is of much less significance in the eastern United States because the mountains are not high enough to intercept significant amounts of moisture from the maritime air flowing in from the Atlantic Ocean.

Forests play an important role in slowing erosion, in reducing the impact of wind, in prolonging snowmelt, and in moderating temperature. In a very real sense forests are the Earth's air-conditioning equipment, and it is a free good if we have sense enough to appreciate it. For example, a 50-foot shelterbelt of trees planted on a flat prairie will help moderate the wind for 3000 feet. Wind velocities are reduced 50 percent after penetrating a dense forest 200 feet.

Preceding pages: Autumn Foliage Display, Mt. Hood, Oregon

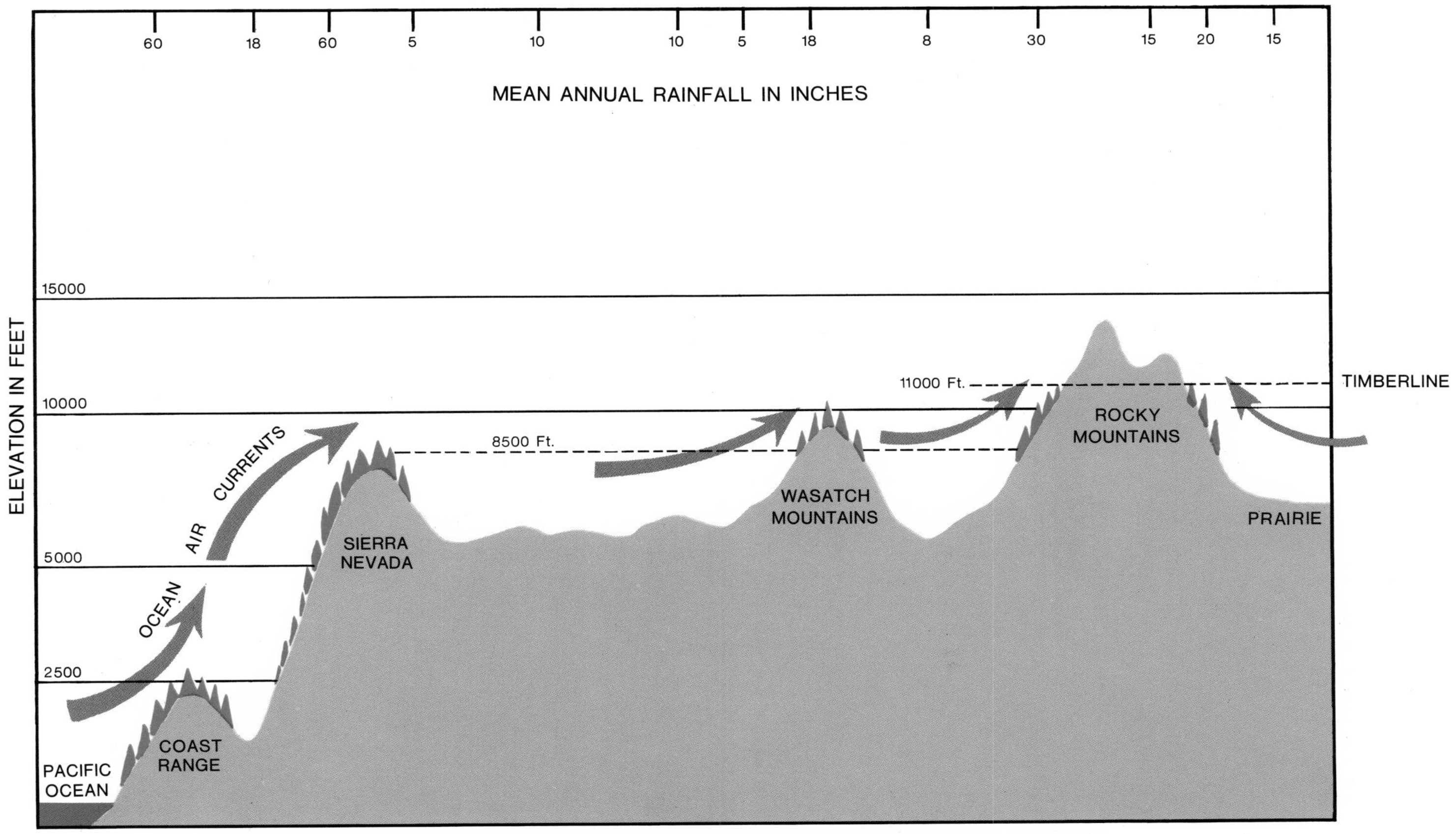

THE EFFECT OF AIR CURRENTS ON FOREST GROWTH

Important as these physical characteristics are, one must really learn to see a forest as a plant-animal community before understanding it as the dynamic ecosystem it is. Animals play important roles which affect the distribution of various tree species, hence the composition of various forest communities, and they speed the turnover of chemical nutrients in the forest. Squirrels, for example, help oaks extend their ranges, often uphill, by their incessant planting of acorns. And so do jays and woodpeckers. The turnover of raw materials in a forest is always impressive when we look at it for the first time. In the deciduous forest of the eastern United States, for example, with its conspicuous autumnal foliage, the "rain" of leaves, twigs, seeds, and animal wastes may amount to over one ton of material per acre per year. In the tropical rain forest of Central America it often amounts to five tons per acre!

Some 225 million acres of land have been set aside as National Forest administered by the U.S. Forest Service. These forests contain about 20 percent of the commercial forest land in the United States, which the Congress has decreed shall be managed on a sustained yield basis—annual cuts not exceeding annual growth. The National Forests are also managed on a multiple use basis. This allows not only regulated lumbering, but camping, hunting, other types of recreation, and grazing of livestock. It is unfortunately often difficult to regulate such uses to avoid abuse, and the National Forests often suffer from the greed of individuals who profit at the expense of all others.

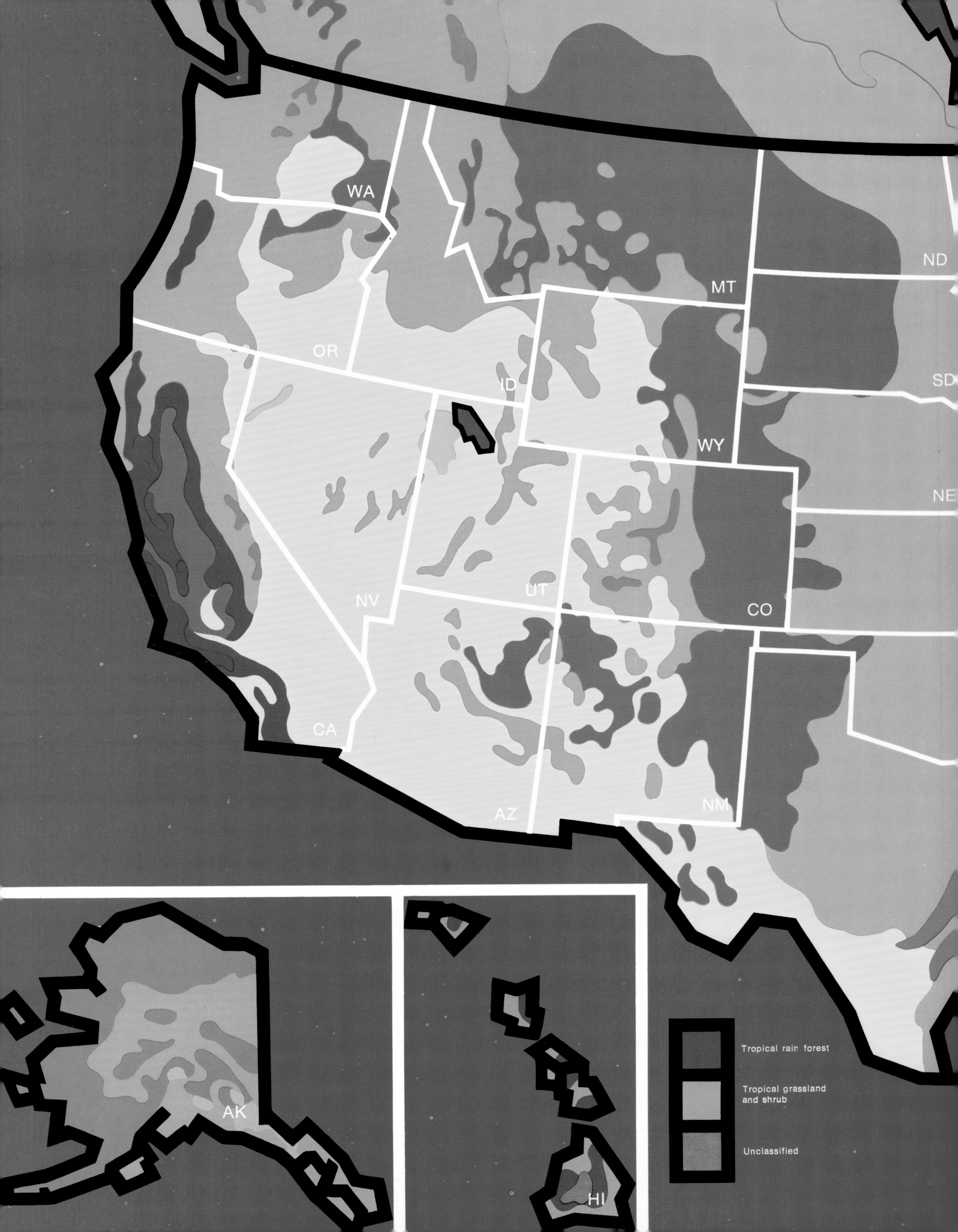
WA
OR
ID
MT
ND
SD
WY
NE
NV
UT
CO
CA
AZ
NM
AK
HI
Tropical rain forest
Tropical grassland
and shrub
Unclassified

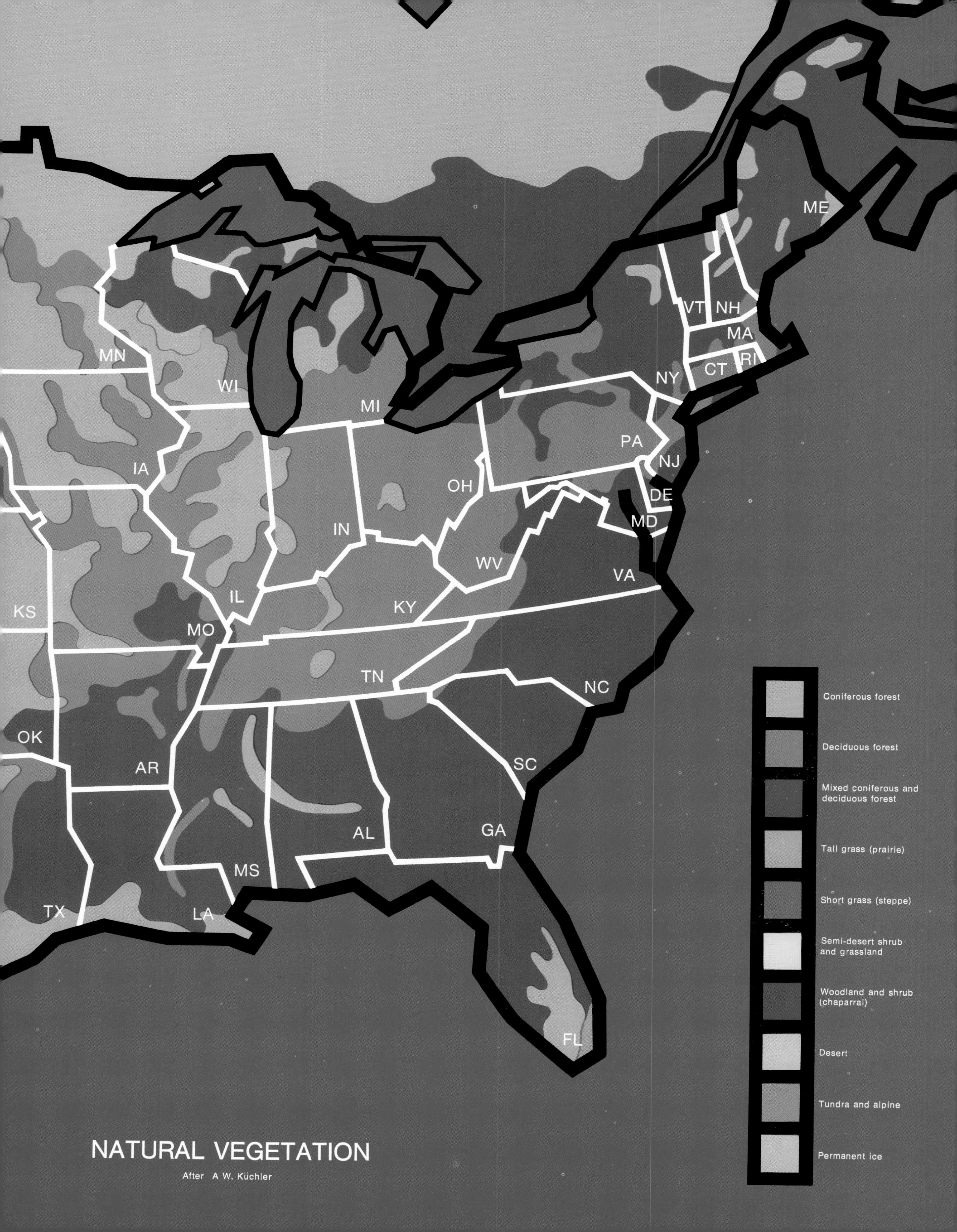

NATURAL VEGETATION

After A W. Küchler

Range Maps of Trees

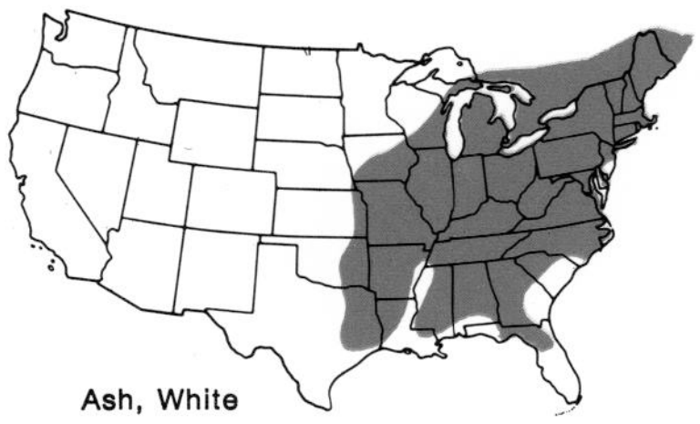
Ash, White

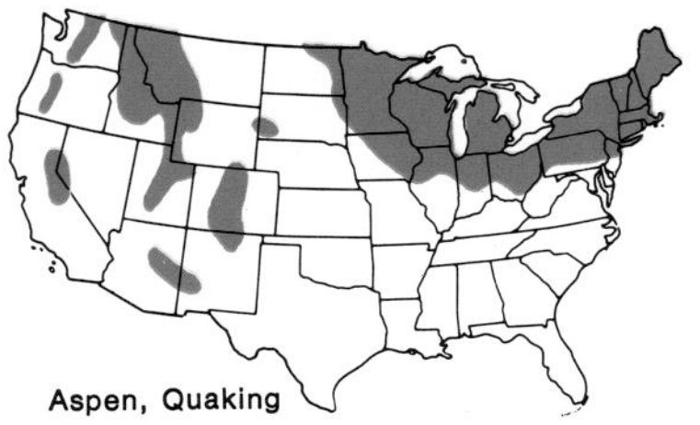
Aspen, Quaking

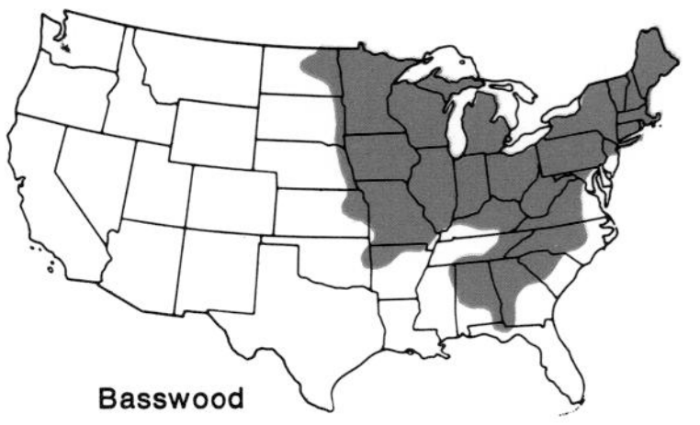
Basswood

Beech, American

Birch, Paper

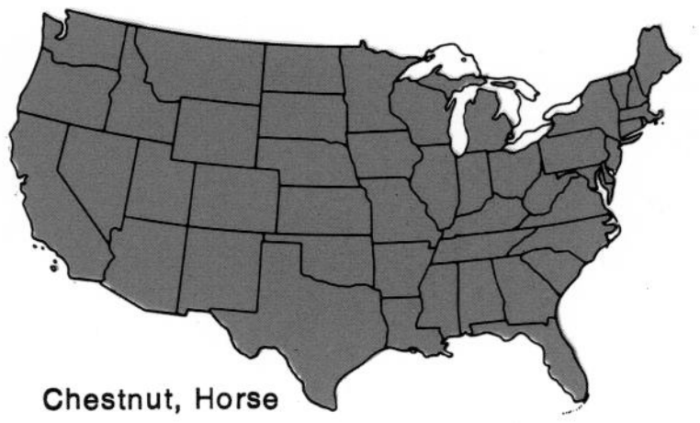
Chestnut, Horse

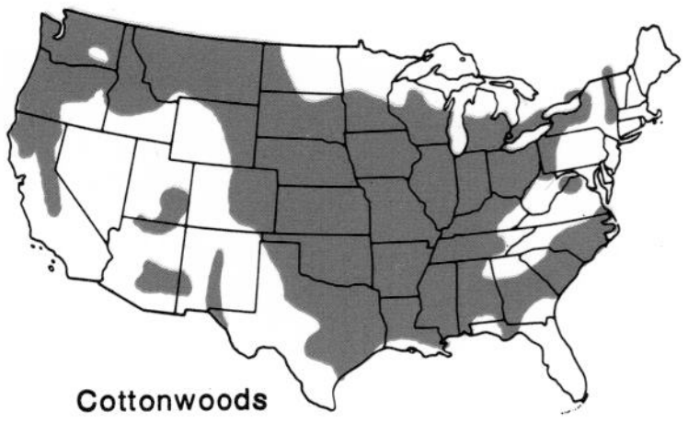
Cottonwoods

Cypress, Bald

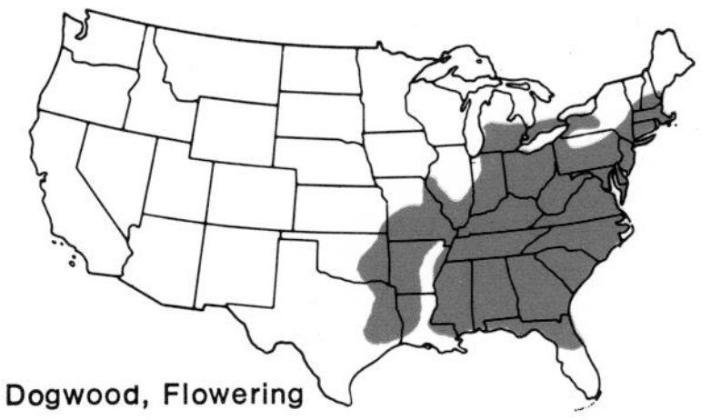
Dogwood, Flowering

Elm, American

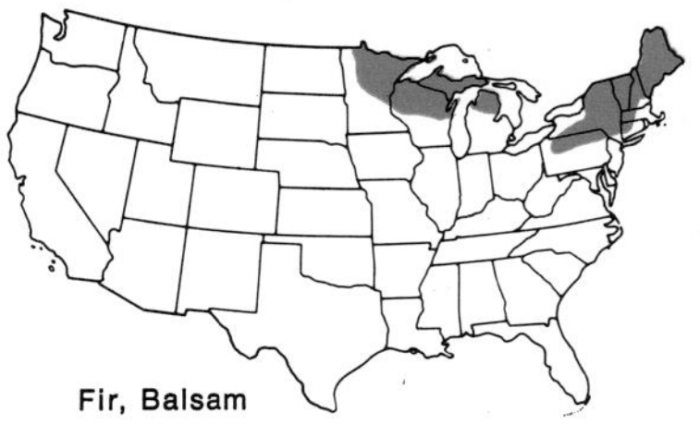
Fir, Balsam

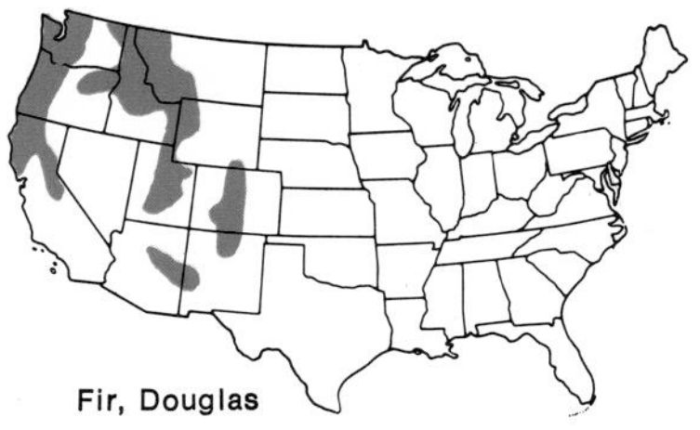
Fir, Douglas

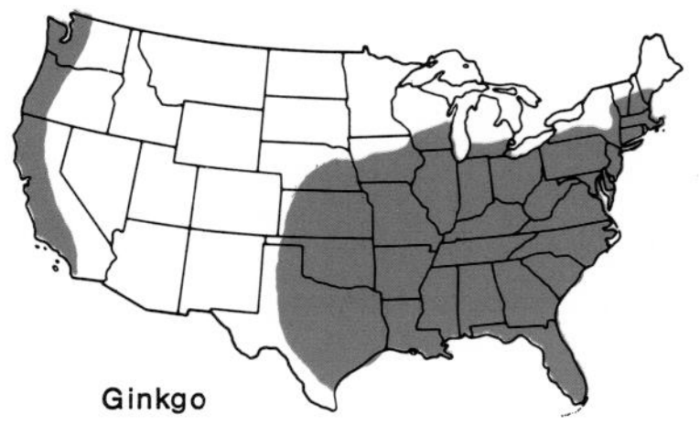
Ginkgo

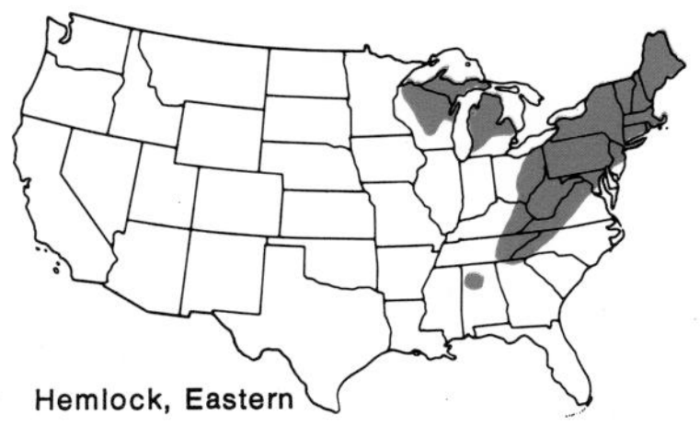
Hemlock, Eastern

Hickory, Shagbark

Holly, American

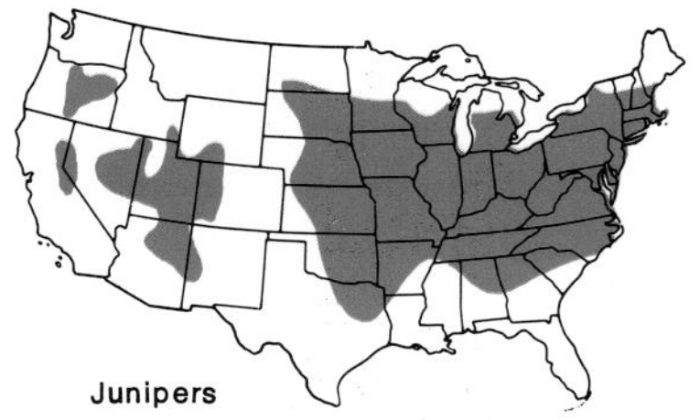
Junipers

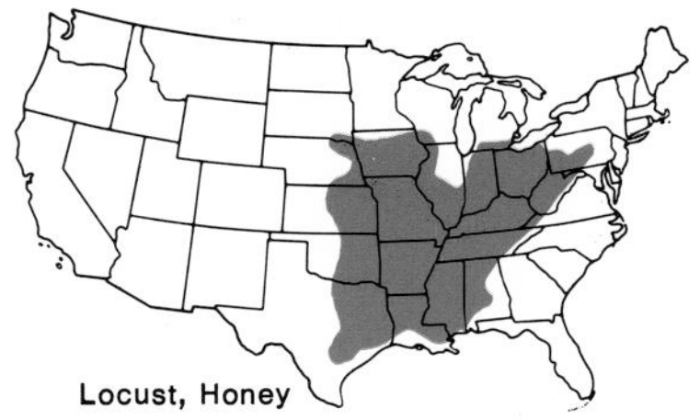
Locust, Honey

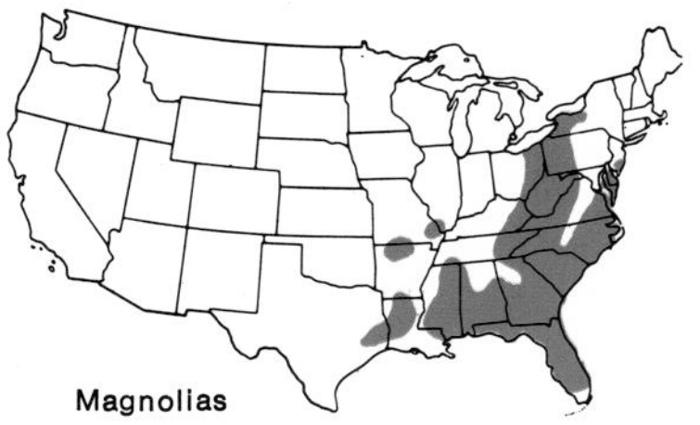
Magnolias

Manzanita

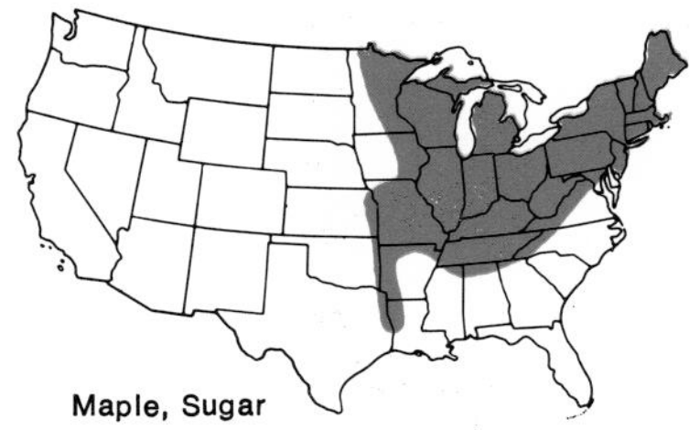
Maple, Sugar

Oak, California White

Oak, Live

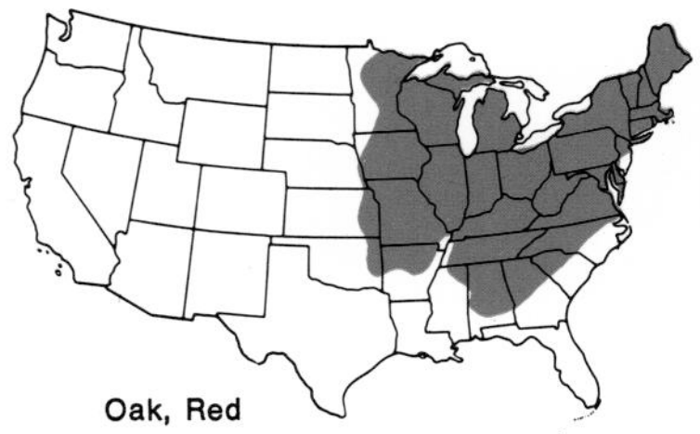
Oak, Red

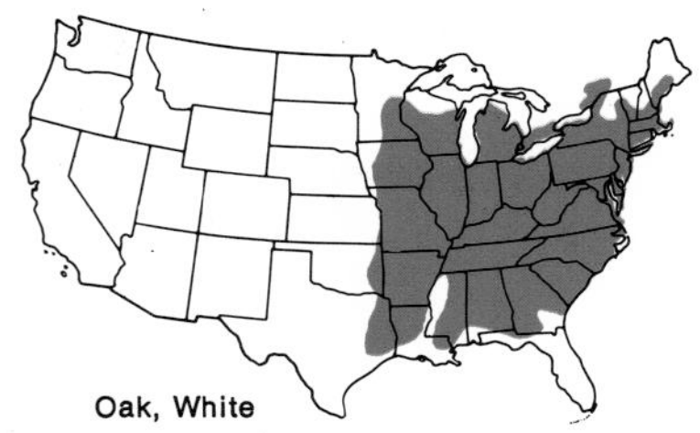
Oak, White

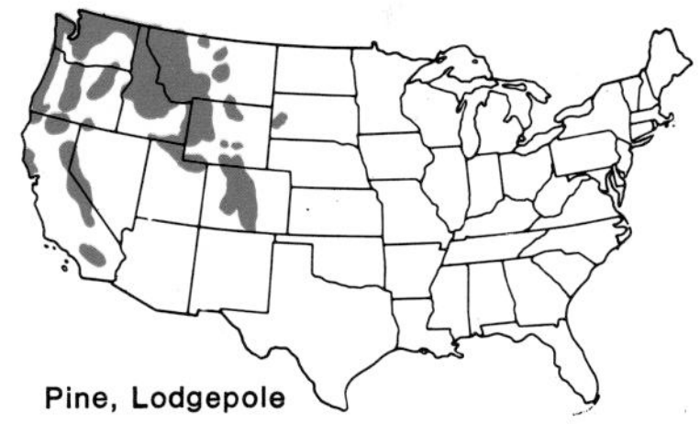
Pine, Lodgepole

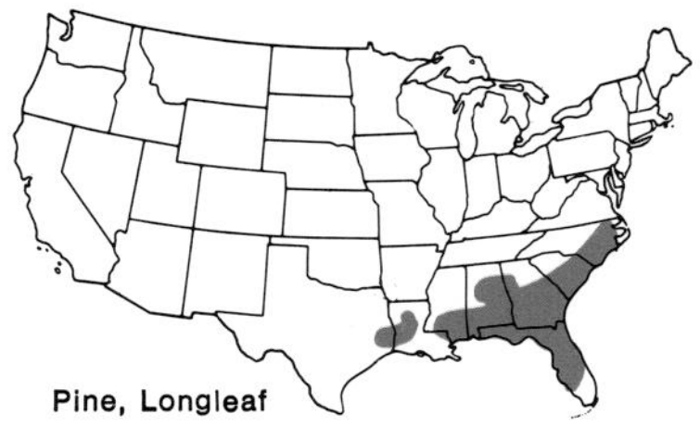
Pine, Longleaf

Pine, Pinyon

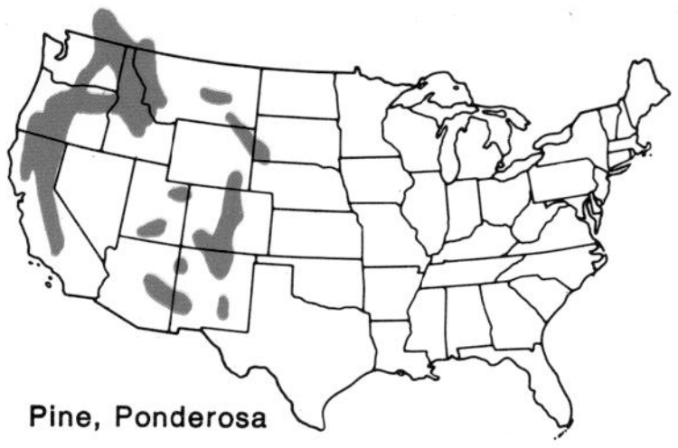

Pine, Ponderosa

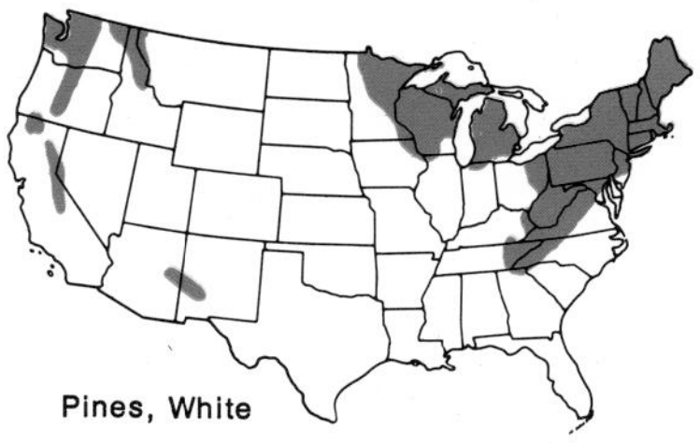

Pines, White

Redwood, Coast

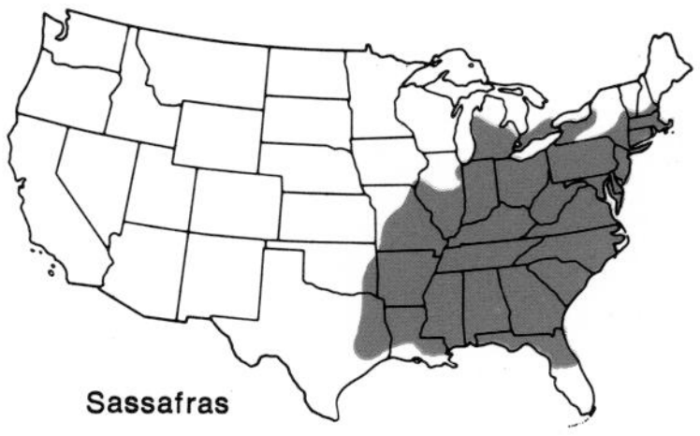

Sassafras

Sequoia, Giant

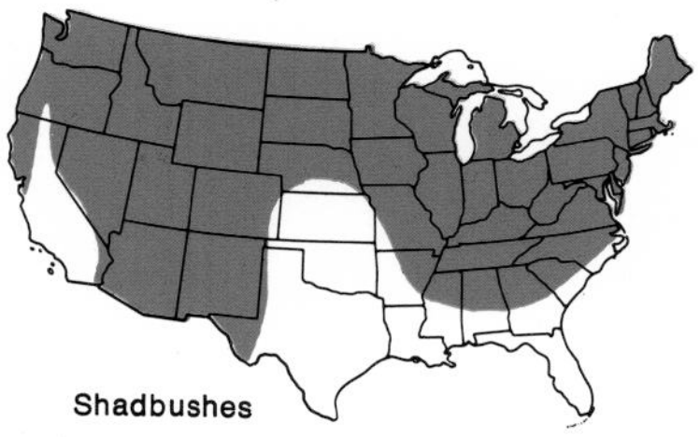

Shadbushes

Spruce, Blue

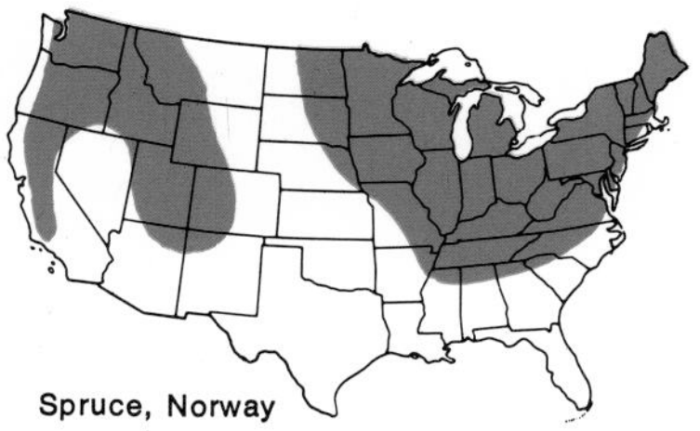

Spruce, Norway

Spruce, Engelmann

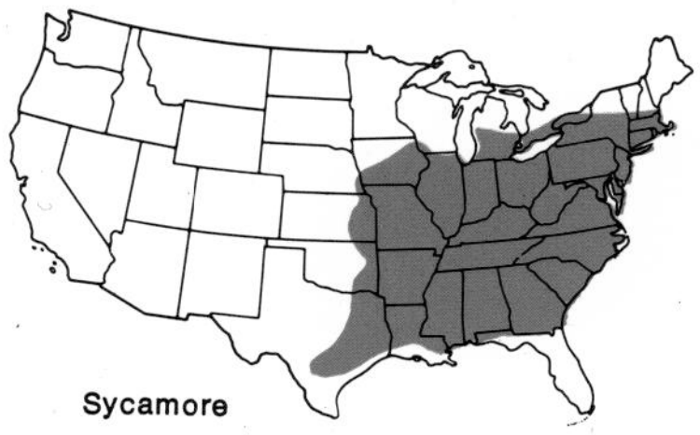

Sycamore

Tuliptree

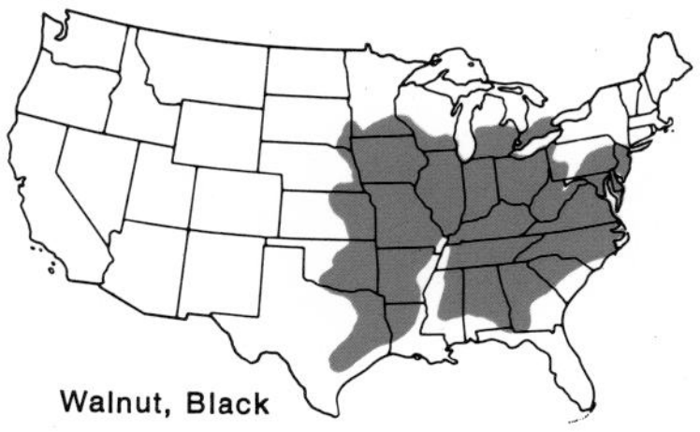

Walnut, Black

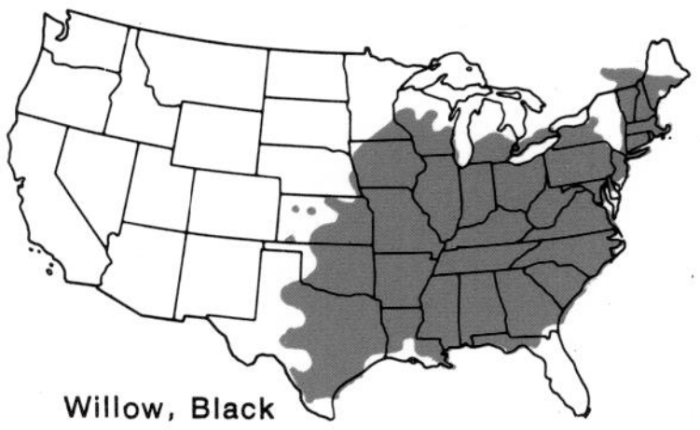

Willow, Black

Eastern White Pine (detail)

Pinyon Pine (rear) with Juniper

WHITE PINES

Once the monarchs of the eastern forest, growing 250 feet tall and six feet in diameter over a span of 250 years of life, the White Pines literally built colonial America. The stock is now much reduced, hardly any of it three feet through or over a hundred feet tall. Today one must look to the great Sugar Pines of California and the Oregon hill country to see how drastic a change the East has suffered. These are five-needle pines, each needle longish (3″–5″) and limber; and as in all pines, they are tied into a bundle at the base. The needles are bluish-green, and the combination of soft foliage and color is diagnostic at almost any distance. White Pines that grow in the open are frequently deformed by weevils that kill the leader twigs. The age of young pines can be measured by the number of whorls of branches. Western are larger than Eastern White Pines.

PINYON PINE

The small nut-pines of the dry Southwest are a distinctive, specialized group. Seldom 20 feet high, they grow in open stands—almost like apple orchards—on gently sloping table lands between 2000 and 8000 feet, depending somewhat on latitude, where the annual precipitation is less than 13 inches and where temperatures range from 110° F. to 25° below zero. One of the two common species **(Pinus edulis)** has a two-needle cluster and the other **(P. monophylla)**, a single needle while two less numerous species have three and four needles. The famous pinyon nuts, which were once a staple of the southwestern Indians' diet, are now marketed as a delicacy, being roasted to prevent spoiling. Stands of these trees are extensive enough to provide habitat for their own species of jay, the Pinyon Jay, which looks like a small, blue crow.

PONDEROSA PINE

Widespread throughout the mountains of the West, open stands of this big, orange to cinnamon, brown-barked pine are among the most pleasant landscapes in America. Most of them occur at elevations between 6500 and 10,500 feet in the Black Hills, the Rocky Mountains, and the West Coast ranges. This is one of the pitch pines, often called Western Yellow Pine, with two to three long needles (5″–10″). The seeds have large wings which help scatter them widely. Young trees —those less than a hundred years old—have very dark bark. The colorful, adult trees may live to be 500 years old, be over 200 feet high, and attain a diameter at breast height over six feet. Today only the Douglasfir of the Northwest and the pines of the Southeast exceed it in the quantity of lumber produced. Despite its attractiveness and adaptability, it is not used horticulturally.

Ponderosa Pine

Lodgepole Pine

Longleaf Pine

LODGEPOLE PINE

Although one of the most widespread conifers in the West, the Lodgepole is most conspicuous and characteristic in a broad band at mid-altitude in the northern Rocky Mountains. Here it forms incredibly dense stands after lightning fires. The stems are pale and straight as arrows after they attain a diameter of three inches or so. They provided ideal poles for tepees all along the upper reaches of the prairie and hence the name. The dense, evenly-aged stands are themselves ripe for the next fire, and since the species grows well under such conditions, it perpetuates itself. The needles occur in pairs, are about two inches long and bright yellow-green. If no fires occur for several decades, the trees thin themselves by crowding, have gray scaly bark, and may grow to good size, perhaps living to be 150 years of age if they escape disease.

LONGLEAF PINE

Three in a bundle, the needles are ten to 15 or more inches long, limber, and drop off every other year. The resulting name Longstraw is used as a common name, as is also Southern Yellow Pine. This is the principal turpentine tree of the Southeast. It is an important commercial tree and provides the best hard-pine timber used in construction for such things as masts, spars, and railroad ties. Mature trees exceed a hundred feet in height and are tall, only slightly-tapered columns, two feet or more in diameter, with papery, orange-brown bark. Cones may be ten inches long, but like most pines, produce good seed crops only every few years. The southeastern pineries are a result of selection by fire, so periodic lightning fires are necessary to prevent invasion by oaks. Now that man is in charge of the landscape, he must use burning as a management tool.

Engelmann Spruce

Blue Spruce

Norway Spruce

ENGELMANN SPRUCE
This is the dominant spruce of the mountains of the West, growing from Yukon Territory to the Mexican border. It occupies a large part of all the forested land in the central and northern Rocky Mountains, including the extensive slopes of Colorado. Because it is shade tolerant, it often occurs in association with Blue Spruce, Lodgepole Pine, or Douglasfir. The needles are dark blue-green, squarish as in most spruces, but more limber than most, and tend to curve forward and upward on the branchlet that bears them. A young tree is often silvery for a while. One non-botanical characteristic is the disagreeable "catty" odor of its crushed needles. This is a handsome tree, and is symmetrical enough to be used in horticulture, even in Europe. It is slow-growing and, because it grows in pure stands, is subject to insect attack and fire.

BLUE SPRUCE
The powder-blue foliage of this handsome tree makes it a favorite ornamental throughout temperate America and Europe, as well. Indeed, so fond are northern Europeans of trees that they have imported almost as many American species as the colonists took with them from Europe. As a native tree, the Blue Spruce has a rather restricted range in the Rocky Mountains, being most numerous—though never in pure stands — in Colorado. Nurserymen have naturally sought to select the brightest-blue specimens and have multiplied colorful types by grafting them onto Norway Spruce rootstock, especially since the latter is a naturally slow-growing species. Because the bright-blue color is in good part due to a powdery covering on the needles, which can be rubbed off, the trees are brightest in early summer when they sport new growth.

NORWAY SPRUCE
Although introduced from Europe, this big spruce is such a favorite that it has been planted extensively throughout temperate America, more particularly as a front-yard tree, to line entrance lanes, or as a farm windbreak and shelterbelt. Even today in much of the Northeast, a pair of large Norway Spruces will mark the site of an old country house, though the house itself may be gone. The needles are shiny, dark green, short and squarish, and emerge from all sides of the twig. Like all spruces they carry a small splinter with them when pulled from the twig—a sure way of distinguishing spruce from fir. As the tree matures its lower branches spread and sweep low to the ground. Like most trees transplanted into a new environment, the Norway Spruce does less well in the U.S. than it does in its native land, where it attains a height of 150 feet.

EASTERN HEMLOCK
Both halves of the country, East and West, have two hemlocks. Of the four the Eastern Hemlock has the most extensive range. It is a handsome tree, with dark-green foliage and gracefully drooping branches, including even the leader. The needles are flat, little more than a half-inch long, silvery below, and arranged in a flat frond. The new growth of the year is a delicate, pale green, always a pleasant contrast. The cone is among the smallest of any conifer, brown and persistent. Here and there in rocky gorges, which made earlier lumbering activities unprofitable, stands of mature hemlocks have persisted in the East. These are today some of the most pleasant wooded places, examples being Mianus Gorge in southwestern Connecticut and Heart's Content in northeastern Pennsylvania. The hemlock's reddish bark has long been used for tannin.

DOUGLASFIR
This great tree combines so many characteristics of other conifers that botanists have given it the hybrid name **Pseudotsuga taxifolia**, meaning "the false hemlock with yew foliage." Actually, the tree is easy to identify because pendant cones show three-pronged bracts that extend beyond the cone scales —an absolutely diagnostic characteristic. This is the last, great timber tree of the continent whose stands have not been cut over at least once. Soon, only what remains in parks and wilderness areas will show its magnificence—a giant that lives a thousand years, soars to 300 feet, and has a ten-foot-diameter trunk. It has, besides, extremely strong wood for its weight. It fortunately grows rapidly, so western timber companies are planting thousands of acres of Douglasfir. Individual trees are used horticulturally across the nation.

BALSAM FIR
All the true firs, and only they, have erect, often purplish, candle-like cones. Pluck a single needle from a fir branch and it will leave a clean, round disk; spruce needles always splinter away. The trunk of a young fir is marked with many large blisters, which contain the clear Canada balsam used in pharmacies and laboratories. The needles are especially aromatic and persistent; and since a young fir is particularly symmetrical, these characteristics combine to make it the best Christmas tree. The southern Appalachians have their own Fraser Fir, and the mountains of the West have several much more impressive species: White Fir, Silver Fir, Grand Fir, Noble Fir, Red Fir, and Alpine Fir. The wood of fir is brittle, however, so it is used very little in construction. Instead, millions of acres of fir—along with spruce—are cut for pulp to make paper.

Eastern Hemlock

Douglasfir

Balsam Fir (detail)

COAST REDWOOD

It is not surprising that most people do not distinguish between the Coast Redwood and the Giant Sequoia; neither did botanists for a long time. Redwoods are restricted to the summer fogbelt of the Pacific Coast, from Monterey County, California, to southern Oregon. There, on small river flats and ocean-facing slopes, dense stands of Redwoods send great shafts skyward for over 300 feet, the tallest living things—taller than a 25-story building! There giants have small cones, more like cedars than pines. Their needles are small, at first stiffly opposite, like hemlocks, but later overlapping like the scales of junipers. Not until 1968 was the nation able to contain its greed for every resource that could be turned to commercial use. It then acquired a mere 16 square miles (4 mi. by 4 mi.) of primeval Redwood forest to add to California's Redwood parks.

GIANT SEQUOIA

How much of our world remains to be explored is well illustrated by California's Big Trees. The Coast Redwood was thought to be the last of an ancient race that flourished well to the north millions of years ago but in the 1940s botanists rediscovered Metasequoia, the Dawn Redwood, in remote valleys of western China. The Big Trees were thought to be the oldest living things until, in 1954, Bristlecone Pines more than 4000 years old were found. This suggests that we should stop making over nature until we have learned much more about our world. Giant Sequoias survive in small basins in the cool middle elevations of the western slope of the Sierra Nevada mountains. Though not so tall as Coast Redwoods, they are perhaps more impressive individually, attaining heights of 250 feet and diameters between 20 and 30 feet.

Giant Sequoia

Coast Redwood

Bald Cypress

Western Juniper

Black Willow

BALD CYPRESS
An inhabitant of wet lowlands, this giant is a relative of the Coast Redwood. But like a larch, it is a conifer that sheds its short needles every autumn, assuming a bald look that gives it its name. As its relationship suggests, the small cones are more like those of sequoias and cypresses than pines. Most of the mature Bald Cypresses have been cut, but the stateliness of old cypress "strands" can still be seen at two Audubon sanctuaries—Four Hole Swamp near Charleston, S.C. and Corkscrew Swamp near Naples, Fla. — and at Okefenokee National Wildlife Refuge. Big trees may live over a thousand years, grow well over a hundred feet tall, and acquire diameters of ten or more feet. The fluted buttresses of big trunks and their cluster of "knees" are impressive features. The wood is highly resistant to decay, but fire kills many stands during drought.

JUNIPERS
Junipers are small to medium-sized trees of dry, rocky, or gravelly sites, and distinctive in many ways. The needles are of two types, the new ones being short and awl-like, the older ones compressed together like overlapping scales. The branches are therefore more prickly than those of other conifers. The bark is fibrous and shreds easily. The wood may be reddish-brown or white. And the bluish-white berries really are small, fleshy cones. Junipers are widespread in the Northern Hemisphere. Many of the species are low, prostrate forms used horticulturally. The most widespread in eastern America is the Virginia Juniper, or Red Cedar, which grows in abandoned pastures and stands like a big green candle. The Utah Juniper is one of several western species that evolved to occupy extremely dry sites in the rain shadow of the Sierra Nevada mountains.

BLACK WILLOW
There are nearly 300 species of willow in the Northern Hemisphere, half of them on our continent and most of them shrubs. Of the 30 or so tree-sized willows, the Black Willow is the largest and attains heights between 50 and 100 feet. It is the only willow that produces measurable amounts of lumber. Although willows are extremely difficult to identify because they frequently hybridize, a large native willow is likely to be of this species. It has long, narrow leaves, usually two to six inches long and a half inch wide. The leaf is dark green on both surfaces (many other species have pale under-surfaces) and tapers to a long point. Another characteristic is the tendency of branchlets to be brittle at the base, though they are strong and supple along their length. As one may gather from the name, the bark is dark, unlike the widely-planted Weeping Willow, which is yellowish.

Quaking Aspen

QUAKING ASPEN

A widespread and an eager colonist of disturbed areas, especially after fire, this small, colorful aspen plays a vital ecological role, though it furnishes no lumber, being reduced to pulp instead. The roundish leaves, less than two inches long, are bright green in summer but turn to gold when autumn's cold hits them. Where aspen stands occur on slopes, as happens in the West and the Appalachians, they account for much of the splendor of autumn. The adjectival name (sometimes Trembling Aspen) refers to the movement of every leaf in the slightest breeze because the leaf stem, or petiole, is both long and flattened like a strap. Most eastern aspens have greenish-gray bark, and western trees are paler and grow to greater size. Everywhere, however, this is a short-lived tree, and is a healer of scars in the landscape, growing to heights of 20 to 40 feet.

Cottonwood Grove

COTTONWOODS

These are fast-growing trees of some importance as timber in the lower Mississippi River valley, but are best known and admired as lonely patriarchs in farmyards throughout the East and up river courses along the prairie. Along western rivers they form distinctive stands that furnished winter shelter to the Plains Indians and today furnish shelter and fuel for wildlife and campers. Mature trees have deeply fissured bark, and bright green, leathery, and conspicuously-triangular leaves. Cottonwoods are poplars and all poplars are members of the Willow Family. As such, the flowers are in long, drooping catkins that produce lots of cotton fuzz. This fluffy, white down is the parachute of seeds and helps distribute them widely. Housewives often object to the cottony down that clutters screen doors for a week or so annually.

BLACK WALNUT

The walnuts, hickories, and pecans all belong to the same Family. The first group includes the Black Walnut and the White Walnut (Butternut), and each can be positively identified as to genus by slicing open a branchlet, lengthwise. The spongy pith within is divided into a series of chambers by thin plates or septa. The big compound leaves usually have more than 15 leaflets. These are almost smooth in the Black Walnut, but hairy and sticky in the Butternut. The fruit, at first bright green, is round, usually over two inches in diameter, hard, and contains the familiar grooved nut, the American equivalent of the Persian Walnut, which is usually marketed as the English Walnut. A Black Walnut will grow over a hundred feet tall and achieve a diameter of three feet. It is our foremost cabinet-making wood, strong, easily matched, and easy to work.

Shagbark Hickory

Black Walnut

SHAGBARK HICKORY
Hickories are differentiated from walnuts by their solid, dark, unchambered pith, and by their smaller compound leaf, usually with five or seven leaflets. The Shagbark is the most widespread and the most important hickory for timber. It is also the most easily recognized because of its distinctive bark. The bark is gray and curls away from the trunk at one or both ends of long strips, a characteristic noticeable a hundred feet away. The trunk is usually straight, grows well over a hundred feet, and attains a diameter of two or more feet The strong, springy wood makes it one of our most valuable trees. Its strength and resilience makes it ideal for axe handles, baseball bats, and other sporting equipment. Pecan is also one of the hickories, and is the most valuable nut-tree in America, even though it is limited to the south-central U.S.

MANZANITA
Throughout the Southwest, where long, dry summers and intense sunshine recreate a Mediterranean climate, grows chaparral, a dense, almost impenetrable and fire-prone brushland at middle elevations. Mostly evergreen, it is composed of several shrubs and small trees. Many people consider the false lilac, **Ceanothus,** and the Manzanita the most attractive and typical of these. The tight-barked purplish trunk and stems of Manzanita are twisted and gnarled, as though tortured into arthritic shapes by the desiccating winds and sun. The leaves are frosted gray-green, and the flowers remind one of the blueberry, because this is indeed a member of the aristocratic Heath Family. Tenacious specimens may stand only a foot high or reach up to 25 feet, depending upon the age of the plant or the nature of the site on which it grows.

PAPER BIRCH
Because it does well in the full light of a clearing, whether after fire or lumbering, the Paper Birch is probably more common today across Canada and the adjacent northern states than it was in colonial days. It grows fast, and the white, papery bark of a young tree peels easily in broad strips. The Amerindians of the Algonquin and Iroquois Nations adapted this resource to their economy by creating birch-bark canoes, one of the important inventions of mankind. This use was functional, but today's stripping of bark is a disfiguring form of vandalism. There are over a dozen other birch species, the most widespread of them being the River Birch or Red Birch. In the northern U.S. two small European species of white birch are extensively planted as ornamentals. The Gray Birch of the Northeast is a short-lived species, with chalky-white bark.

Manzanita

Paper Birch (detail)

American Beech

Red Oak

AMERICAN BEECH
Along with the oaks, pines, and a few others, this is one of the great forest trees of the world, and one of the codominant species of the eastern deciduous forest of America. It is easily recognized by its tight, blue-gray bark; by its rather glossy, straight-veined leaves that bleach to a pale buff in autumn and often persist on the lower branches of young trees throughout the winter; by the long, sharp-pointed red-brown buds; the small, sharp-angled edible beechnuts; and by the habit of sprouting from the spreading root system, so that an older tree becomes surrounded by a ring of saplings. This was once one of the great "mast" trees of the eastern forest, furnishing food for the now extinct Passenger Pigeons, Wild Turkeys, squirrels, and others. The beeches, the oaks, and the American Chestnut belong to the same Family, named for its edible nuts.

RED OAK
Not all mighty oaks from little acorns grow. Some grow from sprouts or from old root systems that have awaited the opportunity for half a century to grow upward again. In general, of course, one still tells a tree by its fruits, and for oaks this means acorns. Assuming a tree is an oak, we must classify it into a black oak group or a white oak group. Most oaks have indented leaves (with sinuses and lobes). In the black oak group each lobe has a spiny bristle at its tip, whereas the lobes in the white oak group do not. Classifying oaks to this point will give one an intelligent layman's grasp of the complexity of life forms, but classifying oaks by species requires consulting a detailed guide. Briefly, the Red Oak's leaves have bristles; their sinuses are shallow; and the bark shows flattened patches, as though someone had pressed it with a hot iron.

WHITE OAK
All oaks with leaves whose lobes are smoothly rounded (without bristles) belong to the white oak group. The White Oak pictured here is the prototype. Its leaves have deep sinuses and its pale-gray bark, which tends to be flaky, makes it easier to identify than most oaks. The principal oaks are great forest trees, and the White Oak is as impressive as any of them. Its long life—up to 800 years with luck—allows it to grow to great size, but it attains its height slowly. One that grows in the open is broader in total outline, with heavy branches low on the trunk. Such a gnarled old giant becomes a landmark because it outlives several generations of men. Forest-grown trees, on the other hand, growing upward more rapidly because they must compete for light, have their lower limbs naturally pruned away by shading, and grow tall and straight.

White Oak

California White Oak

Live Oak (with Spanish Moss)

CALIFORNIA WHITE OAK

The oak-grasslands of California's central hills and valleys are among the most pleasant landscapes in America. The dominant tree, also called Valley Oak, grows best in the rich soils of the valley floors, but because these have mostly been taken up for other uses, the tree is now chiefly on the lower slopes, always in the hot interior valleys, not on cool, ocean-facing slopes. Growing in open stands, since moisture is at a premium, it has a broad crown and is generally graceful in a rugged sort of way. As protection against desiccation by hot winds, the leaves are small, leathery, and covered with fine hairs on both surfaces. They are deeply but narrowly incised. The acorns are long, slender, pointed, bright chestnut-brown, and sweet. Today the Mule Deer and squirrels of these hills are the principal beneficiaries of the acorn crops.

LIVE OAK

Few living species are more variable in form than the Live Oak, which can be a great tree or a shrub, depending on the environment. As most of us know it, this is one of the impressive trees of America. In the southeastern coastal plain it is a massive tree, seldom more than 50 feet high, but spreading twice that far or more. When, as so often in the Southeast, it is shrouded in Spanish Moss, blue-gray and eerie a good part of the time, it is almost awesome, and is the symbolic tree of the deep South. At times no plantings in the world seem more impressive than a double row of these great oaks arching the entrance road to one of the old southern plantations. The name Live Oak of course refers to the persistent foliage. The leaves are a glossy, dark green above and whitish below. Unlike most oaks, they are not indented at the margin.

AMERICAN ELM

This most graceful, most stately of the deciduous trees is fast vanishing from the landscape because of the spread of Dutch elm disease introduced on imported lumber in the 1930's. Despite the spraying of tons of DDT to kill the bark beetles that help spread the disease, the epidemic spread out of control, and the landscape was poisoned for many other life forms. The elm was such a favorite for park and street plantings that its loss in many communities has left disfiguring scars that will take time to heal. We should learn to diversify plantings to avoid such losses. There are still good examples of this tree, especially at the limits of its range—trees that send vase-like trunks upward for a hundred feet. The toothed, parallel-veined leaves are smallish, uneven (one half is larger than the other), rough above, and soft below.

American Elm

Tuliptree

SASSAFRAS

Although potentially the longest-lived tree in the East—up to a thousand years—old trees are scarce today because we have abused the land, fire often being the agent. Even in immaturity, Sassafras is an intriguing species. It tends to be flat-topped; its twisty branches come out horizontally; and the big golden-yellow buds are welcome signs of spring. The bark is reddish-brown, deeply fissured with age and often with a wash of gray. But the twigs and shoots are bright green. Most distinctive of all, however, are the three kinds of leaves found on every tree: simple or lance-shaped; mitten-shaped; and three-lobed, suggestive of the French fleur-de-lis. Its aromatic bark and roots were used as a "spring tonic"—sassafras tea—by Indians and colonists, and even exported to Europe. In parts of the Atlantic coastal plain Sassafras colonizes old fields.

MAGNOLIAS

There are many magnolias scattered throughout temperate and tropical America and eastern Asia, many of them small trees used horticulturally. The Sweetbay and the Bigleaf Magnolias of the southeastern U.S. are among the most pleasing and ornamentally desirable. The leaves of the Sweetbay Magnolia are evergreen, and large—five to seven inches long and nearly three inches wide, bluntly pointed at both ends, and coated with whitish down below. Consequently, even the foliage is used decoratively. The crowning glory of the Sweetbay, and many of its relatives, is its large, creamy-white blossoms, six to eight inches in diameter. These are fragrant, but last only three or four days, after which the numerous petals fall to the ground. Quite aside from their beauty, the larger species are also valued for their timber.

TULIPTREE

The tall, straight bole of this splendid forest tree is so distinctive that it can suffice for identification. Even in winter, the persistent, dry, fruit capsules stand conspicuously erect. All around the tree will be the paddle-shaped seeds, or samaras. Both the common and Latin names refer to the tulip-like flowers — large, orange-spotted, yellow-green blossoms that surprise one on so tall a tree until we learn that this is a relative of the magnolias. The leaves are equally distinctive, dark green, almost glossy, and square-cut. The Tuliptree is one of several species that has developed its own chemical defenses against leaf-chewing insects, and in the Northeast, at least, it is free of caterpillar attack. The wood is usually pale-yellowish and soft, hence the other common names Yellow Poplar and Whitewood. Most of the cut goes into boxmaking.

Sassafras (detail)

Sweetbay Magnolia (with Spanish Moss)

Sycamore

SYCAMORE

This tree reminds one of the giraffe, because the mottled trunk has overstretched bark that is brown, reddish, tan, or greenish against a new background of nearly-white bark. It is thus easily recognized. The Sycamore does not form stands but is a scattered occupant of river bottoms or other areas of deep, moist soil. It often exceeds a hundred feet in height, may be ten feet or more in diameter, and is one of the largest eastern trees when mature. The leaves are broad, sometimes ten inches across, usually with three shallow lobes and bright green above and paler below. The fruit is a dense ball of nutlets, nearly two inches in diameter, and responsible for the tree's other common names, Buttonwood or Buttonball. The European Plane Tree, a close relative, is often planted in the eastern U.S., but has smaller leaves and never attains the dimensions of the Sycamore.

Sugar Maple

Honey Locust

HONEY LOCUST

The locusts—including Honey Locust, Black Locust, and Kentucky Coffeetree—all in different genera, are members of the Legume Family. All have small leaflets on a larger compound leaf, but each has a different seed pod. The Honey Locust is most readily distinguished by the dangerous forked spines that grow out of its trunk, either singly or in clusters. The foot-long seed pods are also the longest of the group. They are cinnamon brown and recurved. Its blossoms are the least showy of the three species mentioned here. The numerous brown and oval beans in the pods are eagerly sought by cattle and several species of wildlife, including both mammals and birds. Its wood resists decay, but since the tree is nowhere common and occurs only as scattered individuals, not much of it is used. The genus occurs in Asia and Africa as well.

SUGAR MAPLE
The maples are a varied tribe and widely scattered across the Northern Hemisphere. None is finer or more valuable than the Sugar Maple, a real triple-treat tree valued for its wood, its sugary sap, and for its flaming orange-red autumn foliage. All maples are opposite-leaved and opposite-branched. Since among eastern trees only the ashes, dogwoods, and the Horse Chestnut also have opposite branching, this is a good clue to identification. The maples also bear seeds in winged pairs, the familiar "maple key" which country children have always enjoyed splitting open and implanting on their noses like a miniature rhinoceros horn. A good tree yields over 15 gallons of sweet sap in early spring, but it takes nearly 50 gallons to boil down to a gallon of syrup. Over ten million trees are tapped annually in the northern U.S. and southern Quebec.

AMERICAN HOLLY
We are so accustomed to seeing holly as a Christmas cutting that we may not realize this attractive foliage was propagated from a bona fide forest tree. On good soil it will attain a height of 40 to 50 feet and a trunk diameter of one to two feet. The wood is white, close-grained, and takes a high polish, so is excellent for wood turning. It is even used as a substitute for ivory in piano keys. The evergreen foliage of tree holly makes excellent ornamental plantings, either as specimen trees or hedges. Because the tree is usually unisexual, however, with only one type of flower per plant, those who wish a berry-bearing plant, must either buy one of each sex, so that fertilization may occur, or get assurance from the nursery that the plant is of the scarcer polygamous type. Robin flocks winter as far north as holly groves occur.

American Holly

Horse Chestnut

Basswood

White Ash (detail)

HORSE CHESTNUT

A native of southern Asia, first imported to Europe, and then to the U.S., the Horse Chestnut is now grown as an ornamental tree in every state. It is a handsome tree, well proportioned, with lush green compound-leaves and a showy open spike of purple-spotted white flowers that bloom in June or early July. The compound leaf has seven leaflets arranged like the fingers of a hand (palmately), five of them large and the two basal ones small. Notice that a compound leaf has a single attachment to its branch and falls as a unit. The leaf scar left by each fallen leaf is large and looks somewhat like a horseshoe print. The terminal bud is large and sticky. There are several tree and shrub relatives of the same genus **(Aesculus)** in America, the principal ones being the Ohio Buckeye (with yellow flowers) and the California Buckeye, all characteristic of their genus.

BASSWOOD

More than two-score species of hardwood trees make up the eastern deciduous forest, the most richly diversified forest of its kind on Earth. Of these, the American Basswood occupies the northern half of the deciduous region, the White Basswood the southern half. Both have characteristic heart-shaped leaves with toothed margins and an abruptly tapered point. The northern tree has a smooth, green leaf, whereas the southern one has a leaf covered with silvery-white hairs below. Both have a spray of small, creamy flowers attached to a leafy bract, and a trio of dry nutlets the size of green peas as fruit. The wood of these trees is nearly white, light, and has such good working qualities that it is highly valued for wood carving. A close relative, the Linden of Europe, widely planted in the U.S., and our own species are good ornamentals.

WHITE ASH

This great tree is even more pleasing during its winter leaflessness than in summer, because in winter the angularity of its opposite branching and the strikingly parallel fissures of its uniformly-gray bark, stand out with a familiar clarity unmatched by any tree. Those who come to know trees usually agree that most of our deciduous trees are as delightful in winter as at any other time. The hard, springy, straight-splitting wood is one of the best hardwoods in the world, and the large size of the tree, plus its wide distribution, makes this one of the leading, commercial species in the East. The compound leaf has five to nine short-stalked leaflets arranged pinnately (on each side of the stalk). The fruit is a drooping cluster of slender samaras (seeds with a paddle-like wing) and a favorite winter food of several birds, especially the Evening Grosbeak.

Flowering Dogwood (white and pink varieties)

Shadbush

SHADBUSHES

We say that a tree is a woody plant with a single stem or trunk. How high? Some say at least 12 feet; others 18 feet. Obviously, there are so many variables that our definitions are arbitrary—merely for convenience in organizing our growing stock of information. Most Shadbushes—also called Juneberry, Serviceberry, Sugarplum — are shrubs, but at least two of them with heights of 25 and 40 feet may be listed either as trees or shrubs. Though each begins with several main stems, they either grow together or only one tends to survive and dominate with age. However classified, they are worth knowing, because their gray-stemmed forms are graceful and their open clusters of delicate white or pinkish-white blossoms are harbingers of spring, appearing before the leaves. The juicy fruit is a favorite of wildlife everywhere.

FLOWERING DOGWOOD

Throughout the deciduous forest of eastern America, the Flowering Dogwood is the dominant and most pleasing understory tree. Hence, it is never a large tree, like many of the others it keeps company with. Its early flowering, before the leaves of the canopy trees cast their shade, lavishes the woodland with showy white blossoms, all the more delightful because they seem suspended within the forest. The leaves are ovate, pointed at both ends, and opposite one another. The best clue to identification, however—remembering the two or three diagnostic traits already mentioned—is the alligator-hide pattern of its bark. The bark itself is often gray, but may be brown or blackish. Interestingly, the showy blossoms are not flower petals, but enlarged white or pink bracts that help display a cluster of small, perfect flowers at their center.

Gingko

GINKGO

Sometimes called Maidenhair Tree because of its lovely, fan-shaped and parallel-veined leaves, this tree is a living fossil, as is the Metasequoia. This means it escaped extinction when all its close relatives became extinct in the past. As the record of the rocks shows, the Ginkgo was both numerous and widespread 150 million years ago. The Ginkgo's age is also attested to by the fact that although it has a broad leaf and is deciduous, it is actually more closely related to evergreen coniferous trees than to such present-day deciduous trees as oaks. Ginkgos were first discovered by American traders in Chinese temple gardens and were so popular during the era of the China clipper trade that they were planted extensively in this country. Male trees are preferred because female trees have a fleshy, plum-like, odiferous fruit that messes up sidewalks.

4.WILDFLOW

ERS

WILDFLOWERS

The title for this group of plants is most artificial because the popular term Wildflowers usually refers to common herbaceous plants with showy flowers. Actually, some trees and shrubs also have showy flowers; some herbaceous plants have inconspicuous flowers; and some, like the Scouring Rush and the ferns, are not flowering plants at all but are, instead, spore-bearing plants.

All this seeming confusion comes from the fact that the Plant Kingdom is a very large one with 150 million years of evolutionary history. Almost every imaginable combination of adaptations to the Earth's extensive habitats and its changing climates has been tried by plants. It is therefore impossible to categorize them neatly.

We can begin by recognizing that, in a sense, a flower is a biological mechanism for effecting the fertilization of egg cells (ovules borne in a pistil) by male cells (pollen produced in a stamen) to produce an embryo, which produces a seed from which a new plant grows. A seed has been described as a baby plant wrapped up in its lunch.

All flowers were originally pollinated by wind, and the pollen was blown from plant to plant. This, of course, requires vast amounts of pollen because it is a matter of chance whether or not a windblown pollen grain will alight on an appropriate pistil. Typical of this method of pollination are the pines and grasses. They emit veritable showers of pollen during their flowering season, enough to dust woodland or prairie ponds with gold. The pollen sinks into the mud and much of it is preserved, or fossilized. This provides a key for the later reconstruction the history of the region's vegetation.

Today's showy flowers are usually an adaptation to insect pollination. This involves showy petals or bracts, bright colors, and nectar-bearing glands which attract insects, who then unwittingly transfer pollen from one flower to another in the process of feeding themselves. This effects cross-pollination and increases genetic diversity within the plant species. Hummingbirds, which feed on flower nectar, also play a role in the pollination of many flowers. In Africa, sunbirds perform this role. It is a challenge to understand how these interdependencies originated and perfected themselves, because comparative studies suggest that none originated fullblown.

The very large Family of grasses, of which there are over 4500 species in the world and 1100 species in the contiguous United States, deserves special mention because of its importance as an element of the landscape and the neglect it generally suffers except among specialists. Grasses not only make up the bulk of the vast areas in wet or dry prairie, veldt, and savanna, but also of many cultivated species which now furnish a large share of mankind's food. Maize (which we call corn), rice, wheat, barley, oats, millet, sugar cane—all these are grasses and basic food crops. Bamboo is also a grass.

Many grasses have fibrous root systems that greatly exceed their above-ground parts, and they thus play vital roles in anchoring soil and in building up organic matter in soil. When mowed regularly, several species of grass make excellent turf, which is why we use them as lawn grasses. In the United States, however, where most of the country has hot, dry summers, too much lawn has been planted. Suburban homemakers struggle to become amateur greenkeepers and waste millions of dollars trying to maintain grass where shrubs and trees would provide a more appropriate ground cover.

Grasses once maintained the tremendous numbers American Bison. Today, they still maintain the great ungulate herds of East Africa and, indirectly, all those other species that are dependent upon them. Lions do not eat much grass, but they would not exist without the grass that nourishes their prey.

Weeds, the farmer says, are plants out of place. But this is a self-centered view that disregards ecological principles. Ralph Waldo Emerson once, more sagely, observed that a weed is a plant whose virtues have not yet been discovered.

Functionally weeds are pioneer plants. They have the special ability to colonize quickly unvegetated raw land. Large or small openings in the landscape are created by floods, landslides, forest fires, bulldozers, the death of other plants, and a thousand other causes. It is these openings that weeds are best equipped to fill. Interestingly, a majority of all U.S. weeds are plants introduced from Europe during the colonial era. In the East, most showy wildflowers found along roadsides are European

Preceding pages: Wildflowers, Olympic Mountains, Washington

weeds; one must look in the forest to find native flora. In the West, or more particularly in the prairie, most native flowering plants and many weeds are found along roadsides and other uncultivated ground because the native prairie has all been plowed up.

The way to fight weeds is to avoid creating raw land and to fill openings with a preferred plant cover. Weed-killing chemical herbicides may kill a crop of weeds but they thereby reopen the landscape to invasion by more weeds. In a lawn, for example, crabgrass and dandelions quickly colonize every opening. If one objects to these—and not all people do—one must not only eliminate them but must plant new seed and nurture it until the turf is dense enough to prevent invasion by weeds.

Like insects, plants come in so many forms that one needs a new vocabulary to find one's way among the descriptions in botanical manuals and field guides. Many of these terms are listed in the glossary of this book, but it may be helpful to pull those applicable to plants together here to show more clearly how plants, and especially flowers, are described.

The conspicuous plants of our landscapes are either plants with woody stems, which include trees, shrubs, and vines, or herbaceous plants, which include a large group of grass-like plants and a great, more or less familiar, variety of small flowering plants.

The grass-like plants include the true grasses, which have round, hollow stems with solid joints (nodes with septa) at intervals; the rushes, which have round, hollow stems but no nodes or joints; and the sedges, which have triangular stems or leaves wrapped together so that they form a triangular cross-section. Since many of these grass-like plants have slender stems, the quickest way to check the type of stem involved is to twirl it in one's fingers. The stem, of course, is that part of the plant which connects the roots with the leafy portion.

Flowers are complex arrangements of plant parts specialized through evolutionary time to ensure cross-fertilization by insects. A perfect flower contains both female and male elements enveloped in a double series of specialized leaves. The lowest, or outermost, cup is formed by small, only slightly-modified leaves called sepals. Together the sepals form a calyx. Within the calyx is a series of larger, often showy, highly-modified leaves called petals. For most people these showy petals are the flower. Together, the petals form a corolla (a crown).

In the center of this double cup (calyx and corolla) is the ovary, a tiny, firm envelop which contains the egg or ovule. Rising above and out of the ovary is a hollow tube called a pistil. The male pollen grain that fertilizes the ovule must pass down the length of the pistil. The pollen grain, in turn, is formed in the anther of a stamen, the latter attached to the outside or base of the pistil by a slender filament. The photograph of the Turk's-cap Lily on page 82 shows the parts in cross section of a perfect flower fairly well.

Imperfect flowers lack one or another of the parts of the perfect flower just described. Sometimes the male and female elements are on separate flowers; sometimes the corolla is missing. Occasionally, showy petal-like bracts (really exaggerated sepals) form what is known as a false flower around the true (usually small and inconspicuous) flower, as do Poinsettia and Flowering Dogwood.

The map on pages 74-75 shows the average annual rainfall and has superimposed upon it lines that show the growing season of plants. This means that after the indicated date, the season will be frost-free at night, except in unusual years, and the daily temperature will be above 50° F., for example, for several hours most days.

The map on pages 224-225 is a more generalized climatic map, and the map on pages 44-45 shows how natural vegetation adapts itself to climate. Indeed, vegetation is a better clue to climate than the climatologist has yet been able to formulate by combining rainfall and temperature data.

In retrospect, it is ironic that the climatic zone we occupy was called a temperate zone. It is actually a zone of extreme temperature contrasts and violent storms, and it is subject to almost unpredictable variation. Always more predictable, the Arctic is never as hot as and is seldom colder than the temperate zone at its coldest. The tropics are seldom as hot, never as cold, and always more predictable.

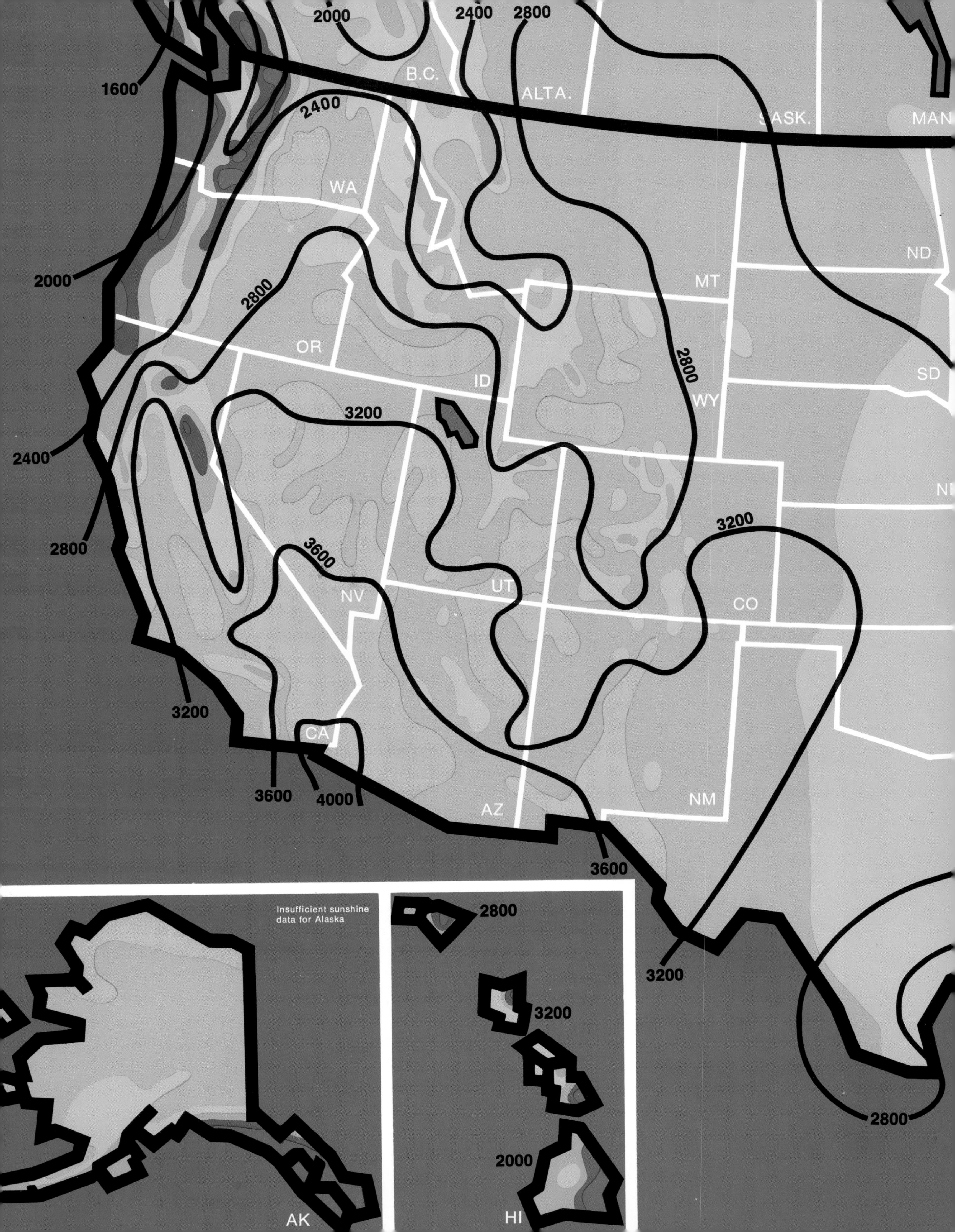

1600
2000
2400
2800
B.C.
ALTA.
SASK.
MAN.
2400
WA
2000
2800
OR
ID
MT
ND
SD
WY
2800
2400
3200
2800
3200
3600
NV
UT
CO
3200
CA
3600
4000
AZ
NM
3600
3200
2800
Insufficient sunshine data for Alaska
AK
2800
3200
2000
HI

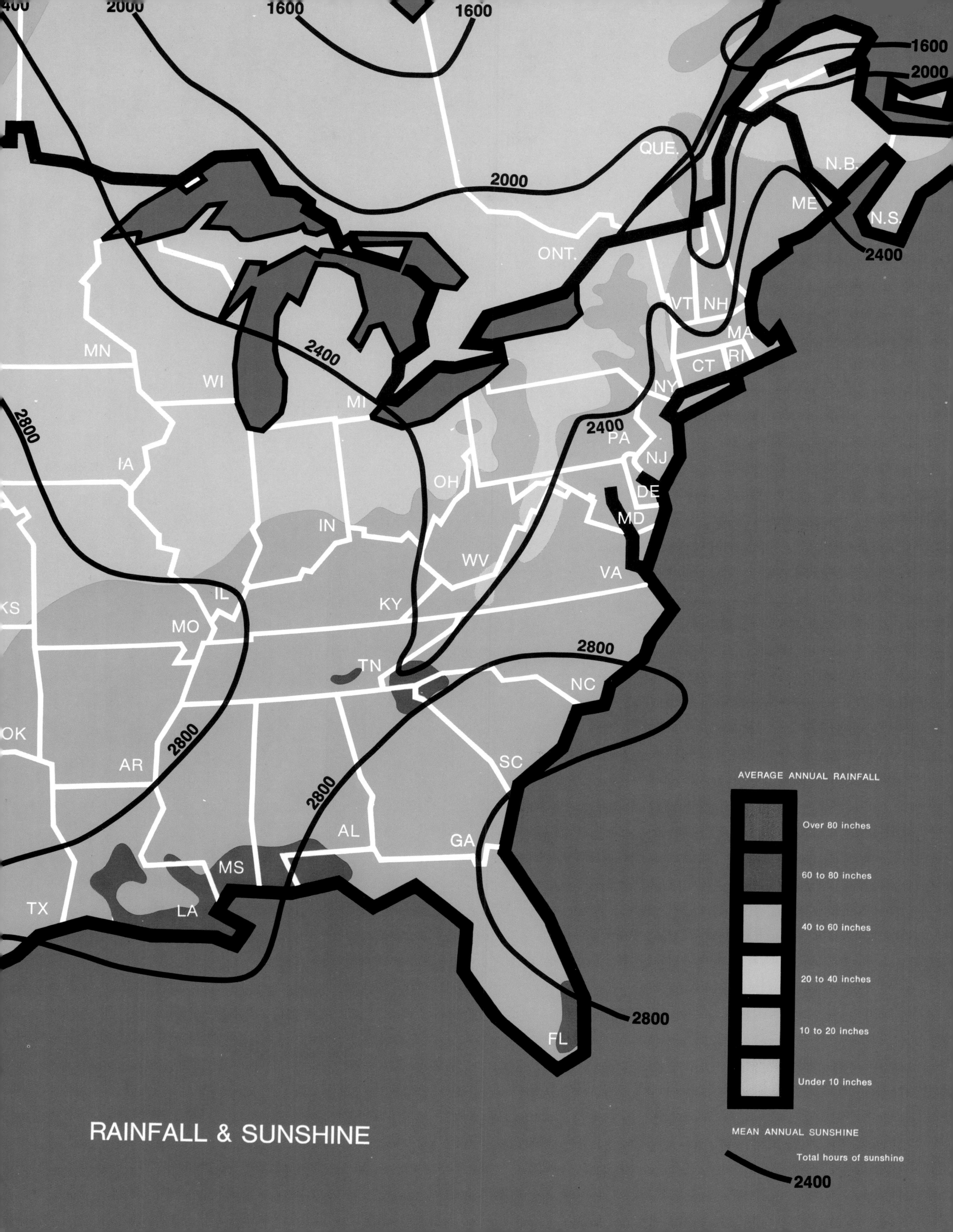
RAINFALL & SUNSHINE
AVERAGE ANNUAL RAINFALL
Over 80 inches
60 to 80 inches
40 to 60 inches
20 to 40 inches
10 to 20 inches
Under 10 inches
MEAN ANNUAL SUNSHINE
Total hours of sunshine
2400
1600
2000
2400
2800
QUE.
ONT.
N.B.
N.S.
ME
VT
NH
MA
RI
CT
NY
PA
NJ
DE
MD
VA
WV
OH
MI
IN
IL
KY
TN
NC
SC
GA
FL
AL
MS
LA
AR
MO
IA
WI
MN
KS
OK
TX

Range Maps of Wildflowers

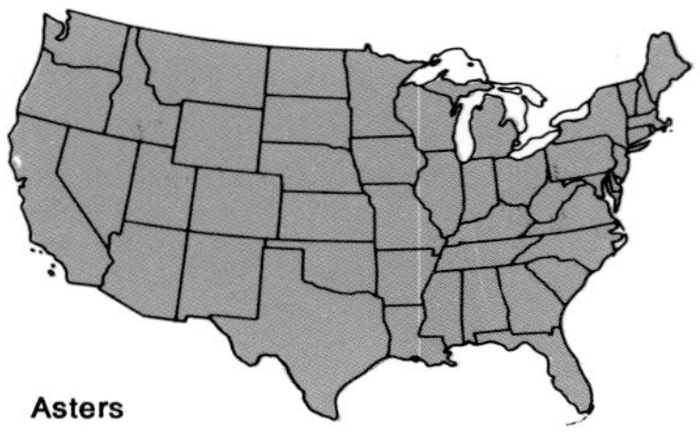
Asters

Bayberry

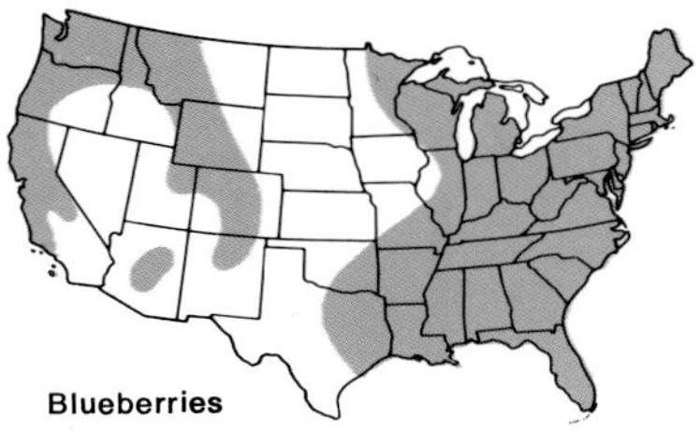
Blueberries

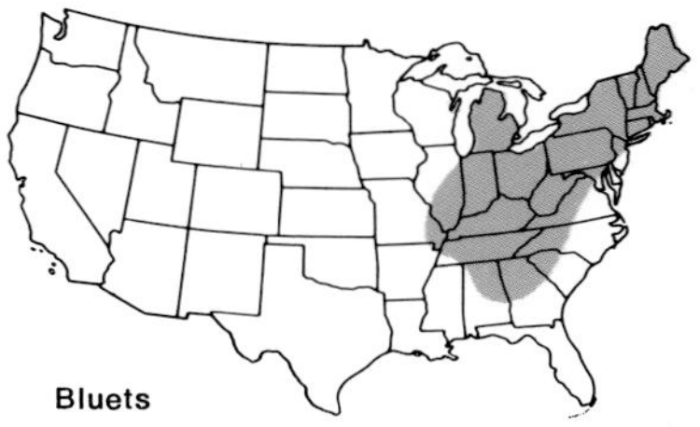
Bluets

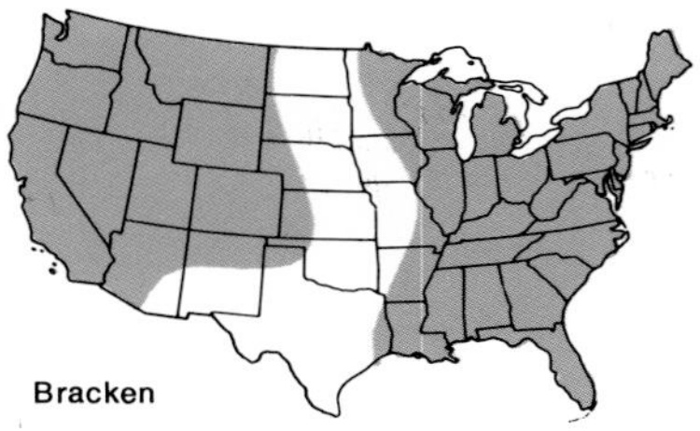
Bracken

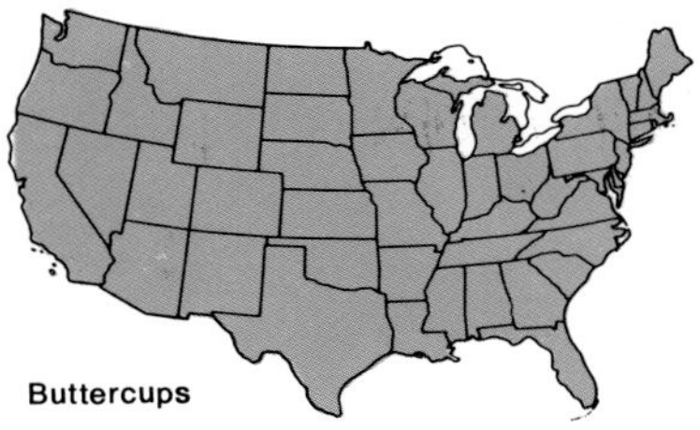
Buttercups

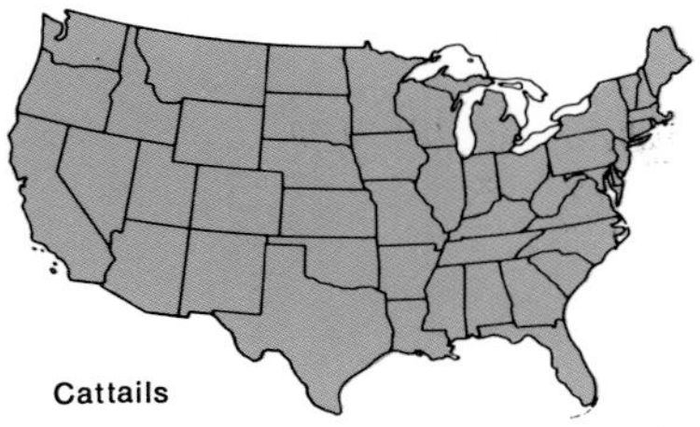
Cattails

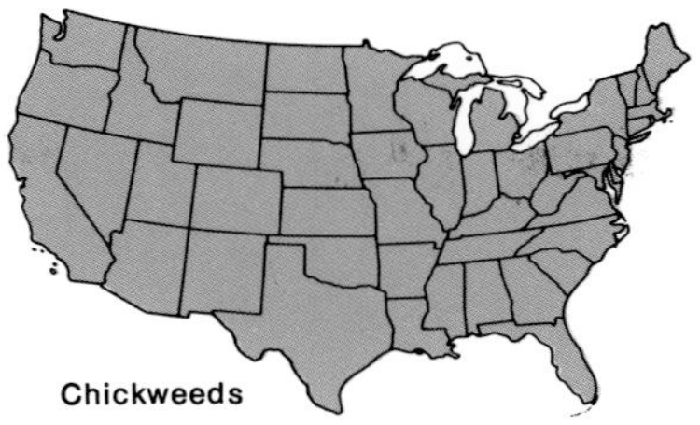
Chickweeds

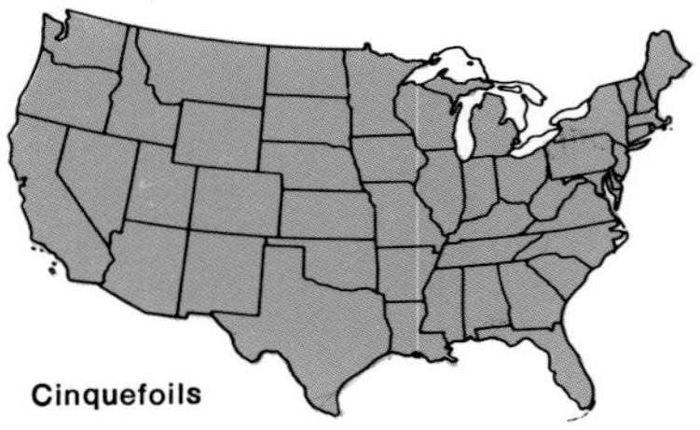
Cinquefoils

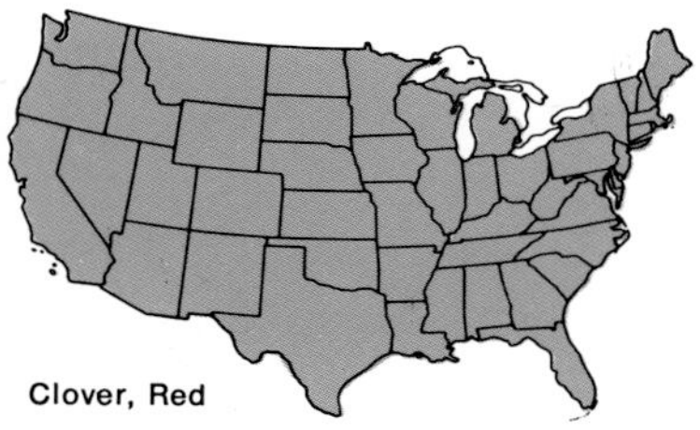
Clover, Red

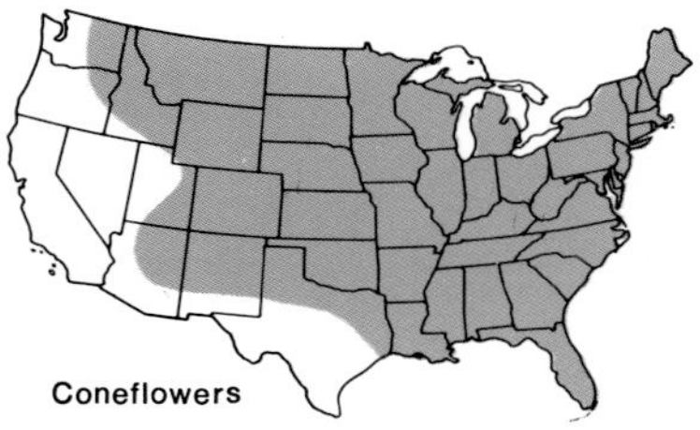
Coneflowers

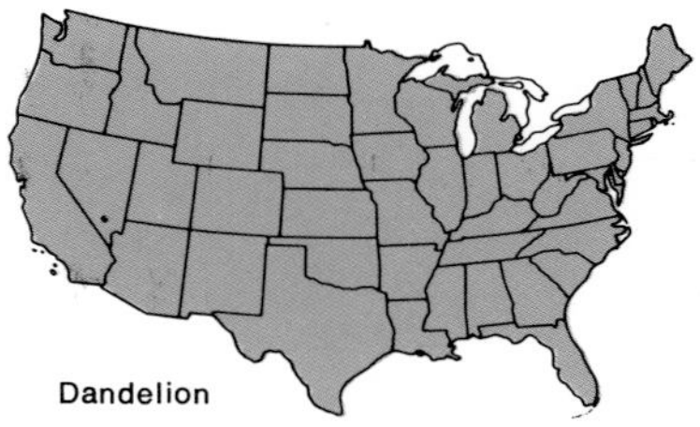
Dandelion

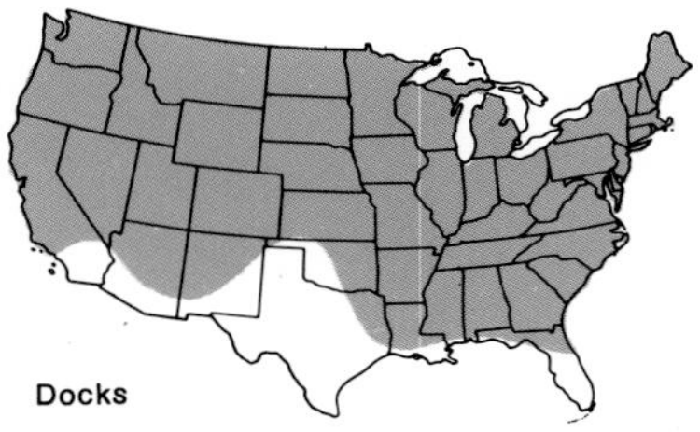
Docks

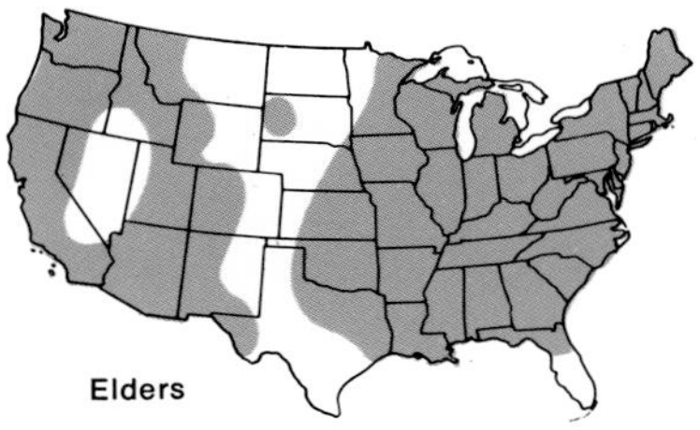
Elders

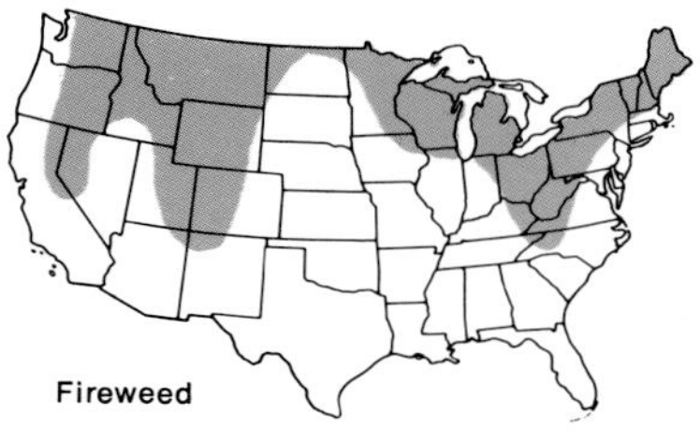
Fireweed

Gentian, Closed

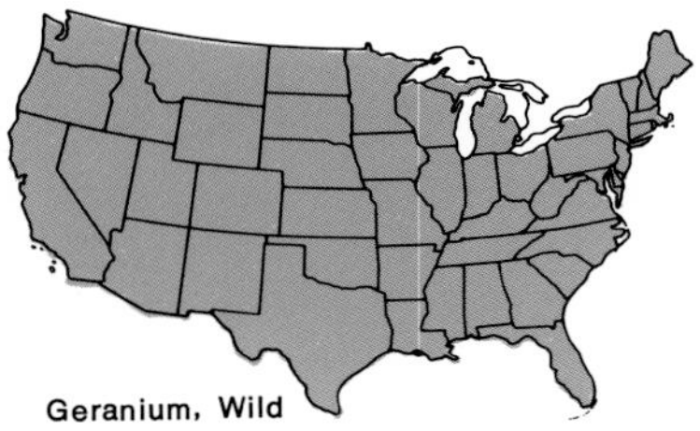
Geranium, Wild

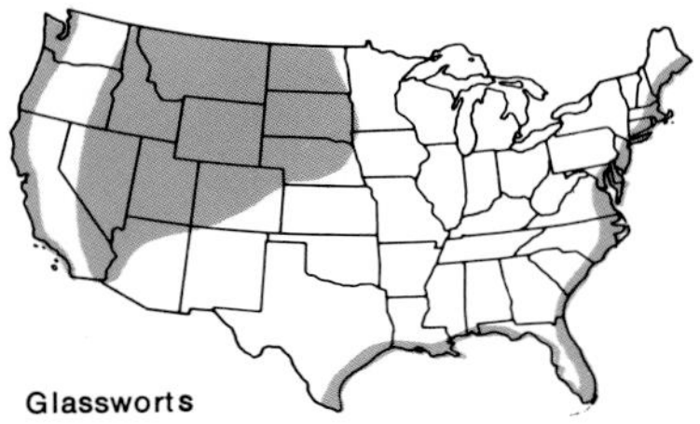
Glassworts

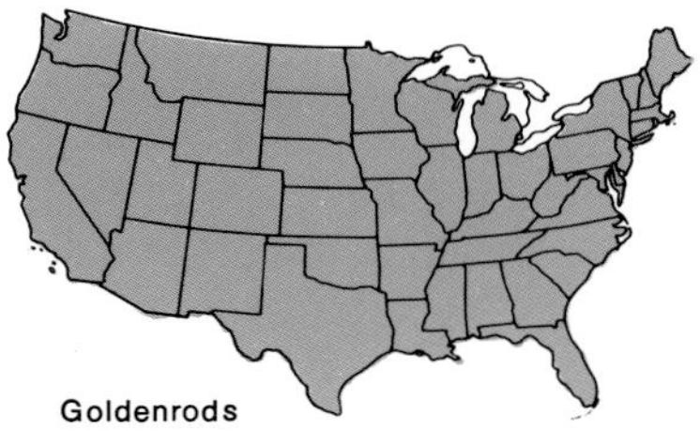
Goldenrods

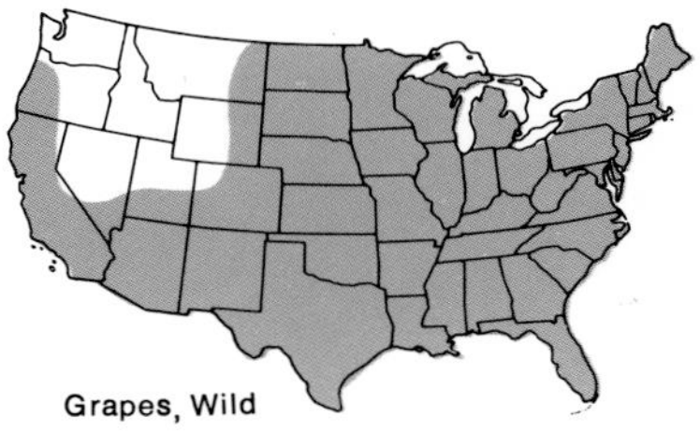
Grapes, Wild

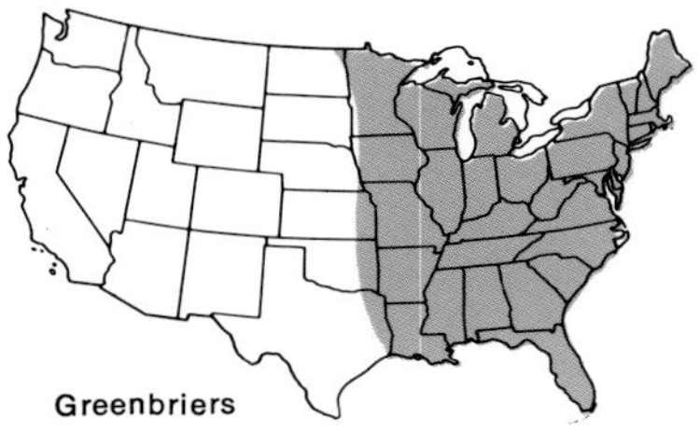
Greenbriers

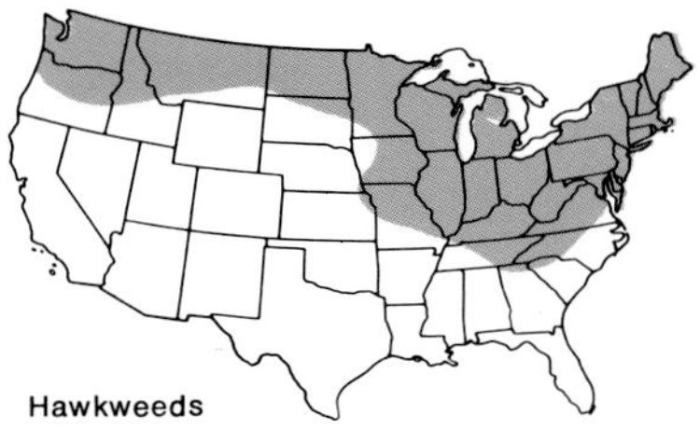
Hawkweeds

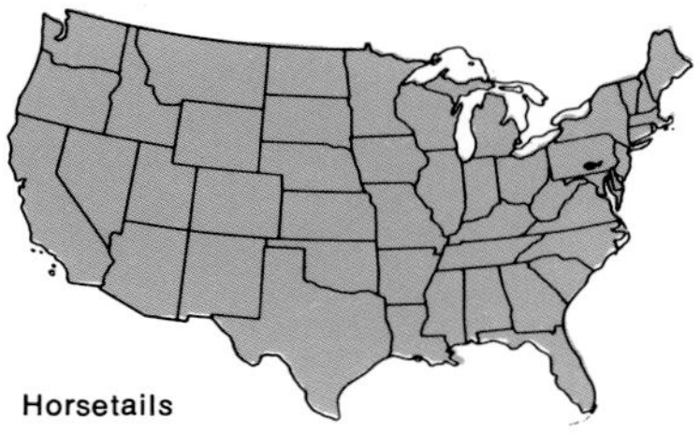
Horsetails

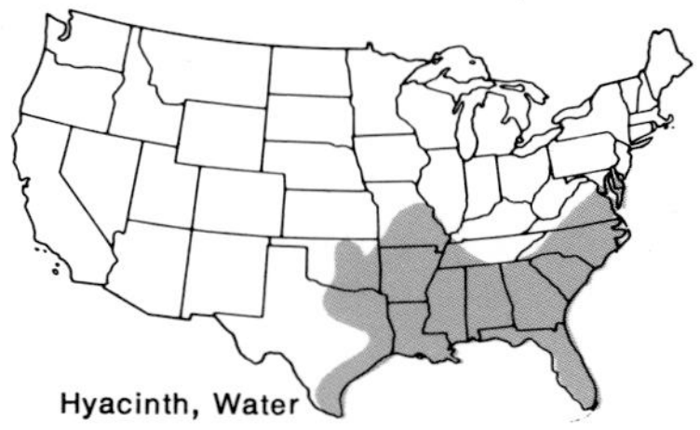
Hyacinth, Water

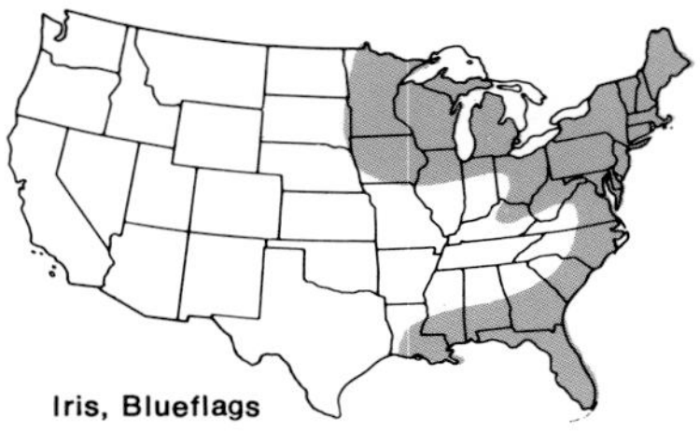
Iris, Blueflags

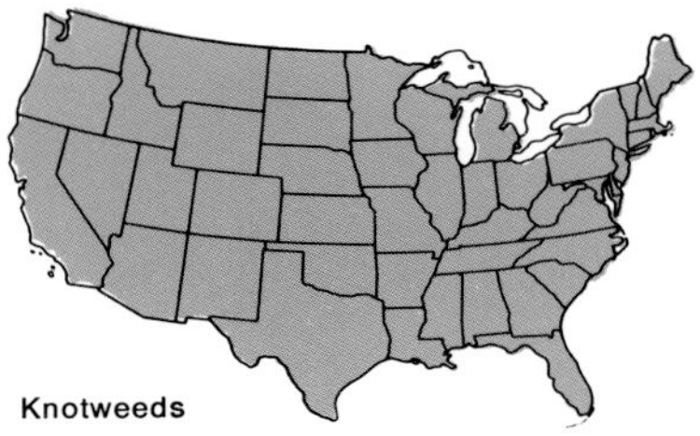
Knotweeds

Lady's Slippers

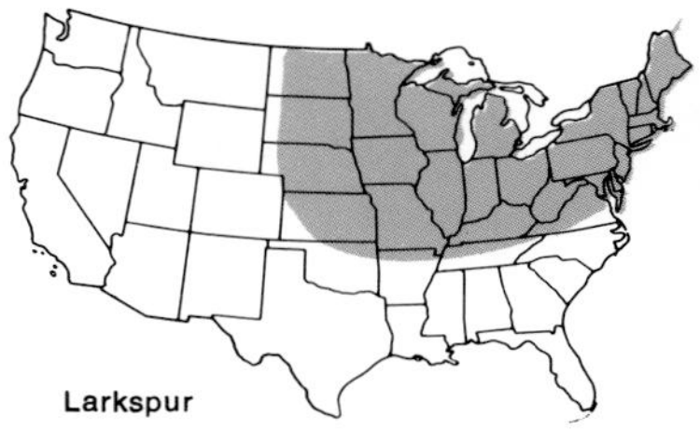
Larkspur

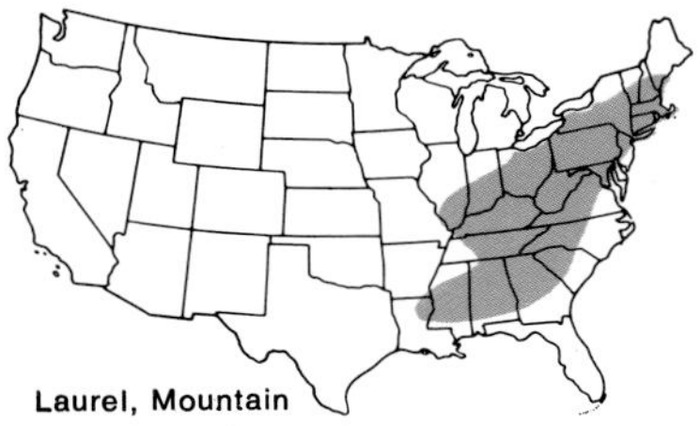
Laurel, Mountain

Lily of the Valley, False

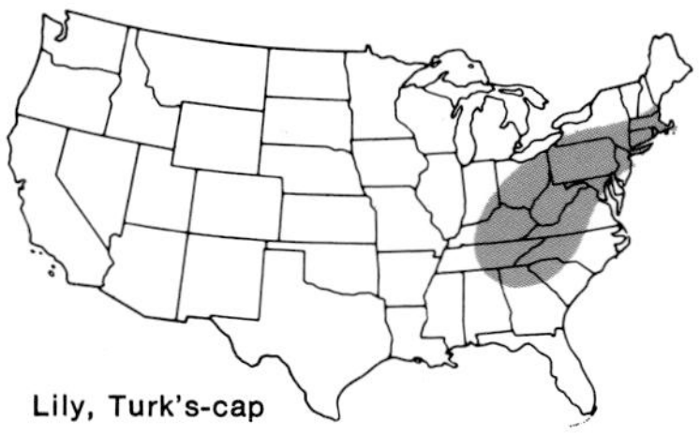
Lily, Turk's-cap

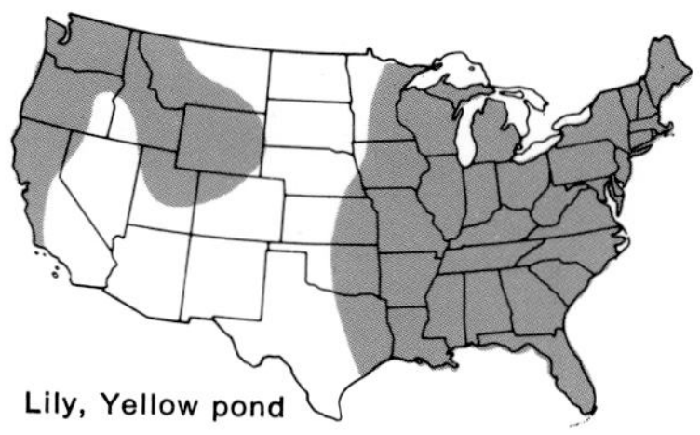
Lily, Yellow pond

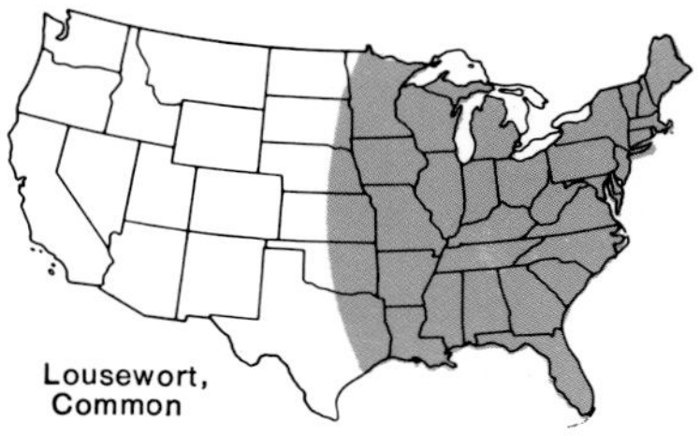
Lousewort, Common

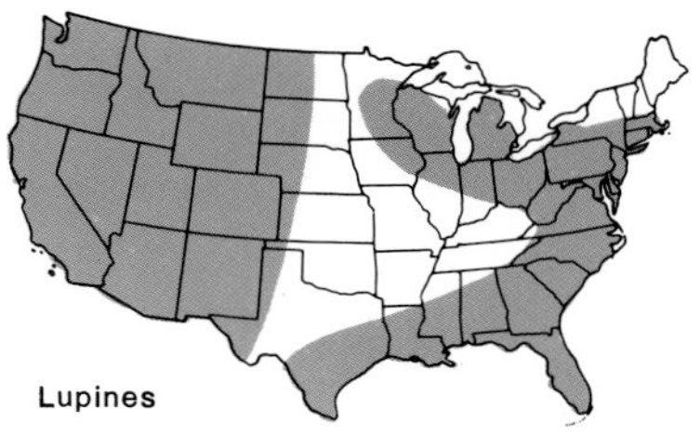
Lupines

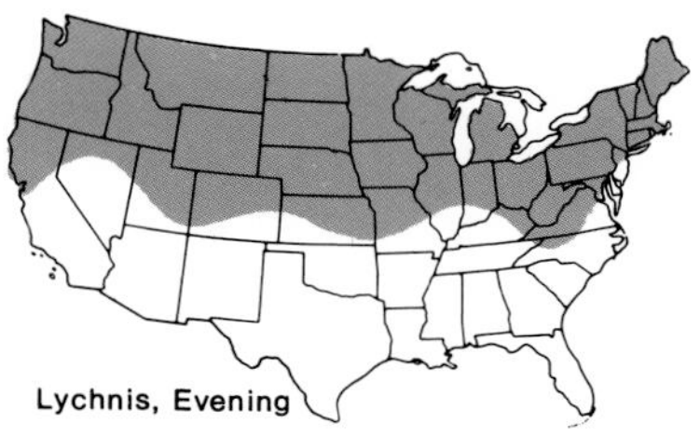
Lychnis, Evening

Mallow, Rose

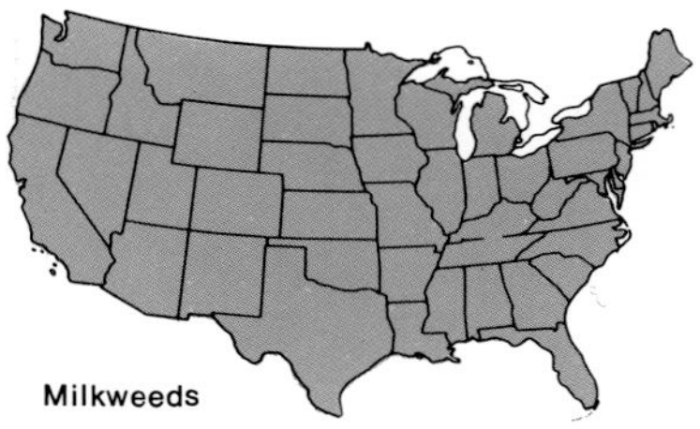
Milkweeds

Morning Glories

Moss, Spanish

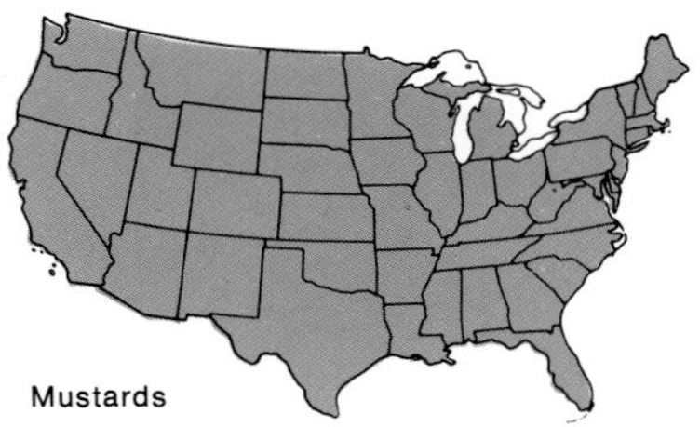
Mustards

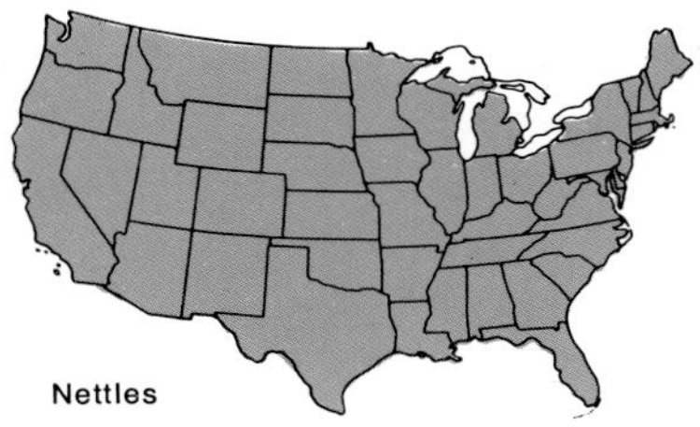
Nettles

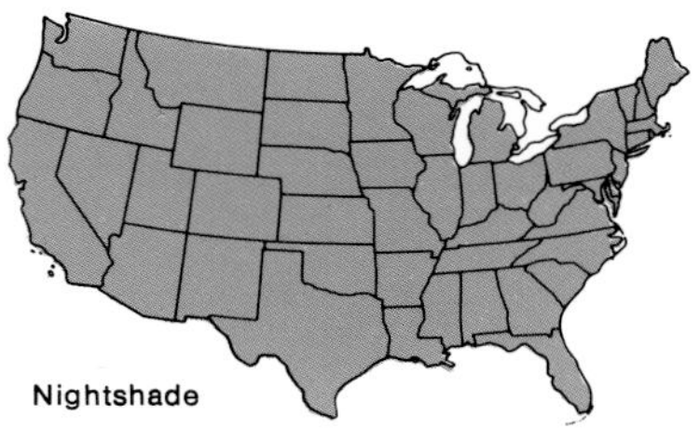
Nightshade

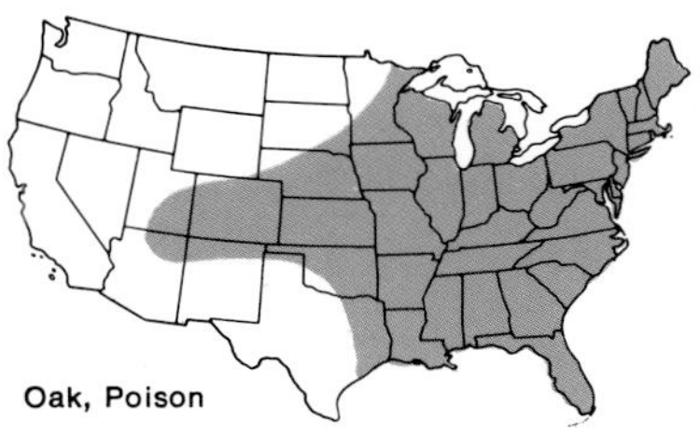
Oak, Poison

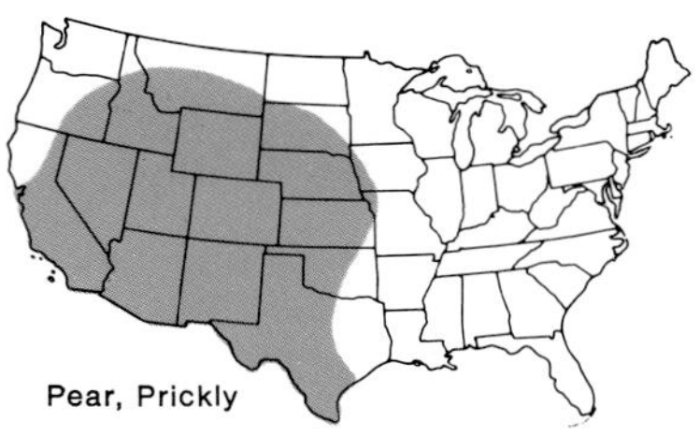
Pear, Prickly

Penstemons

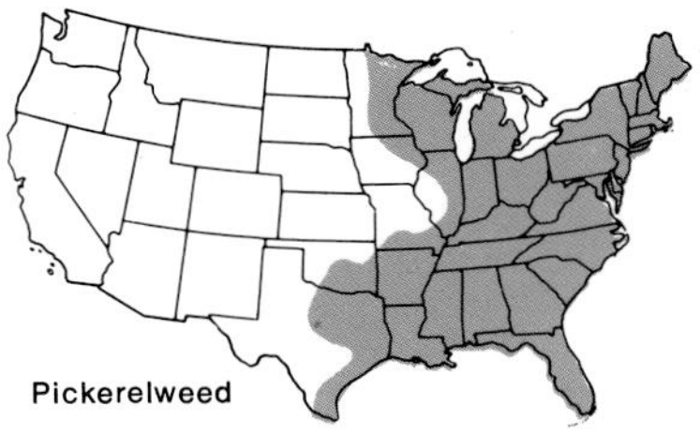
Pickerelweed

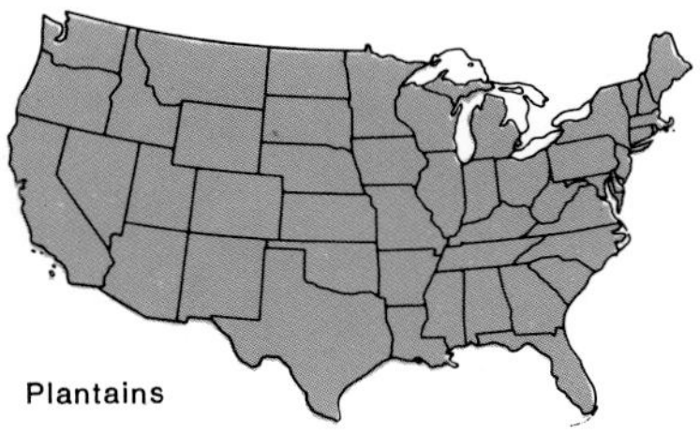
Plantains

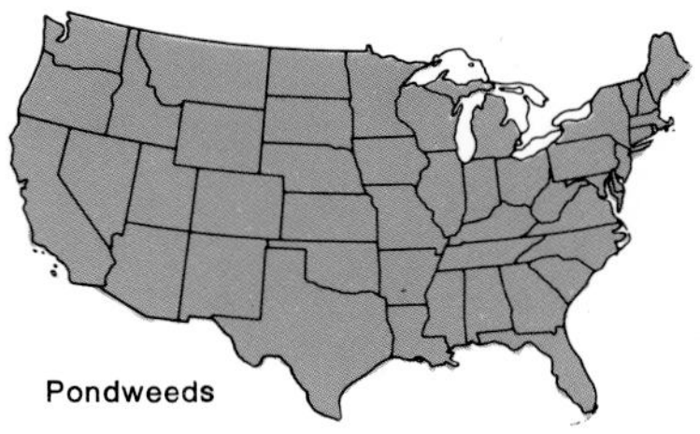
Pondweeds

Poppy, California

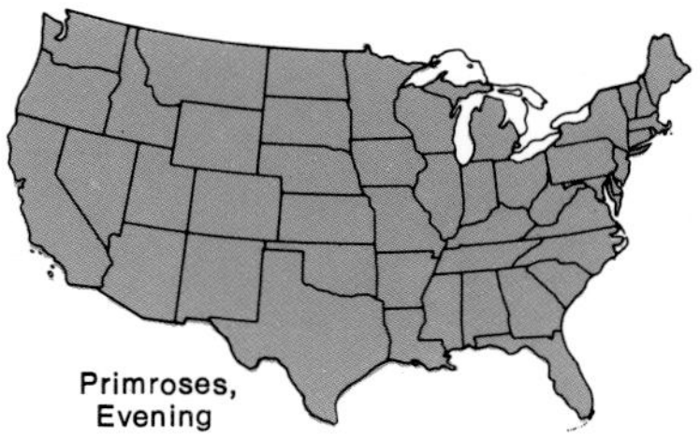
Primroses, Evening

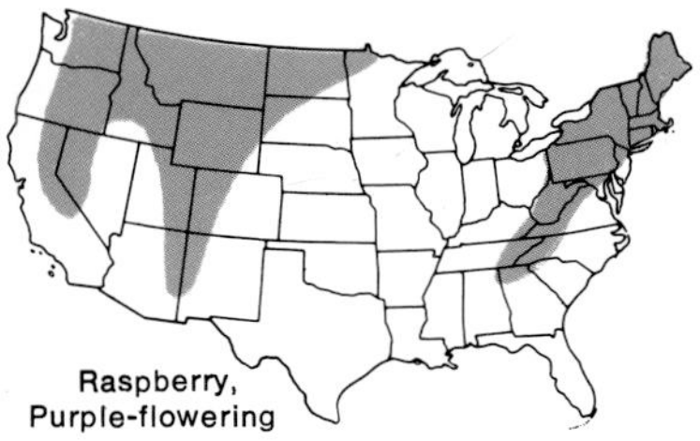
Raspberry, Purple-flowering

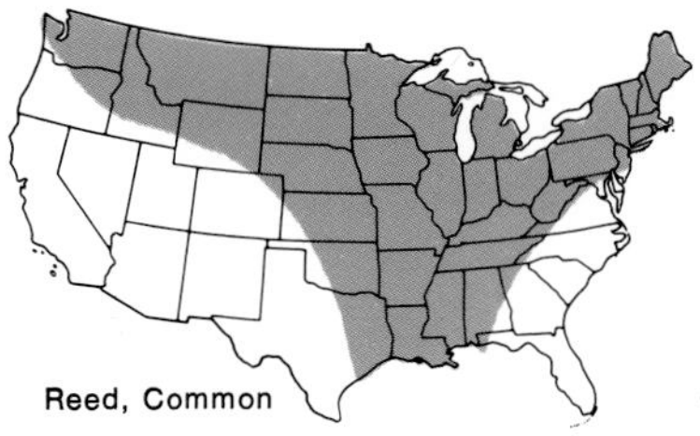
Reed, Common

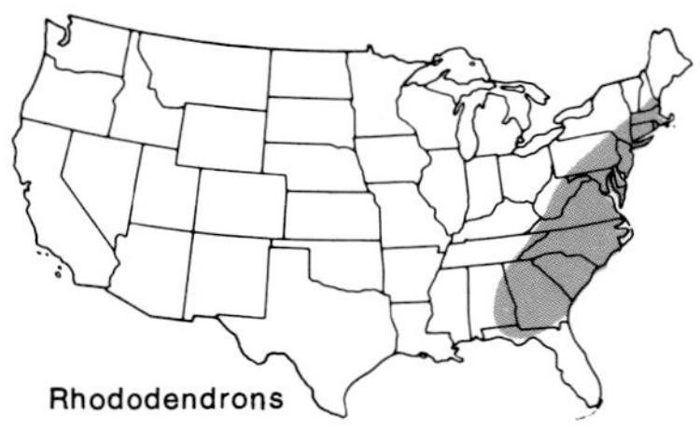
Rhododendrons

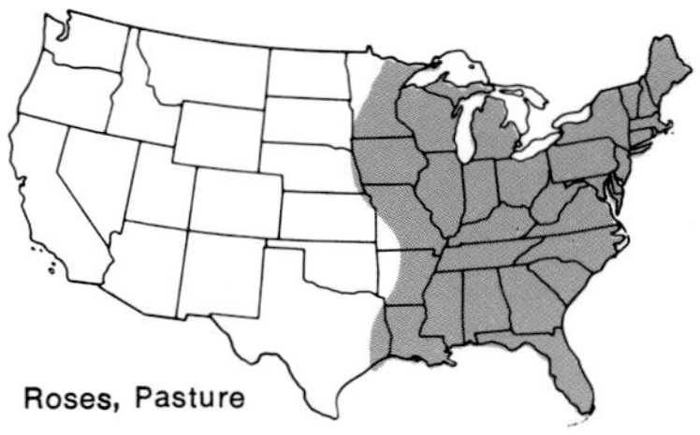
Roses, Pasture

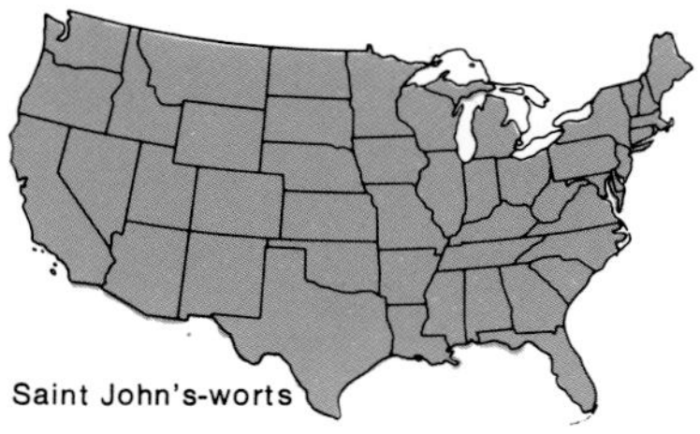
Saint John's-worts

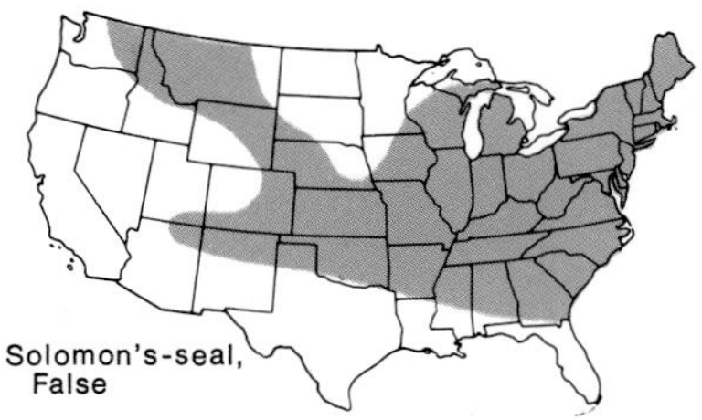
Solomon's-seal, False

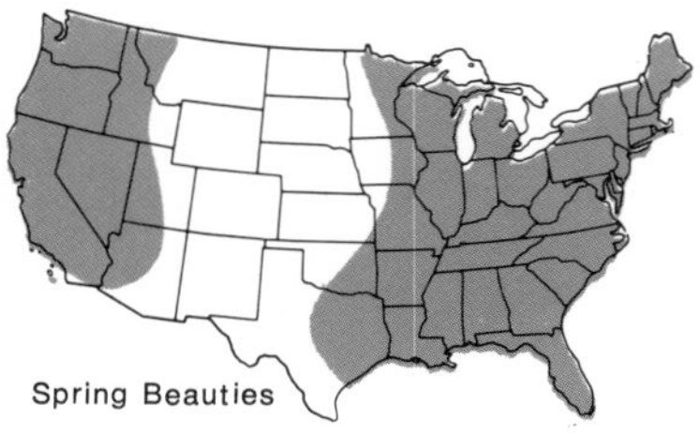

Spring Beauties

Sunflower, Common

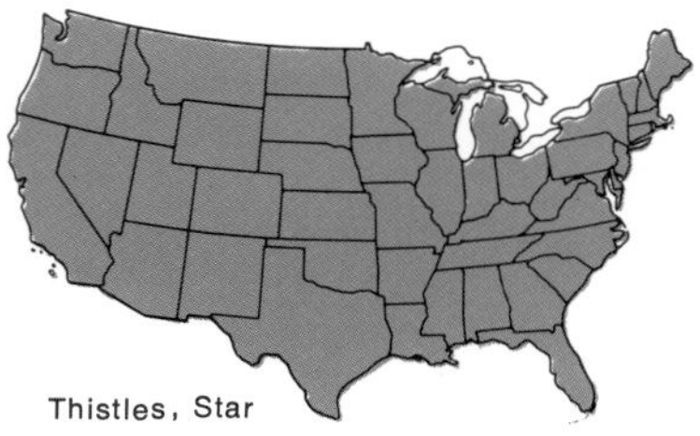

Thistles, Star

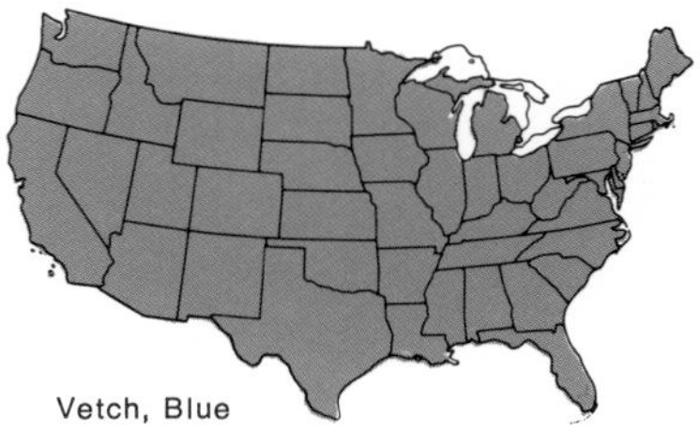

Vetch, Blue

Violets, Wild

Willow, Pussy

Horsetail

Bracken

Cattail (with Red-winged Blackbird nest)

HORSETAILS

Also called scouring rushes, because of the silica in their stem, and **Equisetum,** the genus name, these intriguing plants are included as a reminder that trees and flowering plants by no means cover the Plant Kingdom, though they characterize the conspicuous groups. The jointed mainstem, grooved, hollow, and joined by a toothed collar, is diagnostic. Each segment pops open when gently pulled. Many species have simple erect stems, others have branched stems, and some have depressed and creeping stems. They are usually bright green with darker collars at each node. Fertile stems bear erect cones, similar to pine cones, that shed pollen. These are among the oldest land plants, the last survivors of a great clan that included the hundred foot Calamites of the Coal Age some 300 million years ago. Today only this genus, with about 25 species, survives.

BRACKEN

Called Brake or Bracken in English literature, as well as Eagle Fern, this widespread and conspicuous species occurs across North America, Europe, and Africa. The three triangular fronds arranged in a triangular head are distinctive. It grows both in wet places and on dry hillsides, especially after fires. Man's tendency to overgraze pastures, to clear cut woods, and to be careless with fire has thus created suitable environments for this versatile plant. Bracken communities are valueless as pasture because man's use of the land has already impoverished it. Like most ferns, it bears asexual spores in small, brown clusters on the underside of the frond. Spores are scattered by wind and, when they land on moist soil, they give rise to a second generation—a flat, leaf-like gametophyte. It produces male and female spores, which then produce another fern.

CATTAILS

Key demarcation plants at boundaries between salt-water marshes and fresh-water wetlands, cattails often form extensive aquatic stands. They also occur inland on wetlands. They are aggressive colonizers of shallow-water areas with mud bottoms. In fact, their thickets are great soil-builders, catching sediments brought in by waves and adding to the bulk of their annual tissue production. The flowers are borne in a dense, cylindrical brown spike at the tip of an erect, jointless stem. The stamens appear in a pale, loose, short-lived tuft at the very tip, and the pistils form the principal head. The leaves are long and strap-like. The two widespread species are the Common Cattail, four to seven feet tall with leaves over a half inch wide, and the Narrow-leaved Cattail, seldom four feet high with narrow-spiked leaves less than a half inch broad.

Pondweed

Common Reed

Spanish Moss

PONDWEEDS

Inconspicuous as flowering plants, pondweeds are therefore neglected by most amateur botanists. They are of the genus **Potamogeton** and are well worth taking the trouble to know. They are true aquatics, and have submerged, or floating, leaves and clusters, or short spikes, of small flowers elevated above the water surface by a peduncle. The variations of the leaves developed in their adaptation to aquatic environments are fascinating. Some leaves are thread-like, some grass-like, and others broad. Moreover, some plants grow a variety of leaves to suit the circumstances. One species may grow different types of leaves depending upon whether it grows in quiet water or in running water. Submerged leaves are translucent and either thread-like or broad, and floating ones are broad and thick. The species are consequently difficult to differentiate.

COMMON REED (Phragmite)

This is one of the world's tall grasses, with heights over ten feet much of the time. In the U.S., only sugar cane and bamboo, both planted in the warm South, match or exceed it. Although widespread in poorly drained areas, it is not known by many people except in autumn when its large silvery-buff plumes attract attention. Many are then taken indoors because the flowering heads are persistent and decorative. Since this is the only grass treated here, it should be pointed out that grasses have hollow stems with solid nodes (joints or knees). Other grass-like plants include the rushes, which have round stems but no nodes, and the sedges, which have triangular stems. A Phragmite sends out ten-foot runners which root at intervals and help spread the community rapidly. Other common names are Roseau Cane, Carrizo, and Feathergrass.

SPANISH MOSS

It always comes as a surprise to learn the true relationship between this soft thread-like plant and the trees or even telephone wires from which it hangs in eerie tufts in the humid South. It is called a moss, but it is neither a moss nor a lichen. It is a bromeliad, i.e., a member of the Pineapple Family. Like most members of this tropical Family, it is an air plant (an epiphyte), which grows attached to another plant without being parasitic on it. It may, in time, break limbs off by its weight. To a Northerner, at least, it reminds one of the lichen **Usnea** which hangs in silvery-gray tufts from trees in cool, humid regions and is called Old Man's Beard. It is an amusing sidelight on the process of naming things that Linnaeus, the Swedish classifier, thinking the plant disliked water, named it after a man who walked a thousand miles to avoid a sea voyage.

PICKERELWEED

Whereas a Water Hyacinth is a floating plant not dependent on contact with soil, a Pickerelweed must be anchored in mud to thrive. It forms one of the large group of plants called emergent aquatics. The big, heart-shaped leaves are attractive, and the spikes of short-lived, blue flowers help highlight the shallows in which it grows—haunts of the voracious freshwater fish, the pickerel. Unlike the hyacinth, it is a native species and not a pest, except perhaps where the silting of waterways has provided mud flats, which it is quick to colonize. Unfortunately, we have so carelessly mismanaged the landscape in recent decades that much silting has occurred. It is those who overlook man's impact on the environment who tend to consider Pickerelweed a pest just because it takes over mud flats of our own creation. It begins to bloom in June.

WATER HYACINTH

Since man has taken to ransacking the resources of the whole world to satisfy his appetites, his imports and exports have increasingly significant repercussions. The introduction of new species of plants and insects are some, among others, of the consequences, and once established, they often become pests. The otherwise attractive Water Hyacinth of the Southeast is a prime example. It is a tropical species that has multiplied so uncontrollably that it now clogs many Gulf Coast waterways from shore to shore. This hampers the use of boats; but worse, it prevents sunlight from penetrating into the water and thus greatly reduces other aquatic populations. Millions of dollars are being spent to reduce hyacinth numbers by mechanical and chemical means, but little progress has been made. We should, meanwhile, enjoy their floral displays.

Water Hyacinth

Pickerelweed

Turk's-cap Lily

TURK'S-CAP LILY

The specific name **superbum** suggests that this is indeed the outstanding member of a group of spectacular, damp-woods border lilies with nodding flowers. The group includes Gray's Lily, the Orange-bell of the southern Appalachians, the Wild Yellow or Canada Lily, the Michigan Lily of the Midwest, the Turk's-cap Lily, the Carolina Lily of the Southeast, and the Tiger Lily. They are tall plants, one to two yards high. The nodding flowers range from yellow to orange-red, and vary in their amount of spotting and in the degree to which the pointed petals are recurved upon themselves. They are therefore difficult to distinguish specifically. Not all of them occur in a particular region, so knowing what to expect simplifies the task. These spectacular lilies grow in good soil or wet peat and propagate from bulbs. **Lilium** is probably most common in Asia.

False Solomon's-seal

FALSE SOLOMON'S-SEAL

Called also False Spikenard or Solomon's Zigzag, this conspicuous member of the Lily Family is widespread throughout the eastern forest. It is a perennial herb with a simple stem that grows from a heavy rootstock that extends itself subterraneously and sends up seasonal shoots at its tip. Because the aerial stem dies back each year, the plant migrates across the woodland from new rootstock elongations. The distinctive characteristic used in identification is the terminal head of small white flowers. In the true Solomon's-seal the flowers are distributed beneath the stem, usually singly, rather than clustered at the tip of the stem. The leaves are mostly large, parallel-veined, as in all members of the Lily Family, and arranged alternately at each angle of the slightly zigzag stem. The fruit is a small berry, at first greenish or whitish, but ruby-red when ripe.

FALSE LILY OF THE VALLEY
The long compound name is awkward perhaps but designed to distinguish it from the cultivated Lily of the Valley so popular at Easter time. It lacks the attractive bell-shaped flowers of the cultivated species and is less fragrant, but it is a pleasant ground cover in open deciduous or mixed woodland across much of the continent. The two smooth, parallel-veined, heart-shaped leaves unfurl in early spring —before the foliage of the forest canopy casts its shade—and the white flowers emerge in May and June. A sparse cluster of small berries, at first pale, but later bright red with dark speckling, matures when summer comes. It tends to form extensive carpets, sometimes an acre in extent, because its creeping stems branch extensively, sending up new shoots every few inches, especially where forest clearings provide a shower of light.

False Lily of the Valley

GREENBRIERS
The several, rather similar, common names—Catbrier, Bullbrier, and Horsebrier—attest to the prickly nature of most of the dozen or so species in the genus **Smilax.** This is not, however, the smilax of florists who have improperly applied the name to an ornamental asparagus. Greenbriers are troublesome weeds along the margins of woods, growing from a tuberous root system that resists eradication. Several species have a pair of curved tendrils at the base of the leaf petiole. The leaves show the genus' membership in the Lily Family by their parallel veination or ribbing. The flowers are inconspicuous, but the black or bluish berries (red in one species of the coastal-plain wetlands) are obvious. The most widespread species is the round-leaved Common Greenbrier, a vine-like plant with many tendrils, which attach to other stems, creating impenetrable thickets.

Round-leaved Greenbrier

Larger Blueflag

Yellow Lady's Slipper

BLUEFLAGS

These stately iris are certainly among the most regal wildflowers, hence the frequent use of the French name—especially in French Canada —fleur-de-lis. Considerable confusion exists as to whether the word lis is from the river Lys of Flanders or Louis VII, who made the great yellow iris the national flower of France in 1137. The Larger Blueflag of the northern U.S. and Canada has very erect, pale-green, sometimes almost grayish, leaves. It grows in compact clumps which are all the product of vegetative sprouting from thick, tuberous rootstocks. The southern Slender Blueflag is smaller and has greener leaves that bend over weakly instead of standing closely erect. All the blueflags are plants of wet places—at least seasonally wet places. Too much water on the land will favor the growth of cattails and not enough will favor the growth of grasses.

LADY'S SLIPPERS
(Moccasin Flowers)

These are among the showiest of the orchids and great favorites. The genus **(Cypripedium)** occurs widely across northern North America, northern Asia, and in the Andes of South America. It grows best in somewhat open woods with acid, sandy soil. The two, long basal leaves are sheathed at the base, and from the center of this sheath a long, slender, naked stem rises to bear the single, showy, pink flower. The flower is an inflated sac, with a fissure the whole length of its front, through which a pollinating bumblebee must force its way to get at the nectar. Cross-pollination is effected by this mechanism. The flower sac is marked by an abundance of purplish veins. The flowers do not bear picking and are very difficult to transplant. The Yellow Lady's Slipper grows in rich, black soil in northern bogs.

Yellow Pond Lily

YELLOW POND LILY

Also called Spatter-dock and Cow-lily, this is a floating aquatic plant of quiet shallow waters across the Northern Hemisphere. The rounded leaves are sometimes as large as a man's hand and have a deep sinus on one side. The half-inch thick stem may be three to six feet long, depending upon the depth of the water. Flowers are tight round balls that open only slightly when mature, exposing a thick clump of pistils and anthers that give rise to a ribbed fruit in late summer. This aquatic plant is a favorite food of beaver and moose. The Yellow Pond Lily is so important to moose for food that the northern limit of the animal's range coincides with the plant's. Where it lacks animal harvesting, the Pond Lily may grow rankly in coves and canals and bar boat movement. Overlapping much of the range of the Yellow Pond Lily is the Fragrant Water Lily.

Buttercup

BUTTERCUPS

Few yellows in nature have the golden lustre of buttercups. Throughout the Northeast in early summer, the Common Buttercup lights up damp meadows, growing upward a full three or four feet if crowded by competing grass. This tall buttercup prospers because a grazing animal will not touch it, having become well aware of the bitter, poisonous juice it carries. The flower has five rounded petals and a central cluster of pistils and sepals, all separate rather than attached. The Common Buttercup is an introduced weed of European origin. There are about 275 species of the genus. They occur across the Northern Hemisphere and penetrate southward, down the Rocky Mountain and Andes chain. The leaves are often deeply dissected and give rise to the common name crowfoot. It is necessary to study the small nut-like fruits to be sure of the species.

Larkspur

Mustard

CALIFORNIA POPPY
What the Goldenrod is to the northeastern landscape, the California Poppy is to the far West. Acres of coastal slopes, mountain meadows, and desert flats may be colored bright-orange by its lovely cupped flowers. It occurs from sea level to 6500 feet or so and in such diverse habitats that it may flower from February to September. April is usually the peak month. The Common Garden Poppy is a European introduction of the genus **Papaver,** and though there is a California species of this genus, the California Poppy proper is a member of a native genus, **Eschscholtzia,** named after a surgeon-naturalist on a Russian expedition to the Pacific Coast about 1820. There are many garden varieties of both species. All poppies have yellow-orange, milky or clear, latex sap. Only the large-flowered Opium Poppy of the Old World produces opium and morphine.

LARKSPUR
The name refers to the unusual flower, whose segments project backward in a long spur. Since it was in use before botanists classified plants, the name attests to the fact that people of earlier centuries were excellent naturalists: the name implies they knew a lark had a long hind toe or spur. The genus name **Delphinium** is from the Latin name for dolphin. This is a large group of Northern Hemisphere species that extends into western South America. As is usual among members of the Crowfoot Family, the leaves are deeply dissected and radiate palmately, similar to the fingers of a hand. The plants, depending on the species, may be two to six feet tall and, again according to species, the flowers may be white, greenish, blue, or purple. The seeds are poisonous and, in the West, frequently kill cattle. Few colors are brighter than the blue of larkspurs in the West.

MUSTARDS
Common weeds introduced from Europe, mustards are sometimes planted as a green cover-crop in orchards to prevent wind erosion. The bright-yellow cultivated fields one sees in spring and early summer are usually colored by these weeds. Their intrusion into grain or flax fields brings considerable economic loss because the plants have no commercial value unless specifically grown for their seeds. The Black Mustard is grown for table mustard, the seasoning being extracted from the tiny black seeds. There are several species of mustard, each with a pale-yellow flower and four narrow-based petals arranged like a cross, hence the Family name **Cruciferae**. The seed-pod is a narrow capsule called a silique. After flowering and fruiting, the plants grow rankly, sometimes to a height of four or more feet. Roadside ditches across the country also harbor them.

California Poppy

Cinquefoil

Purple-flowering Raspberry

CINQUEFOILS

The name is from "cinque feuilles," which in French means "five leaves." Some cinquefoils are three-fingered, and a few are seven-fingered. Generalizations like cinquefoil are thus only partly reliable in identification. The leaves of the two most common eastern species are, however, five-fingered. Many mistake the species for wild strawberries because they send out runners, which strawberries do. Strawberries, however, have white flowers, whereas all cinquefoils have yellow ones. Altogether, there are over 30 species in the U.S. The two most common ones are the Canada Cinquefoil, both a roadside and yard weed, and the Silvery Cinquefoil, which grows in wet places and whose leaves have bright, silvery undersides. One woody species, the Shrubby Cinquefoil, is widespread, especially on wet or dry soils derived from limestone.

Pasture Rose

PASTURE ROSES

Whether Gertude Stein had the difficult task of classifying roses in mind when she wrote "A rose is a rose is a rose" is unlikely. But roses are indeed a very complex group. Those of eastern America were, in the past, split into a hundred or more species, but additional study has established only 20 or so extremely variable types. Not all roses smell like a rose. Some have no odor, some smell like violets, and others are musky, peachy, pineapple-like, or even outright disagreeable. The common pasture roses, or wild roses, have large pink flowers. The most widespread species are: **Rosa virginiana,** which is shrubby, up to six feet with curved or hooked prickles on its stems; **Rosa carolina,** a much smaller species never more than three feet tall, with relatively few straight prickles; and **Rosa blanda,** taller, with either no prickles or only a few straight short ones at each end of the stem.

PURPLE-FLOWERING RASPBERRY

The raspberries are members of the Rose Family, and this one, also called Thimbleberry, is the only one with Maple-leaved foliage. Unlike many of its raspberry relatives, its stems are not armed with spines, but the stems, branchlets, and even the calyx of the flowers are variously covered with bristly, usually dark, glandular, sticky hairs. It normally grows six to seven feet high and forms dense tangles, usually along the borders of woods or mixed into thickets of other shrubby plants. Because it is shrubby, it is often left out of wildflower books. The flowers are showy and usually deep pink though sometimes white. The plant, though American, is often planted in Europe. Like most roses, it has five petals and a multitude of stamens crowded in the middle. The rather broad fruit is red and persistent on the stem. It is rather tasteless.

LUPINES

Lupines belong to the very large, world-wide Legume Family, noted for its winged flowers (said to be papilionaceous, after butterfly), its great importance in producing food crops, and the ability of most species to fix nitrogen from the air. Most species produce pea-like fruits in a many-seeded pod, or legume. Lupines are of the genus **Lupinus** (from Lupus, or wolf), reflecting the early notion that lupines destroyed soil. Quite the reverse is true, for the plants fix nitrogen, the most difficult-to-come-by chemical element. They are straight and tall-stemmed, with a long spike of showy-blue, purplish-blue, or rose-and-white flowers. The rosette-like leaves are strikingly-distinctive, delicate, palmate clusters of five to 18 leaflets. They are distributed along the smooth or hairy stems, depending on the species. The Texas Bluebonnet "blues" the West in spring.

Lupine

Red Clover

Blue Vetch

RED CLOVER

All true clovers (genus **Trifolium**) have leaves composed of three leaflets and a tightly-packed roundish head of flowers. The four-leaf clover is a genetic sport and, because of its rarity, people seek it for good luck. Red Clover is distinguished from related species by the pair of leaves immediately below the flower. The other species have flower heads on a naked stalk (peduncle). Both Red and White Clovers are naturalized European species. The White Clover and the Alsike Clover have shamrock-like leaves (indeed, the Irish shamrock is a White Clover), but the Red Clover's leaflets are oval and somewhat pointed at both ends. The florets of Red Clover are tightly closed and, for the most part, are pollinated only by bumblebees strong enough to open them. It takes an estimated two and half million bee visits to make a pound of honey.

Wild Geranium

Poison Oak

BLUE VETCH

Also called Cow Vetch, this species has the typical papilionaceous flowers of the Legume Family. Instead of being arranged in an erect spike, as is a lupine, or in a globular head, as is a clover, the flowers are arranged on a completely one-sided spike. The leaves are pinnate (leaflets on either side of a petiole), with eight to 12 pairs of small, narrow, leaflets, often felted with soft hairs. The tips of many leaves have tendrils that anchor the growing plant as it spreads up to six feet from its base. Vetch makes good hay. The common Eastern species were all introduced from Europe and are now widely naturalized. In Europe the Blue Vetch is cultivated as a garden plant. In the U.S. thousands of acres of Blue Vetch are planted to serve as a cover crop to prevent soil loss by water and wind erosion. There are about 130 species of vetch. Few are limited to North America.

WILD GERANIUM

This geranium quintuples everything. It has a big leaf which is deeply dissected into five parts; five deep rose-colored petals supported by a calyx made up of five sepals; and there are ten stamens in two circles of five each. Even the pistil and the fruit, seen in cross section, have five divisions. The members of the genus **Geranium** are also called Cranesbills (Cranesbill Geraniums), which is merely an English translation of the scientific name that refers to the Greek name for crane, because the shape of the dry fruit suggested the long, pointed bill of the bird. Indeed, the beak-like fruit of this group is unusual. Its valves curve upward on drying and then throw the seeds some distance. The common Wild Geranium of the East **(Geranium maculatum)** grows about two feet tall and highlights the early spring woodlands with its blossoms.

POISON OAK

The four species of **Rhus** that are poisonous to the touch are often indiscriminately labelled Poison Oak by those who do not trouble to distinguish them. Such people are therefore in danger of being poisoned again and again. The poisoning causes a painful dermatitis. Poison Oak **(Rhus toxicodendron)** is a small shrub with slender, erect stems. Each leaf is made up of three leaflets that have lobed margins. The leaf petiole is long and velvety. Poison Oak grows in sandy barrens and pinelands, mostly on the coastal plain. Poison Ivy **(Rhus radicans)** also has three leaflets. But they are more triangular, with wavy margins and a glossy surface. It is brilliant red and yellow in autumn. The other two species, Poison Dogwood **(Rhus vernix)** in eastern swamps and a falsely named Poison Oak **(Rhus diversiloba)** in California, are tall shrubs.

WILD GRAPES

There are nearly 500 species of these climbing vines called grapes because of their fruit. They occur mostly in Europe and the U.S. The vines climb by the attachment of coiling tendrils that grow opposite each leaf. The brown bark tends to pull loose from the vine as it grows, coming off in long ropy shreds. The roughly heart-shaped leaves are large and moderately toothed. They vary greatly among species in thickness, color, and felting on the under surface. The flowers are small and occur in fragrant clusters. Except for the Fox Grape of the northern U.S., whose grapes are often three-quarters of an inch in diameter, most American species have small fruit, with varying numbers of seeds. Most of the native grapes are acid to the taste, but the Fox Grape and a few others sweeten late in the season, especially after the first frost hits them.

ROSE MALLOW

The delicate blossoms are often six inches across, flared openly, and bright pink. Usually near water, the plant stands five to eight feet tall, and its rose blossoms are often seen against the reflected blue of the sky or against the sky itself. Its delicate bloom is late flowering, from late July to early October, and is almost alone in the summer scene. The leaves are large and commonly three-lobed. Both the stalk and the lower surface of the leaves are hoary with short, pale, woolly hairs, though the upper surface of the leaves is dark green and smooth. The flowers of all mallows are exceptional: the stamens give the appearance of a beard on the pistil, because they are joined to form a sheath which surrounds the growing pistil. This **Hibiscus** has several cultivated relatives including the hollyhocks, the Rose-of-Sharon, and the cotton plant of commerce.

SAINT JOHN'S-WORTS

The most common species is the weed introduced from the Old World **Hypericum perforatum,** which became a serious agricultural pest in 1900 in the far West. There it is called Klamath Weed. By 1950 it had contaminated 2.5 million acres of pasturage, whose land values declined. Cattle who eat it develop skin irritations and sore mouths, and lose weight. The plant is not a pest in Europe because two species of beetles feed on it exclusively. These beetles were imported to the U.S. and, within ten years, brought the weed under control. It now maintains itself in small numbers along roadsides and in neglected fields. The Common Saint John's-wort is a bushy herb up to three feet high, with small opposite leaves and numerous yellow flowers, each with an abundance of stamens. The flower petals are slightly uneven in outline.

Wild Grape

Swamp Rose Mallow

WILD VIOLETS
Some 300 species of violets are currently recognized, mostly in the temperate zone. Field guides list about 25 species each for California and Quebec and 50 for the eastern U.S. Species are difficult to determine partly because violets are variable and hybridize considerably. This variability points out that the concept of species is much less clearly-defined in plants compared with animals. This is partly because plants often reproduce asexually. Many species of violets have heart-shaped leaves. Some have roundish, kidney-shaped ones, and others have dissected ones, or some variation thereof. Flowers may be violet, yellow, or white, usually with a contrasting center. The flower petals are unequal. The lowest of the five is set rather flat (horizontally), prolonged backward like a spur, and thus serves as a landing platform for bees who come to pollinate.

Saint John's-wort

Wild Violet

Prickly Pear

PRICKLY PEARS

The cacti of the genus **Opuntia,** sometimes called beavertail cactus, are among the most widespread of this unique Family. There was such a craze in Europe for this unusual group of plants in the 1600s that everyone grew them. The genus is now naturalized in the Mediterranean region. There are over a thousand species, all difficult to distinguish. There are two principal groups in the genus: the prickly pears (or beavertails), which have flat jointed pads, and the cholla (pronounced cho-ya) or cane cacti, which have cylindrical, jointed stems. All of them have showy flowers imbedded in the plant, mostly at the margins of the newer segments. Flowers range in color from yellow (often with a red center), rose-pink, to purplish-red, or occasionally white. Some have reddish bristles that detach easily, and others have dangerous spines.

Fireweed

FIREWEED

Also called Great Willow-herb, great patches of this tall, colorful herb light up the upper reaches of the Northern Hemisphere with a magenta glow from July to September. Four to six feet tall, its stems are crowded with narrow lance-shaped leaves that may be from three to eight inches long, dark green above and much paler below. The plant is crowned by a long, open head of flowers. Wherever raw land is exposed within the realm normally dominated by spruce-fir forest, especially after fires, the first healing growth will be Fireweed. When acres of downtown London were bombed out during World War II, Fireweed surprised and consoled the people with its pastel blooms. The tall flowering head matures one row at a time, beginning at the bottom. A floret lasts only about 48 hours, but there are over a hundred on a large spire.

EVENING PRIMROSES

This complex group hybridizes freely and is thus full of variants that have confused botanists for generations. The flower, however, is distinctive. It always has four petals, and the tip of the pistil is split into four conspicuous, cross-shaped arms. The four lobes of the calyx (sepals) point away from the flower. The widespread Field Primrose illustrates well the variability of the group. It is a biennial, and the first year it simply grows a large rosette of long, elliptical leaves that have a good deal of purple mixed with green. The second year the rosette sends up a stout, simple or branching, stem which attains a height of four or five feet. Again, the greenish stem is tinged with purple. It is leafy—though the leaves are short—and topped by a narrow flower spike. When the flower drops off, the capsules are often mistaken for new buds.

Evening Primrose

RHODODENDRONS

These are some of the great flowering shrubs of the world. The genus is common in central China and in the wet monsoon belt of eastern Asia, including the Himalayan front. The English and the scientific names of the genus are the same. Also called great laurel or rosebay, rhododendrons are large shrubs, sometimes almost straggling trees. In the rich soil of mountain coves in the southern Appalachians, they may attain heights of 30 feet. The leaves are thick, evergreen, four to ten inches long, dark green above and paler on the underside. The leaf petioles are sticky when young. The flowers come in generous clusters, each flower bell-shaped and about one and a half inches across, usually rose-pink and white, though some are all-white or all-purplish. The spectacular purplish-flowered plants are used in horticulture. There is an American Rhododendron Society.

Great Rhododendron

MOUNTAIN LAUREL

Also called Calico-Bush, Spoonwood, or Ivy-Bush in the South, this is a small edition of the Great Laurel or Rhododendron. It is usually four to six feet high and forms dense tangles on the acid soil of rocky hillsides, especially after a fire. The evergreen leaves are flat, leathery, and not more than four inches long. The flowers are in open, rounded bunches near the top of the shrub. Each flower is a deep cup about one inch across and a marvel of ingenuity. The ten stamens are strongly recurved and attached to a dimple in the flower cup. When fully mature, the dimples collapse, one after another, and each stamen rebounds upward, releasing its cloud of pollen. It begins flowering in May in the South and reaches a peak in New England (and on the higher slopes of the Appalachians) in June, when its blossoms highlight acres of woodland.

Mountain Laurel

Blueberry

BLUEBERRIES
Members of the Heath Family, the blueberries, billberries, and cranberries are all members of the genus **Vaccinium.** There are about 130 species in the Northern Hemisphere, 40 of which are in North America. The flowers are plump, slightly more than a quarter inch long, and creamy-white or pinkish. They produce luscious blueberries that, in some species, may be a half inch in diameter, usually with a pale bloom that rubs off. Unfortunately, the species of true blueberries hybridize and are therefore difficult to identify in many cases. By a combination of characteristics, however, including growth habit, habitat, leaf, and flower, one can get to know them. Any one region is unlikely to have more than ten species. In the East, the Highbush-blueberry grows mostly in damp woods, attains a height of 12 feet, grows in clumps, and has the sweetest fruit of all.

Closed Gentian

CLOSED GENTIAN
Gentians are widely admired for two reasons: because their blossoms are both colorful and intriguing in form and because they are late-flowering. The most widespread species is called Closed Gentian, or Bottle Gentian, so called because its one and a half-inch flowers seem to remain unopened. Some experts insist that they do open briefly, however, when the sun is bright overhead. Bees then make haste to enter but often become entrapped. Sometimes they chew their way out of the sides of the flowers. Two to five plump, deep- or purplish-blue flowers make up the terminal clusters. The pointed leaves are two to four inches long and opposite one another. The plant itself may be one to two feet high. Although it is said to prefer damp meadows, it will do well in most grasslands. A large genus of northern regions, many are favored by rock gardeners.

Milkweed

Nightshade

MILKWEEDS

The Milkweeds are rather coarse herbs with a sticky, milky sap that is a rubbery latex. Plants are from one to six feet tall and may have their leaves arranged singly, in whorls, or in pairs. The latter is the most common. The flowers are in tight bunches, which form insect traps for many species that try to feed at them, because the five stamens are attached at their tips. Only the strongest insects can pull themselves away from the waxy entanglement once they enter. The seeds are as notable as any other part of these striking plants. The pointed pods split down the side when ripe and reveal row upon row of flat, brown seeds with pale margins, each one tipped with a silky parachute. This silk was collected as a substitute for kapok during World War II. The Common Milkweed has a slightly more extensive range than the Four-leaved Milkweed.

NIGHTSHADE

Purple is rare in nature, and so the purple and yellow flower of this European species makes it readily recognizable, especially for those who know the flowers of the Irish Potato, also a member of the large genus, **Solanum.** In late summer, the drooping clusters of translucent, elliptical, red berries are so attractive that they were eulogized by Thoreau who wrote, "They hang more gracefully over the river's brim than any pendant in a lady's ear." Weedy in growth habit, this species tends to become a woody climber. The leaves tend to be trilobate, i.e., with a large, pointed, central leaflet and two small, ear-like lobes. Often called Bittersweet or Deadly Nightshade, its reputation for being poisonous has been widely exaggerated. The genus is mostly tropical in distribution and consists of nearly a thousand species. Few species are native.

MORNING GLORIES

Two genera and a great many species are involved when talking of morning glories. Properly, a Morning Glory is of the genus **Ipomoea**. But **Convolvulus,** which refers to Bindweed, is often referred to as a Morning Glory, since most of us are uncritical botanists. Both produce attractive vase-shaped flowers that grow on a vine. They are therefore widely used as trellis climbers.. The color of the flowers also varies widely, some being white, red, or blue, or a combination thereof, yielding purple and pink. Whether native or introduced, they escape cultivation readily. Bindweed is an especially troublesome weed due to its deep root system which branches readily. It thus spreads rapidly and resists eradication because new plants grow from sections of the root system that have been isolated by attempts to cut it back. The Ivy-leaved Morning Glory is a southern species.

Ivy-leaved Morning Glory

PENSTEMONS
They are also called beard-tongues because of a sterile fifth stamen which is often long and bearded. The showy flowers are tubular, often abruptly dilated at the throat, and have five lips. In most of them the lips are unevenly divided: two above and three below. The predominant color is blue or lilac, but some are red or even white. The plants may be only a few inches high (in alpine forms) or up to three feet tall. The simple leaves are opposite each other and are usually clasped across the stem. Because there are some 230 recognized species—most of them in the West—all a beginner can do is to learn to recognize the genus, whose scientific name is similar to the English name used here. The West seems to have a species for every habitat, from prairies to high alpine areas, usually on well-lighted slopes with adequate moisture and drainage.

COMMON LOUSEWORT
The strange name, Lousewort, is repeated in the genus name **(Pedicularis)** as one more example of the early intimacy between people and plants. In this case the name fixed the mistaken notion that this woolly plant incubates lice that are found on cattle. Most of the 500 or so species are high altitude or high latitude herbs of the Northern Hemisphere, but the Common Lousewort is widespread in small clearings throughout the eastern U.S. It is anywhere from six to 16 inches tall and crowned with a tight-packed head of strangely-beaked (overarching) yellowish flowers that are often touched with red. The leaves are three to four inches long, with edges scalloped like those of ferns. The stems usually occur in tufts, and the entire plant is hairy. In the West, some of the species, often red-colored, are called Indian Warrior and Elephant's Head.

Common Lousewort

Penstemon

English Plantain

PLANTAINS

Along with the Dandelion, these are major lawn weeds. Like the Dandelion, the leaves form a basal rosette. They survive mowing by growing flat on the ground and flowering at the same level instead of growing upward a foot or so, as they do normally when not mowed. They also have a deep taproot. It is the adaptability to unfavorable circumstances that makes a plant a weed. To make matters worse, the pollen of plantains may cause hay fever. There are six species of plantains in the U.S., but the two most common ones are the Narrow-leaved Plantain, with a short, green flowering spike on a long stem, and the Broad-leaved Plantain, which has a considerably longer flower spike. The flowers are tiny and densely crowded in their spike. They must be looked at closely to be appreciated at all. The Narrow-leaved Plantain is also called Buckhorn.

Bluet

BLUETS

When Mrs. William Starr Dana wrote about the northeastern flora in 1893 she said, "No one who has been in New England during the month of May can forget the loveliness of the bluets." And no wonder, because almost as soon as the snows melt, carpets of delicate, pale-blue or lilac flowers, each with a yellow eye, light up grassy slopes. Loosely tufted, the stems are about four inches long, with a few basal leaves and two or so pairs of tiny, opposite leaflets. Each flower is less than a half inch across. May is the month of mass flowering in New England, but individual plants may flower until an October frost. Earlier Americans called bluets Quaker Ladies. There are ten members of the genus in the U.S. The bedstraws are close relatives and so is the Buttonbush. All are members of the Madder Family which includes trees that produce coffee and quinine.

Common Elder

ELDERS

Also called elderberries, these attractive shrubs are useful horticulturally. They are attractive to birds, their berries make a good wine, and the soft pith of their straight canes is easily hollowed for whistles. The leaves are opposite and compound, and the flowers are in a terminal bunch. The European Elder, with lustrous black fruit, is used extensively in parks and formal gardens, but sometimes escapes domestication. The native U.S. species are black- or red-berried. The Common Elder **(Sambucus canadensis)**, a smaller species, is usually less than five feet high. It is scarcely woody and has a white pith. It has five to 11 narrow, sharply-toothed leaflets. Its flowers are in a white, aromatic umbrella spread, appearing in June well after the leaves come out. Its small fruits are purple-black, juicy berries. The more northern Red-berried Elder **(S. pungens)** is taller.

Goldenrod

GOLDENRODS

Unlike most wildflowers, which mark the coming of summer, the bloom of the goldenrods marks its end. They burnish the autumn landscapes, especially in old abandoned fields on the Northeast Coast. We all know goldenrod and either begrudge its augury or welcome its adornment of the annual transition. Though many know the genus, few persons have the patience to recognize the different species, because there are over a hundred of them, each difficult to recognize at first glance. It is said that they are so closely related to the asters, which bloom in autumn, that their characteristics grade imperceptibly. Despite their reputation as hayfever pollen-purveyors, they should be considered as landscape elements for open country planting as suggested in Warren Kenfield's book, *The Wild Gardener In The Wild Landscape.*

Coneflower

Star Thistle

ASTERS
The asters, like the goldenrods, are another large group that tests even a professional botanist's identification skills. The 250 or so species, centered chiefly in the eastern U.S., are so variable, both within the species and as a result of habitat variations, that some, even in herbarium, have not been identified. We can at least know that most of them belong to genus **Aster,** though identifying the different species requires great application. The enveloping sepals that hold the flower are thin, somewhat dry, bracts arranged in overlapping rows, like shingles. The ray florets that make up the false corolla are blue, lavender, purple, pink, or white. They are less than a quarter of an inch long. The central flower-head is small, in comparison to the total flower, and usually yellow, often turning reddish. The plants are from a few inches to six feet high and are all late-flowering.

CONEFLOWERS
In one sense these are small sunflowers. They belong to the same large tribe but are a separate genus **(Rudbeckia)**. Like other members of the Composite Family, the "flower" is really a compressed head of many florets, wherein the showy orange-yellow petals are really sterile ray florets that surround the true flowers of the brown inner-head or cone. Unlike true sunflowers, where the flowers are arranged on a flat disc, coneflowers have a raised, or coned, flower-head. The flowers of the related prairie coneflowers (genus **Ratibida**) are arranged on a very conspicuous, thumb-like cone. There are two widespread groups, one with simple, lanceolate leaves, of which the countrywide Blackeyed Susan, with prickly-hairy stems and leaves, is typical, and the other with deeply dissected leaves, like the Cut-leaved Coneflower. The Black-eyed Susan invaded the eastern U.S. after 1830.

STAR THISTLES (Knapweed)
There are nearly 500 species of this genus **(Centaurea)**, native mostly to the Mediterranean basin but now widespread through cultivation, of which at least 20 occur in the U.S., mostly on the West Coast, though every state has some species or other. Some are troublesome weeds in croplands. The flowers are typical composites, emerging from a swollen, greenish or brownish capsule (the button of bachelor's-buttons). The petals are usually rose-purple, and the central head is either darker pink or yellow. Some western species have entirely yellow flowers and are, on the whole, more prickly than eastern ones. Identification of the species usually requires careful scrutiny of the flowering heads. Most plants are from one to three feet tall and usually many-flowered. The leaves are alternate, simple or fern-like. Star thistles have been widely cultivated.

Dandelion

Hawkweed

DANDELION
This could well be called the weed for all seasons. Valued, loved, or hated, it grows everywhere openings occur in seasonally moist soil. The silky parachute of its seeds—borne in a downy cluster—provides wind dissemination, and the long tap root enables it to sprout after repeated mowings. The attractive, slightly fragrant, compound yellow flowers are used for home winemaking. The flattened or lushly erect rosette of toothed leaves is picked for table greens when young and tender. Its dried roots have often been used as a coffee substitute. Bees sip the nectar of its flowers, and birds, especially goldfinches, appear to relish its ripened seeds. Many of today's suburbanites wage relentless war on weeds. To eliminate dandelions, slice off the taproot when the flowers first appear and seed the open spot to prevent recolonization.

HAWKWEED
This bright, yellow or orange-red member of the Composite Family is a troublesome weed introduced from the European Alps about 1875 and now widely spread throughout the East. From eight to 30 inches tall, the leafless stems and the rosette of leaves are covered with dark hairs. Entire fields may be colored deep orange where hawkweed has taken over, and such fields are then useless for pasturage. Interestingly, the European species seem to be in an explosive phase of differentiation, mostly by asexual vegetative reproduction. They are confusing in the extreme when it comes to classification. The several native U.S. species, mostly woodland plants, are not so variable, however, and neither are those introduced from Europe a century or more ago. Where the hawkweed is not wanted, frequent mowing will retard its spread and eventually eliminate it.

COMMON SUNFLOWER
Not many species can span the climates of the U.S., but the Common Sunflower does. It occurs from Nova Scotia to California. It is the state flower of Kansas and is most abundant in prairies. Elsewhere it grows mostly in waste places and roadsides, but, when allowed, in rich soils. The cultivated sunflower, with the giant flower disc, is a variety of this native plant. Unlike a majority of the 60 or so other species, the Common Sunflower is an annual herb. The rough stem grows upward six to nine feet and may be simple or branched. The leaves are unusual: they are opposite low on the plant and alternate above. They are rough to the touch on both sides. Sometimes they are heart-shaped, but more often they are finely-toothed pointed ovals. They always have a petiole. The seeds are used in huge quantities to feed birds at home feeding stations.

Common Sunflower

5. MAMMALS

MAMMALS

To be a mammal means to be a particular kind of animal: one that has hair, even if only a few bristles, as does an Armadillo or a whale, and that suckles its young on milk. When, therefore, we wish to refer to cats, dogs, horses, and people, as a group to distinguish them from birds, fish, insects, reptiles, and amphibians, which are also animals, we should use the more specific term, mammal.

The distinction between mammals and other animals is rather new. It was not until 1695 that anyone thought of distinguishing between the egg-laying animals (such as birds, snakes, fish) and those that bear live young. Even then, however, the whales were left among the fish. Not until 1758 did the great Swedish naturalist Carl von Linné (known commonly as Linnaeus) see that having both mammae and hair indicated a closer relationship than the division between laying eggs or bearing live young. The Duck-billed Platypus of Australia is a mammal that lays eggs even though it has hair and has mammary glands without nipples.

It is a sad commentary on the heedlessness of our civilization that most of us first get to know mammals as victims killed by automobiles. There is a veritable geography of roadkills. In the northern coniferous forest, for example, the mammal we are most likely to see dead is the Porcupine. In the temperate zone, whether prairie or deciduous forest, the skunks and the Raccoon are the principal victims. Farther south the slow-moving Opossum is the most common. And in the Southwest the Armadillo and the Antelope Jack Rabbit are the indicator species.

In geological terms, mammals are the most recent Class of animals to appear on Earth. Even so, the fossil record shows that some of them originated about 150 million years ago, when dinosaurs were at their peak. Many of the several types of mammals now in the United States came from the Eurasian continent across land bridges connecting with North America at what is now the Bering Strait. One notices, for example, that many northern species in Alaska and Canada are either similar or closely related to those in Siberia.

The number of species in any given region—at least where not seriously disturbed by man—appears most closely related to the number of habitable environments present. For that reason the far North, which is locked in ice a good part of the year, has the smallest number of mammals. The temperate regions have three times as many. And the tropical regions, where there is an abundance of vegetation that both feeds and shelters animals, may have ten times as many species as the far North. This tendency to increase the numbers of types within a large Class, such as mammals, to take advantage of environmental diversity suggests, of course, a continuing evolutionary process.

One sees this rather clearly in the present distribution of the species within the United States. In the East, which has a gently diversified landscape, there are less than a hundred species of mammals. But the West, with its several mountain ranges, having great altitudinal reliefs

Preceding pages: Bighorn Sheep

—from below sea level in Death Valley to over 14,000 feet at the summit of Mount Whitney—and its corresponding variety of climates, soil types, and vegetation, has over 300 species. This multiplication of species results from the fact that mountains and their associated ecological diversity create a set of barriers which tend to isolate populations into island-like environments.

We know that the young of every population tend to do a great deal of exploring of new environments, partly because the adults who dominate their home environments limit opportunities for the establishment of new families. Many of these exploratory young fail to survive in the less favorable environments available to them. But those who succeed in reaching a new and favorable environment are then largely isolated from their parental populations. Their own innate differences will be magnified by inbreeding within their smaller pioneer population. The new environment will favor different combinations of characteristics, and the pioneer population will gradually accumulate physical and behavioral changes that will distinguish and isolate it further from the old parental group, at which stage it may be recognized as a new species. The test of a new species is that if, by chance or experimentally, offspring of the pioneer population are brought together with offspring of the old parental group they will not interbreed.

The Great Plains, extending from the Mexican Plateau to central Canada, constitutes a mid-continent barrier that only a relatively few species of mammals—or other groups—can bridge because it forms a great north-south zone of quite different climate, soil, and vegetation. And the American Southwest, because of its great diversity of landscapes, probably has more subspecies of mammals than any other area of comparable size in the world. Being a geographical subpopulation which has begun accumulating differences of its own, a subspecies is a new species in the making. The American Southwest is thus an evolutionary melting pot.

Whether the American Bison would have survived the inroads made by the Plains Indians after the 1700s, when they acquired horses, is a moot point. There is no question, however, that the only wildlife spectacle left in the world which compares with the bison herds of a century and more ago is that of the East African savanna. We now expect the people of that picturesque country to accomplish what we were unable to do—to organize themselves, limiting their numbers if necessary, in order to prevent a second major natural-history tragedy that would reduce the elephant, the wildebeest, and the zebra to the status of zoo animals.

It may be useful for Africans to notice that in less than a century, since we eliminated the bison and the Plains Indians from the American prairie, we have retired over 50 million acres of land from agriculture. And the experts tell us that even now four million acres are kept in wheat that should be returned to grassland. Even so, we have remained unwilling to create a proper Prairie National Park.

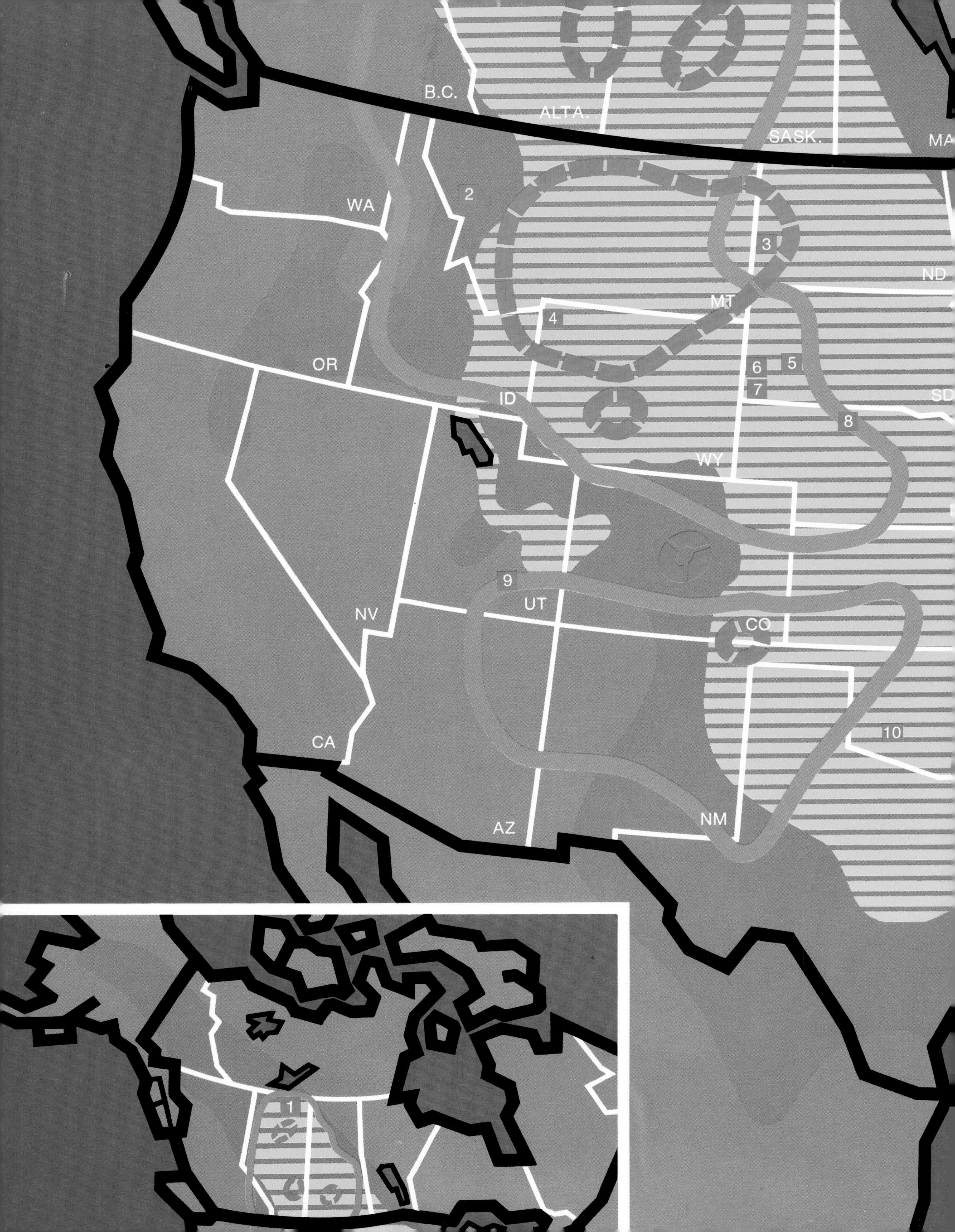
B.C.
ALTA.
SASK.
MA
WA
2
3
ND
MT
4
OR
6
5
7
ID
SD
8
WY
9
UT
NV
CO
CA
10
AZ
NM
1

BISON

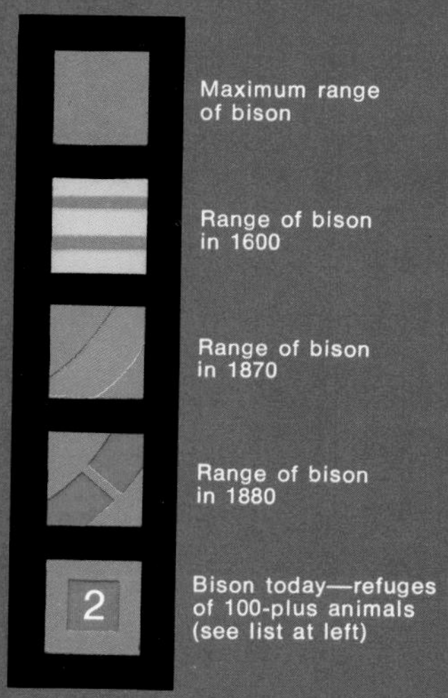

1 Wood Buffalo National Park
Canada

2 National Bison Range
Montana

3 Theodore Roosevelt National Memorial Park
North Dakota

4 Yellowstone National Park
Wyoming

5 Badlands National Monument
South Dakota

6 Custer State Park
South Dakota

7 Wind Cave National Park
South Dakota

8 Fort Niobrara National Wildlife Refuge
Nebraska

9 Henry Mountains
Utah

10 Wichita Mountains National Wildlife Refuge
Oklahoma

Range Maps of Mammals

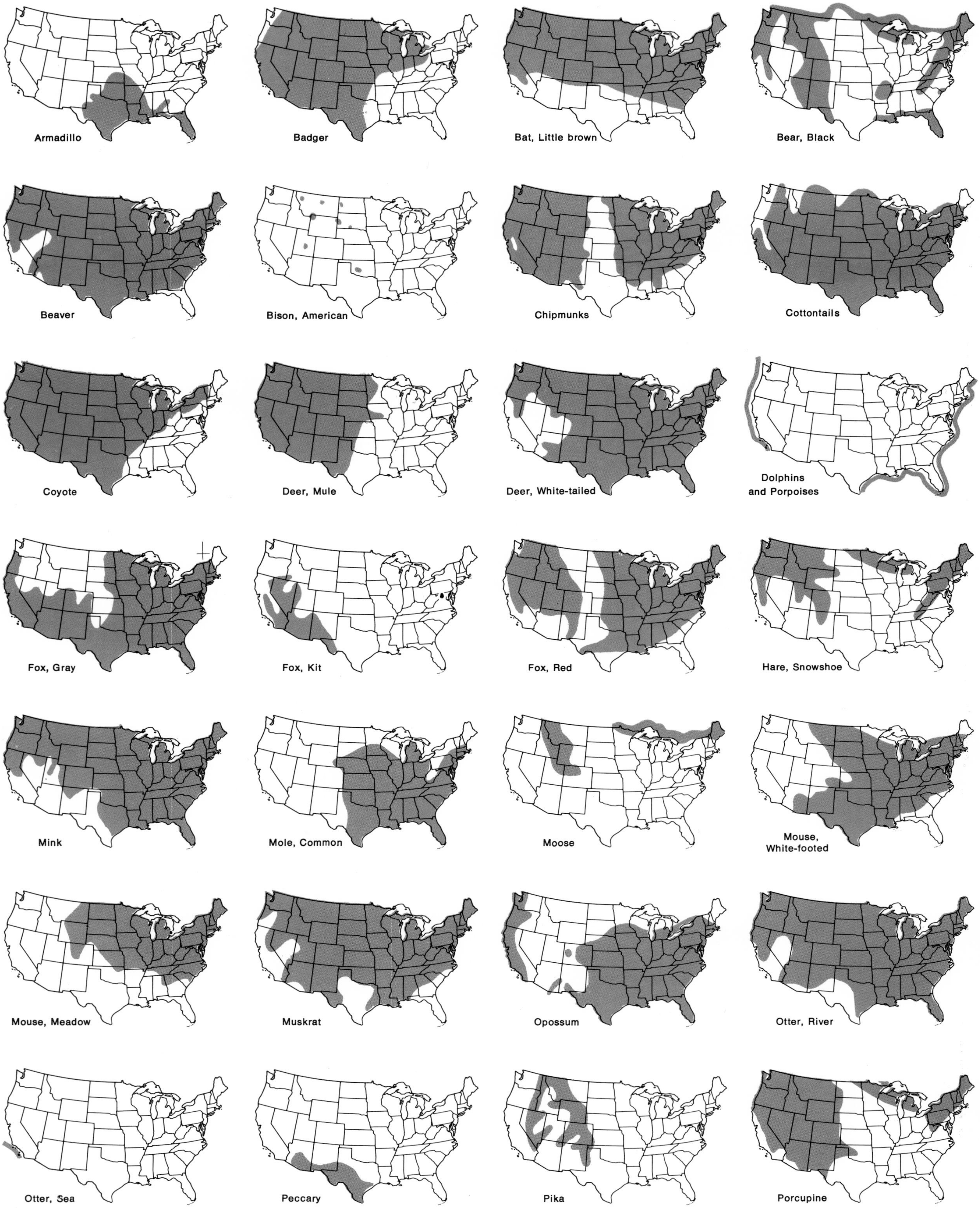

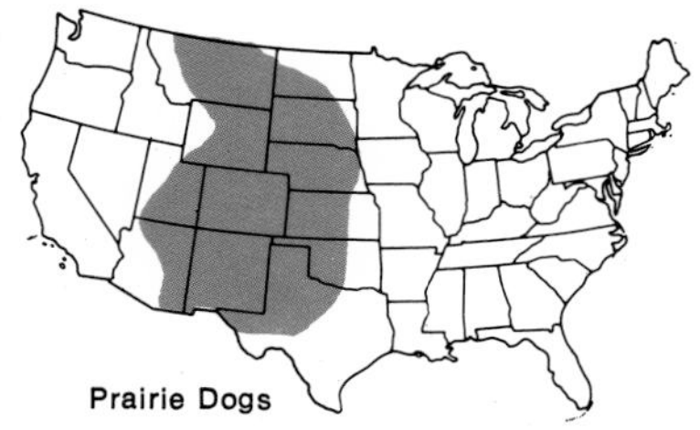

Prairie Dogs

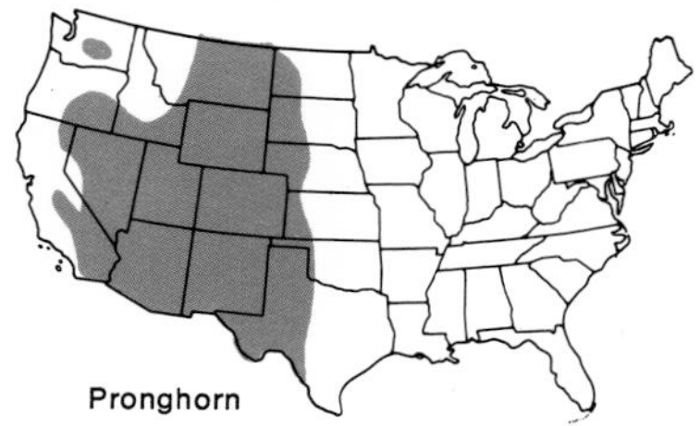

Pronghorn

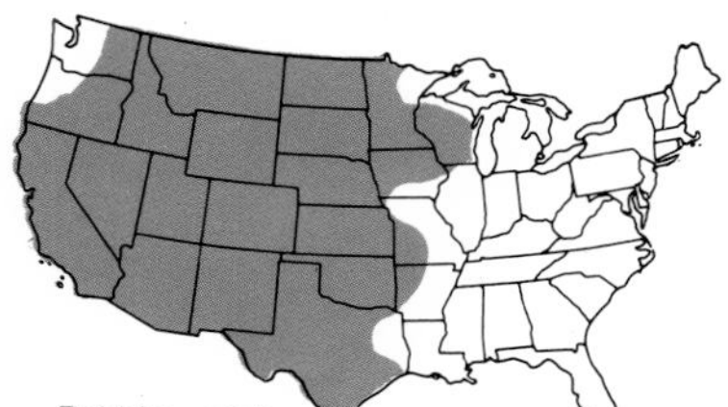

Rabbits, Jack

Raccoon

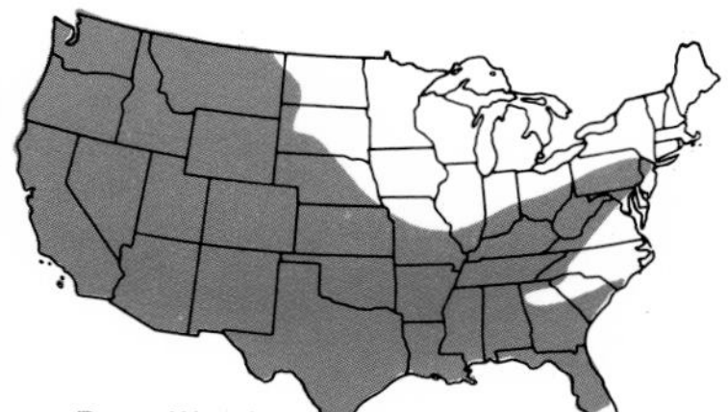

Rats, Wood

Sea Lion, California

Seal, Harbor

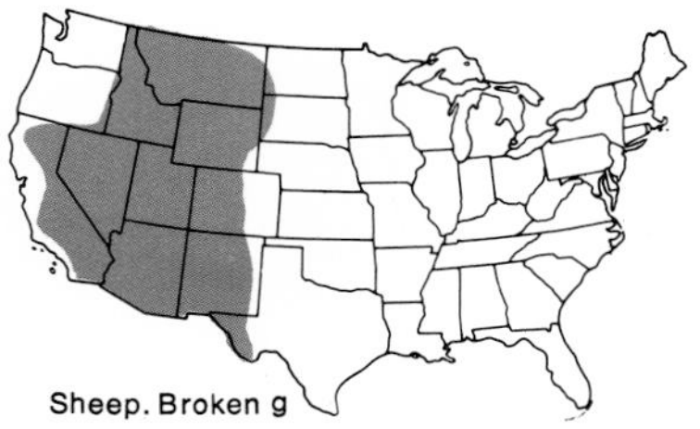

Sheep. Broken g

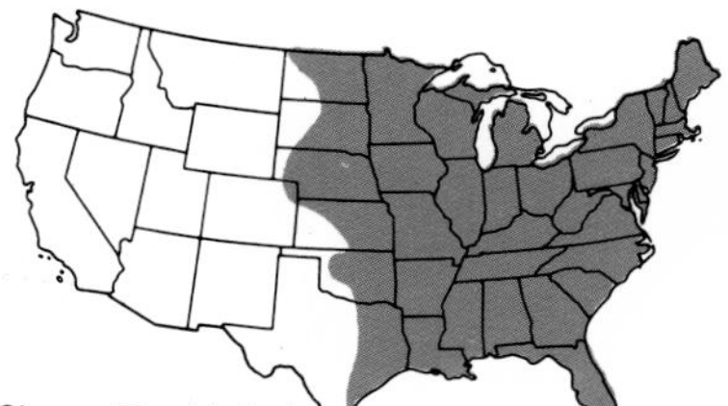

Shrew, Short-tailed

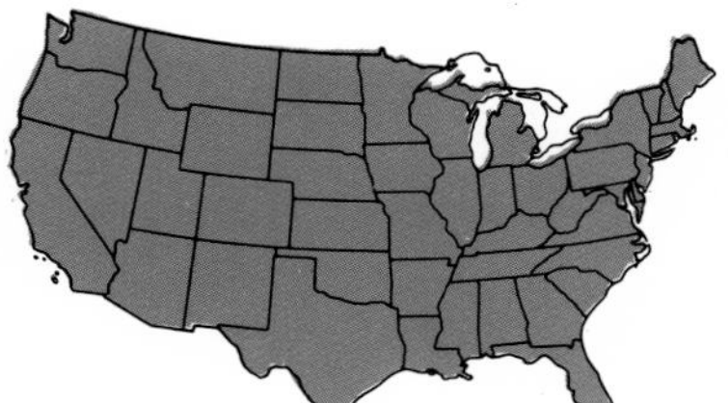

Skunks

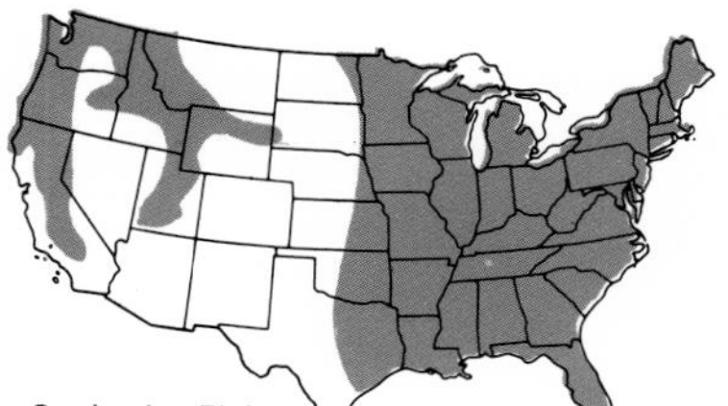

Squirrels, Flying

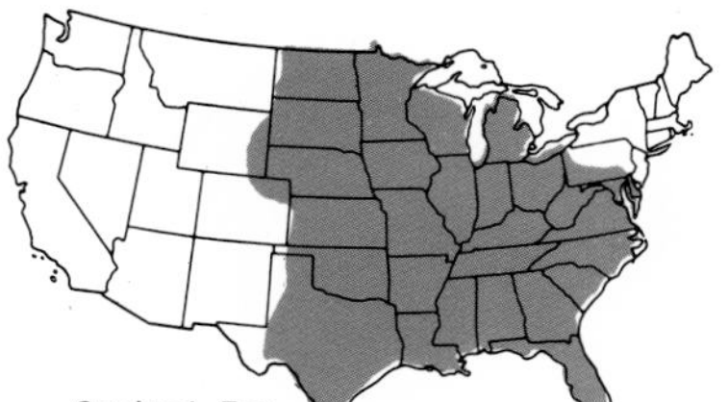

Squirrel, Fox

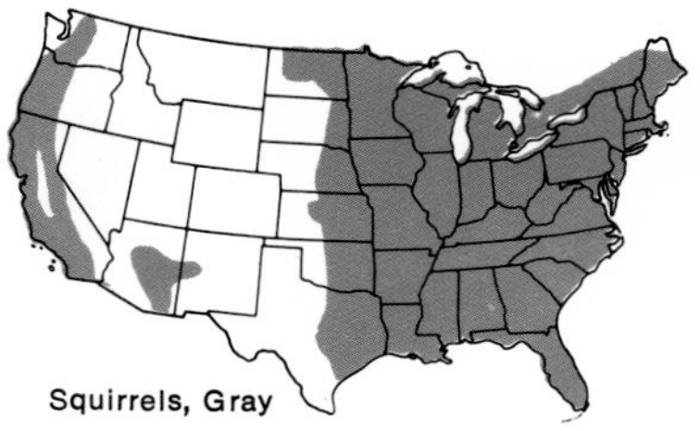

Squirrels, Gray

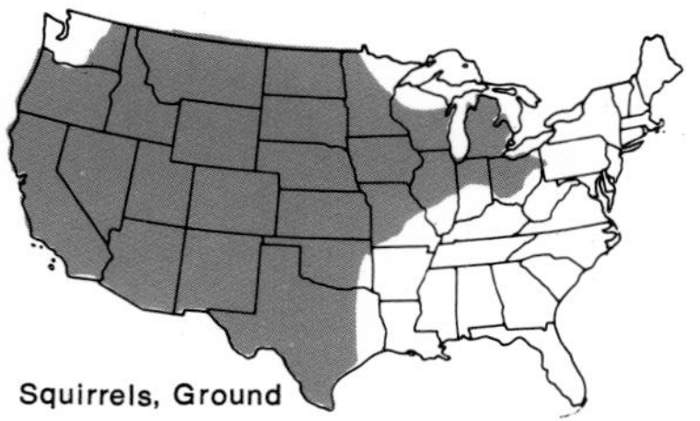

Squirrels, Ground

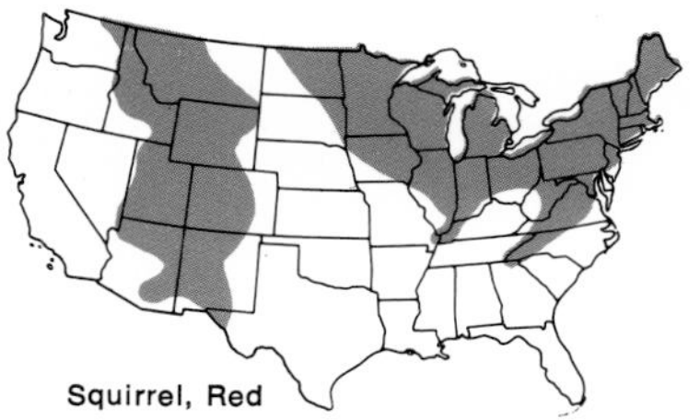

Squirrel, Red

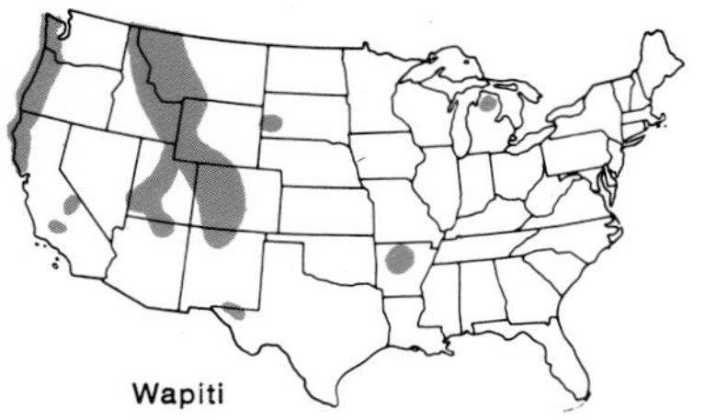

Wapiti

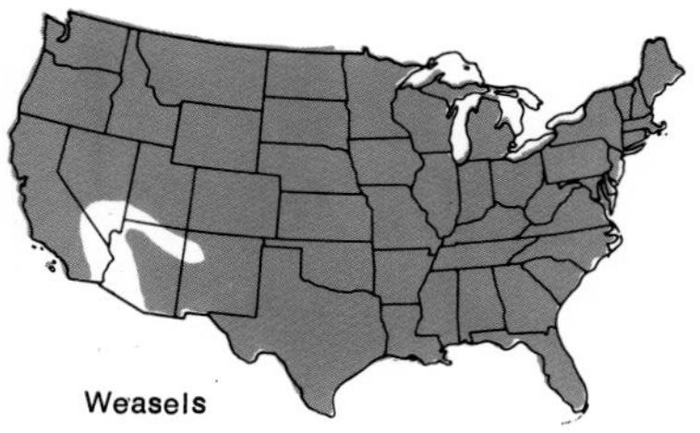

Weasels

Whale, Gray

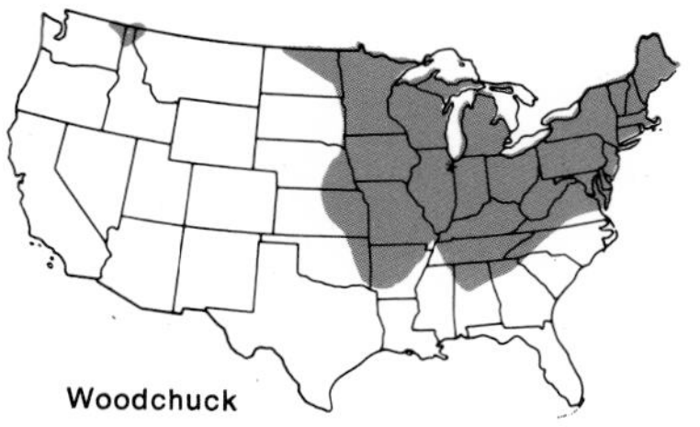

Woodchuck

Opossum (with young)

Common Mole

Short-tailed Shrew

OPOSSUM

Cat-sized and pale-gray, the Opossum is a marsupial, that ancient Order of pouched mammals so much more spectacularly represented by the Koala and the kangaroos of Australia. Equipped with almost finger-like toes and a long, naked, prehensile tail, the 'possum is equally at home in trees as on the ground. Young opossums occur in litters of ten or so, are born before being fully developed, and are carried in their mother's abdominal pouch for about ten weeks before they can scramble about to feed at night on small animals (mostly insects) and wild fruit. The habit of playing dead when cornered or injured is a unique adaptation. Unfortunately, this does the slow-moving 'possum little good in confronting automobiles. Opossums appear to have originated in South America, and the single U.S. species is spreading from coast to coast.

COMMON MOLE

A small (6″–7″) subterranean mammal, stoutly cylindrical, with a pointed snout and barely visible eyes and ears, it has tremendously enlarged forefeet which it uses to tunnel through the ground, usually just below the surface. The fur is velvety brownish-black, and reversible when stroked. Moles, like their relatives the shrews, are carnivorous. They feed on insect grubs, earthworms, and even mice that fall into their tunnels. To keep moles out of a lawn, their mounded tunnels should be packed down when they appear and a mothball inserted near the edge of the lawn they have invaded. The Common Mole **(Scalopus)** occurs throughout the central and eastern U.S.; and the similar Western Mole **(Scapanus)** all along the Pacific Coast. None occur in the mountains of the West. Two other genera, the Hairy-tailed and the Star-nosed Moles occur in the East.

SHREWS

All native shrews are smaller than moles but, like them, have velvety fur and small eyes and ears. Unlike moles, their front and hind feet are roughly the same size, and the teeth of shrews are stained chestnut at the tip, a completely diagnostic feature. The Short-tailed Shrew of the genus **Blarina** lives in leaf litter on the forest floor and is carnivorous, eating such small animals as insects, earthworms, and occasional mice. Normally abundant, it goes through great population ups and downs throughout its range. The slightly smaller Least Shrew of the genus **Cryptotis** overlaps the range of the Short-tailed Shrew south of the spruce forest, except in New England. As is true of many small mammals, an examination of the dentition is essential to identification. **Blarina** has 32 teeth; **Cryptotis** has 30. Many are eaten by snakes and owls.

Little Brown Bat

Raccoon

Black Bear

LITTLE BROWN BAT

Of the world's 750 species of bats 37 occur in the U.S., of which this species and its close relatives in the genus **Myotis** are the most widely dispersed and occur in summer north to Labrador and Alaska. Bats are a remarkably specialized Order of flying mammals (not related to mice) of very ancient lineage. The tropics have several large fruit-eating bats and a few blood-sucking bats, but all U.S. bats are small insectivores and harmless, though they may, of course, bite if handled. They consume prodigious quantities of small insects which are captured on the wing by dint of radar-like, ultrasonic sounds whose reflections lead them unerringly. They often roost hanging head down, closely packed together to preserve body heat, in caves, hollow trees, or old buildings. Many hibernate or migrate to escape winter's stress.

RACCOON

Although largely nocturnal, the chunky, ring-tailed and neatly-masked Raccoon is so often tame and so widely distributed up and down North America that it is easily the most familiar carnivore in the U.S. Suburban populations raid garbage pails and are often fed as wild pets. The Raccoon prefers wooded areas near water because frogs and crayfish are favorite foods, though the species is omnivorous. A large Raccoon weighs about 20 pounds, and a young animal half that. It mates in mid-winter and drops three to six young in early spring. It climbs well and leaves distinctive tracks in mud, like miniature human foot prints. As in most widely-distributed species, the northern animals are larger and darker than southern ones. There are several small, grayish sub-species on the island chains of the southeastern United States.

BLACK BEAR

The husky, flat-faced, brown, bluish, or black bear stands about two feet at the shoulder, may be five feet long and weigh over 300 pounds. It once occurred throughout wooded America except in the Southwest, but is now restricted to the extensive wooded areas where it has been adequately protected. It is still common in Great Smoky Mountains National Park, occurs in deep swamps in Florida and Louisiana, and is found across the northern tier of states and throughout forested Canada. A good tree climber, it is omnivorous and peaceful when left alone, though it occasionally gets into mischief by breaking into camps. Although in the north it often takes a "long sleep," it is not a true hibernator. Cubs may number three, are tiny at birth, and are usually born in February. Do not be among those who get out of cars to photograph park bears.

Long-tailed Weasel

Mink

WEASELS

Twenty or more species of weasels occur across North America and range in size from the six-inch Least Weasel with a one-inch tail to foot-long animals with over seven inches of tail. They include the two-foot-long Black-footed Ferret once associated with prairie dog towns but now very rare because of poisoning campaigns against prairie dogs throughout the West. All weasels are long, thin-bodied, short-legged, and swift rodent-hunters who feed mostly on mice, though larger ones take rabbits. An occasional weasel may raise havoc in a chicken house. Most weasels are sleek, chocolate-brown above, and white or yellowish below. North of the latitude of Pennsylvania weasels turn white in winter (all but the black tip of the tail), and the fur is then called ermine, once highly valued by royalty for trimming garments. Weasels include the smallest true carnivores.

MINK

A Mink is really a larger, more heavily built, white-throated, but otherwise almost uniformly colored, semi-aquatic weasel. About two feet long, including its eight-inch furry tail, it is dark lustrous-brown, sinuous, and such a good swimmer that it can catch trout. A large male weighs about two pounds, and a female half of that. A tireless wanderer, it hunts along the edges of streams, lakes, and marshes, feeding on a variety of small animals including young Muskrat. A Mink builds a den among tangled roots or rocks at the edges of such water bodies across the continent (except in the drier parts of the Southwest) and bears four to eight tiny young in mid-spring, which remain as family groups well into summer. The single species has been divided into 11 subspecific populations by mammalogists. It is more widely distributed than most people believe.

Sea Otter

River Otters

RIVER OTTER
This is the clown of the weasel tribe, over three feet long, low-slung, a hefty 20 pounds, a rich glossy-brown color (paler below), with a stout tail which leaves telltale marks in snow. A master of its aquatic realm, it feeds on fish, crayfish, and even turtles when ice locks up too much of its hunting grounds. An otter always finds time to play, and its mudslides down a steep bank, or the equivalent in snow, are worth watching for the privilege of sharing the exuberant enjoyment of life this animal displays. When going cross-country in snow, its trail shows as a broad furrow every time there is an opportunity to slide downhill. Although brutally persecuted by people with mistaken notions that every fur-bearer is a threat to someone, otters still occur widely where clean fresh-water and solitude exist, exactly what man needs to preserve his health.

SEA OTTER
When H. E. Anthony wrote his little classic, *Field Book of North American Mammals*, in 1928, he despaired that his readers would ever see a live Sea Otter. The comeback of this fascinating marine mammal is thus one of the triumphs of modern wildlife conservation. Today at many points between Monterey and Cayucos, California, and especially at Point Lobos State Reserve, anyone can see Sea Otters lolling among the big kelp of the Pacific Coast and diving for crustacea or shellfish, their principal food. People enjoy watching the remarkable feeding adaptations they have developed. They eat floating on their backs, using their bellies as a table, and often bringing up a rock against which to pound and get at the last bits of meat. The otters again need help, because abalone fishermen covet their feeding grounds. Friends of the Sea Otter will welcome support.

Striped Skunk

BADGER

This squat, husky, specialized member of the weasel tribe is over two-feet long, half as wide, and weighs 12 to 20 pounds. Usually a grizzled gray, the Badger has conspicuous face markings and a shuffling gait that make it easy to recognize. It is one of the best hole-diggers in existence, so that even when one does not see it, its presence is well advertised. The holes, of course, are dug in search of food, usually for one of the several kinds of ground squirrels. This makes the Badger one of the intermediate-sized predators of the grassland community of interior North America, feeding on the abundance of rodents this grassland produces. But whereas the Coyote, its partner in the economy of this community, can prey only on the surface, outrunning or outwitting its prey, the Badger digs it out. The Old World Badger is gregarious and inhabits woodlands.

SKUNKS

The strong, offensive odor these animals emit from paired anal glands when alarmed or injured is the trademark of skunks. The scent glands can emit their liquid at some distance, which is a great defense against dogs and other predators but not, alas, against automobiles. There are three skunks in the U.S. The widespread Common Skunk is a husky, bushy-tailed species of the genus **Mephitis.** It is black with two broad white stripes down each side. The smaller Spotted Skunk, of the genus **Spilogale**, has several broken white stripes that give it a spotted appearance like a small house cat. Skunks are more southern animals in the East, but widely scattered in the West. The husky Hog-nosed Skunk of the genus **Conepatus,** with a broad white dorsal stripe, occurs along the Mexican border and the Texas coast. Skunks are mostly nocturnal and are omnivorous in diet.

Badger

Gray Fox

Red Fox

Kit Fox

Coyote

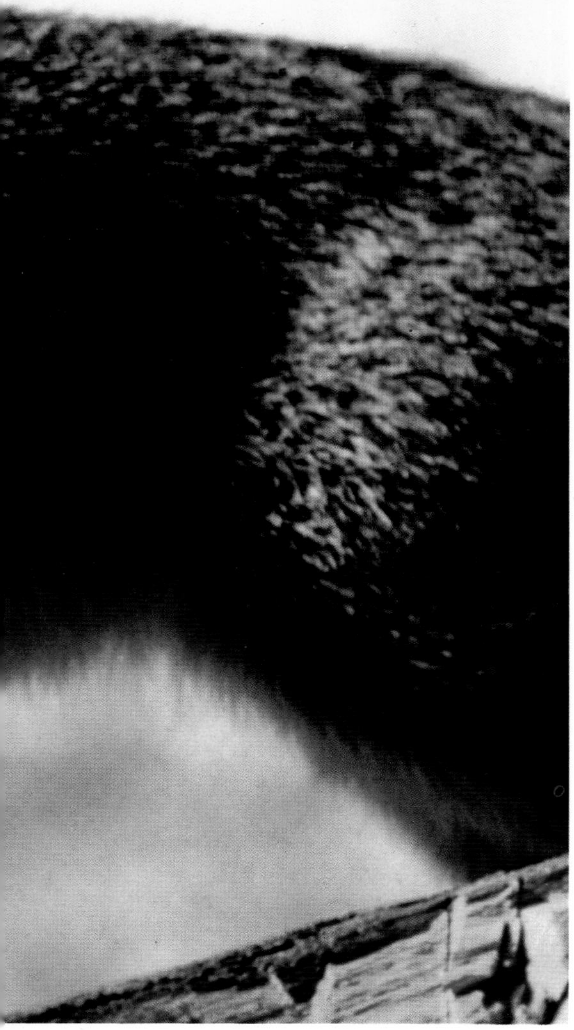

GRAY FOX

The Gray Fox is of a different genus **(Urocyon)** than its somewhat larger Red cousin, and in itself this indicates a different anatomy. This is evident in the shorter legs and the much flatter, almost cat-like face. Its color is much more a pepper-and-salt gray, with patches of reddish brown on the ears, neck, and ankles. It also climbs trees more readily than other members of the Dog Family, and when chased by dogs it will climb a tree or disappear into some favorite hole much more quickly than a Red Fox who seems to enjoy the chase as much as the dogs. Again comparing it with the Red Fox, the Gray Fox is more a warm-country animal, though it does occur in small numbers north to the Great Lakes and the St. Lawrence basin. It is the common fox in the South and is widespread in the West, even including some desert areas.

RED FOX

The Red Fox of the U.S. and Canada is of the same genus as the European fox **(Vulpes)** and is really a small wild dog with a sharp-nosed muzzle and a long, bushy tail. The long-haired coat is a rich reddish yellow with various amounts of black. The very black (melanistic) form is called Silver Fox and is bred commercially for fur. Its tail is tipped with white in all pelages. Few weigh more than 12 pounds. The Red Fox likes diversified landscapes and is both a temperate zone and a subarctic animal. It feeds mostly on mice, takes berries when available, but eats almost any small animals it chances upon, occasionally raiding chicken houses. It is alert, clever, and becomes cautious under persecution, showing impressive survival ability. A yippy bark is heard during the breeding season, and a litter of four to ten pups is born in a den in early spring.

KIT FOX

Though of the genus **Vulpes,** this is a much smaller animal than the Red Fox, is more buff-colored, and has larger ears and a black-tipped tail. It occupies the dry plains and deserts of the West. Being an open-country animal, it stays in its den most of the day. Being, unfortunately, much less wary than the Red Fox, it has fallen prey to rodent poisoning campaigns and varmint shooters who spotlight it at night after luring it out with mechanical calls or sound recordings of its voice. Also called Swift Fox, this little animal shows well the strong molding that environment imposes on a species. In this case selective pressures have favored small size, pale coloration, and big ears in very much the way the Fennec, an evolutionary counterpart half way around the Earth, has been molded by similar semi-desert environments in the Middle East.

COYOTE

A Coyote is a small prairie wolf, less than 50 inches long (including its 15″–18″ tail) in contrast to the Gray Wolf of the North which is over 60 inches. A Coyote thus resembles a lightly built German shepherd dog, but can run much faster and is a superb hunter of small animals, subsisting mostly on rabbits, mice, and whatever else it can catch. The yapping howl is distinctive and, as H. E. Anthony says, is of "an indescribable quality . . . which sets it apart from the obnoxious disturbance of a night-howling dog," and like its larger relative is considered by many to be a true voice of the wilderness. The aggressive production-mindedness of American agriculturists is now eliminating the Coyote from the landscape as drastically as it eliminated wolves a generation or two ago. Coyotes have spread into the Northeast in recent decades.

California Sea Lions

Harbor Seal

HARBOR SEAL

Sometimes called Hair Seal, this is the small seal found off both U.S. coasts, on occasion south to North Carolina and to Baja California. Unlike the considerably larger Fur Seal and the much larger Sea Lion, a Harbor Seal cannot rotate its hind limbs forward and is therefore very clumsy out of water. For this reason it hauls out onto rocks at high tide and suns itself during the lowering tide. A male is up to five feet long and weighs up to 300 pounds, and a female is not much smaller. The color is extremely variable, running in the young from a yellowish-buff to a yellowish-brown or dark gray with darker spots, to almost black in the adult. Although this seal gathers in small herds when not molested, it does not form harems. Pups are born in late spring. The Harbor Seal feeds on fish and shellfish and, unfortunately, often gets tangled in fishermen's nets.

CALIFORNIA SEA LION

This very large seal—a male weighs up to 500 pounds and a female less than 200—is nevertheless swift and graceful in the water, and can scramble onto the shore much better, for example, than the Harbor Seal. The species is fortunately still fairly common, especially south of San Francisco and on Pacific islands south to the Galapagos Islands. It gathers in herds, barking and honking, and a bull maintains a harem of five to 20 females. The single pup, born usually in June, remains with its mother nearly a year. Though a California Sea Lion looks black when wet, the fur is light to dark-brown when dry. Its agility and playfulness make it the best, and nearly the only, circus seal. In California its populations are overlapped by the even larger Stellar's Sea Lion, which runs to 1500 pounds or more and ranges northward to the Bering Strait.

WOODCHUCK (Marmot)

The familiar Woodchuck, a conspicuous summer resident of meadows throughout the temperate East and Canada, is really a large ground squirrel. Also called a Ground Hog in the East, it is a warm-brown, sometimes rufous, animal. It is chunky, about ten pounds in weight, but agile enough to climb trees occasionally. Its den systems are extensive, with a prominent mound of dirt at one of the entrances, but also with unobtrusive plunge holes for quick escape from such predators as foxes, dogs, or hunters. A Woodchuck fattens up on grass and other greens all summer and hibernates through the winter. One that comes out on Ground Hog Day, Feb. 2, is searching for a mate and not forecasting the weather. Throughout the West, mostly at temperate elevations, the very similar Yellow-bellied Marmot may startle visitors with its loud whistle.

GROUND SQUIRRELS

Almost everywhere in western North America, from the Arctic to Mexico, and eastward to Ohio, one or another of the 23 species of this variable genus **Spermophilus** (formerly **Citellus)** occurs in open country. The most widespread is the Thirteen-lined Spermophile, named for the alternating light and white-spotted dark stripes on its back. It occupies most of the prairie, including its eastern tongue to Ohio. The widespread Golden-mantled Ground Squirrel of the West looks like a big chipmunk but lacks striping on the face. All ground squirrels dig burrows, staying close enough to dive away when startled. They often sit upright, whistle, and twitch their tails nervously. Some store food—seeds, grass, insects—and most of them hibernate several months, though desert forms may estivate, becoming dormant during the hot, dry season.

PRAIRIE DOGS

These stout rodents, named prairie dogs because of their so-called bark, are really large ground squirrels. Once the most widespread, the Black-tailed Prairie Dog occupied the high plains from southeastern Arizona and western Texas to Montana. It formed extensive towns in these former bison grasslands, and its burrows were also homes for many other species. Today, even though experts tell us that we have four million acres of surplus wheat agriculture, prairie dogs have been poisoned almost out of existence. A few parks and Indian reservations, at the western edge of the prairie, still have small towns. Three other somewhat smaller species occur at higher elevations in the Rocky Mountains: the White-tailed Prairie Dog in Wyoming and northwestern Colorado; Gunnison's Prairie Dog in southern Colorado, New Mexico, and Arizona; and the Utah Prairie Dog.

Woodchuck

Ground Squirrel

Black-tailed Prairie Dogs

Eastern Chipmunk

Red Squirrel

Gray Squirrel

CHIPMUNKS

These are colorful, saucy, playful, little, striped squirrels that neither dig like other ground squirrels nor climb like tree squirrels. They live in the in-between realm. Their shrill chirps and chatterings are often mistaken for bird notes until a better acquaintance is developed. The Eastern Chipmunk (genus **Tamias**) is somewhat stouter, brighter, with a slightly shorter tail, than the western chipmunks. It lives in the eastern deciduous forest, northwestward to Lake Winnipeg and northeastward to the Maritime Provinces. It readily adapts to the suburbs, where it occasionally pilfers gardeners' bulbs, and it hibernates through the northern winter. Western chipmunks of the genus **Eutamias** seldom hibernate. They occupy 11 western states and most of Canada, and have evolved 16 species and 59 described geographical races or subspecies.

RED SQUIRREL

This is the arboreal squirrel of coniferous forests. It is smaller than the Gray Squirrel of the East, rusty-red above and white below. A bold, scampering sprite, it scolds every passerby. The seeds of conifers—spruce, fir, pine—are its principal foods, and its presence is well marked by stripped cones or great middens of cone scales and cores. It is active mostly in daylight and spends the night in old woodpecker holes or in tight twig nests it builds for itself. Since the northern coniferous forest covers most of Alaska, Canada, the Rocky Mountains, the lake states, and the Appalachian region, this is the range of the Red Squirrel. Another species, the Douglas Chickaree, or Squirrel, occupies the more humid coniferous forest of the Northwest. It is a darker, chestnut-red and has yellow underparts, as becomes a resident of cool, damp climates.

GRAY SQUIRREL

Wherever acorns grow in the eastern half of our continent—in forests, river-bottom woods, city parks, or suburbs—there are usually Gray Squirrels. It is therefore among the best known mammals we have, since so many of us are urbanites and suburbanites. A typical arboreal squirrel, it has many relatives (all of the genus **Sciurus**) south to Argentina and throughout Eurasia. Acorns are its staple food, but other fruits, mushrooms, insects, even birds' eggs are eaten. The Gray Squirrel buries nuts as security against food scarcity, but many of them are never recovered, making this squirrel a major factor in the spread of oaks and hickories. The Gray Squirrel has been introduced into Great Britain and South Africa where, as often happens to an exotic species, it has increased rapidly and is considered a pest. It builds bulky nests of twigs and leaves.

Fox Squirrel

Flying Squirrel

Beaver (feeding on Aspen)

FOX SQUIRREL
It is seldom that two very similar species occupy the same range, but the Fox and the Gray Squirrels do, except in the Northeast, where there are no Fox Squirrels. Both were formerly very abundant, but the Fox Squirrel is now much scarcer, though still widespread in semi-open woods, parks, and suburbs. This is the largest tree squirrel, almost two pounds in weight, instead of one pound as is a Gray Squirrel, and much more colorful, though variable. A Fox Squirrel almost always has a black head with a pale-buff nose; the back and tail, however, may vary from gray, more often rusty-buff, to black. It is tamer than a Gray Squirrel, especially in city parks, more leisurely in movement, and appears more confident. It too buries nuts, builds large twig and leaf nests in tall trees, and remains active the year around, though it will sleep out a storm.

FLYING SQUIRRELS
Almost everywhere Red and Gray Squirrels occur in good woodland, one may expect also to find the beautiful little flying squirrels. Hardly a foot long and only three ounces in weight, their dense fur is soft and silky. The eyes are large, dark, and lustrous, as becomes strictly nocturnal animals. For that reason, few people get to know them, but the effort to do so is worthwhile. Flying squirrels spend the day sleeping in shredded bark nests in large woodpecker holes, or in suitable bird nesting boxes placed higher than usual, or even in the attics of country houses. Persistent scratching on a nesting tree may induce two or three of them to poke their heads out, or even to "fly" away. They do not really fly, but volplane on tightly drawn folds of skin between front and hind legs. Glides of a hundred feet or more appear to be not uncommon.

BEAVER
The lure of Beaver pelts led in the exploration of Canada and the U.S. This big aquatic fur-bearer, the largest rodent north of Panama (60 lbs.), once lived on every stream that had trees along it, except in the extreme southwestern U.S. and Florida. Its drastic decline illustrates how much we have altered North America. Fortunately, conservation measures in recent years have re-established it in many places, especially in the Northeast, so that Beaver ponds are again within a half day's automobile drive for millions of people. The Beaver is a noted engineer, fells trees, floats them on connecting canals he has dug, builds stout dams across small valleys, and then builds big winter lodges of sticks and mud in the resulting pond. Its big flat tail slaps an alarm on the pond when an intruder approaches. Its favorite food is the innerbark of poplar.

WHITE-FOOTED MOUSE

Although many small mammals can vie for the title, the 27 species and 150 subspecies (north of Mexico) of the genus **Peromyscus** are the most widespread group. Names such as Deer Mouse, Brush Mouse, Cotton Mouse, Oldfield Mouse, and Canyon Mouse attest to the variety of habitats and regions occupied. All members of this genus have long noses, big ears, and long tails. The southern forms are nondescript, but the northern ones are an attractive two-tone or a bicolor—various shades of warm buff above and pure white below. Those who know them usually consider them delightful animals, clean, dainty, and easily tamed. The northern species build their winter homes in old birds' nests several feet off the ground. Others may chew up paper or curtains for winter nests in the drawer of a dresser in a summer cottage. They eat seeds, nuts, and insects.

WOOD RATS

Although proportioned very much like the unpleasant, introduced Norway Rat of cities, the woods rats, or pack rats, of North America are attractive and intriguing rodents, softly furred, gray to buff or even rufous-spotted, with hairy or actually bushy tails, and mostly white below. The seven different species of them are occupants of rocky hills in temperate, desert, or even alpine regions. And as one would expect of such a wide-ranging group, the species are divided into many subspecies. These are highly social animals, and among their interesting habits is that of building huge nests, sometimes a yard across, of sticks or cactus spines in rock crannies, trees, or even abandoned sheds. Wood rats are notorious for taking bright objects, for which they often trade pebbles, from the camps or deserted country houses they visit, mostly at night.

MEADOW MOUSE

Wherever rank grasses grow south of the Arctic the Field Mouse, or Vole, occurs. This is a medium-sized, dark, gray-brown mouse, short-tailed, with very short ears, and the usual prominent, paired incisor teeth that characterize the Order of rodents. Its presence is marked by inch-wide tunnels in grass and piles of cut hay, by middens of droppings at convenient intervals, and domed grass nests in winter. This is a weed species, fluctuating greatly in numbers every three years or so—to over a thousand mice per acre from the usual 300. Such population explosions are understandable from the fact that they may have a dozen litters of six or so young per year. Gestation is only 21 days. Such irruptions are, of course, destructive to agriculture, since they are grass eaters. Legions of flesh-eaters consider this vole a staple food, however.

MUSKRAT

The Muskrat is now the principal animal in the U.S. fur trade. With a range almost as extensive as the Beaver's once was, it has probably always been more numerous because it occupies more habitats, especially the shallow fresh and brackish marshes the Beaver never occupied. It is a big brown water-rat that weighs three or four pounds and has large hindfeet with stiff fringing hair that make swimming easy. It builds Muskrat houses in marshes, which are mounds of cut or plucked vegetation about three feet across and rising somewhat less above the water. Where conditions are unsuitable for houses, it burrows into banks. This may make it a serious nuisance where it has dug into an earthen dam. Its principal predator is the Mink. In Florida, the much smaller Round-tailed Muskrat forms a link between true Muskrats and Meadow Mice.

PORCUPINE

This big, prickly rodent weighs ten to 20 pounds and is today restricted to the spruce forest and the northern hardwoods immediately south of it. Here and there a few animals descend wooded river valleys. Slow-moving, and prone to climb trees when pressed, it does most of its feeding at night, chewing the inner-bark of trees, buds, and young pine needles. It can be a serious nuisance around a camp because it will chew up anything made salty by human perspiration, like axe handles or the straps of a pack sack. It usually dens up in small rock caves, where its presence is marked by oblong, capsule-like scats. The dangerous, two- to three-inch quills are almost hidden in the long, black-and-white or yellowish fur, but are erected in a big pin-cushion when the porky is alarmed. Quills are not thrown but can be imbedded deeply with a swat of the well-armored tail.

PIKA

The little Rock Cony, or Little Chief Hare as Indians called it, is a charming, short-legged member of the rabbit tribe. Only about seven inches long, chunky and brownish, with rounded ears and no visible tail, it is perhaps best known for its loud calls—half bleat, half whistle—that echo from the rock piles or talus slopes at high elevations in the mountains of the West. It occurs at decreasing elevations as one goes north, especially in Canada. As one might expect, the several upland populations, each made insular by dissected mountain masses, are now recognized as different subspecies—35 of them. A separate species occupies Alaska, and other pikas extend across Asia to the Ural Mountains of Russia and down to the Himalaya Mountains. This little rock-rabbit cuts and cures hay for winter use since it does not hibernate like its neighbor the Yellow-bellied Marmot.

White-footed Mouse

Desert Wood Rat

Meadow Mouse

Muskrat

Porcupine

Pika

Snowshoe Hare

Black-tailed Jack Rabbit

SNOWSHOE HARE

Throughout the spruce-fir and other coniferous forests of Canada and the high country of the U.S. this hare with its big hind feet, which give it the name Snowshoe Hare (or rabbit), is the basic food supply of the large owls and medium-sized carnivorous mammals such as foxes, bobcats, and lynx. Indeed, its importance is reflected in fur trade annals because every ten years or so the high Snowshoe Hare population crashes to a low point, and so then do the numbers of the dependent predators. After such a crash, the litter size of the hare may grow to ten young, though the usual litter is two to six. The snowshoe-like hind feet are an adaptation to living on snow for half the year. Even more striking, however, is the change of pelage, from grayish-brown in summer to pure white in winter, hence its other name, Varying Hare. The ear-tips, however, stay black.

JACK RABBITS

As is so often the case, the popular name is a misnomer. These are true hares, not rabbits, i.e., their young are born in the open rather than in a nest, with eyes open, are fully haired, and able to run almost immediately. There are three species, all western and large (5 lbs.—6 lbs.), with tremendous ears and long hind legs. The White-tailed Jack occurs from Iowa to the Great Basin and north to Washington (east of the Coast Range) and Saskatchewan. The Black-tailed Jack is slightly smaller and much more numerous all throughout the West except Montana. It is also a great runner and it zig-zags through sagebrush, often leaping high to look over its shoulder. The Antelope Jack of the Arizona desert occurs southward into western Mexico and is the palest of the trio. These jack rabbits are the principal food of eagles, coyotes, and bobcats.

COTTONTAILS

Like all true rabbits, the medium-sized cottontails bear naked, blind, and helpless young which they keep safe in small fur-lined depressions in the ground. Because they feed mostly at dusk and at night, rabbits spend much of the day in a den, usually an old woodchuck burrow. The Eastern, or Florida, Cottontail is the most widespread species. It often the tamest, commonest, and one of the best-known small mammals, occupying field borders, lawns, and brook bottoms. The largest species is the Swamp Rabbit, a darker brown animal of the Southeast. The Western Cottontail is more often a brush rabbit; and the smallest of the group, the Pigmy Rabbit, occupies the sage-brush flats of the Northwest. Other cottontails occur all the way to Argentina. They are preyed upon by almost all meat-eaters, especially by foxes, hawks, and owls.

Wapiti (bull)

Cottontail

Peccary

PECCARY (Javelina)
These little wild pigs are semi-desert dwellers, living in the cactus and mesquite areas of western Texas and southern Arizona; hence the Spanish name preferred in that region. But the species also occurs all the way to Patagonia, a remarkable geographic and ecological range. The Texas form is smaller (about 20″ at the shoulder) and a dark, grizzled gray. The Arizona subspecies is paler and larger. All have bristly fur, stumpy tails, slim legs, and small hooves. A musk gland on the lower back emits a powerful odor. They appear immune to rattlesnake poison, a fortunate adaptation since they live where rattlesnakes are most numerous. Javelinas almost always occur in groups of five to 20, move quietly in single file except when feeding or alarmed. Then they show great agility, speed, and courage. They feed mostly in the cool of day.

WAPITI (Elk)
This splendid animal is closely related to the Red Deer of Europe. A stag is five feet at the shoulder, weighs 700 to 1000 pounds, has a conspicuous mane, and may have a rack of antlers that spread five feet in two directions. The head, neck, and legs are chestnut-brown, the body grayish, and the rump straw-colored. A female is smaller, weighs about 500 pounds, and is less distinctly marked. More properly called Wapiti, the elk is now restricted to the mountains of the West, where it feeds mostly in alpine meadows in summer and descends to increasingly restricted valleys in winter, at which time many starve despite an annual take by hunters. The Tule Elk of Owens Valley, California, is a remnant, but thriving, population of a smaller species. Merriam's Elk of the southwestern mountains was shot to extinction.

WHITE-TAILED DEER

Once the food and fiber staple of eastern Amerindians, and for a while of the early colonists, this graceful deer is so wide-ranging, so abundant and relatively tame that it is the best-known large mammal in America. A buck may exceed three feet at the shoulder and weigh over 200 pounds. It has simply-branched, forward-directed antlers. A doe is smaller and lacks antlers, and a fawn is spotted. Primarily a denizen of the eastern deciduous forest, it now occurs in increasing numbers northward because pulpwood cutting in Canada has opened up the forest to its liking. Other White-tailed Deer occur southward into South America. The Whitetail profited greatly from the farm abandonment of the last century in the East. Its peak of abundance is passing rapidly, however, since mature forest has less browse and cover than young woodland.

MULE DEER (Black-tailed Deer)

This is the open-country deer of the West, ranging well up into the hills in summer, and down to grass and shrub flats in winter. It is more huskily built than the White-tailed Deer, has larger ears, hence is called Mule Deer, and has a black-tipped tail. The antlers are normally distinctive, forking first into two main prongs which may in turn carry smaller, rather uniform prongs. The Black-tailed Deer bounds much more than the Whitetail, a useful trait in the rough country it favors. Because of such differences, though their ranges overlap considerably, these two species generally occupy different habitats. Although deer in good country can stand lots of hunting, it is time the states managed them more equitably for hunters, non-hunters, and their natural predators, where these still exist, or could exist. The name Blacktail is favored in its northern range.

MOOSE

This is the largest of all deer and it once occurred throughout the northern coniferous forest, where lakes, streams, and attendant thickets furnish abundant food, either as aquatic plants for summer use, or willow, alder, and other shrubs for winter browse. Biologists now call this a spruce-moose biome. Six feet at the shoulder, up to 1400 pounds, of ungainly proportions with great humped shoulders and a broad, pendulous muzzle, it is dark brown except for its pale legs. Despite its great size, broad hooves carry it quickly, gracefully, almost stealthily, through its swampy habitats. Much restricted in range today, the same moose occurs across northern Scandinavia and Siberia (where it is called elk by Englishmen), but centuries of selective trophy hunting in Europe has greatly limited the impressive palmate antlers that make the American Moose so distinctive.

PRONGHORN

A member of a unique American Family, the dainty Pronghorn is our short-grass plains' representative of the antelopes that grace the savannas of Africa. Now much restricted in range, it occurs mostly in the drier portions of the West, though a few ranchers now nurture small herds for hunting purposes elsewhere. Nearly three feet at the shoulder, a rich tan above and white below, a buck has a black face and black throat patch. Both sexes have small straight horns. Those of a doe are smaller, in keeping with her generally smaller proportions. Pronghorns are very curious, and hunters take advantage of this trait to lure them within gun range. They cruise easily at 30 miles per hour, can run at 40 if pressed, but seldom run long distances. The barbed-wire fences of agriculturists are a serious obstacle to them, since they can not jump like deer.

Moose (bull)

Mule Deer

Pronghorn

White-tailed Deer

AMERICAN BISON

In 1750 this great beast—a big bull standing nearly six feet at the shoulder and weighing nearly a ton—was nature's supreme monument to the life process inherent to the North American continent. Symbolically, its only rivals were the Passenger Pigeon, the Plains Indians' civilization, and the California redwoods. Nurtured on the best grassland in the world, herds wandered north into Saskatchewan in spring and retired to milder climates in winter. So numerous and so vigorous were they in the face of all vicissitudes that they overflowed eastward to the piedmont region and southward into Mexico. American Bison probably numbered well over 50 million animals before white men began the slaughter that reduced them to a mere 514 individuals in 1889. A few herds have been rebuilt, and some day they may be given a proper Prairie National Park.

BIGHORN SHEEP

This large, heavy-set wild sheep, once widespread throughout the rough country of the 11 western states, is now restricted to the wilder mountainous areas where adequate protection is afforded it. In some of the Rocky Mountain parks, however, and in adjacent hills, Bighorn ewes and their young become quite tame. It is a real sheep, of the genus **Ovis** from which domestic sheep originated over 5000 years ago, but the coat is hairy rather than woolly. A ram is an unmistakable animal with a brownish coat and a pale rump patch. It has massive curled horns, stands about 40 inches at the shoulder, and weighs up to 300 pounds. A ewe also has horns, but much more slender ones; it is smaller (about 150 lbs.) and has a paler coat. Smaller, paler subspecies occur in the desert hills of the Southwest and adjacent Mexico including Baja California.

ARMADILLO

This unusual, cat-sized, armored mammal is of tropical origin and now appears to be spreading northward like the Opossum and other species, taking advantage of the milder climate of more recent years. The bony skutes that form the armor occur in overlapping rings, so that the animal can curl up into a tight protective ball when alarmed. The young are born with soft skin that gradually becomes ossified. An Armadillo feeds mostly on insects by snuffing and rooting through ground litter like a small pig. It digs many burrows that make useful dens for other species, and its presence is otherwise indicated by droppings (scats) which look like clay marbles. Although it can dash away quickly, an Armadillo is particularly vulnerable on highways because of the habit of jumping up when startled. Even so, it is prolific enough to expand its range.

American Bison

Dolphins

Bighorn Sheep (ram)

Armadillo

DOLPHINS and PORPOISES

About 60 species of small whales qualify for these two terms. They differ enough to be classified in 18 genera. Dolphins have a beaked snout, and porpoises have a blunt snout. They are agile, speedy (up to 25 knots), sometimes playful, and often gather in schools. Some species are intelligent or docile enough to be trained to jump for fish, and they apparently often assist one another when in trouble. For example, they will nudge wounded or sick companions to the surface to breathe, and they will jointly ram a shark to death. The notorious Killer Whale is also a porpoise who is predatory on his own kind. They inhabit all the world's oceans, a few species inhabit large river systems, and several come into estuaries. Of the latter, the Common Porpoise and the Bottle-nosed Dolphin are the most likely visitors to the Atlantic and Pacific coasts.

GRAY WHALE

Of the world's 90 species of whales and porpoises—most of them hard-pressed by exploitation—this is the only one regularly and commonly seen from land. Some ten thousand now migrate south from the Bering Sea in autumn and breed in the warm lagoons of Baja California. In 1971 Mexico made Scammon Lagoon a National Park for them. The months of passage in southern California are December and January for the southbound movement and March to May for northbound whales. Monterey and San Diego have become noted whale-watching areas. This is a baleen whale which feeds on sardines and krill. Dark gray, with pale patches of barnacles, it has no dorsal fin, and its spout is quick and less than ten feet high. Usually in groups of two or three, it migrates at about four knots per hour and submerges for five minutes between surfacings.

Gray Whale

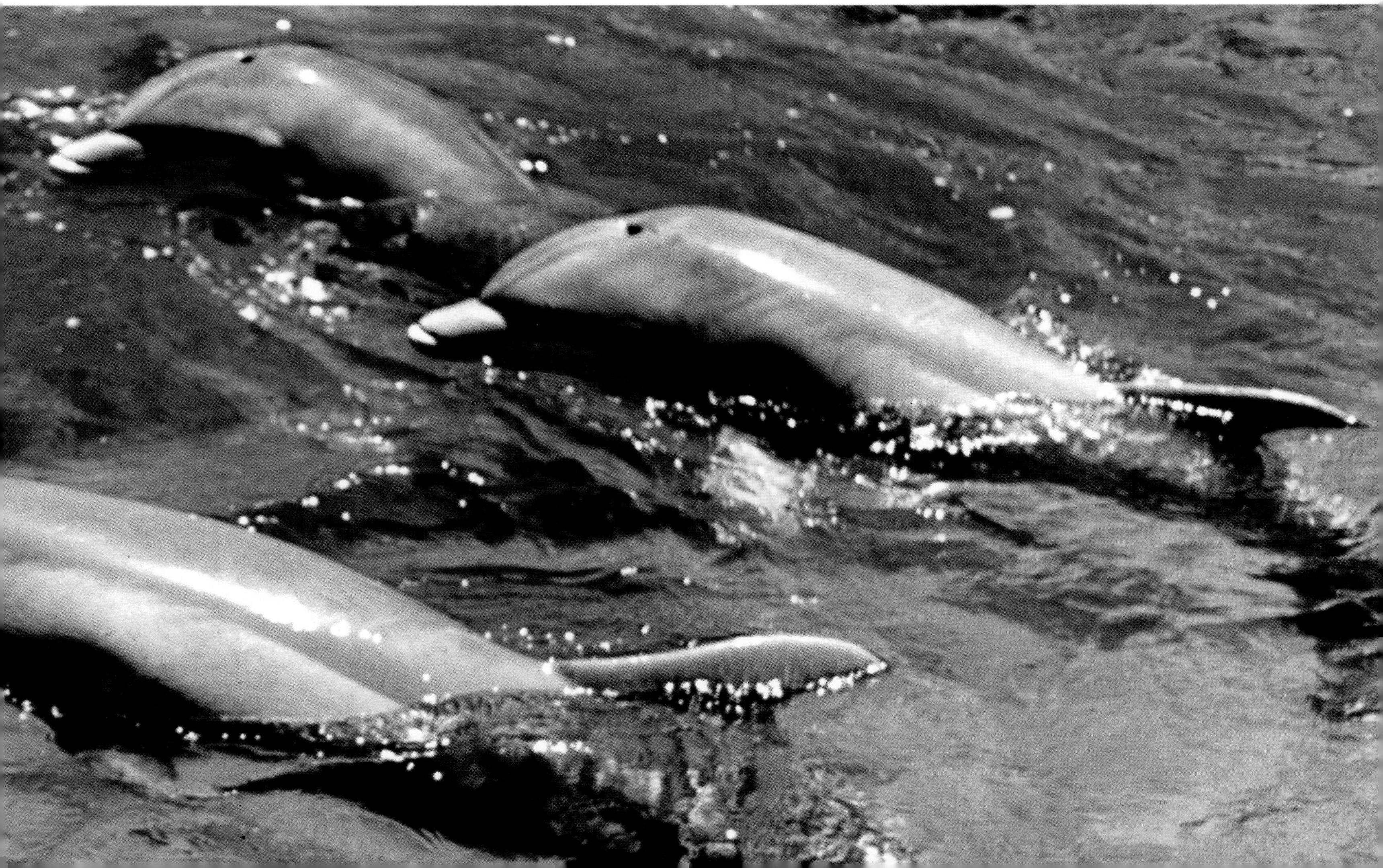

6. BIRDS

BIRDS

For most people, birds are the ideal introduction to nature because they have so many attributes similar to our own. We find them especially interesting because they are colorful, they sing, they dance, they are often great travelers, and their domestic life, though mostly seasonal, seems to us devoted and peaceful. Few of us envy the instinctive simplicity of the lives of other animals, but many of us wish we could soar like an eagle or sing with the abandon of a wren. There is then much that is superlative in birds. They add so much to the world by the way in which they recombine and utilize the same elements we more or less have common access to. This is the marvelous side of the evolution of life—it explores and actualizes so many potentialities. We can learn much about our own potential by observing not only other people, but nature in general, and birds in particular.

Altogether our planet has about 8000 species of birds. Although a few more, it is thought, remain to be discovered in the less-explored tropical regions, this number is unlikely to grow in our time. Unfortunately, the rapid growth of human populations is likely to push more species into extinction than will be discovered. In addition, as we learn more about many of the species of birds, we discover that many of them are more closely related than originally thought, and we therefore lump many of them together as mere races of particular species. This is helpful for both the amateur and the professional because it simplifies the task of learning so many species. And the clues to the relationships provided by this more conservative art of classification are also of interest. It becomes intriguing to see how variable, or plastic, many species can be. For example, Song Sparrows in North America vary greatly from large, dark birds in the humid Northwest to small, pale birds in the deserts of the Southwest. Until one has learned how to distinguish Song Sparrows from other sparrows, it would be easy to assume that the extremes just mentioned represent different species. When we study them carefully, however, we find that these extreme types are merely the two ends of a graded series of related forms—subspecies rather than full species. On the other hand, many other wide-ranging species hold true to type despite the widely different climates in which they live.

As Chandler S. Robbins and his colleagues point out in their excellent *Birds of North America*, although North America makes up nearly 17 percent of the world's land area, it has less than eight percent of the world's bird species, i.e., about 1780. Because the tropics are richest in birds, only about 645 species nest north of Mexico. One reason for this relative poverty of northern species is that so much of the northern United States, and almost all of Canada, was completely covered by glacial ice during the last million years or so until some 15,000 years ago, or less, when the continental ice retreated once more. There simply has not been time for much of the northern landscape to be revegetated adequately. Also, since winters are still very long, northern lands are populated only seasonally except for a few animal groups that were able to evolve specially-adapted species to occupy the harsh environment year around.

North America, however, has large numbers of many of its species, simply because so much of the northland provides millions of acres of similar habitat. The wood warblers occupy the vast spruce-fir forest of Canada, and great legions of waterfowl and shorebirds nest on the Arctic tundra whose prairie-like landscape blooms

Preceding pages: Bald Eagle

profusely during the 24-hour daylight of the brief Arctic summer. As a result, Robbins *et al.* accept the figure of 20 billion individual birds for North America (north of Mexico) in late summer, when annual broods of young are added to the population. This is thought to give us about 20 percent of the world population, which is slightly more than the 17 percent area would lead us to expect.

It is exactly because so much of North America can be occupied only seasonally that such spectacular seasonal migrations have developed. This is a strategy for taking full advantage of an abundant food supply during the short, northern summer. Northern nesters retire to the tropics and subtropics or cross into the south temperate zone for winter. They nest only once, however. The number of species that nest south of the equator and winter in the northern summer is much smaller.

Several of our species have oval migration routes, moving north through the interior of North America in spring and southward along our coasts, especially the Atlantic Coast, in autumn. Various points along both coasts, such as Cape Cod, Cape Hatteras, Point Lobos, and Point Arena, are therefore good migration-watch areas. Inland, long ridges parallel to the direction the birds want to travel become flyways. One of the most famous of these is Hawk Mountain in the Kittatinny Ridge of eastern Pennsylvania. Here, each fall, ten to 20 thousand migrating hawks, a few eagles, and many other birds are recorded by observers who man the lookouts daily from August to November.

The trick in coming to identify birds at sight is to learn first the principal groups—the Orders. There are only 19 of these in the United States, no great task for anyone's memory. Orders are subdivided into Families, and nine of the Orders have only one Family each. On the other hand, the perching birds **(Order Passeriformes),** most of them fine singers, are divided into 27 Families in the United States, many of which are nevertheless very distinctive.

Size, which is best estimated by comparison with some familiar standard—a crow, pigeon, robin, sparrow—is important. Most helpful as a clue to relationships is the type of bill—whether long or short, curved or decurved, thin and tweezer-like or stout and conical. After that comes color pattern including conspicuous field marks such as shoulder patches and white outer-tail-feathers. The relative length and shape of the wings, legs, and tail are of course also helpful. In short, a bird has to be characterized in order to be identified by comparison with an illustration in a field guide.

The way to become an expert is to learn what is already known about the birds of one's own region, and later the birds of larger regions one wishes to specialize in. There is, however, so much to learn about birds today, that real experts acquire a good general background and then specialize in some phase of ornithology—either in a group of birds or some aspect of the biology of birds.

Although it is possible to learn a great deal by oneself, since there are now good books and good binoculars to make it easier than it was only a generation ago, the ideal way is to learn from someone who already has a good beginning in bird study. This way one will learn faster and avoid mistakes that might otherwise be confusing for years. Colleagues can help one another enjoy bird study either as a pastime or serious hobby, or even as a profession if one becomes really good at it.

WA
OR
CA
NV
ID
MT
WY
UT
AZ
CO
NM
ND
SD
AK

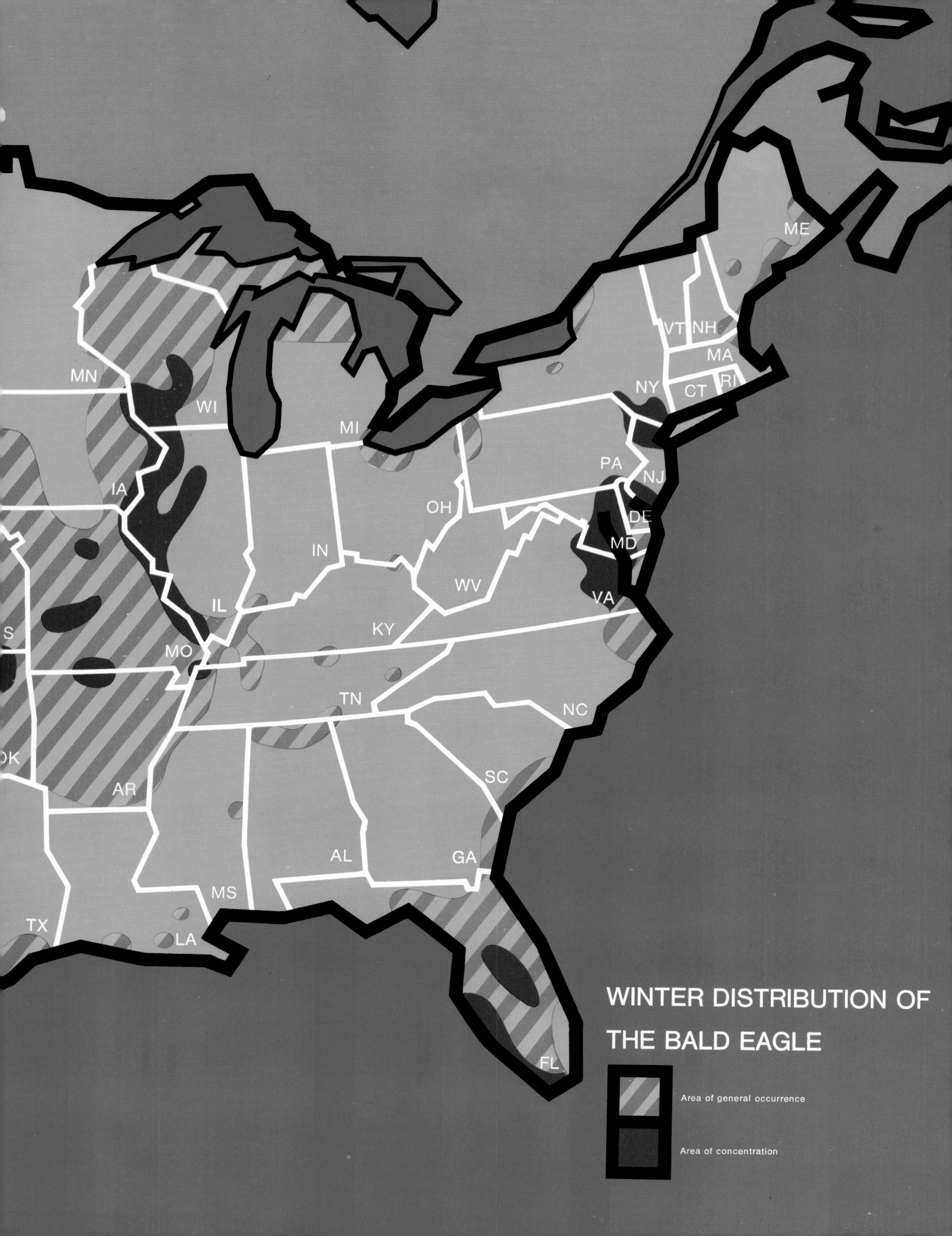
WINTER DISTRIBUTION OF
THE BALD EAGLE
Area of general occurrence
Area of concentration
ME
VT
NH
MA
NY
CT
RI
PA
NJ
DE
MD
MN
WI
MI
IA
OH
IN
IL
WV
VA
KY
MO
TN
NC
SC
GA
AL
MS
AR
LA
TX
FL

Range Maps of Birds

Summer Winter Year-round

Avocet, American

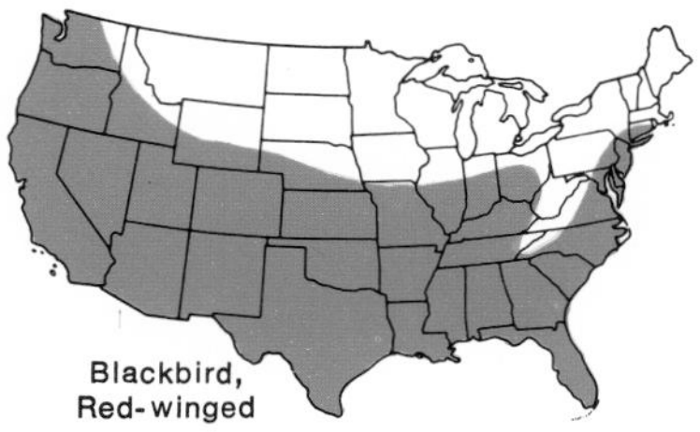
Blackbird, Red-winged

Blackbird, Yellow-headed

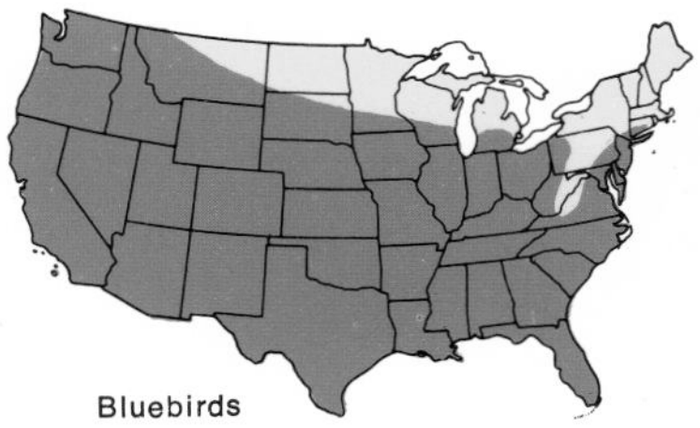
Bluebirds

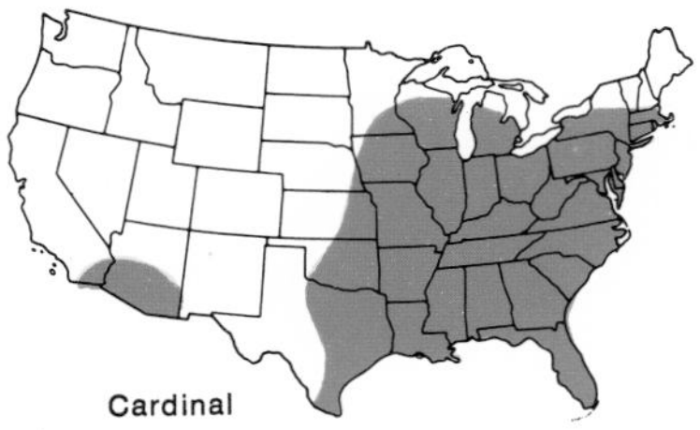
Cardinal

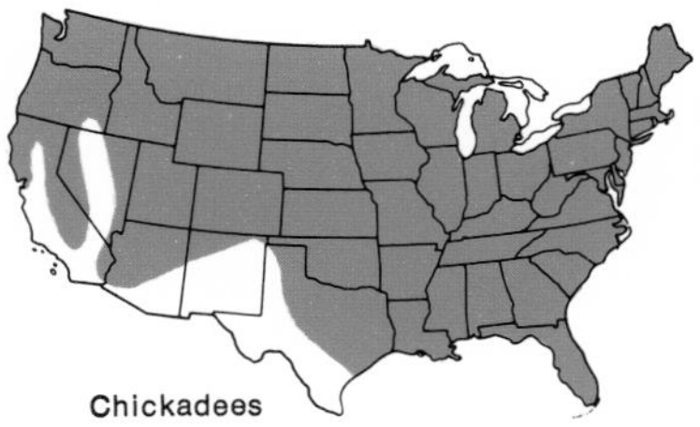
Chickadees

Coot, American

Cormorant, Double-crested

Crane, Sandhill

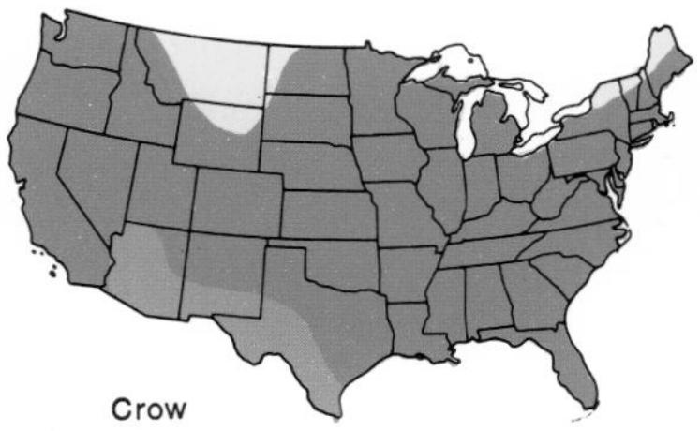
Crow

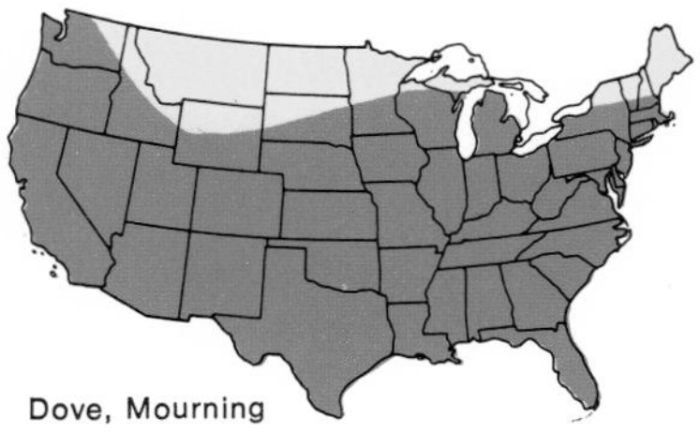
Dove, Mourning

Duck, Canvasback

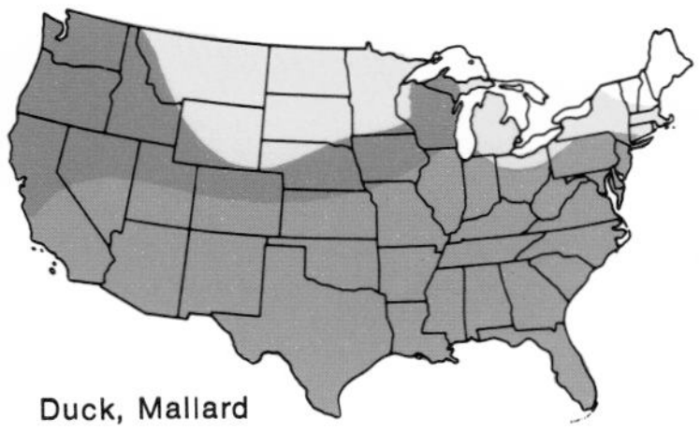
Duck, Mallard

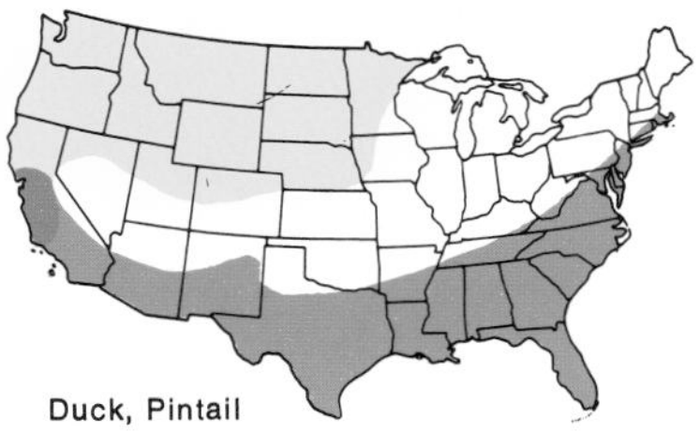
Duck, Pintail

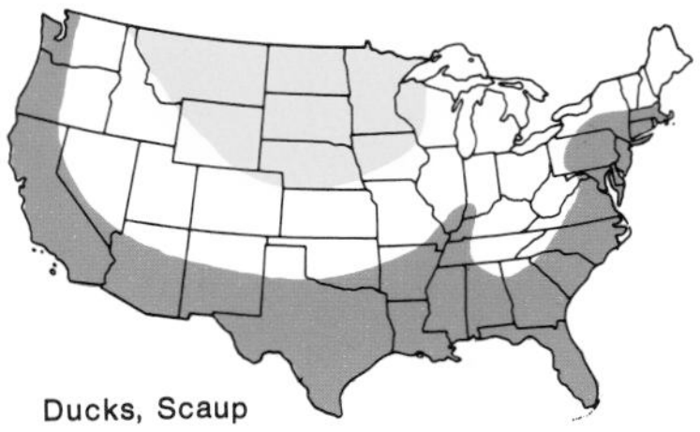
Ducks, Scaup

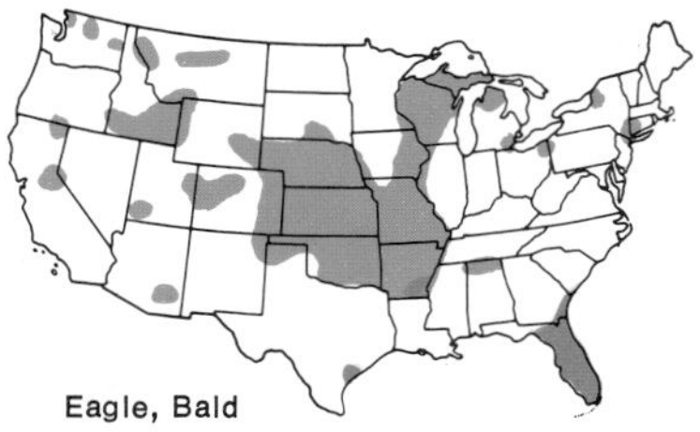
Eagle, Bald

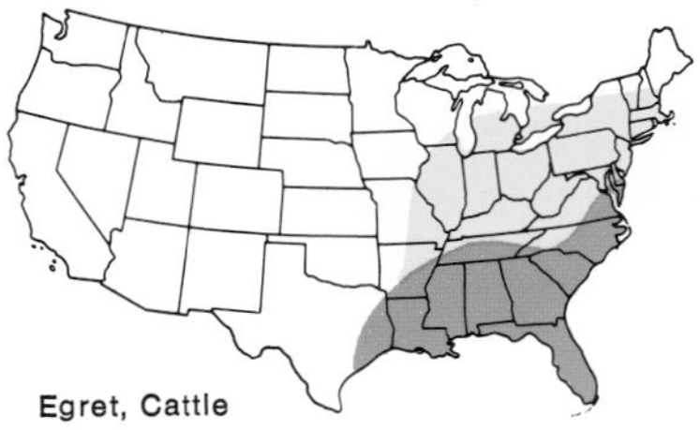
Egret, Cattle

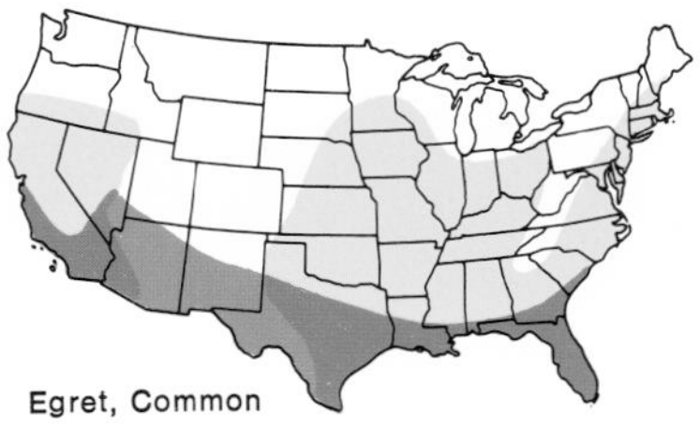
Egret, Common

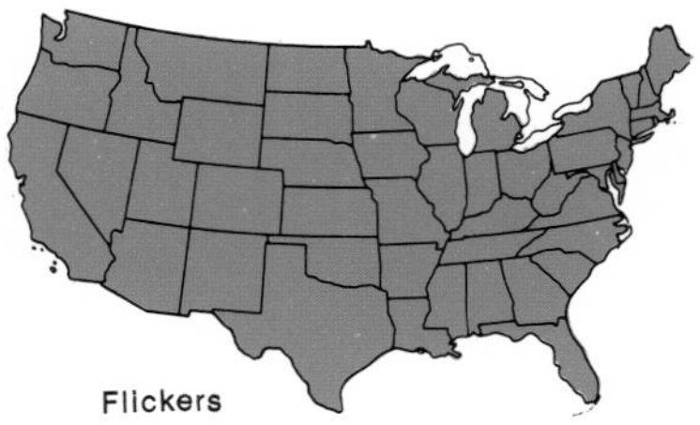
Flickers

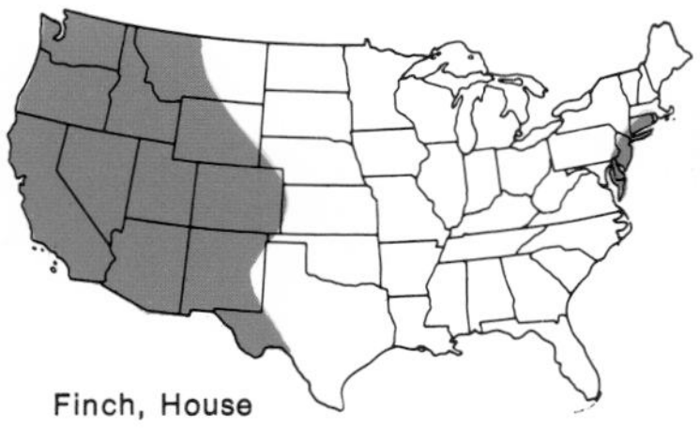
Finch, House

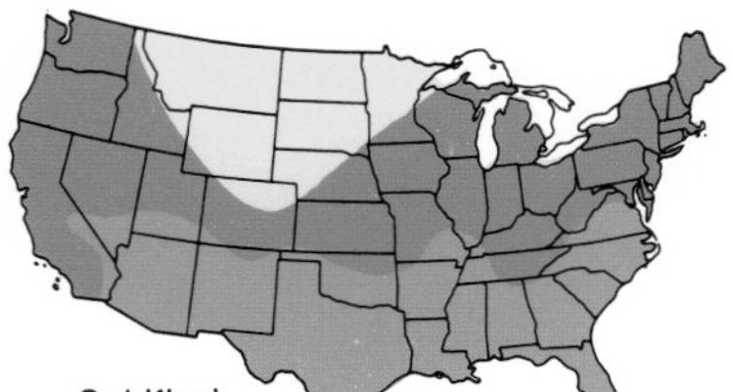
Goldfinch, American

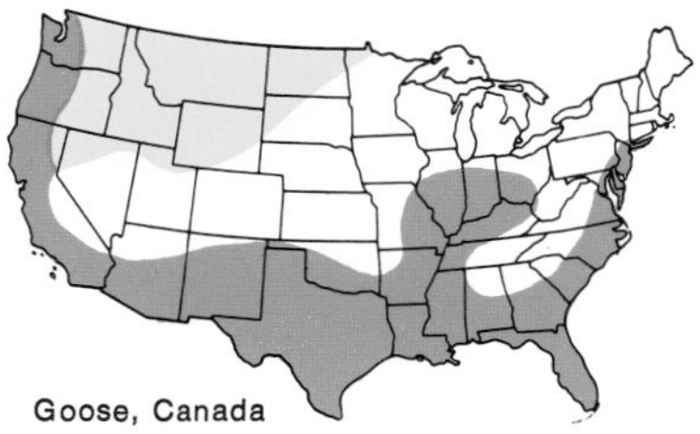
Goose, Canada

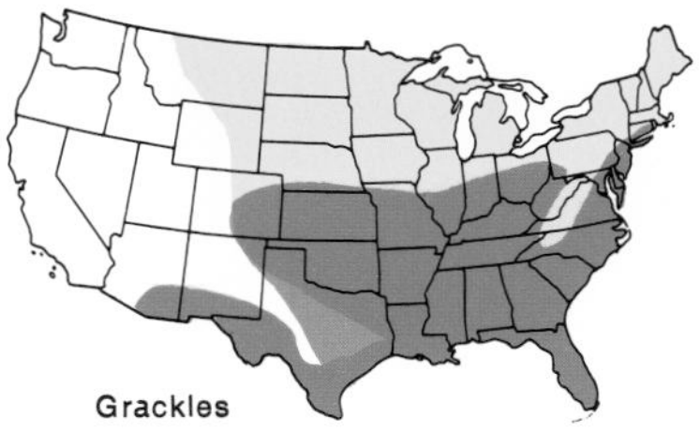
Grackles

Gull, Herring

Gull, Laughing

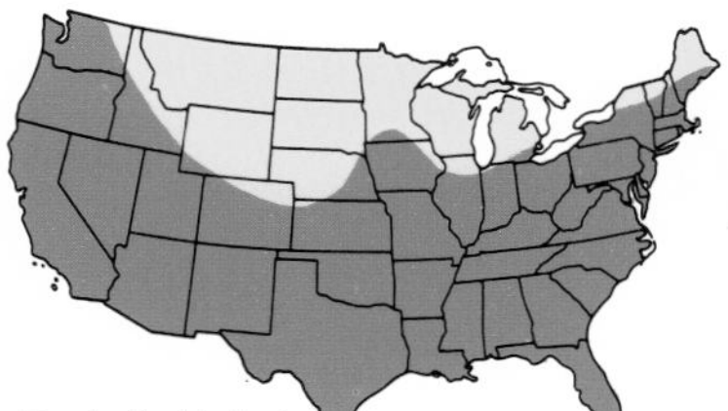
Hawk, Red-tailed

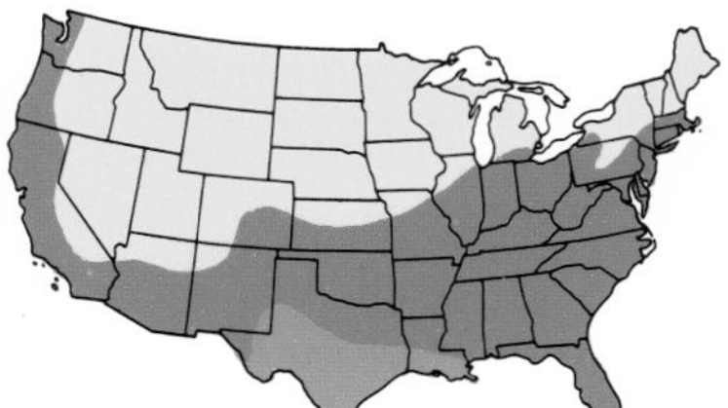
Hawk, Sparrow

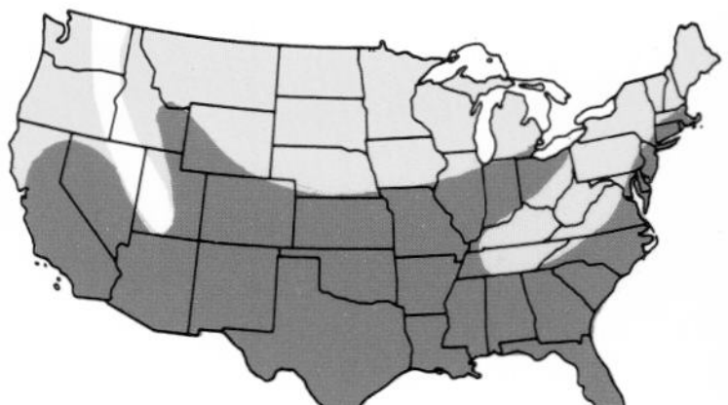
Heron, Great blue

Hummingbird,
Ruby-throated

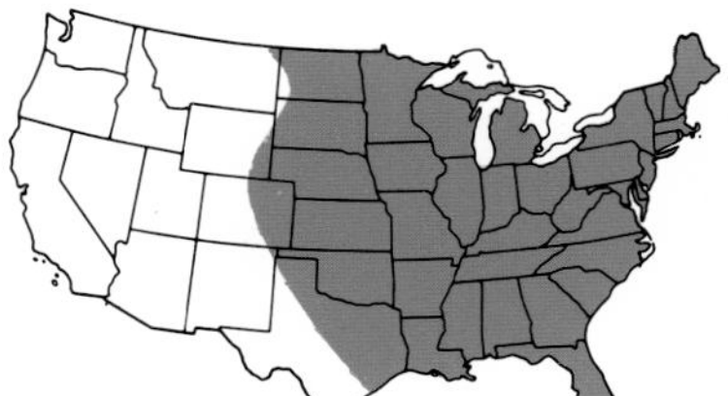
Jay, Blue

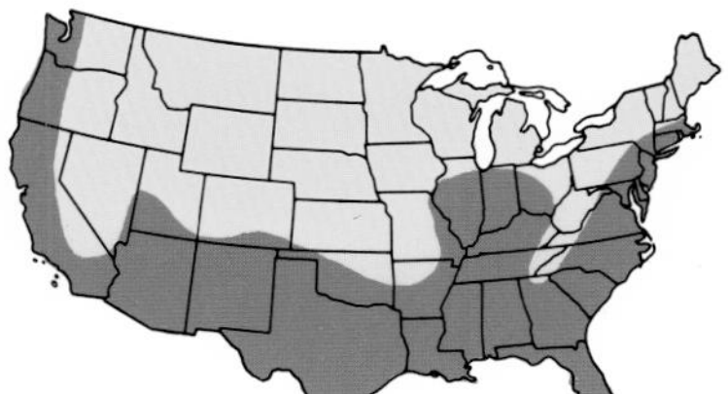
Killdeer

Kingbird, Western

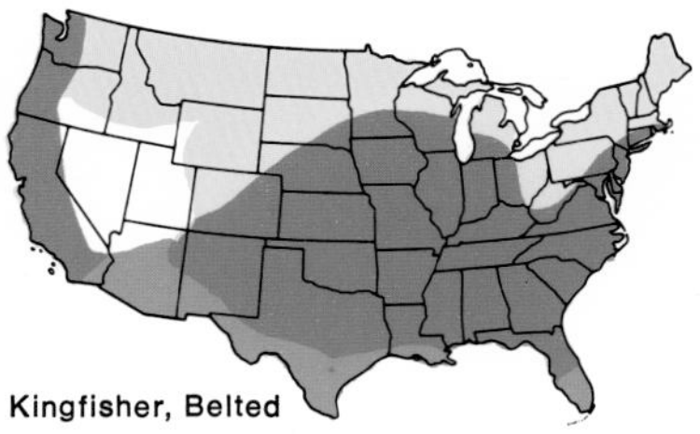
Kingfisher, Belted

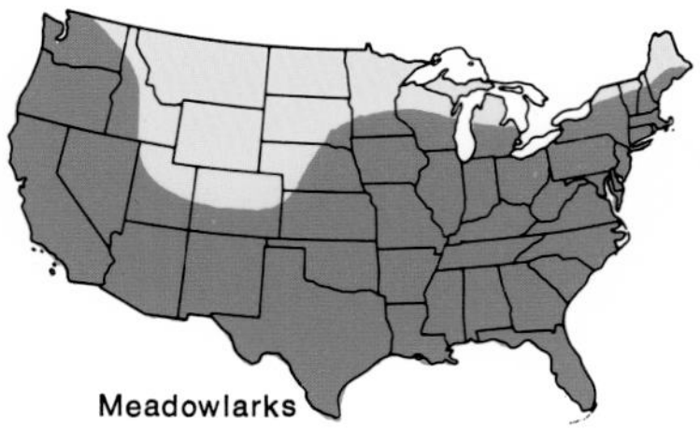
Meadowlarks

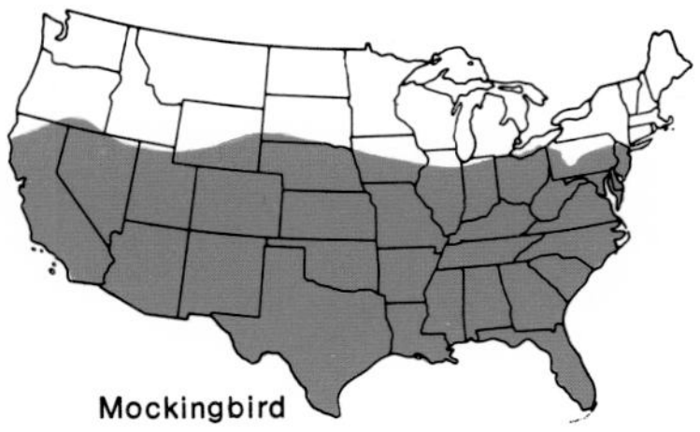
Mockingbird

Nighthawk

Oriole, Baltimore

Oriole, Bullock's

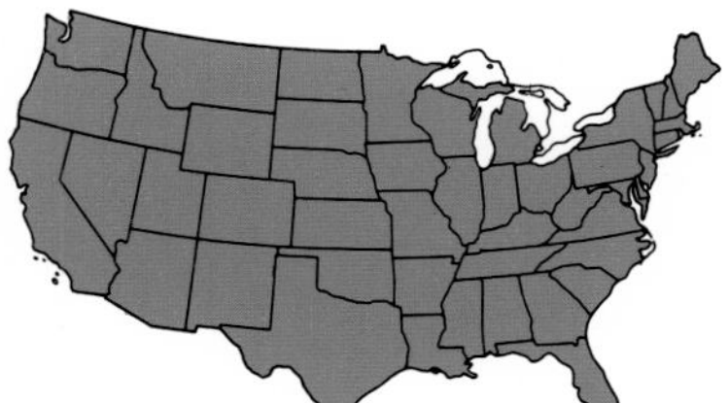
Owl, Great horned

Pelican, Brown

Pelican, White

Pheasant,
Ring-necked

Quail, Bob-white

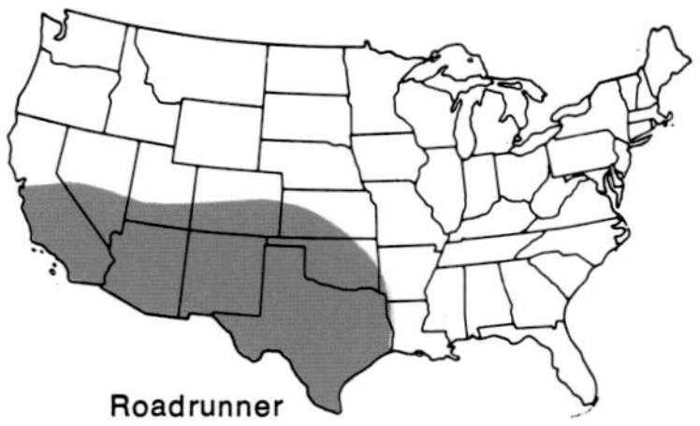
Roadrunner

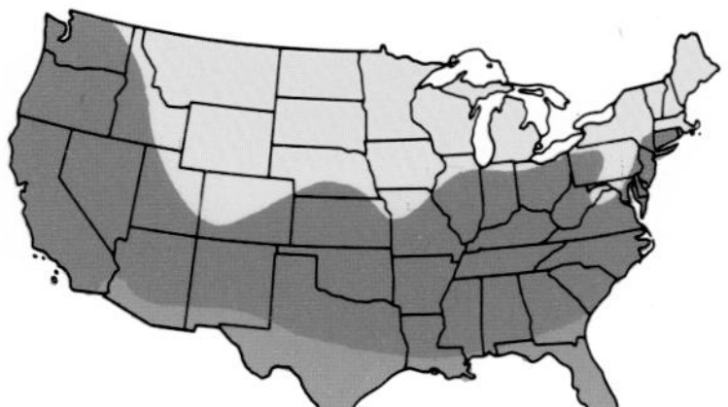
Robin

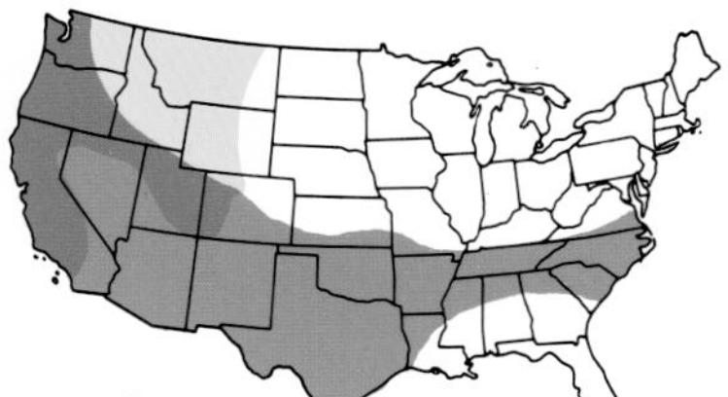
Sparrow,
White-crowned

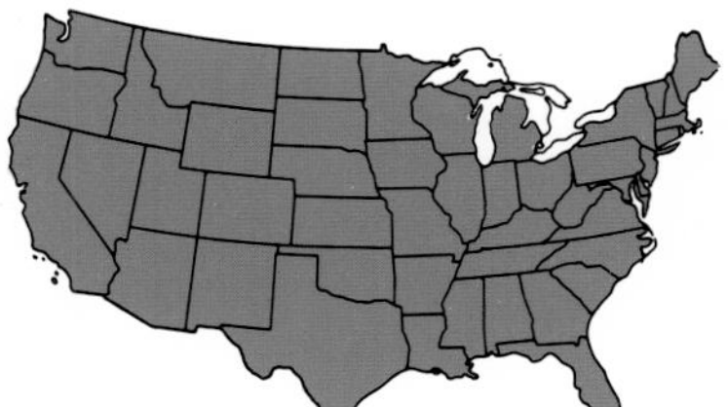
Starling

Swallow, Barn

Swallow, Tree

Swan, Whistling

Tern, Common

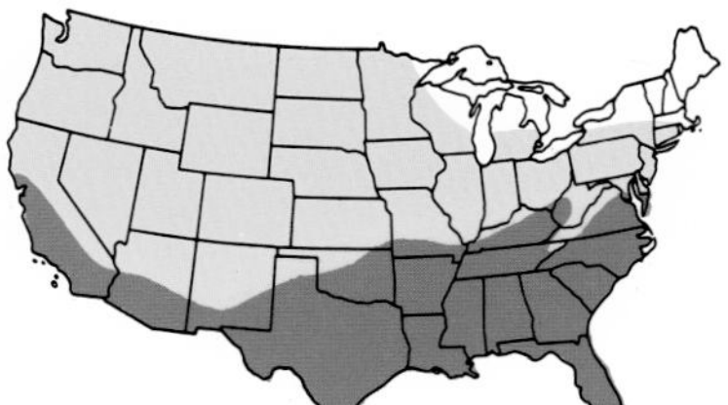
Vulture, Turkey

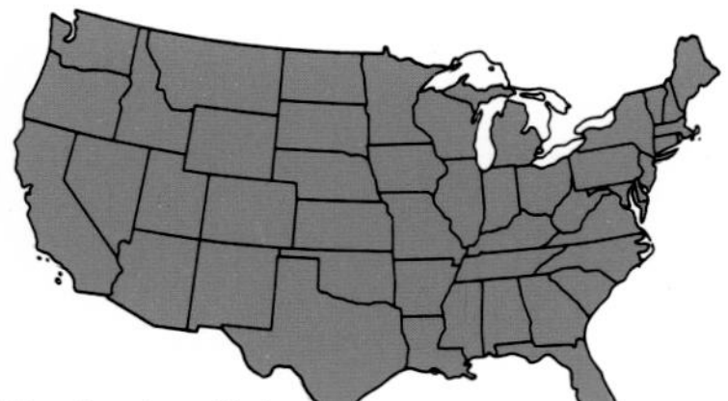
Woodpecker, Hairy

Woodpecker,
Red-bellied

Wren, Cactus

Yellowlegs

White Pelicans

Brown Pelican

Double-crested Cormorant

WHITE PELICAN
Even larger than its cousin the Brown Pelican, the White has a wingspread over nine feet. It is a most impressive flier, but never dives for fish from the air. Instead, it fishes cooperatively, several birds lining up abreast, then swimming with their heads down until they crowd a school of fish enough to scoop them up with their big bills. This performance is as graceful as a dance. Whereas the Brown Pelican is a coastal bird, the big White nests on interior lakes in the western U.S. and Canada. It winters near the coasts after long overland flights. One colony nests on the Texas coast. Pelicans are colonial nesters, the White on the ground on islands, the Brown usually in low trees. The sexes are indistinguishable afield. Pelicans are mostly silent except for occasional grunting or croaking sounds. The young feed by reaching into the pouch of one of their parents.

BROWN PELICAN
This is the smallest of the six or so pelicans that occur on all the continents, but mostly in tropical regions. Even so, this is a large bird, with a wingspread over six feet. Notice the distendable chin-pounch which gave rise to the joke-ster's question, "How can a pelican's bill hold more than its belly can?" All pelicans are fish-eaters. They are impressive fliers, usually arrayed in long lines, often low over the water, flapping then sailing. This one fishes by diving from heights 30 feet above water, entering with a big splash, and always bobbing up facing away from the direction of flight. This species may be very tame, and when not molested will haunt the waterfront of fishing communities. The Brown Pelican is unfortunately in trouble because the use of DDT has caused many birds to lay thin-shelled eggs that perish easily.

DOUBLE-CRESTED CORMORANT
Cormorants are large, blackish, usually gregarious, aquatic birds. They sit very upright and have long necks and slender hooked bills. They ride lower on the water when swimming than typical waterfowl. They often fly in lines or wedges like geese, but are silent. Cormorants dive for fish from the surface, then climb or fly to some perch and hang out their wings to dry, a very characteristic pose. There are 30 species scattered around the world, one of them a famous fishing assistant of Japanese fishermen who keep them on long leads, with leather collars to prevent the birds from swallowing the fish they capture. The Double-crested Cormorant—so named for its small tufts of nesting-season plumes—is the common cormorant of the East Coast and interior lakes, but also occurs on the West Coast, where Brandt's Cormorant is more numerous.

Whistling Swan

Canada Geese

WHISTLING SWAN

Swans, along with geese and ducks, make up the typical waterfowl that hunters enjoy pursuing in autumn. Swans are much the largest members of the tribe. The American species have all-white plumage and wingspreads over six feet. The species are difficult to tell apart, however. The Whistling Swan nests in the western Arctic and winters on the middle-Atlantic and California coasts, plus a few western lake areas. It has a slender, black bill with a yellow spot between each nostril and eye. On the Northeast Coast the equally-large Mute Swan is locally common. It has a reddish bill with a large black knob. It was introduced from Europe by estate keepers but spread from domesticity and is now wild. And in the far West, around Yellowstone National Park, in British Columbia, and Alaska, is the Trumpeter Swan, the largest, with a large all-black bill.

CANADA GOOSE

Geese are between swans and ducks in size. All of them have webbed feet. Although there are six distinct geese and brant in the U.S., this species is the wild goose, the honker whose great skeins flying low or high overhead are heralds of the seasons for all those who are attuned to the outdoors. There are several subspecies of Canada Geese, some large, some medium, and some small. In keeping with the diversity of the continent, the East enjoys only one large form, and the western half of the continent all the others. In one form or another, large honkers occur across the continent. They have a five-foot wingspread and weigh nine pounds or so. The black stocking neck, white cheeks, and an otherwise brown plumage are distinctive. These are splendid birds, wary, devoted to one another, and guided by tradition in their long migrations.

Pintail Duck

PINTAIL DUCK
This slender, graceful duck is the most widely distributed waterfowl of all, and also the most numerous on a worldwide basis. The female is drab, as are most female birds that nest on the ground. Their camouflaged coloring provides protection against roaming predators. Being slender, they are also fast fliers. Like most ducks, a Pintail goes through an unusual feather molt called eclipse plumage. The drakes drop their distinctive feathering after each mating season and are then flightless and resemble their mates. After staying in their drab plumage about a month, they molt again and acquire another bright coat typical of their sex. Eclipse plumage is most apparent in species having strikingly different plumage according to sex. No other bird Family has an eclipse plumage, because only waterfowl can afford to lose their flight for a while.

MALLARD DUCK
Common to both the Old World and the New in the Northern Hemisphere, this is probably the world's best known waterfowl, because it is widespread and because it is the progenitor of the domesticated duck. Often called a Greenhead in prairie country where it once nested in great abundance, it is the favorite duck among hunters, if only because it has provided the most birds in the bag throughout the West for generations. Today, however, with the incessant drainage of the countryside, even this bird's numbers are declining. This is a tip-up duck, or puddle duck, feeding by dabbling —head down and tail up—in shallow water. The principal foods are seeds of such aquatic plants as sedges and knotweeds. As do all puddle ducks, it also jumps from the water on take-off. Females are unlike drakes in plumage, being plain streaky-brown with an orange bill.

Mallard Duck

Canvasback Duck

Turkey Vulture

Red-tailed Hawk

Lesser Scaup Duck

Bald Eagle

Sparrow Hawk

CANVASBACK DUCK
Unlike puddle ducks, which jump from the water into flight, the Canvasback and its cousins among the diving duck clan must run and flap on the surface in order to take off. They are called diving ducks because they dive to the bottom in deeper water instead of tipping up in shallow water as the Mallard and its relatives do. Also called bay ducks, they winter in coastal bays, where they feed on mussels and other marine organisms. The Canvasback, the most regal of the clan, is a big round-headed duck with a long, tapered, bluish bill. The pattern, which shows black fore and aft, is also typical of other bay ducks, but the Canvasback is larger and shows more white whether sitting or in flight. This bird nests in rushes in fairly deep ponds on the northern prairie and winters on both coasts, principally in Chesapeake Bay and San Francisco Bay.

SCAUP DUCKS
Called bluebills by hunters, scaups are the most numerous diving ducks. Chunky and lively, they bunch or raft together so tightly that this is a distinguishing field mark. When large flocks feed together, smaller units leap-frog over one another. And even when they wheel off they tend to bunch in flight. The Greater Scaup is a northern nester and winters on salt water on both coasts. The more numerous Lesser Scaup nests on the prairie and winters mostly on fresh water across the southern United States. It is the common duck of Florida's fresh-water lakes and occurs in winter all the way down to Panama. The Greater has a long, white wing-stripe, wheres the Lesser has a short one. Females of both species are brown with a white ring around the base of the bill, which gives them a distinctive white-faced appearance at a considerable distance.

TURKEY VULTURE
This bird is often called a buzzard, especially in the South, which is an unfortunate monicker based on the ornithological incompetence of the early colonists. It would be well to abandon the term buzzard and substitute the more proper term vulture. This bird is among the most graceful fliers of all, matched or exceeded only by the kites. A Turkey Vulture has a longish tail, holds its wings up in a good "V," and actually rocks from side to side on air currents to show what a master of the airways it is. An adult has a naked, red head, and an immature bird has a black head. The nakedness helps it to keep clean while doing sanitary squad chores. Its southern cousin, the Black Vulture, has a short tail and a hesitant, flapping flight. Together they clean up the highway kills that careless people leave behind them in their speeding vehicles.

BALD EAGLE
It is worth a special trip to go see the national bird—now unfortunately much decimated by man's careless use of the landscape. Study the map of its winter distribution on pages 144-145 for a convenient location to go see it. The adult's white head and white tail make it unmistakable; but for its first three or four years, a young bird is dark brown and looks like a big hawk. This is why so many Bald Eagles are still shot annually even though they are protected by Federal and state laws. Lots of people who use guns have yet to learn to tell one species from another and to stick to bona fide game. Along with losses from DDT poisoning and disturbance at nesting time, this can eliminate birds from whole regions. Since this eagle is principally a fish eater, look for it along lakes, large rivers (below big dams in the Midwest), and coastal bays.

RED-TAILED HAWK
An Englishman would immediately recognize this as a buzzard, which it is. The English had first call on the name, so we should not misapply it to vultures. We sometimes call it a **Buteo,** one of that genus of broad-winged, fan-tailed, mouse-eating hawks that spends lots of time circling in the sky and perching on telephone poles where people who do not know any better shoot at it. It is a heavy-shouldered bird. The adult has a red tail, and the immature has a nondescript, finely-barred, grayish-brown tail. Indeed, all immature Buteos are difficult to distinguish, but all Red-tailed Hawks have a dark belly-band that is diagnostic in any plumage. Despite its husky form, this bird has a rather weak, high-pitched, hissing voice that can hardly be called a scream. Being a mouse eater, this hawk has suffered less than its relatives from DDT poisoning.

SPARROW HAWK
Better called Kestrel, as in England, this little raptor is a falcon, and the small male is not much bigger than a robin. All falcons have long, pointed wings and longish tails. This one is unusual in being so brightly colored, nesting in old woodpecker holes, and feeding principally on grasshoppers. As is usual among birds, the male is more brightly colored than the female; but the reverse is true when it comes to size—another surprise. A female is larger than a male. This is so, probably, because if the female lost her mate during the nesting season she would have to be big and strong enough to hunt for the whole family—otherwise all the young would starve. This little bird's relatives, the big falcons, are the noblest birds of all—the legendary Peregrine, now so much decimated by DDT poisoning, and the great White Gyrfalcon of the Arctic tundra.

BOB-WHITE QUAIL

This racy little game bird with the familiar whistled call *bob-bob-white* is, along with the several colorful quail of the Southwest, a member of a distinctive American sub-family of the Pheasant Family. The short, stiff, rounded wings of this quail make for explosive take-offs and fast flights. It is not otherwise a strong flier and soon alights after a quick flight. The take-off is like that of a Ruffed Grouse, but quail are much smaller brushland birds, and have a short, rounded tail. They are also social birds, occurring in coveys made up of family groups, sometimes numbering up to 30 birds in winter. On cold nights they roost together to keep warm, crowded tail to tail like leaves in a rosette. The California Quail and Gambel's Quail in the West are dark-gray, black-faced birds, with a conspicuous black and recurved top-knot feather.

RING-NECKED PHEASANT

All across middle America—almost from coast to coast—this naturalized foreigner has made itself at home. All pheasants are from Asia, and this one from China was first introduced in Oregon in 1881. Several hybrid strains are mixed in across the country, so they vary a bit. The pheasants do best in corn country, but even in the Corn Belt, where millions were shot a few years ago, land use practices have reduced the bonanza to ordinary proportions. The Ring-necked Pheasant becomes very tame in suburbs if fed corn in winter, and its stately form, with its long tail etching the snow, is a very welcome sight. A hen is much less fancy than a male in coloring, being plain brownish-tan, but has a longer tail than other native members of the same gallinaceous bird clan. The common chicken, like the Jungle Fowl it came from, is also a pheasant.

Bob-white Quail

Ring-necked Pheasant

Cattle Egret

Great Blue Heron

Common Egret

COMMON EGRET
Egrets are herons, long-legged and long-necked, and have the characteristic habit of pulling the neck back into an S-curve in flight. The legs then trail behind. The Common Egret, formely called the American Egret, is large and white-plumaged. It is identified certainly by the combination of a long yellow bill and black legs. Like other herons it eats small fish and other aquatic animals, which it stalks slowly or still hunts by standing immobile in the shallows until a prey species comes close enough. The long neck and bill then come into play in a flash, darting out to capture a meal. The egret was rescued from the threat of extermination by the plume trade by Audubon Societies at the turn of the century. It came back in numbers for a few decades, but is again declining because man is taking over so much of the landscape for himself.

CATTLE EGRET
A small egret with a butter-yellow bill and, in spring, buff patches on the breast and the back, this is a meadow bird rather than a wading bird as are the other herons. It feeds on grasshoppers flushed out of the grass by moving cattle and will often perch right on the cows it associates with. At nesting time, however, it joins other egrets and herons in large heronries (often misnamed rookeries—which are for rooks, an English bird not found in the U.S.)—building bulky nests of sticks high or low in a grove of trees. The amazing, fascinating thing about this bird is that it did not invade North America until this century, apparently first crossing the Atlantic from Africa to South America and then moving up the Antillean island chain to Florida. It has colonized half the U.S. in one of the few unassisted invasions man has witnessed.

Sandhill Crane

GREAT BLUE HERON
Often misnamed crane by people who cannot distinguish one Order of birds from another, this is our largest dark heron, with such broad wings and heavy flight that it often suggests an eagle until its long legs and retracted neck (folded on the chest) are noticed. Big and solitary, except at heronries and during fall migrations, it is a conspicuous bird of waterway margins, both on inland fresh water and along coastal salt marshes, where it feeds on such things as fish, crayfish, and fiddler crabs. In winter it sometimes hunts Meadow Mice in open fields. When alarmed it flaps off heavily, often with a series of deep, complaining vocal croaks or squawks. It is otherwise silent. This bird is closely related to the Gray Heron of the Old World. Some experts even consider the Great White Heron of southern Florida a color phase of the Great Blue.

SANDHILL CRANE
Cranes and herons are often confused, but there is little reason for this if one remembers that cranes always fly with the neck outstretched. Herons pull in their necks. True, when a heron first jumps up, especially if it plans to alight quickly, it may keep its neck outstretched, but never if it flies more than a few rods. A Sandhill Crane, also called a Little Brown Crane, stands about the same height as a Great Blue Heron, but it is always more uniformly colored, sometimes a warm brown and sometimes a steely bluish-brown. Its flight is a distinctive, snappy stroking of the air alternating with a glide. It is normally a social bird, and the musical rattling call is one of the grand sounds of the outdoors. The rare Whooping Crane is one of the grandest birds of all, and a flight of either Sandhills or Whooping Cranes should excite anyone.

American Coot

AMERICAN COOT

A duck-like, slate-gray bird with a china-white bill can be only this bird. It is common to the point of being disliked by waterfowl hunters who have a low regard for both its flesh and its sporting qualities. Though it suggests a duck at first glance, it is not of that Order but is closely related to rails and gallinules instead. This is most evident when a coot flies, since its flight is rather typically rail-like—a fast but weak flapping that barely lifts the bird above the water, with the legs trailing behind. The coot has very distinctively lobed toes which help it walk on mud and to swim. It is a versatile feeder—on shore like a rail, by diving in shallow water like a duck, or by attending a group of tip-up ducks and helping itself to the overflowing mouthfuls the ducks often bring up from the bottom. There are ten coot species around the world.

American Avocet

AMERICAN AVOCET

One of the most dashing of the large Order we call shorebirds (the British call them waders), the Avocet is still common and rather widely distributed in the West. It is so distinctive that the Avocet and the Stilt constitute the separate Family **Recurvirostridae,** named after the recurved bill of the Avocet. When feeding, the Avocet strides or dashes about in shallow water, either in fresh or brackish ponds, and scoops up small fish, crustaceans, or insects, frequently with a side-to-side sweeping of its long bill, like a man with a scythe. It is more social than most shorebirds, usually feeding in groups and nesting in small colonies. Like many of the Order of shorebirds, it has intriguing, stylized, ceremonial displays as part of courtship. These displays may involve only the mated pair or may be veritable dances by several birds together.

YELLOWLEGS
Typical sandpipers, though larger and longer-legged than most, the Greater and Lesser Yellowlegs are grayish-brown birds with bright-yellow legs and slender bills. Though they differ a good deal in size, size alone is an unreliable identification point unless the two species are almost side by side. The surest field characteristics are their calls: three or more loud notes for the Greater Yellowlegs and only two softer notes for the Lesser Yellowlegs. Both yellowlegs, and most shorebirds, nest in the far North—on the muskeg or the tundra—and engage in tremendous annual migrations that take them to the pampas of Argentina and back. The marvelous thing about these long flights is that they are done without guidance. The parent birds migrate first, leaving their young behind. The young later take off on their own and rejoin their kind 8000 miles away.

Greater Yellowlegs

KILLDEER
This is a plover, which is a medium-sized shorebird distinguished from a sandpiper by a short neck and a short bill with a swollen tip. The Killdeer—so named for its cry—has the widest nesting distribution of any plover within the U.S. Rather than nesting near watercourses or on open tundra as most others do, a Killdeer lays its eggs in the gravelly patches of open fields and in the ruts of unpaved roads. This, of course, exposes it to considerable disturbance by people or cattle, but it has evolved an interesting trick to decoy disturbers from its eggs and young. The parent bird approaches an intruder and drags a wing in front of it, seeming to be hurt, and thus lures away a curious visitor. Once the intruder is safely away, the parent bird abandons its ruse and flies off. Only a thoughtful observer is aware of what has happened.

Killdeer

Herring Gull

HERRING GULL

Although related to shorebirds, gulls are considerably larger with shorter legs and webbed feet. The Herring Gull is what is commonly called a sea gull, occurring around all extensive bodies of water. But the U.S. has 15 other gull species which require expert scrutiny to differentiate. The Herring Gull is among the largest. It is silvery and white with pink legs. The leg color distinguishes it from the very-similar but slightly-smaller California Gull and Ring-billed Gull. An immature bird is chocolate brown in the first year and gradually acquires the adult's silvery plumage after four years of molting. Telling one immature gull from another is a real challenge, but it can be done most of the time by those willing to master details. The Herring Gull has the interesting habit of dropping clams onto a hard surface from the air in order to break the shell and get the meat.

LAUGHING GULL

Three different black-headed gulls are seen in the U.S. regularly, and three others visit the shores less frequently. All of them are graceful birds, and the Laughing Gull is the largest and darkest of the group. It is largely a bird of the Atlantic Coast. In winter all these birds lose the black on their head and then can be recognized only by wing patterns. The Laughing Gull is no more than a summer resident north of Chesapeake Bay, but nests and occurs year-round on the beaches of the Southeast. Inland, this bird's place is taken by the very similar Franklin's Gull. Distinguishing the two is a task for experts, but a Laughing Gull seldom occurs more than 50 miles inland, whereas a Franklin's Gull is rare on the coast. The Franklin's Gull is the one that follows the plow and the gull to which the Mormons erected a monument.

Laughing Gulls

MOURNING DOVE
Doves and pigeons form a large Family, some species hardly larger than sparrows, but one as large as a hen turkey. The terms dove and pigeon are used somewhat interchangeably, although dove is more often applied to the small, long-tailed species and pigeon to the stocky, fan-tailed birds. All doves and all pigeons coo in some way that is usually diagnostic. The Mourning Dove is the most widespread. The white borders on its long, tapered tail are especially notable when the bird jumps from the ground, where it does most of its feeding on weed seeds or grains. The whistling of its wings is diagnostic. The considerably larger Passenger Pigeon, which once clouded American skies, was exterminated by greed and ignorance at the turn of the century. The Mourning Dove, though heavily hunted, faces no such danger.

Common Tern

COMMON TERN
Terns are small, gull relatives, and most of them are much more delicate. They have narrow, pointed wings, very short legs, and a pointed bill. They cruise waterways, with their bills pointed downward, and dive into the water for the fish or insects they feed on. They are all colonial nesters and normally feed and migrate in flocks. Their buoyancy, pointed wings, and forked tails make the often-used term sea swallows appropriate. All U.S. terns have black caps during the breeding season, which they lose, however, in autumn. Since there are several other species, identification is difficult except where a combination of markings, season of occurrence, and range are used. The voice of each species is different and very useful in identification. Knowing what to expect is half the battle. The Common Tern is best told by its black-tipped red bill.

Mourning Dove

Roadrunner

ROADRUNNER
Throughout the Southwest this big, ground cuckoo with a long, floppy, white-tipped tail is a familiar, often amusing sight in the arid, cactus-dotted country it frequents. There it is often called Chapparal Cock. A Roadrunner seldom flies, but runs with long-legged strides and often climbs into mesquite bushes or cactus clumps. The spring song is dove-like, on a descending scale. Its principal food is lizards, but it will take birds' eggs when the opportunity occurs. A Roadrunner is famous for its ability to trample snakes, even mastering small rattlesnakes on occasion. The black, floppy-tailed Ani of crossword puzzles, south Florida, south Texas, and Mexico is a relative. There are two other fairly common North American cuckoos, a Black-billed Cuckoo and a Yellow-billed Cuckoo, both slender woodland birds. In the Old World the Common Cuckoo is parasitic.

Nighthawk

RUBY-THROATED HUMMINGBIRD

Hummingbirds are strictly American and mostly residents of the humid tropics, though some occur high in the Andes. The Rufous Hummingbird of western North America occurs as far north as Alaska. The Ruby-throated is the only one found east of the Mississippi River and then only in summer. This is a most amazing bird. It is one of the smallest of the high vertebrate animals and is the fastest on the wing. It is capable of backward flight, as well as straight upward and downward movements, and has about 50 wingbeats per second. Hummingbirds have some of the most resplendent plumage in the bird world, most of which is due to structural iridescence rather than to pigment. Despite its small size and high metabolism, the Ruby-throated Hummingbird is capable of flying across the Gulf of Mexico.

GREAT HORNED OWL

Its technical name is **Bubo** and shows its relation to the Eagle Owl **(Bubo bubo)** of the Old World. Soft-feathered and thus silent in flight, a Great Horned Owl is the most powerful winged predator of the night. It feeds mostly on mice, but may take almost anything up to the size of a skunk or a crow. For that reason, all the birds hate it and gather around to scold when its silent form is discovered perching close to the trunk of some pine or spruce during the day. Crows, especially, will heap abuse on the big owl at every opportunity. This owl —and most owls—is easily distinguished from a hawk by its large round head and short tail. The eyes of this species are large and yellow and fixed in a facial disk. Since they cannot look to the side, owls turn their heads much farther and more easily than other birds. They can see in daylight, but prefer dusk.

NIGHTHAWK

Not a hawk at all—though it swoops or "hawks" for insects in flight—this is a relative of the Whip-poor-will which is known to more people by its voice than by sight. The Nighthawk is also called a Bullbat in the U.S. and a Nightjar in England. In spring and early summer it often occurs in cities, because it then nests on gravel roofs as well as on ridges in open country. The long wings with the white patches called windows, its long tail, and the distinctive sounds it makes allow certain identification. A Nighthawk has a twangy *peent* call, and its wings make a deep-humming sound when the bird pulls out of a dive. Intriguing as each is individually, Nighthawks are most impressive when they gather for their autumn migrations. When hundreds or thousands of birds cruise past, feeding as they go, they make a pleasant demarkation of the season.

Ruby-throated Hummingbird

Great Horned Owl (immature)

Belted Kingfisher

BELTED KINGFISHER
The U.S. species is one of the largest members of a diverse, widespread Family. Bright blue above, it is big-headed and has a stout bill. If it were not for its loud rattling call, this solitary bird would often go unnoticed as it perched by some stream or lake, waiting until a passing fish attracted it or hunger set it off on a hunt. Once it sees a fish, it hovers overhead, then dives headfirst into the water and seizes its prey. Then it flies back to the perch and eats it. Both male and female are crested and have a blue chest-band, but the female has, in addition, a rusty band below the blue band. The Belted Kingfisher nests in a burrow in a stream bank it digs itself. There are several other kingfishers around the world. Some of them are dry-land birds that feed on insects, rather than fish. The Kookaburra of Australia, of which we sing, is also a kingfisher.

Red-shafted Flicker

FLICKERS
Flickers are ant-eating and therefore are mostly ground-feeding woodpeckers of medium size. The best field marks are their conspicuous white rumps which show well when the birds fly away upon being disturbed. There are three U.S. species, each heavily spotted underneath and with black breast-bands. But the eastern bird has bright-yellow underwing linings (so is called Yellow-shafted) and a black mustache-stripe; the western bird is red-shafted and red-mustached; and the southwestern bird, the slightly smaller Gilded Flicker, is yellow-shafted, has a red mustache, and lives in tall cactus stands. Like other woodpeckers, flickers have an undulating flight, rising when they beat their wings, sinking when they glide. And although they feed on the ground, all of them drill holes three inches in diameter into trees or Saguaro-type cacti for nesting.

Red-bellied Woodpecker

RED-BELLIED WOODPECKER
There are several small woodpeckers, and this is one of the noisiest of them. Though not diagnostic, this actually helps to identify it. The call includes hoarse churring notes, a variety of rattlings, and other sounds. Its back, including the folded wing, is barred like a zebra, and the whole crown and nape of the male is bright red. In the female only the nape is red. Do not confuse it with the Red-headed Woodpecker, in which the whole head is red. There are two species of the same zebra-back genus in the Southwest: the Golden-fronted Woodpecker, usually a denizen of river bottoms, which shows only a small, red crown and orange spots on both nape and forehead, and the Gila Woodpecker, of giant-cactus desert-country, which is the plainest bird of this trio of species. A male has a small red patch on its crown, but a female is plain-headed.

Hairy Woodpecker

HAIRY WOODPECKER
The Hairy and Downy Woodpeckers are so much alike, except for size, that it is essential to check the length of the bill to be sure which is which. The Hairy's bill is almost as long as its head, whereas the Downy's bill is much shorter and looks much like a stubby little pick. Their voices are also different. The Hairy's is louder and rattly, as one might expect from a larger bird. The males of each species have on the back of the head a small red patch, which the females lack. Although both species wander a good deal and may be seen almost anywhere there are trees, the Hairy Woodpecker prefers more mature woodland and is almost restricted to it during the nesting season. The Downy, on the other hand, likes more open woods, so is more commonly found in suburbs. It was most common in apple orchards until they became chemical traps.

WESTERN KINGBIRD
Although a typical tyrant flycatcher, this kingbird is somewhat less aggressive than its eastern cousin. Its diagnostic field mark is the pair of white outer-tail feathers it carries. Because it lives in more open country, where there are fewer perches, it is much more often seen perching on telephone wires or barbed-wire fences. Otherwise, the habit of making sorties after insects from some favorite perch, or a series of perches, is much the same. Its voice is softer, not the scolding rasp of the Eastern Kingbird. The Southwest has, in addition, two somewhat similar species. These are the plainer, less energetic, Cassin's Kingbird, which lacks the white outer-tail feathers, and the Tropical Kingbird of south Texas and Mexico, which has a bright-yellow belly but also a plain tail. Southern Florida has a Gray Kingbird that looks like the Eastern Kingbird.

Western Kingbird

Tree Swallow

TREE SWALLOW
This little white-bellied swallow lacks the dash and aeronautical skills of a Barn Swallow, but it is gentle, trusting, and delightful. Its back is a metallic green that shows up well only in direct light. In the West it may be confused with the very similar Violet-green Swallow, a bird best distinguished by its white flank-patches. Both of these swallows are hole-nesters, using old woodpecker-holes in trees or nesting boxes erected for them. They occupy these singly rather than colonially as do the larger, darker Purple Martins. The young of both white-bellied swallows are brown above and white below. In the autumn on the Atlantic Coast, thousands of swallows, southbound on their migration but wind-drifted toward the coast, crowd along dunes and marshes where they rest until suitable weather speeds them southward again.

Barn Swallow

BARN SWALLOW
This single species is probably known to more people than any other among the world's more than 8000 birds. This is because it nests straight across the Northern Hemisphere and migrates southward to northern Argentina, South Africa, Ceylon, and even Australia. In the U.S. and Canada it is the only swallow with a deeply-forked tail. Dark blue above and cinnamon-buff below, it is a dashing bird that flies strongly, seldom glides as other swallows do, and often flies closer to the ground than other species. It is, of course, an insect eater and takes all its food in flight, cruising the air much like a whale does the ocean for krill—each a specialist in its own way. This is the swallow that nests in garages or on rafters in barns, whose doors or windows have been left open, where the surrounding country is open enough to furnish insect fare.

Blue Jay

BLUE JAY

Although often considered a common scold, since it does indeed devote a lot of energy to tending the neighborhood's business, this jay is a very handsome bird. It is a bird almost solely of the deciduous forest, where its numbers fluctuate with those of the acorn crop. Lots of acorns, lots of jays. They are, however, omnivorous. It is true that a jay will steal another bird's eggs, but this predation is a minor factor in the population success of the smaller birds it victimizes. Except in the Maritime Provinces, the Blue Jay is a year-round resident. There is, nevertheless, a heavy fall migration of jays along the East Coast. At Hawk Mountain Sanctuary, Pennsylvania, their loose flocks are a conspicuous feature in October. Central Park in Manhattan also experiences this movement, the birds wending southward until they confront the cement and brick canyons.

CROW

Jays and crows belong to the same Family and thus share many characteristics, such as omnivorous feeding, the victimizing of smaller birds, and the mobbing of hawks and owls. But crows are all-black, larger, more social, and caw. Crows deserve their reputation for sagacity. They post sentinels when a flock is busy feeding and are thus seldom surprised. Hunters deceive them, however, by decoying them with stuffed owls, or by imitating their calls. Even so, crows maintain their numbers despite generations of persecution. The conclusions of some scientists suggest that persecution is unwise. For example, though crows eat the eggs of wild ducks, duck populations are not hurt. The pilferage actually forces the ducks to extend their egg-laying, thereby providing a protection against losing the year's production during flooding and grass fires.

Crow

Chickadee

Cactus Wren

Mockingbird

CHICKADEES
There are several kinds of chickadees across the North American continent, all of them very small birds with black bibs and dark caps. They stick close to woody vegetation, in which they feed on such items as insect eggs and seeds. They are so fond of sunflower seeds that they are now the principal visitors of feeding stations in wooded regions and can, with a little patience and a gentle approach, soon be induced to feed from the hand. Chickadees are acrobats, often feed upside down, and are tame and friendly, partly, one supposes, because their small size and agility make them self-confident. The Black-capped Chickadee is the most widespread species. In the spruce-fir forest there is a brown-capped species. The Mountains of the West enjoy the Mountain Chickadee, and the eastern U.S. south of New Jersey has the Carolina Chickadee.

CACTUS WREN
Most wrens are small, elusive, and thus difficult to know. Not so the Cactus Wren. It is as large as the largest sparrows, bold, noisy, and hardly to be overlooked in the southwestern desert-country which is its home. Wrens are a large tribe, mostly based in tropical America, and comprised of 60 species in all. The Winter Wren, the smallest species, has been a great colonizer. It pushed north into Canada and Alaska a million or so years ago and crossed the Bering Strait to Asia. Then it spread westward across Siberia, across Europe, to Iceland, going nearly full circle. Ornithologists are fairly certain that if the Icelandic population now invaded westward and reached Canada, the invaders could not breed with the old parental stock in Canada, even though all the populations in contact with one another do interbreed.

MOCKINGBIRD
Birds play an important symbolic role in our lives—especially the dove and the eagle. In the U.S., the Mockingbird symbolizes the South even more than the Bald Eagle, the national bird, symbolizes the Nation. Live oaks, magnolias, Spanish Moss, and Mockingbirds are all firmly interwoven in the nostalgic fabric of life in this region. The environment does not determine our lives but it certainly colors and enriches them. This is a gladsome bird, bouncing around its neighborhood, flashing its big white wing-patches, flicking its long tail sideways, and singing day and night. It is a superlative mimic, often with a repertoire of 20 or more songs of other birds. But it always repeats phrases at least three times, and this gives it away. Along with thrashers and the Catbird, it makes up a separate Family called Mimic Thrushes. It is a resident where it occurs.

ROBIN

Familiar though we all are with the Robin, most of us know it only from a few traits we let stand for it in our memories. It is "robin redbreast." But in England, whence that name came, it means quite another bird, in fact, perhaps the world's best-studied bird, as those who will read David Lack's *The Life of The Robin* will see. Our robin is a large thrush, particularly chesty—something to be noticed especially when the bird alights. It then always sticks its chest out and runs a few steps to absorb the last impetus of flight. The habit of pulling worms from lawns in spring is one man has made unsafe by spraying trees with DDT for 25 years. A Robin cocks its head to peer at the worm with one eye and not to hear it, as was once thought. The mud-lined nest is distinctive, as also the cheery caroling, *cheeri-up cheeri-up,* and the loud scolding.

BLUEBIRDS

Between them, the three species of bluebirds found in the U.S. blanket much of the continent at some time of year or other. Both the Eastern Bluebird and the Western Bluebird are red-chested, but the Eastern Bluebird lacks the red shoulders of its western cousin. Much as easterners love their bluebird, they are invariably enthralled by the ethereal appearance of the Mountain Bluebird on first acquaintance. It is much the handsomest of the trio, the male deep sky-blue all over, the female and the young sky-blue above and gray underneath. The Mountain Bluebird is also longer-legged than its cousins and seems more sprightly in behavior. It "stands up" more, i.e., leans forward instead of hunching up as the others do. It spends more time catching flies on the wing, does more hovering, sometimes just off the ground, and is a quieter bird.

STARLING

If success in life is measured by ability to colonize new lands, this is one of the world's most successful small birds. But for those who know the many beautiful starlings of Africa and Asia, it is a double tragedy that this least attractive of them all was introduced into America by people who wanted another "familiar" bird—as though to gild the lily—though America was already so rich in bird life. Now the bird is a pest, congregating in large winter roosts in cities or the countryside, sometimes up to a million birds we do not know how to control. In spring they spread into the country and compete with more attractive native birds, such as flickers and bluebirds, for nesting cavities in trees or bird houses. Starlings look like short-tailed blackbirds, with wings swept back pointedly in flight. The glossy-green adults are speckled in winter. The young are brownish and noisy.

Robin (feeding young)

Western Bluebird (female)

Starling

House Sparrow

HOUSE SPARROW
One has to have a grudging admiration for this ragamuffin bird. It has the dogged persistence of the human race itself, scrapping and courting where the soot of dirty cities has blackened it, even where, for example, it has had to fly up 12 stories to a nest tucked in a chink of the stone and brick canyons that are so much a part of Manhattan. This is by no means any longer a house sparrow. It has spread from cities and towns and occupies the countryside, not only across the United States but well up into Canada and deep into Mexico. It was first introduced in the 1850s and became so numerous that for a while Michigan placed a bounty on its head. The black bib, white cheeks, and chestnut plumage of the male make it easy to identify. A female is difficult to identify. It is plain brown, with a pale eye-stripe and a yellowish bill, and is best told by the company it keeps.

Western Meadowlark

MEADOWLARK
The black V on the bright-yellow chest and the conspicuous white feathers on either side of the short tail make this an unmistakable bird. It is strictly a meadow bird, prefering grass of medium height, and is usually found in loose flocks. It does a good deal of singing and sunning on fence posts. Its flight is also distinctive because the bird uses shallow wing-strokes and glides a great deal, never rising very high. The confusion of common names among birds and other living things is well exemplified by this species which is not a lark, though it reminded the early colonists of the Skylark of England. Instead, the Meadowlark is a member of the American Blackbird Family, to which orioles and grackles also belong. The blackbird of the U.S. is most unlike the blackbird of England, however, since the latter is a thrush, as is our Robin, and is all black with a yellow bill.

RED-WINGED BLACKBIRD
The blackbird tribe has many distinctive males. The bright orange-red epaulets of this blackbird make it easy to recognize. A female is a streaky-brown bird that looks like a big sparrow until one notices the longer, sharp-pointed bill, characteristic of several of the blackbirds and orioles. A Redwing nests in both fresh-water marshes and tall-grass pasture. The more that wetlands are drained, the more it must shift to pasturage. This has brought the bird into increasing conflict with agriculture, especially corn farmers in the northern U.S., but, fortunately, only in certain places. In fall and winter it congregates in huge mixed flocks which may be troublesome to rice farmers at the southern edge of its range. Male Redwings push north in spring as soon as the ice melts and arrive two weeks before the females. Their *con-cho-ree* is a sign of spring.

Red-winged Blackbird

YELLOW-HEADED BLACKBIRD
A male of this striking species has a bright golden-yellow head and a stout black body with conspicuous white spots at the bend of the wing. The female is slightly smaller and brown except for a white throat and a yellowish breast. This is a bird of the tule, or cattail marshes, of the upper Midwest and the West, where it forms large, noisy, nesting colonies in early summer. After the nesting season, it scatters across the countryside, mixing in with other blackbirds—whether Redwings, grackles, cowbirds, or starlings—and together they feed on waste grain in open country, especially near barns because manure often contains extra waste grains and the barns provide a lee from wind and snow. The less conspicuous females and young males are easily overlooked but can be sorted out with a little patience. The songs of this blackbird are raspy.

Yellow-headed Blackbird

GRACKLES

The blackbirds come in three groups—the long-tailed grackles; the short-tailed starlings (not true blackbirds however); and the medium-tailed blackbirds, including the Redwing, the Brown-headed Cowbird, Brewer's Blackbird of the West, and the Rusty Blackbird of Canada. Grackles have very iridescent plumage, varying from bronze to purple, with blue and green mixed in. Since these are structural colors, however, they are fully appreciated only in direct sunlight. The females and the young are slightly smaller and brownish. Both the grackles and Brewer's Blackbird have yellow eyes. In spring, the male grackles' long tail is folded upward at the sides to form an open trough-shaped structure. The tail is exaggeratedly keeled in the considerably larger Boat-tailed Grackle of the Atlantic (from Cape May, N.J., southward) and Gulf coasts and Mexico.

Boat-tailed Grackle

BALTIMORE ORIOLE

For Easterners, this is one of the most colorful summer birds, with a delightful, clearly-whistled song, sometimes rendered as an emphatic *Edith, Edith, look here!* No other oriole in the U.S. or Canada is black-headed and orange at the same time. Many of the tropical orioles are remarkably skillful nest weavers, some building pendulous baskets over a yard long. The Baltimore Oriole and Bullock's Oriole both build less ambitious, but carefully constructed, hanging-nests which they tie to the tip of a drooping branch well off the ground. Taken by itself, there seems to be little purpose of so intricate a nest, but when one learns the Baltimore Oriole is the most northern member of a tropical Family, the pendant nest then makes sense. It is an escape from the many nest predators of the tropics and is a habit the bird has retained.

Bullock's Oriole

BULLOCK'S ORIOLE

This is the bright oriole of western U.S. and Mexico, distinguished by the large, white wing-patch and the black eye-stripe across its orange-yellow face. A female oriole is a much plainer bird, grayish below, but recognizable as an oriole by its sharp-pointed bill and, in spring, by the company it keeps. All orioles are good vocalists, this one somewhat less innovative than the others. The American orioles (to distinguish them from Old World orioles of a different Family) are a richly diversified group and are especially numerous in the tropics. Since they are in the same Family as the American Blackbirds, the assemblage is referred to as Icterids (from the Family **Icteridae**) by ornithologists. This wide diversity of species is a result of their having colonized a wide variety of habitats, from marshland to desert, and grassland to high tropical forest.

Baltimore Oriole

CARDINAL

The specialists would like us to call this bird a Cardinal-Grosbeak because it is so closely related to the such other grosbeaks of tropical origin as the Rose-breasted Grosbeak and the Blue Grosbeak. Actually, there are so many species of these small to medium-sized, finch-like birds in the Americas that their relationships are still puzzling. It may be a comfort to know that even the experts still have a lot to learn. Meanwhile, the bright-red Cardinal, or Cardinal-Grosbeak, is as striking as any and further distinguished by its crest. The female and the young are less red than the males, washed with browns, but even they have a crest. This is a bird of tangled vegetation, where the woody plants are interspersed with grassy openings. The Cardinal spends a good deal of its time feeding on the ground. The song is a clear, loud whistling, like a man calling his dog.

Cardinal (male)

HOUSE FINCH

Although originally western, the House Finch has become established in the Northeast and is spreading rapidly. Since it is well established in the principal population centers—in California and on the East Coast—it is at least potentially familiar to more people than many historically familiar species. A typical finch, it is a sparrow-like bird with a notched tail, but with a heavier bill and a more undulating flight than most sparrows. The problem is how to tell the House Finch from the very similar and related Purple Finch. Except in cities with a great many trees, such as Washington, D.C., it is likely that when one of these raspberry-colored finches occurs in a city, it is a House Finch. In the suburbs, take a hard look and consult a good field guide and some more experienced birding friend. The Purple Finch nests in cooler climates.

House Finch

American Goldfinch

AMERICAN GOLDFINCH

There is no mistaking this truly golden-yellow finch which travels in small flocks in open country, visiting weed patches to feed on thistle seed, sunflower, and dandelion. It is a true northern finch, with a notched tail and undulating flight. If any American bird deserved the name wild canary, this is it. The real canary of the cage-bird trade is the related Serin of the Canary Islands, the Azores, and Madeira. Distinctive as it is in summer dress, the Goldfinch is widely overlooked in winter, when the male loses its bright plumage and then looks like a female or young, i.e., a greenish, little notched-tailed finch with two white wing-bars. This is the common plumage, when they visit suburban feeding stations. The Southwest has two other goldfinch species, both of them darker birds often seen along highway borders. A song rendition is *per-chic-oree.*

White-crowned Sparrow

WHITE-CROWNED SPARROW

The Americas have a great variety of sparrows—little brown jobs, or LBJs as they are called by those impatient with the mastery of detail required to identify all of them in the field. But the White-crowned Sparrow is a cut above the average in size and markings and somewhat easier to know, at least in the West. The eastern White-crowned is a subarctic nester and, since it does not sing in its winter quarters, it is a silent but abundant bird of brush piles across the southern U.S. On the Pacific Coast, however, the White-crowned is a year-round resident whose numbers are augmented in winter by more northern forms. These mixed populations occupy every little open space that has grass, a few bushes, and a tree or two. As a consequence, one can hear White-crowned Sparrows sing in downtown San Francisco almost every month of the year.

7. REPTILES &

AMPHIBIANS

REPTILES & AMPHIBIANS

Some 350 million years ago a strange, fish-like creature emerged from the waters in an attempt to take up life on land. It takes only a very few words to tell this, but it must have taken the species hundreds of thousands, if not millions, of years of evolving to actually accomplish it. First it had to develop some means of absorbing oxygen from the air, and then it had to develop some method of moving on land. Whatever this creature may have been, it was the first backboned animal to join a terrestrial fauna, until then limited to insects, snails, and other invertebrates. But despite its successful arrival on land, the creature had to return to the water to breed and start its life as a gill-breather before it could live, as an adult, on land. This double life, translated into Greek, is amphi (double) and bios (life)—amphibian.

Today's amphibians, with very few exceptions, still lead a double life and their development, called metamorphosis, apparently follows the course of their ancestor's evolution, re-enacted in a matter of months, however, or even weeks. The eggs are laid in water, and from them emerge gill-breathing larvae that bear little, if any, resemblance to adult forms. A larva cannot live for more than a few minutes out of water, in which it moves by means of a tail. In time, however, it develops legs and lungs, and, if a frog or toad, the tail disappears and it is ready to take up life on land.

In the United States two groups, or Orders, of amphibians occur: the salamanders, and the frogs and toads. The most obvious difference between the two Orders is that salamanders have tails, and frogs and toads, in the adult stage, do not. This difference is reflected in both the Greek and the Latin scientific names of these Orders, which mean tailed and tailless. But perhaps the most descriptive term, and most commonly used scientific name, for frogs and toads is the Latin word "salientians," meaning "the jumping ones."

Amphibians are among the few vertebrates that are truly naked. Unlike scaled, feathered, or furred animals, they have no protective covering on their skin. And yet skin is one of their most important organs. It contains the mucous glands that keep the skin damp on land and lubricated in water. It also contains the granular glands that secrete an irritating fluid which, in some amphibians, is capable of killing predators and without which the creatures would be virtually helpless. The skin is also a breathing mechanism, particularly important for the lungless salamanders, and it also absorbs water, a vital service, since amphibians do not otherwise drink. Water is the most essential need of amphibians because, while they can live for a great length of time without food, they will quickly die if they are denied access to water. It must always be remembered by anyone who keeps an amphibian in captivity that a dish of water, in which the amphibian can soak, must be in the cage at all times. Amphibians shed their skin several times a year but most of them do not discard it as do snakes. Instead, they use their mouth to pull the skin off the body, and then they swallow it.

Amphibians scored a very important evolutionary first in the nearly silent world into which they emerged: the first sound ever produced by means of vocal cords was made by a creature resembling a frog or a toad. The only other sounds produced by living creatures at that time were the chirping, rasping, and buzzing of insects which are not made by vocal cords. The sounds produced by today's frogs and toads vary greatly, for each species has its own particular call. The high-pitched whistle of the Spring Peeper and the bass rumble of the Bullfrog are familiar to all who have even a fleeting awareness of the outdoors. There are many calls—croaking, whistling, snoring, clicking, chirping, trilling, grunting—that are as helpful in identifying the various species of frogs and toads as is a bird call in identifying a particular bird. Salamanders do not have vocal cords, so the sounds they produce are usually faint and squeaky, but most male frogs and toads have, in addition to vocal cords, resonators which intensify the sound of their calls. The resonator, or vocal sac, is an extension of the mouth lining into which air is

Preceding pages: Hog-nosed Snake Eating a Toad

pumped, and if the skin around it is loose enough it will balloon into one or two bubbles. While frogs and toads may call at any time for various reasons, they are most vociferous during the breeding season.

Except for a few species, such as the Spotted Salamander, the courtship of salamanders is secretive and not too often observed. But the courtship of most frogs and toads is a noisy, crowded, public affair. They congregate in large numbers in breeding waters, where males call not only to attract females, but to assert their claim to territory. Females are larger than males and heavy with eggs. A male mounts a female, clasps her with his forelegs, and fertilizes the eggs as she lays them. This method of external fertilization is common to all frogs and toads in the United States, with the single exception of the Tailed Frog of the Pacific Northwest. This frog lives in swiftly-flowing mountain streams whose waters would wash away its eggs before they could be fertilized. Therefore, the male Tailed Frog possesses a tail-like appendage with which it effects internal fertilization of the female's eggs. While virtually all frogs and toads lay their eggs in water, there are exceptions. The Greenhouse Frog of southern Florida lays its small, thick-shelled eggs on land, and from the eggs emerge not tadpoles, but tiny, fully-developed froglets.

Salamanders also practise external fertilization, but in a different manner. A male deposits sperm capsules on the bottom of a pond or brook, and a female picks them up in her cloaca and retains them in a sperm chamber until the eggs are ready to be fertilized. With few exceptions the eggs are laid in water and, within a short time, the larvae hatch. Woodland salamanders, however, select damp logs, or deep moss, as a nursery in which to lay their eggs. From here fully-developed salamanders emerge. Some salamanders retain the larval stage, with gills, as long as they live.

All amphibians, as well as all reptiles, are cold-blooded. They have no internal mechanism with which to regulate their body temperature. Consequently, they are susceptible to exterior temperature changes. In hot regions they must seek shelter, and some desert dwellers, such as the Spadefoot Toad, bury themselves deep in the ground. In cold regions all reptiles and amphibians must hibernate in the winter.

The amphibians were on Earth more than 150 million years before the first reptiles appeared. Of the reptiles only turtles have retained their identity. All other early forms evolved into the some 6000 species of crocodilians, lizards, snakes, and birds that exist today. These reptiles are on a much higher evolutionary plane than the amphibians. Fertilization of eggs is internal, and young undergo no external metamorphosis. Most reptiles lay eggs, but many, such as vipers, bear live young. In either case the young resemble their parents in every respect except size. Reptiles are completely free of the amphibians' need for water, and although many are aquatic in the sense that they live in water, they must come to land to lay their eggs.

The most apparent difference between reptiles and amphibians is the skin. At a quick glance a small woodland salamander and a small lizard look very much alike, but the salamander has smooth skin and the lizard has scales. Reptiles do not depend on their skin for the same functions amphibians do. No mucous glands are needed because the scales help to hinder dehydration. Nor do reptiles need the protection offered by granular glands. They have other and more powerful weapons of defense, whether a virulent poison or just a painful bite.

Both reptiles and amphibians perform important ecological functions. Amphibians not only serve as food for many higher forms of life, but many of them, particularly toads, are highly beneficial to man because of the great quantities of insects they devour. Snakes are very effective in keeping rodent populations in check. While poisonous snakes should be treated with respect, they should not be recklessly destroyed. Most of them will do their best to avoid a confrontation with man. Like all creatures of the wild, they deserve our protection.

WA
OR
ID
MT
WY
NV
UT
CO
CA
AZ
NM
Black-tailed rattlesnake
Sidewinder
Mojave rattlesnake
Speckled rattlesnake
Tiger rattlesnake
Rock rattlesnake
Twin-spotted rattlesnake
Ridge-nosed rattlesnake

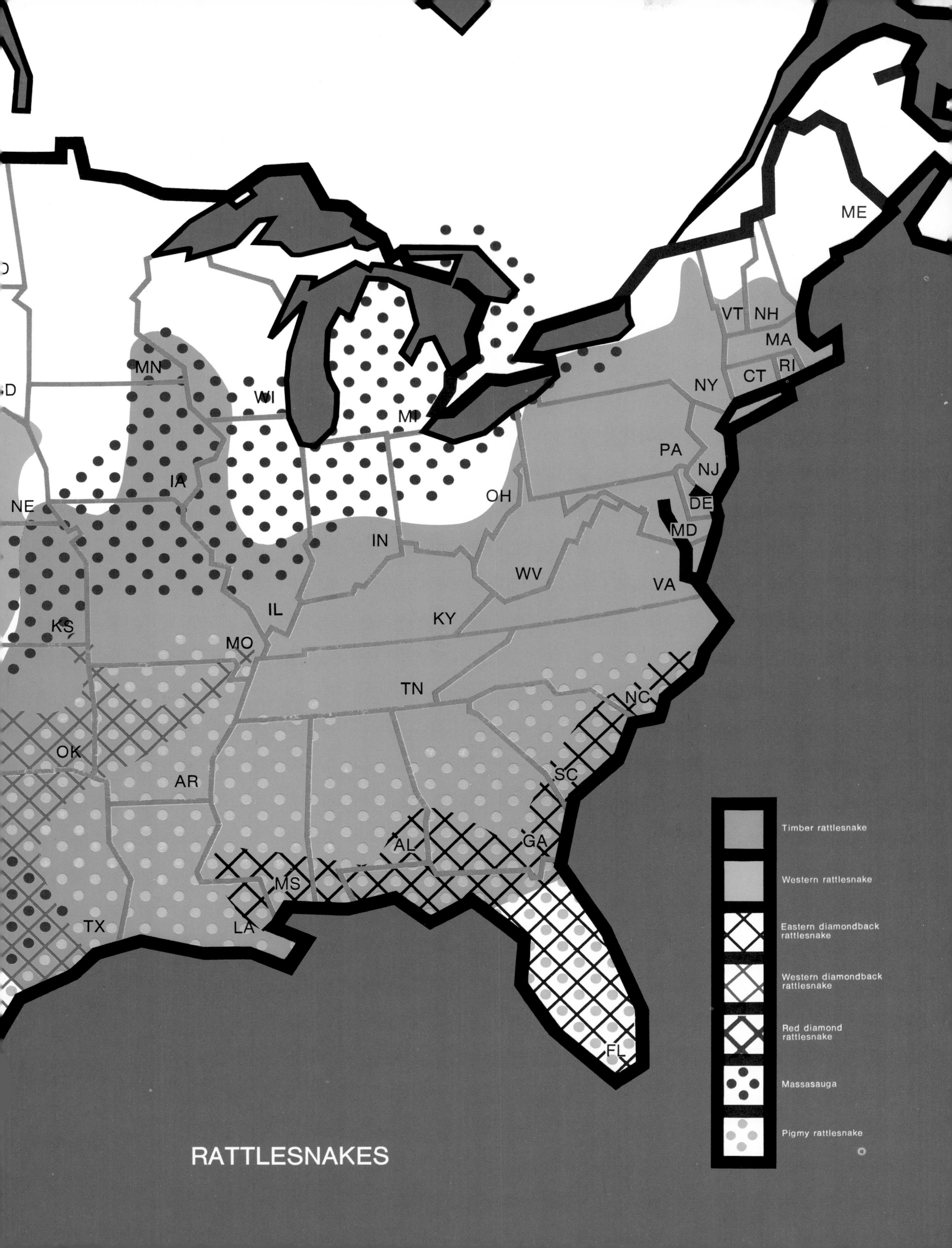

RATTLESNAKES

Range Maps of Reptiles & Amphibians

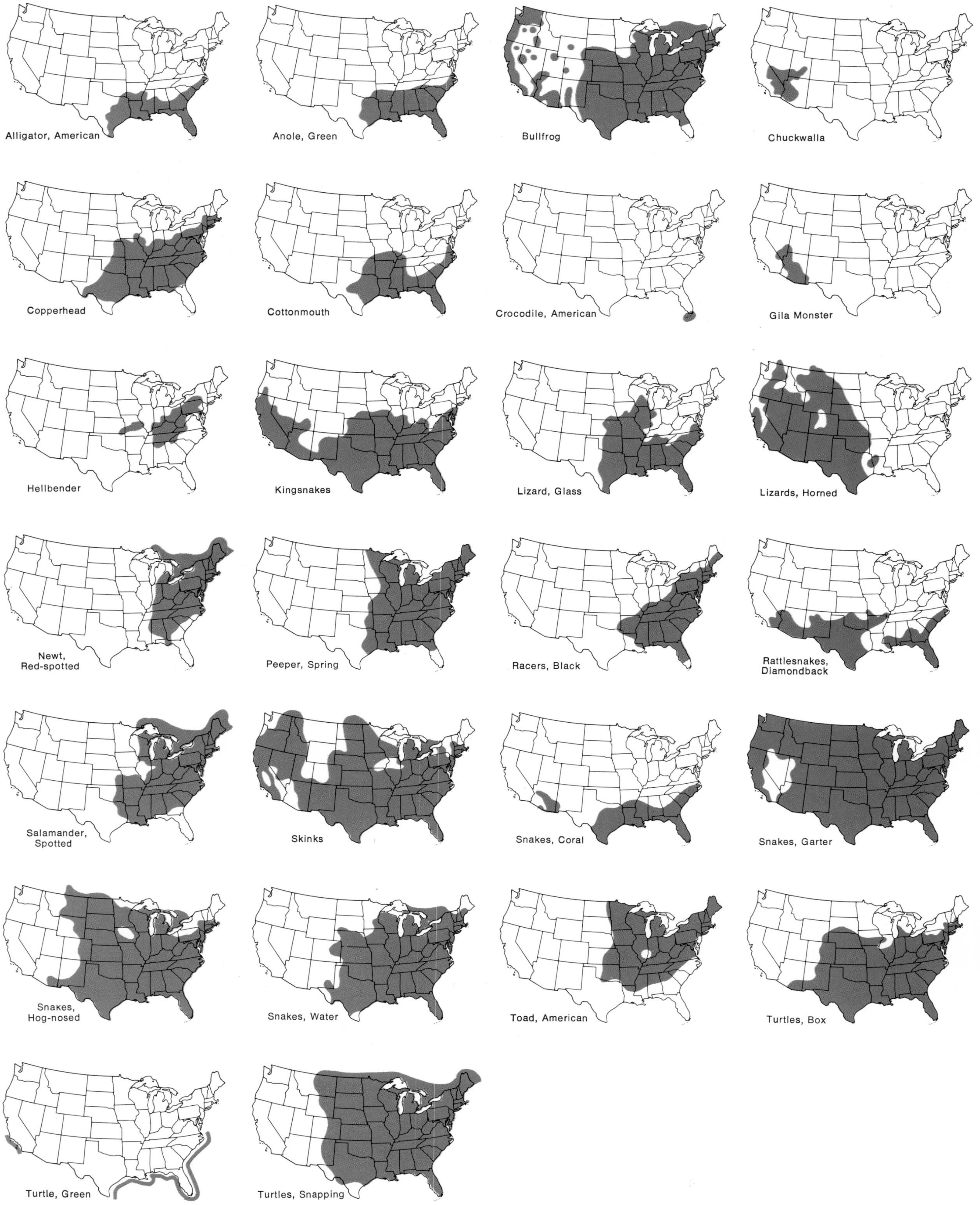

Alligator, American
Anole, Green
Bullfrog
Chuckwalla
Copperhead
Cottonmouth
Crocodile, American
Gila Monster
Hellbender
Kingsnakes
Lizard, Glass
Lizards, Horned
Newt, Red-spotted
Peeper, Spring
Racers, Black
Rattlesnakes, Diamondback
Salamander, Spotted
Skinks
Snakes, Coral
Snakes, Garter
Snakes, Hog-nosed
Snakes, Water
Toad, American
Turtles, Box
Turtle, Green
Turtles, Snapping

American Alligator

American Crocodile

AMERICAN ALLIGATORS

Although most reptiles are voiceless, the roar of a bull alligator during courtship remains one of the awesome sounds of swamp and bayou nights in the southeastern U.S. It is always one of the joys of swamp prowling to discover an alligator basking on a log or swimming by with only its eyes and nostrils protruding from the water. An alligator feeds on all sorts of aquatic animals, and on whatever terrestrial animals blunder into it along the banks where it spends so much time sunning. As many as 30 eggs may be laid in a nest made of a mound of aquatic vegetation and guarded jealously by the female. Young alligators grow rapidly. Born about ten inches long, one is often four feet long at age two, and may attain 14 feet if it lives long enough. Habitat destruction and over-hunting for the market have greatly reduced numbers in recent years.

AMERICAN CROCODILE

Alligators and crocodiles are very closely related. A crocodile is distinguished from an alligator on sight by its tapered snout and by the fact that the fourth tooth on either side of the jaw protrudes; whereas an alligator has a bluntly-rounded snout and no protruding teeth when the jaws are closed. Also, a crocodile may live in salt water, as does the American Crocodile, whereas an alligator does not. The gavials of Southeast Asia are crocodile relations; whereas the caimans of Central and South America are alligator relatives. The leather trade has unfortunately placed the threat of extinction on the great beasts, and they will survive in few places unless all countries agree to regulate the take carefully. With sound management programs they could be brought back in numbers and serve as a valuable resource. Failing this, the species may be lost for all time.

Snapping Turtle

Eastern Box Turtle

Green Turtle

SNAPPING TURTLES
Snapping turtles, found in many fresh waters, may attain a length of more than 15 inches, weigh more than 35 pounds, and may often have a very nasty temper. They are easily recognized because of the large head, long tail with a jagged ridge, and a shell that seems too small for the body. It is their powerful jaws and very aggressive manner that should warn one to keep away, for they can sever a man's finger with one bite. Snappers feed on practically anything, and in the spring many a young duckling is pulled beneath the surface to be eaten. The largest American fresh-water turtle is the Alligator Snapping Turtle of the Southeast, which can grow to 150 pounds. This turtle usually lies in wait for its food, mouth agape, wriggling the small worm-shaped piece of flesh that is attached to its tongue to attract curious and incautious fish which may become food.

BOX TURTLES
Being land turtles, with a strikingly domed shell, box turtles are well known and not infrequently seen in damp open woods, nibbling on a toadstool or stripping berries from the lower branches of a bush. Adult male turtles frequently have red eyes, while the females usually have brown. The domed shell comes in an assortment of light patterns on a dark ground and gives the turtles their name for, when threatened, an adult is able to enclose itself completely in its shell. The lower shell, or plastron, is hinged to allow the two shells to close together so tightly that the turtle is imprevious to practically anything but being run over by an automobile. Although box turtles live on land they go into shallow waters, and summer heat will send them burrowing into mud, where they may remain until cooling showers arrive. The western species is called the Ornate Box Turtle.

GREEN TURTLE
Like almost all sea turtles, a Green Turtle attains an enormous size, sometimes weighing over 300 pounds, but legend claims that it grew much larger long ago. It ranges widely through the warm ocean waters through which it can swim with great speed by means of powerful flippers that are its front limbs. Although, surprisingly, the Green Turtle sometimes basks, like a small pond-turtle, on oceanic islands, it usually visits land, leaving a trail like the track of a tank, only to lay its clutch of more than 150 eggs in a large, deep nest it has dug. Later the turtle smooths over the nest with dirt, in order to hide the eggs from predators. The Green Turtle and its eggs have been hunted so ruthlessly for food that the future of this fine species is now considered endangered throughout much of its range. Fortunately, sanctuaries are being set aside to protect nesting sites.

Green Anole

Skink

Horned Lizard

GREEN ANOLE (Chameleon)

The perky acrobatic, slim green chameleon of the Southeast, sold by many circuses and pet shops, is actually an anole, one of the lizards. It is probably its ability to change color rapidly from bright-green to brown that has caused it to be named for the more dramatic, true chameleons of the Old World. It is an attractive little creature, five to seven inches long, with a bright-pink throat-fan that is erected during aggressive or courtship displays. Some displays are as ritualized as those of birds. The chameleon also has toe pads that enable it to run swiftly across fences or through trees, where it will battle other chameleons until one, or both, tumble to the ground, usually unhurt. Captive anoles should be kept warm and fed live, small, soft insects and spiders. Since chameleons will not drink from a dish, water should be sprayed into the cage for them.

SKINKS

Skinks are a very large Family of agile, glossy lizards, of which the 17 species in the U.S. range from a delicate, shy creature only two inches long, to one which is about a foot long. Most skinks are drab in color but some have a red head. Some have brightly colored tails which, like the tails of many lizards, are easily broken off. This is a fine protective device, for a predator will grab at a skink, only to find the tail wriggling in its mouth while its prey escapes. Skinks occur in all tropical and warm-temperate regions and in most habitats. Whether they are found in woodlands or along ocean shores, burrowing in sand or climbing trees, there is usually some moisture nearby. It is fascinating to notice that the lower eyelids of some skinks contain a small transparent disk that serves as a window when the eyes are closed.

HORNED LIZARD

For a creature that blends so unobtrusively with the ground cover of the arid and semi-arid areas of the West, the Horned Lizard has a most dramatic appearance. It has a number of horn-shaped spines fringing the back of its head, and sharp pointed scales on its back and scalloped ones on its sides. Its squat body, flattening in time of danger until it looks as though it had been stepped upon, and its square-jawed look cause it to be called, incorrectly, a Horned Toad, but it is a true lizard. If its resemblance to a prehistoric creature is not enough to discourage a predator, the Horned Lizard has the unusual ability of being able to squirt a small amount of blood from the corner of its eyes. Horned lizards are widely sold as pets but most of them die quickly, for they need a special diet, rich in ants and spiders, to provide adequate proteins.

Glass Lizard

Gila Monster

Black Chuckwalla

GLASS LIZARD

It is very easy, at first glance, to mistake this slim, shiny creature for a snake. But then it blinks its eyes, which is a sign it is not a snake but a legless lizard, for true snakes have no movable eyelids. A Glass Lizard also has ear openings which, again, a snake does not have. The Glass Lizard is particularly interesting because its very long and brittle tail breaks easily, sometimes into several pieces, each of which seems to have a life of its own, for each piece continues to move about on the ground for several minutes. This is a great protective device, for predators are usually distracted by the wriggling segments long enough to allow the lizard to escape. The legend that the broken pieces will rejoin the tail is, of course, fiction. A new tail will eventually grow but it will never attain the length of the original. It feeds on such items as spiders, birds' eggs, and snails.

GILA MONSTER

The Gila Monster is the only poisonous lizard in the U.S., where it inhabits the southwestern desert, most abundantly in Arizona. The heavy body, thick tail in which fat is stored, short limbs, and vividly patterned bead-like scales distinguish this species from all other lizards. The Gila Monster finds its food less by sight than by smell and taste, following a trail by means of the scent gathered by its flickering tongue. It is a shy and slow-moving creature but when it finds itself threatened, it will grip the attacker with its powerful jaws and hang on with bulldog tenacity. Then, from the glands located in the lower part of the jaw, venom flows into the mouth, through the grooved teeth, and into the wound. Compared to the hypodermic-like fang of a rattlesnake, this is a primitive mechanism for transmitting venom. The rare fatalities are more often from shock.

CHUCKWALLA

Throughout the southwestern desert a Chuckwalla can be seen sprawled in the sun on almost every rocky hillside and outcropping. It is one of the largest lizards in the U.S. It has a flat, dark body, although its young have conspicuous cross stripes. Along its neck and sides the lizard's rough skin falls into loose folds, as though it were wearing the skin of a much larger animal. Unusual among lizards, the Chuckwalla is a vegetarian, feeding on available desert plants, especially the ubiquitous creosote bush of that region. Like most lizards when threatened, the Chuckwalla flees for safety into crevices in rocks, but it has an added safety feature. Once within its stronghold the Chuckwalla swallows air and inflates its body until it is no longer able to get through the opening. An attacker would have to pry open the hole to drag out the Chuckwalla.

Red-bellied Water Snake

Eastern Garter Snake

Hog-nosed Snake

WATER SNAKES
Although not poisonous, water snakes are quite belligerent and, when threatened, will flatten the head and body and strike savagely. They can inflict a painful bite and, if seized, they will discharge dreadful-smelling musk from anal scent glands. The adult Northern Water Snake is a large, thick, dark snake that reaches a length over three feet. When young it is clearly patterned with wide, dark bands on a lighter ground. It lives in most of the waters—bog, pond, or flowing stream—in the East, as far south as North Carolina and west as Colorado. The Water Snake can often be seen basking on top of a muskrat house or on logs and rocks along the shore, but when alarmed it immediately takes to the water. In the South care should be taken not to confuse a water snake with the venomous Cottonmouth, but fortunately both snakes try to elude people.

GARTER SNAKES
Among the most widely distributed snakes from coast to coast, garter snakes are the best known, for they live in almost all habitats: meadows, woods, farms, swamps, and city lots. The several species vary greatly in size, but average adults range from 20 to 30 inches and have stout bodies. They were supposedly named for the garters that were once popular, for most of these snakes are striped lengthwise, and many are attractively colored. When aroused, they flatten their bodies, thus accentuating their pattern and colors. Garter snakes are harmless, but when annoyed they may strike and even bite. They will smear their captor with feces and expel musk from their anal scent glands, as their relatives the water snakes do. Garter snakes have a varied diet, including frogs and toads, mice, birds, and even carrion. In general, their role is a constructive one.

HOG-NOSED SNAKE
Probably the greatest actor among reptiles is the Hog-nosed Snake, whose heavy, blotched body and threatening manner belie its true harmlessness, for it is not poisonous and it rarely bites. Its name comes from its upturned nose which, it is believed, is used to help dig up toads, which are this snake's favorite food. Its acting has given it such erroneous names as Puff Adder and Blow Viper, for when it believes itself in danger the Hog-nosed Snake flattens its head and neck to resemble a cobra and strikes and hisses at its attacker. If this does not prove discouraging, the snake appears to go into convulsions, opening its mouth, writhing and twisting a few times, and then turns on its back and seems to fall over dead. As soon as the danger passes the snake comes to life and crawls away, none the worse for its experience.

Kingsnake

KINGSNAKES

Kingsnakes are constrictors. They stalk their prey until they are close enough to grab it with their jaws, then they coil themselves around the animal's body and firmly squeeze until it dies of suffocation, after which it is devoured. A snake is able to swallow an animal larger than its own head because the two halves of its lower jaw, connected by an elastic ligament, can be widely separated. The kingsnakes' diet consists largely of small rodents, but also birds, frogs, lizards, turtle eggs, and snakes, including even rattlers, since they are apparently immune to their poison. The Eastern Kingsnake, which occurs from southern New Jersey to Florida, is a large, strikingly beautiful, black or dark-brown snake with a white or cream chain-like pattern encircling its body—which accounts for its vernacular name Chain Snake. It is also called Swamp Wamper.

BLACK RACERS

Like garter snakes, these are widely-distributed harmless snakes everyone should know. They are rather long (30″ to 60″), satiny black above and below, but with a white chin and throat. Eastern specimens are larger and more uniformly black than those of the West. Western ones tend to be olive-brown, bluish, or dark-gray to black. The shiny look is because the back scales are smooth, rather than keeled down the middle, as are those of garter snakes and other species with which they might be confused. Young black racers are strikingly different from adults in marking: they have numerous reddish blotches on the back. No other U.S. snake shows such an age contrast. Black racers are active, alert, and fast-moving. They hold the head and neck high as they slide along. They are most often found in woods or along woodland borders.

Black Racer (with eggs)

Eastern Coral Snake

CORAL SNAKES

The highly poisonous Eastern Coral Snake is the U.S. representative of a Family that includes such infamous members as the Cobra, Krait, and Mamba. It is a small snake whose shining red, black, and yellow bands should be enough to warn anyone of its potent venom, but its colors and pattern are mimicked by such non-poisonous snakes as the Scarlet Kingsnake and various milk snakes, all of whom, however, have a black band separating the red from the yellow. Since this detail can easily be overlooked, great care should be taken whenever a brightly-banded snake is encountered. Because the coral snakes have a small mouth and very short fangs, they inflict most of their bites on a human's toes or fingers. Although the Eastern Coral Snake is normally hidden beneath forest logs, it goes foraging in early morning. The Arizona Coral Snake does not grow as large.

COPPERHEAD

A Copperhead snake has a coppery-red, flat, triangular head and distinctive dark markings on a copper-colored body. It is a pit viper, as are all of our poisonous snakes except the Coral Snake. Pit vipers have two facial pits, one on each side of the head below the eye. These are heat sensors that guide the snakes to their warm-blooded prey. The Copperhead inhabits wooded hillsides and rocky areas and often lies quietly in dry leaves, where an unwary hiker may step on it. While a Copperhead is not an aggressive snake it will bite when aroused. Then venom flows from a venom gland to a pair of hollow teeth, or fangs, that can be folded back against the roof of the mouth when not in use, but which can be quickly erected when the mouth is opened wide. In the fall, Copperheads congregate in dens below the frost line where they hibernate.

Eastern Cottonmouth

COTTONMOUTH (Water Moccasin)
A Cottonmouth, or Water Moccasin, is a highly venomous and very dangerous pit viper that frequents the lowland waters from Virginia to Florida and Alabama. It is a large, dark snake that can easily be mistaken for a non-poisonous water snake with which it shares much of its range. Therefore, in any area where the Cottonmouth occurs, any aquatic snake should be viewed with suspicion. The Cottonmouth is very aggressive and, when aroused, it vibrates its tail wildly, rattling everything in its path, throws up its head, and opens its mouth wide, exposing the white interior that gives it the name Cottonmouth. Even though the Cottonmouth is an aquatic snake, it often comes on land to feed on birds and rodents, but its main diet consists of fish, frogs, small turtles, baby alligators, and other snakes. Most snakes lay eggs, but the Cottonmouth bears live young.

Western Diamond Rattlesnake

DIAMONDBACK RATTLESNAKES
To come unexpectedly upon a large specimen of the largest poisonous snake in the U.S., with its thick body tightly-coiled, and its broad, triangular head moving, and to hear the angry buzz of the rattle, is to recognize the personification of the terror some people feel when they hear the word snake. This association is unfortunate, because most snakes slip away quietly when people approach. These pit vipers are dangerous, however, and those who live in rattlesnake country should learn their habits and respect them. The pit behind the nostrils is a highly heat-sensitive organ which allows accurate striking of small mammals at night. The number of buttons in the rattle is not a true index of age except in a minimum sense. The map on pages 180-181 shows the overlapping ranges of the rattlesnakes in the U.S., most of them in the arid Southwest.

Copperhead

Hellbender

Spotted Salamander

Red-spotted Newt

HELLBENDER
The Hellbender, a large, gray, awkward looking salamander with a flattened head and a thick, wrinkled fold of skin on each side of its body, is the American representative of the giant salamanders. The Giant Salamander of Japan is the world's largest, attaining a length of five feet. In contrast, the adult Hellbender is about 20 inches long. The Hellbender is a strictly aquatic salamander, inhabiting swiftly-flowing rivers and streams from New York west to central Missouri. Despite its aquatic life an adult has no external gills and has to rise to the surface of the water to breathe. It will eat anything it can swallow. Its 300 to 500 eggs are laid in long gelatinous strings which the female Hellbender pushes onto a submerged stone or log to which the eggs adhere until the larvae emerge. The Hellbender is thereby eliminated by water pollution.

SPOTTED SALAMANDER
Although the handsome, black and yellow Spotted Salamander often attains a length of more than six inches and ranges widely over the East, it is rarely seen. It is only during the breeding season that salamanders flock to ponds where they twist and tumble around each other, rubbing noses and touching bodies, and make the water look like it is boiling. The males deposit small, pyramid-shaped sperm capsules which the females take into their bodies. In a few days the pond contains small balls of what appears to be tapioca pudding, but which are actually eggs, laid in a gelatinous mass which swells upon touching water. The larvae that emerge from the eggs are very delicate, with feather-like gills, but within three months they develop into tiny salamanders, which then leave the pond to take up life on land.

RED-SPOTTED NEWT
The Red-spotted, or Common, Newt is usually seen as an olive, red-spotted swimmer undulating across a pond, its arms and legs trailing behind, or walking casually over the pond bottom, or else as an orange, waddling eft on the leafy forest floor of the woodlands of eastern Canada and U.S. Unlike most other amphibians which have two life stages—a gilled aquatic larva and then a terrestrial, or at least air-breathing, adult—a newt has three stages. It too starts life as a gill-breathing larva and then develops into a small terrestrial salamander, or eft, ranging in color from light orange to dull red. After roaming the woods for about three years the eft's color darkens to olive, its tail broadens and, as a newt, it returns to the water, to live permanently. Early students of American salamanders considered the eft a separate species.

AMERICAN TOAD

The American Toad is a member of a Family of most delightful creatures that live throughout most of the world. Toads may be found in forests, in deserts, and on mountain tops. They also inhabit fields and gardens, where they are of inestimable value because of the enormous quantity of insects they eat. Depending on the species, adult toads range in size from barely one inch to more than six inches, and their color is as varied. An American Toad is usually brown, but other species may be vividly patterned. However, almost all toads have a chunky shape, dry and warty skin, and two large glands (paratoids), one behind each ear. Frogs, on the other hand, have smooth, moist skin. Toads gather in water in great numbers during the breeding season. The flute-like trill of an American Toad is one of the most beautiful sounds in nature.

SPRING PEEPER

This little treefrog, barely an inch in length, is well known as one of the heralds of spring. On any warm spring night its shrill whistle-like call can be heard coming from swamps and ponds. It produces the call by pumping air into a vocal sac in its throat, which then inflates into an enormous bubble, almost the size of the frog itself. Like all treefrogs, the tips of the Peeper's toes are equipped with adhesive disks, which enable it to climb swiftly on any surface. Although other treefrogs clamber about in treetops, a peeper usually remains in low bushes or on rushes, where its protective coloring of brown or beige allows it to remain unseen. The characteristic field mark of the Spring Peeper is an "X" on its back. This gives the little frog the scientific name of **Hyla Crucifer.** The Cricket Frog and the Chorus Frog of the South are close relatives.

BULLFROG

An adult Bullfrog can frequently be recognized by its size alone, for it is the largest frog in the U.S., often reaching a length of more than six inches. It has a relatively smooth skin, a body much slimmer than a toad's, and long hind legs that make it an excellent jumper and a better swimmer. Its rolling, sonorous *jug-a-rum* is familiar even to an infrequent country visitor. Like almost all true frogs, a Bullfrog is rarely found far from water and usually can be seen sitting stolidly at the edge of the pond. A female lays enormous numbers of eggs that float on the surface of the water like a net. A Bullfrog tadpole may take two years to transform, but other species of frogs and toads complete their metamorphosis in a much shorter time. A Bullfrog is a voracious eater of insects, snakes, birds, and other frogs. A male Bullfrog is larger than a female.

American Toad

Spring Peeper

Bullfrog

8. FISHES

FISHES

There are more than 20,000 kinds of fish in the world, ranging from the Philippine Goby, less than three quarters of an inch at maturity, to the huge Whale Shark, which may reach 50 feet or more. Fish come in all shapes, from sinuous snake eels to fish that use their fins to walk on land like seals. Fish are found from near-freezing polar waters to desert sinkholes with temperatures over 100°F., and from ocean depths to mountain heights. In 1960 from the bathyscaph *Trieste*, Jacques Piccard saw a flatfish at the bottom of the Mariana Trench, 35,800 feet down (over six miles) at the Pacific Ocean's deepest point. Fish also occur at altitudes over 14,000 feet in mountain streams and meadow pools of the Andes. In fact, fish are more widely distributed than any other vertebrate group on Earth. What were the adaptations that enable fish to survive such diverse habitats and conditions? How has this group come to dominate the 70 percent of Earth covered by water?

Fish are the oldest of all the vertebrates; their origins go back over 600 million years. Early fishes lacked jaws and made their living by routing in the bottom, sucking in food as well as mud. Fish really did not come of age, however, for 200 million years until the Devonian period, called the age of fishes, during which their numbers and species increased tremendously. Most of the characteristics of modern fish, such as functional fins and jaws equipped with sharp teeth, evolved during this period. In the evolutionary process many groups have either disappeared or are now reduced to a few relic species. The very primitive, jawless fishes, for example, are represented by the lampreys and hagfishes.

Since Darwin's time we have all realized our close relation to monkeys, but our relation to fishes goes much further back. Land-dwelling members of the formerly abundant group of fresh-water predators called lobe-finned fishes are believed to have evolved into the amphibians that later evolved into reptiles. Birds and mammals (including us) evolved from reptiles.

The lobe-fins became extinct about 100 million years ago—or so everyone thought until 1938 when a fisherman off South Africa brought up a perfectly-alive five-foot, 127-pound lobe-fin. Over a dozen of these lobe-fins, called coelacanths (pronounced seal-a-canths), have been caught since.

The world's waters may contain more fish today than at any other time. Two groups dominate: the sharks (including sharks, skates, and rays), whose skeleton is made of flexible cartilage, and the teleosts, or bony fishes, whose skeleton is calcified. There are only about 250 species of sharks as compared with more than 20,000 species of bony fishes. But the shark species play the same impressive and unchanged role that they have played for over 400 million years. The largest of the sharks, the White Shark, is the most awesome predator in the world. No other species so formidably combines militance with mass. A 20-foot specimen may weigh over three tons, and there are unconfirmed reports of specimens up to 35 feet long. Judging from fossil teeth, a comparable relative 20 million years ago may have been 60 feet long and may have weighed over 50 tons; a person could probably have swum into the stomach of one of these monsters without even touching its throat. Fortunately, most sharks do not have the disposition of the White Shark.

As land animals do, fish need oxygen to live. To obtain oxygen, fish must pump water into their mouths over paired gills containing numerous, minute blood vessels which absorb the oxygen dissolved in the water and release carbon dioxide into the blood. Because the amount of dissolved oxygen in water increases with a decreasing temperature, water temperature is an extremely important factor in fish distribution. Trout are adapted to clear, cold water and feed by eating insects, crayfish, and other fish whole. If a dam is built that releases water warmer than the river, a trout downstream must pump more water and thus work harder to extract the same amount of oxygen. Sediment in the water clogs the gills and creates additional problems. A carp, which requires less oxygen, would be perfectly content in the same situation. If additional oxygen was needed it could go to the surface and gulp air. Being a filter feeder and browser, a carp is used to separating its food from heavy sediments. Any change in the temperature or quality of the water results in a change of advantage for one species over another. The change may not be great enough to eliminate the

Preceding pages: Pike

trout, but loss of energy put into obtaining oxygen may result in slower growth or lower reproduction.

Mudskippers and lungfish have solved the oxygen problem by taking oxygen directly from the air to the gills or into an air bladder, similar to our lungs. In most bony fishes this bladder is used as an internal float to keep the fish, which are denser than water, from sinking. Sharks have no air bladder and must keep in constant motion to stay in surface water.

The sense of smell is the most acutely developed of all fish senses. The pitted, paired nostrils on the snout are extremely sensitive to minute chemical changes. An experimentally blindfolded shark can still find its prey by smell alone. A shark hunting at night or in murky water is apt to bite an interesting smelling object that he might otherwise avoid if he could see it clearly. Perhaps this is why many shark attacks have occurred in the evening or in murky waters. In the perpetual night of the deep ocean smell may be a prime method of locating prey.

Because they have no taste organs in the mouth and taste buds may be located on the head or on any other part of the body, most fish probably taste their food before they gulp it down. The vacuum cleaner syndrome is well documented by sharks, which seem to eat almost anything they consider interesting. Glass floats seem to be particular favorites, but tin cans, automotive parts, wicker baskets, and beer bottles have been found in shark stomachs.

Sight in fish is generally thought to be good; no trout fisherman would say otherwise. Color vision, once discounted in fish, is of some importance although it is doubtful that fish can see the same bright hues we do on a coral reef. Some flatfish, such as the flounders, can change color to match the bottom pattern and foil their predators. In lightless environments sight becomes expendable. Many deep-sea fishes and cave-dwelling fishes have reduced vision, and some have lost their eyes completely.

One unique adaptation is the development of a sixth sense that can feel the presence of food, enemies, obstacles, or other schooling fish. A series of minute, pressure-sensitive canals form a line running down the fish's sides. This lateral line constantly monitors the pressure changes associated with water flow over the fish's body informing the fish of adjacent objects. This is why, among thousands of schooling fish, not one fish bumps into another. Although fish have no external ears, they are able to hear by sensing the pressure waves associated with sound. A fisherman who approaches a stream bank too noisily will have to wait before the fish are willing to take a fly.

A wary stream-fish might not hear a fisherman approach if it is asleep. Because fish have no eyelids they must sleep with their eyes open. Most fish sleep suspended in the water, although some, like tuna, seem never to sleep. Some species sleep deeply and soundly lying on the ocean floor. Parrotfish on Caribbean coral reefs have even been handled at night by divers without awakening.

After survival, including sleeping and eating, a fish's strongest instinct is to reproduce. The usual rule observed in nature is that the more parental care required the fewer the number of young produced. Most fish, being indifferent parents, lay great quantities of eggs, cod up to six million, turbot up to nine million, ling up to 30 million, and an Ocean Sunfish up to 300 million. These fish, like most that travel in large schools, are broadcast spawners. At the proper season and temperature conditions for development of young, females release their eggs into the water where they are fertilized by males. A single school of millions of herring in the North Sea can turn the water cloudy with their eggs and milt. Once fertilized, the eggs either float to the surface or sink to the bottom where they begin to develop into adults. Many fresh-water species are more conscientious parents and care for both eggs and young. Regardless of the number of eggs produced only two need survive to maintain the species.

Because fish are so widely distributed, diverse, and abundant, they serve as excellent indicators of the environmental health of the nations' waters. Dam building, channelization, and pollution have already severely damaged many sport and commercial fisheries. The return of trout and salmon to rivers and streams from which they have been eliminated and the protection of existing populations is a worthwhile goal for us all.

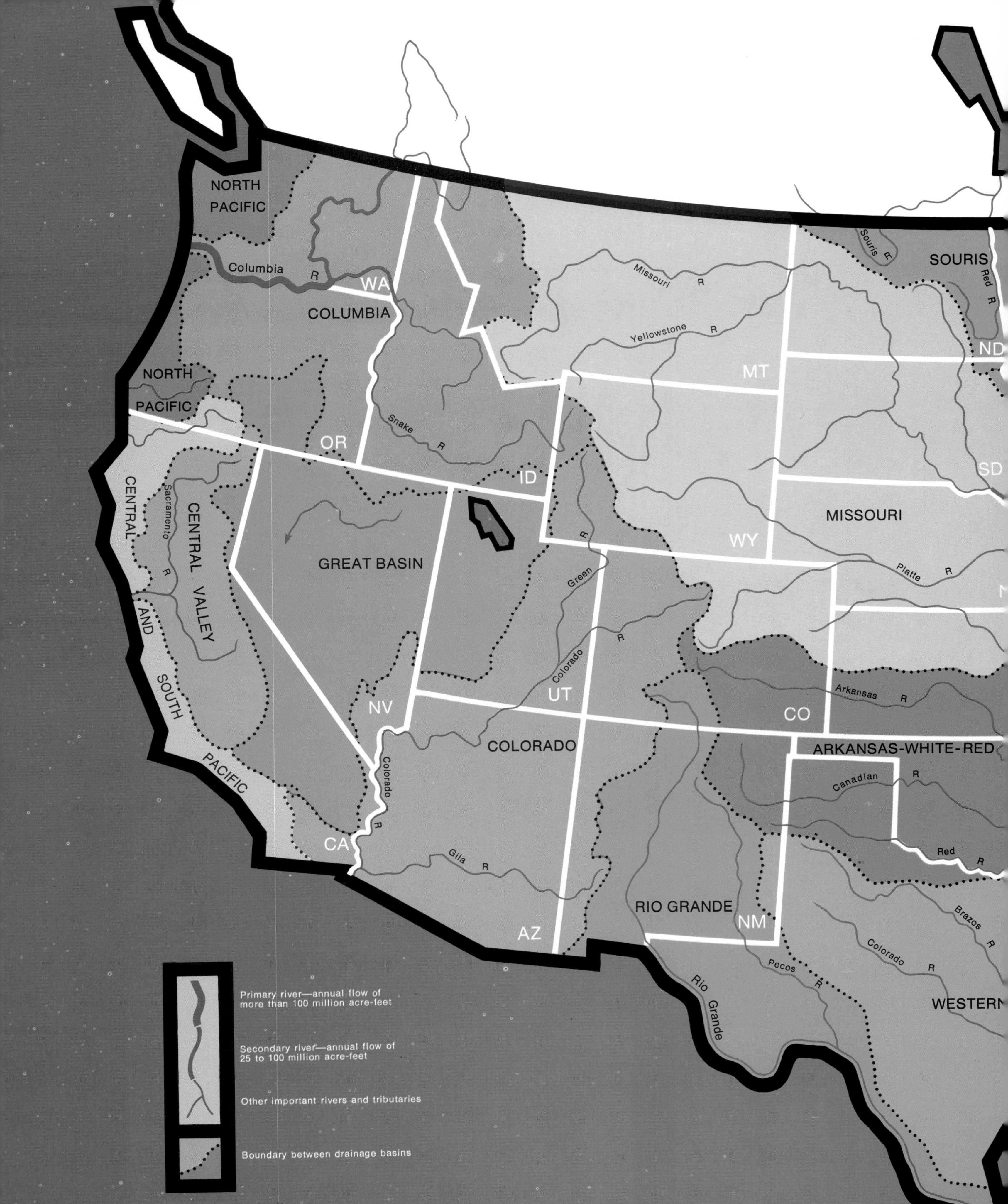

PRINCIPAL RIVER BASINS

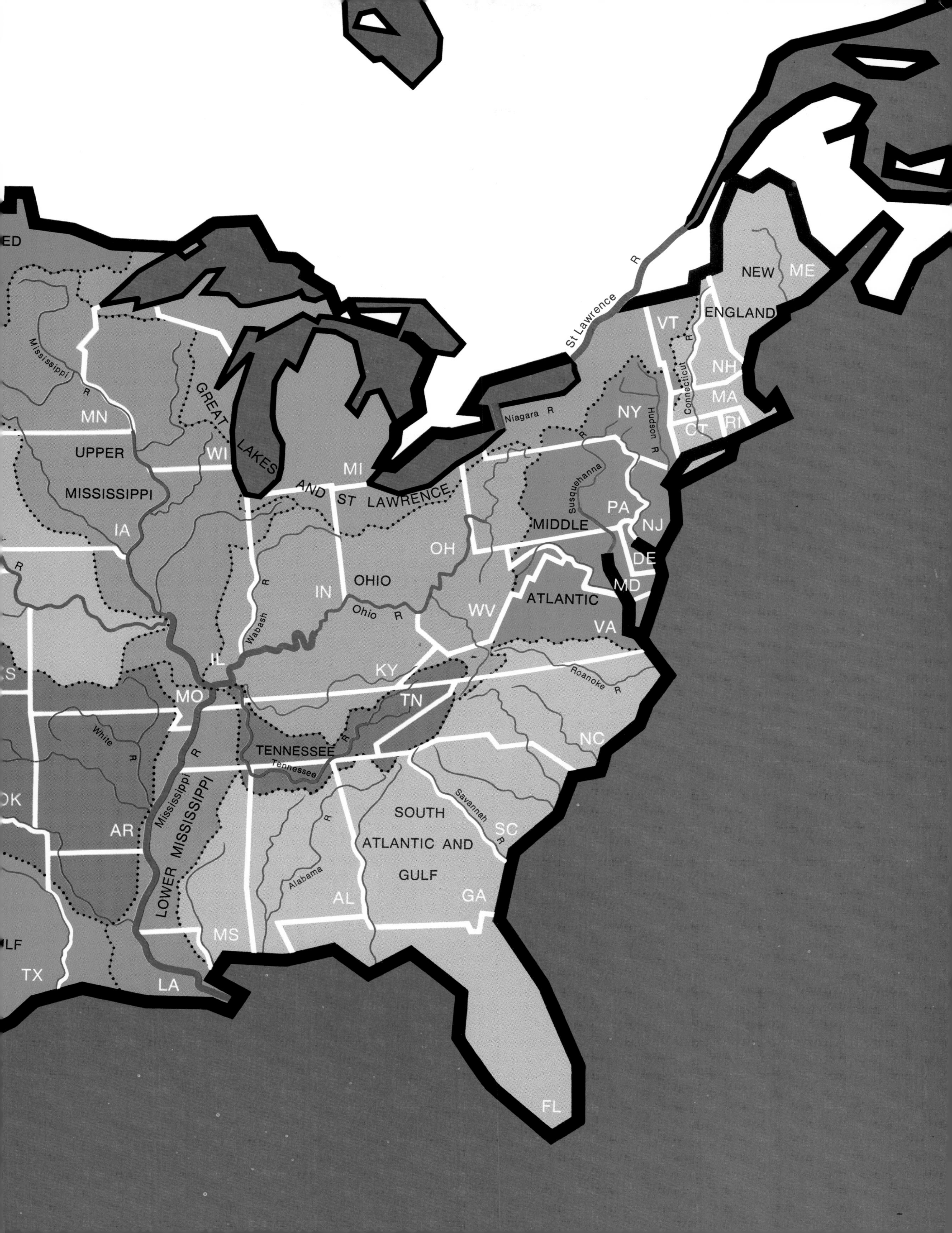

ED
Mississippi R
MN
UPPER
MISSISSIPPI
IA
WI
GREAT LAKES AND ST LAWRENCE
MI
St Lawrence R
Niagara R
NEW ENGLAND
ME
VT
NH
MA
Connecticut R
CT
RI
NY
Hudson R
Susquehanna R
PA
NJ
MIDDLE
ATLANTIC
DE
MD
VA
WV
OH
OHIO
IN
Wabash R
Ohio R
IL
KY
MO
TN
TENNESSEE
Tennessee R
White R
Roanoke R
NC
SOUTH ATLANTIC AND GULF
Savannah R
SC
GA
AL
Alabama R
MS
AR
Mississippi R
LOWER MISSISSIPPI
LA
TX
OK
LF
FL

Range Maps of Fishes

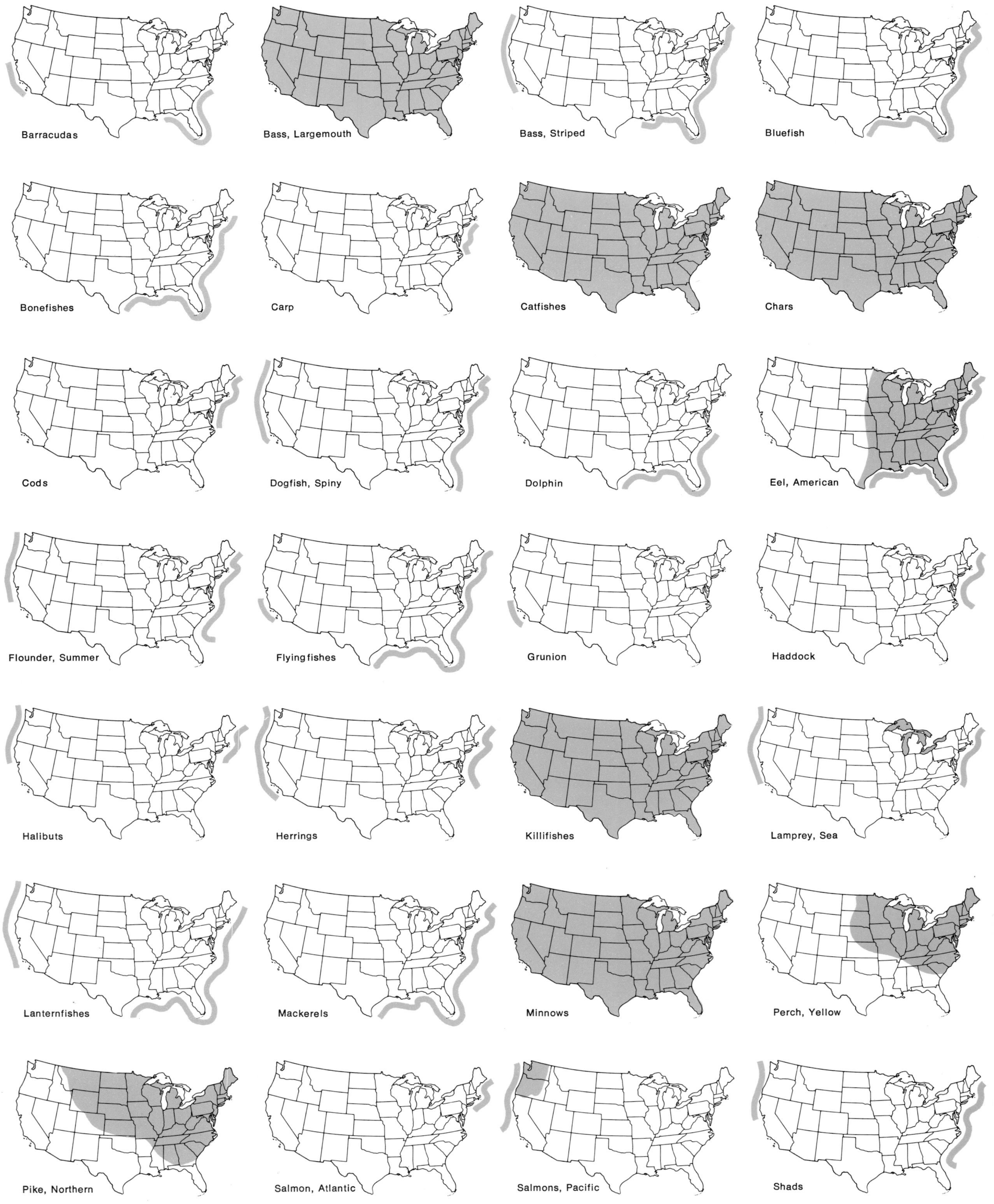

Shark, Blue

Shark, Hammerhead

Skates

Smelts

Sturgeons

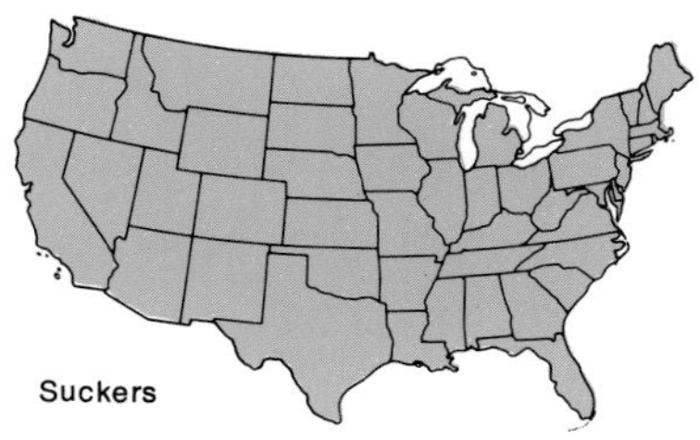

Suckers

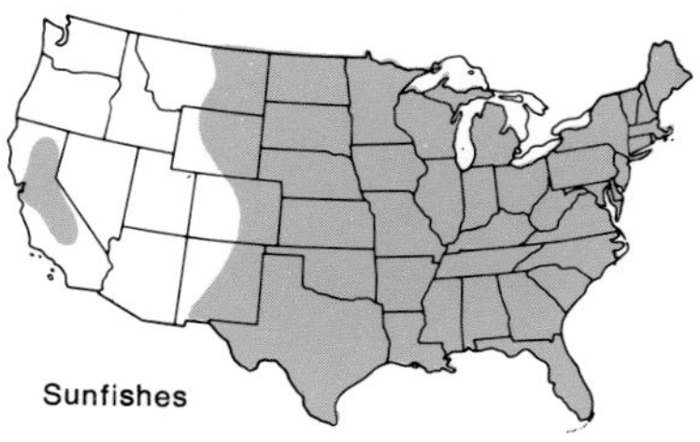

Sunfishes

Swordfish

Tarpon

Tunas

Viperfishes

Whitefishes

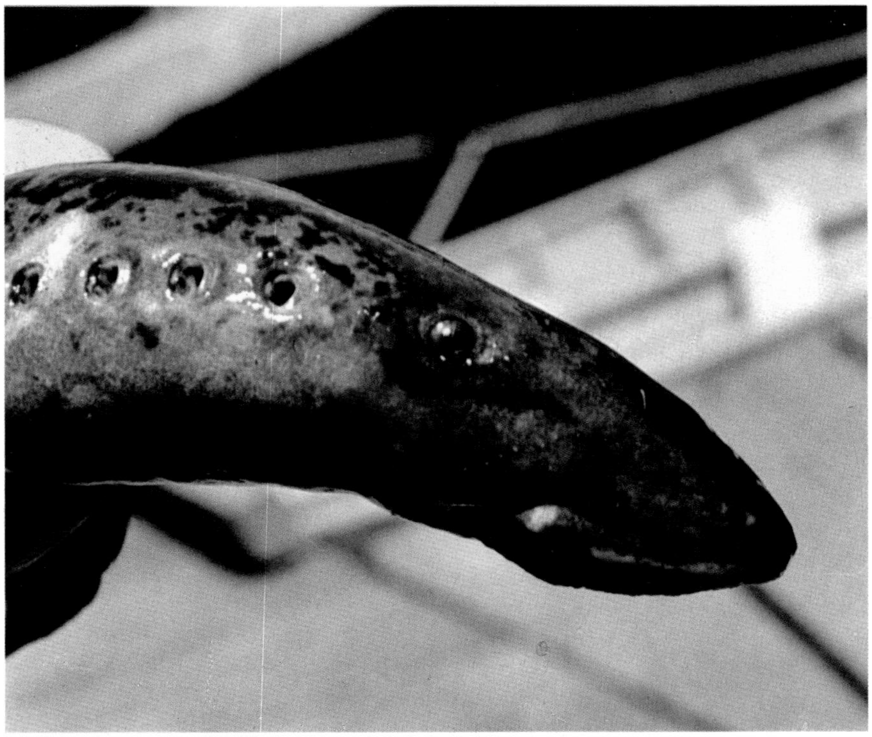

Sea Lamprey

SEA LAMPREY

There are about 15 species of lampreys north of Mexico. Because of its large size (3′) and abundance, the Sea Lamprey is the best known. A Sea Lamprey is an eel-like fish that feeds by attaching itself to a living host. Its suction-cup mouth is filled with over a hundred, pointed teeth which it uses to rasp a hole in its unfortunate victim. A lamprey stays attached, sucking blood from its host, until the exhausted fish, no longer able to catch food, dies. The Sea Lamprey occurs naturally on both the Atlantic and Pacific Coasts. Its invasion of the Great Lakes did not occur until after 1829, at which time the first canal to Lake Erie was being built. The depredations of the Sea Lamprey reached a peak in the 1950s with the elimination of the once-great Lake Trout commercial fishery. Vigorous control measures have been effective but have not eliminated this pest.

Sturgeon

STURGEONS

The White Sturgeon, up to 1200 pounds and 12 feet long, is the largest fish found in North American fresh water. The nine North American species are all greatly valued for their eggs (roe), which are sold as caviar, and for their flesh, which is smoked. Sturgeon enter rivers and streams, each one laying up to five million eggs. Growth is slow, and sexual maturity may not come for 20 years. Sturgeon abundance is now much reduced because dams and water pollution have kept them from their ancestral breeding areas. Unlike salmon, sturgeon cannot climb fish ladders. Despite their size, sturgeon are peaceful fish that feed on snails, clams, and other invertebrates found on river bottoms. They are aided in locating food by sensitive barbels hanging down from their snout, just ahead of the mouth. The Soviet Union supports the largest commercial sturgeon fishery.

BONEFISHES

Despite its small size, averaging less than five pounds, the bonefish **(Albula vulpes)** found in warm, shallow-marine, U.S. waters is one of America's most sought-after game fish. Its miraculous runs and lightning turns are a joy to fishermen. Bonefishing requires both patience and cunning, since the fish is very wary and flees at any disturbance. In Florida, bonefish are stalked by fishermen on shallow tidal flats where they feed on bottom crustaceans, worms, and shellfish. The size of the food consumed is restricted by the size of its small, unusually bony mouth. There are two species, one distributed in all warm, shallow seas, the other confined to the West Indies. Because bonefish cannot be captured in large quantities there is no commercial fishery. The flesh is tasty, but fine bones make its enjoyment hazardous. Bonefish scales were once used for decoration.

Bonefish

HERRINGS

Herring may be the world's most important and abundant food fish. The Family contains over 190 species, including the abundant Alewife, menhadens, and Pacific Sardine. In the past, the economy of some nations was founded on strong herring fisheries, and the importance of such fisheries continues today. U.S. fishermen land over 175 million pounds of Atlantic Herring yearly. Although the Atlantic Herring grows over a foot long and weighs a pound, most fishermen seek fingerlings to smoke, pickle, and salt as sardines. All herrings have energy-rich, oily flesh which makes them a valuable food. The demonstration of the herrings' role in the ocean ecosystem is one of the classic works of marine science. Herrings are important foods for seabirds, marine mammals, and many other fishes. One female lays up to 40,000 sticky eggs.

Herring

Atlantic Salmon

Shad

Pacific Salmon

SHADS

One of the more popular fishing activities in the eastern U.S. is the pursuit of the American Shad. Shad are members of the Herring Family and may grow to two feet and weigh more than ten pounds, although specimens average four pounds. Spring shad fishing has occurred since colonial times. Indeed, so abundant was it in colonial days that laws were passed forbidding the feeding of shad to servants more than two days a week. The demand for shad roe is increasing greatly with the severe decline of sturgeon. Each spring shad enter fresh-water streams from Florida to Maine, each to deposit up to 150,000 eggs. The fast-growing fry do not go down to the ocean until the autumnal fresh-water temperature dips below 60°F. During the spawning season, shad take little or no food and live on stored fat. Shad have been introduced to the Pacific Coast.

PACIFIC SALMONS

Salmon are universally respected as the finest combination of sport and food fish. There are five species on the Pacific Coast, which follow similar life histories. Eggs are deposited in fresh-water lakes and streams and, hatched young spend a few months to several years there, depending on the species, before migrating to the sea. After reaching maturity at sea, salmon return to their hatching area to spawn and die. The migration back upstream varies from a few miles, for the Pink Salmon, to 2000 miles, for the Sockeye. The migrations may include having to jump up waterfalls, swim up rapids, or to climb fish ladders at dams. Most species weigh between ten and 20 pounds, but the largest species, the Chinook, may be five feet and weigh over a hundred pounds. The Sockeye Salmon supports the largest commercial fishery in Alaska.

ATLANTIC SALMON

The Atlantic Salmon, Steelhead, and Pacific Steelhead, are actually not salmon but sea-going trout. The Atlantic Salmon is found in clear coastal water or deep lakes on both sides of the Atlantic Ocean. Spawning runs in the U.S. are restricted to Maine, but formerly occurred elsewhere in New England and New York. Unlike the true salmon species of the Pacific Coast, not all sea-going trout die after spawning. Many return to the sea and spawn two or three times before they die. Eggs are usually laid in spring, but fall runs occur. The young spend several years in fresh water before entering the sea to mature. Adults usually spend several years in the open ocean before returning to spawn. The harvesting of open-ocean Atlantic Salmon by other nations is a cause for concern to state and federal governments. Landlocked salmon are smaller.

Char

CHARS

The fact that Brook Trout and Lake Trout are not true trout but chars (lacking teeth on their palate) makes little difference in the enjoyment of these fine fish. A Brook Trout is usually under a foot long and weighs less than a pound. It lives in clear, cold streams and feeds on insect larvae, small fish, and crustaceans. Chars do not migrate to spawn, but lay their eggs in the lakes and pools where they live. The female makes a depression in the gravel bottom with her tail in which she lays her eggs. As soon as the male fertilizes them the female covers them with a layer of gravel for protection. The young live on the yolk in the eggs until they can swim free of the gravel and feed. A Lake Trout is large and weighs up to a hundred pounds. It once provided a large commercial fishery in the Great Lakes, but was destroyed by the Sea Lamprey.

SMELTS

There are more than a dozen different kinds of smelt, including the American Smelt of the Atlantic Coast and the Eulachon of the Pacific Coast. Superficially smelt resemble immature salmon. Most are under ten inches and weigh less than eight ounces. Like salmon, smelt come into coastal streams to spawn. Each winter small, sticky eggs are laid on the stream bottoms in large numbers. The young generally go to sea each spring very soon after hatching. At sea, crustaceans appear to be the major food source. In some areas, the American Smelt has become landlocked. Smelts have been introduced to man-made lakes in the hope they will eventually provide a valuable resource. The Eulachon is about a foot long and extremely oily. It is sometimes referred to as the Candlefish because Indians tied it dried to sticks for torches.

Smelt

Barracuda

Mackerel

MACKERELS

Mackerels are sleek, fast fish and a small relative of the tunas. The Atlantic Mackerel, weighing between four and seven pounds and about two feet long, is eaten by any predator, it is believed, that is fast enough to catch it. Mackerels are ready prey of tunas, sharks, and dolphins. In turn, they prey on herrings, alewives, and menhadens. The Atlantic Mackerel migrates from deep waters off Chesapeake Bay in April, north to Maine by July, and south again in September. A female lays up to a half million eggs while schooling each spring. The buoyant eggs develop and hatch near the surface. The erratic abundance of mackerel is possibly due to the effect of the broad, yearly range of current temperatures on eggs and larvae. The Pacific King Mackerel and Spanish Mackerel of the Gulf Coast are equal to the Atlantic Mackerel as sport and food fish.

BARRACUDAS

To a novice skin-diver the sight of an inquisitive barracuda provides an uneasy thrill. In shallow water a barracuda may treat a diver as an object of special attention and always seems to be lurking somewhere behind. Barracudas are well-equipped, effective predators. Their teeth are long and sharp, and their bodies torpedo-like and fast. Barracudas are solitary predators and have proved their danger to swimmers. Because they appear to feed by sight rather than smell, most barracuda attacks may be inadvertently triggered by a sudden movement or by a glint of a diver's watch. The Great Barracuda grows to ten feet and can weigh over a hundred pounds. It is best to be cautious and avoid it. There are five species in American waters, four in the Atlantic, and one in the Pacific. One makes a tasty meal and is a savage fighter on a light line.

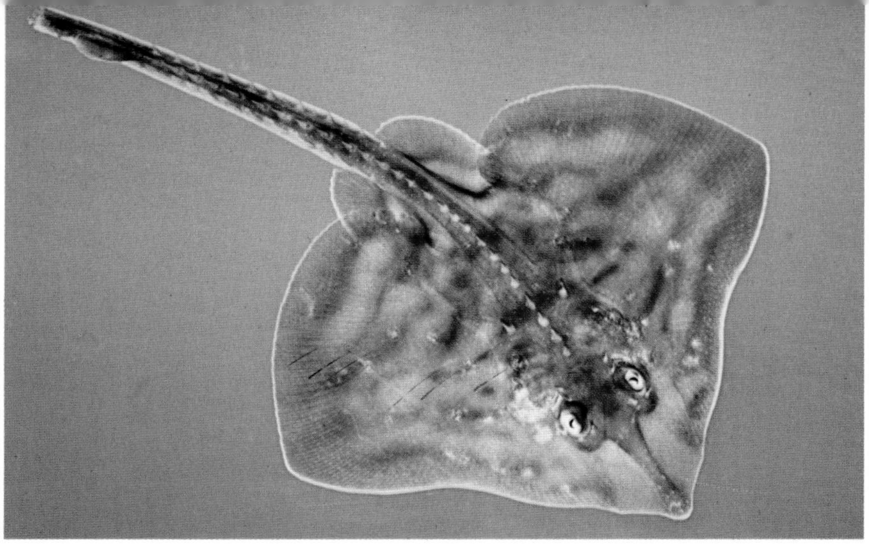

Skate

Tuna (immature)

Swordfish

TUNAS

A Bluefin Tuna is one of the mightiest fishes in the sea. It may attain a weight of 1800 pounds and a length of 14 feet. It feeds voraciously on related species of tuna, mackerel, flyingfish, and other surface feeders. The Bluefin is abundant in the North Atlantic and, like most tunas, is found in all warm and temperate waters. Its only natural enemies may be toothed whales, which hunt it in organized packs. Unlike most fish, tunas maintain a body temperature higher than that of the surrounding water. They evidently are in constant motion and would sink without active swimming. The most valuable fishery in the U.S. is the Yellowfin Tuna of the Pacific. More than 200 million pounds are caught annually. Schools are spotted by the leaping of dolphins which accompany them. The smallest and most desirable commercial tuna is the Albacore.

SKATES

A swimmer may often be surprised by an unexpected encounter with a skate in shallow marine water. Skates are easily recognized by their broad, flattened bodies and pectoral wings, which give them bat-like silhouettes. They are related to sharks and rays and, like them, have skeletons of cartilage rather than bone. Their teeth are small and numerous. Worms, clams, snails, and crustaceans are principal items in their diet; a few species also capture fish. Skates attach their black, rectangular egg-cases to rocks, shells, or seaweeds. Sometimes called mermaids' purses, they are often found abundantly scattered along a beach after a storm. Two to four months after being laid, each purse will hatch into a light-colored version of an adult skate. Most of the nearshore American species are two to four feet wide, but a Two-eyed Skate may be twice as large.

SWORDFISH

The spectacular Swordfish may grow to 15 feet and weigh more than a thousand pounds. The hard, flattened bill may comprise a third of the fish's length. Like most large predators, a Swordfish hunts singly or in pairs, using its sword to attack schooling fish. There is only one species of Swordfish, and it is found in warm, marine waters throughout the world from the surface to a depth of at least 2000 feet. Before the early 1960s Swordfish were harpooned like whales from small boats. This was exciting fishing, because a wounded swordfish can be a dangerous foe. Swordfishing today is conducted by setting out lines of baited hooks in warm waters where Swordfish abound. If it were not for the fact that Swordfish is less in demand because of its high mercury level, this efficient fishing method might have all but eliminated it.

BLUEFISH

Although a Bluefish averages under two feet long and weighs less than 12 pounds, it is a more voracious and bloodthirsty killer than a shark. While most fishes stop killing when they have eaten their fill, a Bluefish will continue to kill any fish in reach. Well-equipped for its role as a predator, a Bluefish is a fast swimmer, armed with numerous sharp teeth and strong jaws. Menhaden are the principal food of a Bluefish, but any defenseless schooling species is subject to attack. Large schools can be found in all warm seas. Moving northward with increasing temperatures, Bluefish schools arrive off the Northeast Coast in early summer and provide a real treat for fishermen. Often fishermen find, amid the lightning rushes and dives, that their lines have been cut by a Bluefish's sharp teeth. It is very tasty, and the demand always exceeds the supply.

SUNFISHES

Except for the Largemouth and Smallmouth Bass, also in the Sunfish Family, most of the 30 sunfish species weigh under a pound and are less than ten inches long. Although originally confined to North America, many species have been introduced around the world. Because the sunfishes are small and are eaten by many fish, including other sunfishes, they are most abundant in quiet fresh-water where protective vegetation abounds. Male sunfish build nests into which attracted females lay their eggs. After driving off the females, the males guard the eggs and young until they can survive on their own. Adult sunfish are usually recognized by their nearly-circular bodies, the high dorsal fin, and the ear lobe on the gill cover. These brightly-colored, attractive, small fish are excellent for home aquaria, because they are adaptable to many conditions.

CODS

The fishery for the Atlantic Cod is among the world's oldest and most productive. Each year hundreds of trawlers from many nations around the world, including Portugal, France, Japan, and the Soviet Union, converge on the Grand Banks off New England to fish for cod. All but one of the 150 species of cod are marine, 23 of which are found in U.S. waters. The largest and most important species is the Atlantic Cod, which reaches six feet in length and weighs over 200 pounds. Adults of most other species, however, average 15 to 25 pounds. Cod are cold-water fish found predominantly in the Northern Hemisphere where the bottom life on which they feed is abundant. The Atlantic Cod is extremely prolific, and one female may lay up to 10 million eggs in a season. The eggs float for three weeks, and the young stay in plankton over two months before going to sea.

Bluefish

Sunfish

Atlantic Cod

Flounder

Haddock

Halibut

HADDOCK

Most people eat Haddock without ever knowing it. With an annual catch over 150 million pounds, Haddock is a favorite for fish chowders, fish sticks, and fish and chips. The smoked version is finnan haddie. Unlike cod which is salted, Haddock is usually brought to market freshly frozen. The bones are few and large, and the taste is excellent. In appearance Haddock is much like cod, with soft fins and a prominent chin barbel; however, it is much smaller. The average weight is about four pounds. A Haddock feeds on invertebrates lying on the ocean floor and swims in huge schools. During the spring spawning season one female may lay up to two million buoyant eggs. The tightly-schooled Haddock are caught commercially by large bottom-trawlers. Although not a game fish, it is much sought after by saltwater charter boats.

SUMMER FLOUNDER

Flounders are a marvel of camouflage. Immersed in sand, they present only eyes to a spearfishing skin-diver. Off U.S. shores there are two major commercial species of flounder, the Summer and the Winter Flounder. Initially they appear to be quite similar, since each is broad and flat, with a dark surface and white belly. There are major differences, however. Summer Flounder is generally a warm-water fish and retreats to deep water to avoid freezing, inshore temperatures. The cold-loving Winter Flounder can be caught even in February. A Summer Flounder is large, up to 20 pounds, lies on its right side, and has eggs that float and mature at the surface. A Winter Flounder barely reaches five pounds, rests on its left side, and has eggs that sink and mature on the bottom. The combined catch of the two species is over 30 million pounds a year.

HALIBUTS

The comeback of the Pacific Halibut is one of the success stories of marine conservation. Through research and proper management the International Halibut Commission has restored this important species once decimated by over-fishing. Halibut are valuable fish that change from upright to flatfish in the larval stage by the migration of the left eye to the right side of the body. Halibut formerly could be caught on most areas of the continental shelf and were especially common on banks and in underwater depressions. With protection of the nearshore spawning areas where the young mature, halibut are now repopulating areas of former abundance. Female halibuts, up to 700 pounds in the Atlantic and 500 in the Pacific, may be ten times the size of males the same age. Halibut appear to be omnivorous feeders, eating cod, herring, crustaceans, and clams.

BLUE SHARK

After the Whitetip Shark, the Blue Shark may be the most common shark. It is a member of the Requiem Shark Family which includes the deadly Bull and Tiger Sharks. A Blue Shark may be considered dangerous by virtue of its grim relatives, but there are no confirmed fatalities. The Blue Shark is handsome, with long pectoral fins, and an indigo, dorsal color that grades into a snow-white underside. This slender shark may weigh only 70 pounds at seven feet and 150 pounds at nine feet. The largest record is 12 feet seven inches, and there are unconfirmed tales of some 15 to 20 feet. Blue Sharks are found in temperate waters and are especially abundant off the northeast U.S. coast during the summer. They were so abundant during the last century that they could quickly devour a dead whale: hence another common name, Whale Shark.

FLYINGFISHES

Although at first glance these fish certainly appear to be flying, anatomical examinations show that they do not have the necessary fin muscles. Slow-motion movies confirm that the tail acts like an outboard motor and provides the energy needed to get one airborne. The fins act as glider wings to keep them aloft for some 30 seconds at speeds up to 35 miles per hour. This ability to leave the water is an important escape mechanism since flyingfishes are a major part of the diet of such open-ocean predators as tuna, bonito, and dolphin. The California Flyingfish is the largest of the 14 North American species and grows to 18 inches. This species, similar to the 12-inch Atlantic Flyingfish, is one of the four-winged types having both pelvic and pectoral fins adapted for gliding. Flyingfish are edible, but most are caught for tuna and billfish bait.

Flyingfish

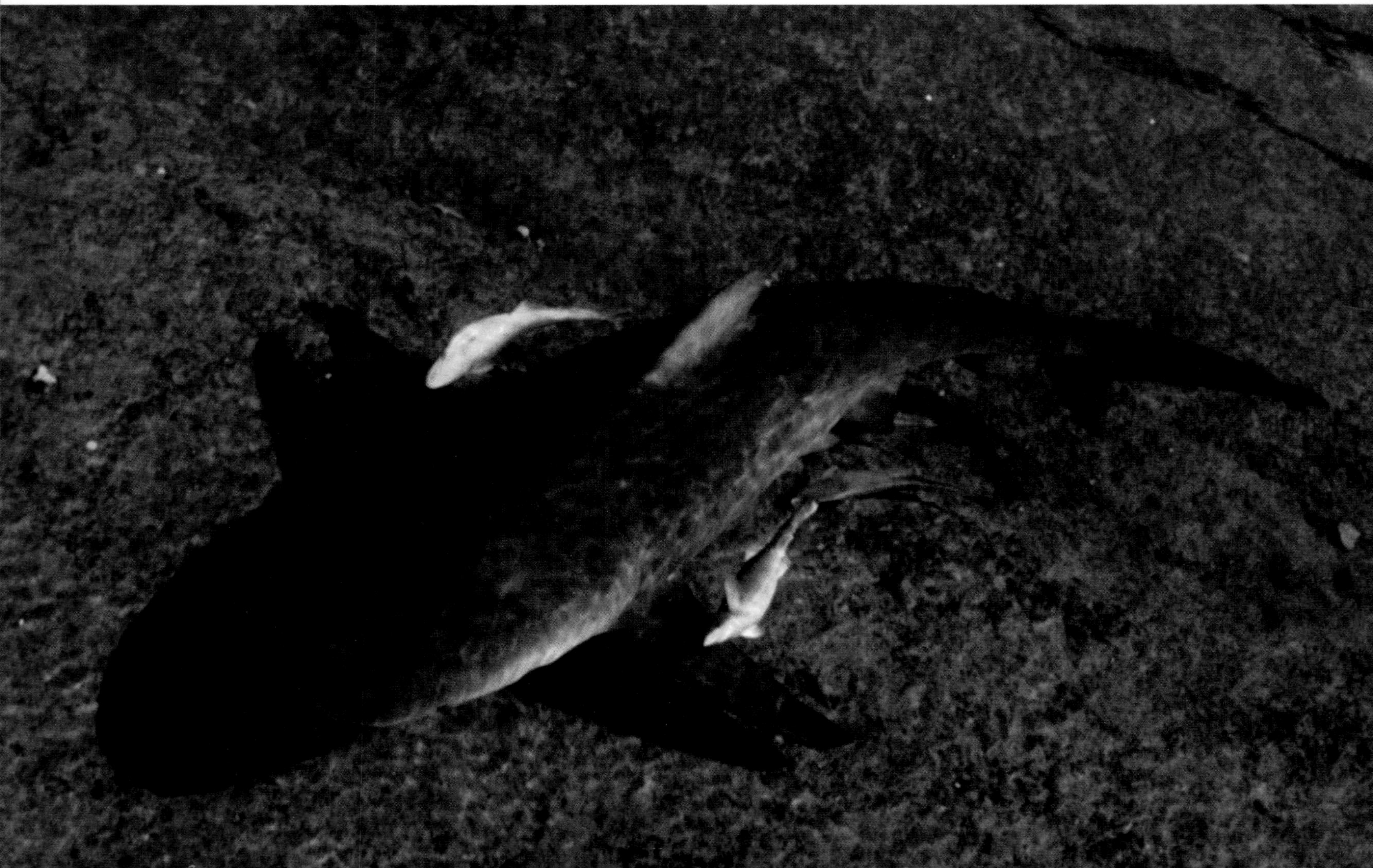

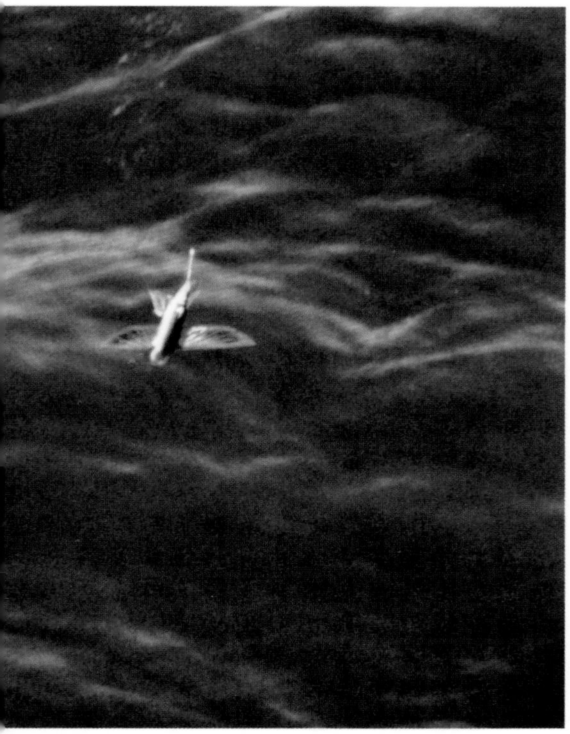

Hammerhead Shark

Spiny Dogfish

HAMMERHEAD SHARK
The Hammerhead is the most easily identified shark. It has eyes mounted on the tips of the rectangular extensions of its head and is a great threat to swimmers and spearfishermen. A 15-foot Hammerhead may weigh up to 1500 pounds and have a hammer three feet wide. This man-eater can be particularly dangerous when harpooned or attacked from a small boat, since it will not hesitate to charge and capsize the boat. It is usually found in warm, temperate waters. It occurs off southern Florida and migrates up the East Coast to New England each summer. Before vitamin A was synthesized, a large Hammerhead Shark was valued at several hundred dollars for its vitamin-A-filled liver. A Hammerhead seems to have a feeding preference for skates and poisonous stingrays. One captured specimen had 54 spines embedded in its throat.

SPINY DOGFISH
This three-and-a-half-foot, ten-pound shark is the most economically destructive fish. The dogfish attacks hooked and netted fish, rips nets, fouls lines, and steals bait. When it schools, almost all sport-fishing stops, and commercial fishing often becomes unprofitable. The names Spiny Dogfish, Spurdog, or Piked Dogfish refer to the poisonous spine at the base of each dorsal fin. The Spurdog is commonly sold as fish and chips in Britain, but in the U.S. it is considered unmarketable. Dogfish, in spite of its abundance, is not prolific. Females carry the young longer than any other vertebrate, up to two years, before giving birth to four to seven pups. Worldwide in temperate waters, a dogfish may travel thousands of miles for food. It attacks larger fish and eats herring, cod, haddock, and menhaden, as well as some invertebrates. It may swim in swarms of many thousands.

Blue Shark

American Eel

AMERICAN EEL

For many years the life history of the American Eel was one of the great mysteries of science. An American Eel spends four to seven years of its life in fresh-water rivers, lakes, and streams before migrating, apparently without feeding, 3000 miles to the Sargasso Sea in the central Atlantic. Here, in the saltiest part of the sea, at a depth of 1500 feet, the eel spawns and dies. One female may carry up to 10 million eggs. While each larva grows, it is carried for a year by the Gulf Stream to American shores where, as a small eel called an elver, it enters fresh water. A European Eel larva remains in the current and is carried for three years before entering fresh water. Eels are captured coming downstream when they are fattest before the long sea trip. The eel harvest in the U.S. has greatly declined, but in Europe it is a multimillion dollar fishery.

Whitefish

Northern Pike

WHITEFISHES

Whitefishes were a major fishery in the Great Lakes until destroyed by overfishing and the depredations of the Sea Lamprey. In 1890, over 12 million pounds were harvested, in 1920, 6 million and by 1950, the fishery was gone. Whitefish are generally dull in color and behavior. They have small, weak mouths with few or no teeth, tarnished silver scales, and they lack a fighting spirit. Preferring cold, deep water, they are usually caught in gill nets set down to 300 feet. Whitefish seldom take a baited hook. Truly adapted to lake living, they spawn up to 35,000 eggs each fall in the lake's gravel, in sandy, inshore areas. After five months the eggs hatch, and the young seek shelter in the shallows before moving to deep water. Whitefish feed on insect larvae, mollusks, and other invertebrates. Occasionally 15 pounds, most whitefish caught are between three and four pounds.

NORTHERN PIKE

If a Northern Pike attacked a person, it would seem like a barracuda. The voracious, solitary Northern Pike can eat up to 20 percent of its weight each day and will gladly accept fish, frogs, fowl, or small mammals for food. This deadly hunter lies in wait in weedy shallows and darts out to grab any passing fare. The beautiful, cylindrical, gray and green pike is a worthy opponent for any angler. From the first violent lunge to the removal of the hook, the angler runs the risk of losing the fish, his gear, or even a finger! Its sharp, powerful teeth can cut through everything but a steel leader. The flesh is delicious and led Isaac Walton to declare that it should be reserved only for anglers and honest men. Pike is found in the cold waters of northern Europe, Asia, and America. It may weigh over 50 pounds. Spawning occurs very early in the spring.

LARGEMOUTH BASS

Most fishermen across America have their favorite fishing hole for bass. Found in every state but Alaska, the Largemouth may reach 20 pounds or more and provides excellent sport fishing. Artificial impoundments such as dikes and dams have hurt most fresh-water fish but have helped the spread of this flat-water game fish. A Largemouth Bass is an overgrown sunfish and, like its smaller cousin, it builds a nest and guards both eggs and young. This does not last forever. Once the young leave the father's protection, their next encounter might result in his eating them. Large, solitary, adult bass will eat most aquatic organisms, including fish, frogs, insects, crustaceans, or young ducklings. The small, less widely distributed Smallmouth Bass is reputed to be more wary than the Largemouth and, when hooked, is a stronger fighter.

Largemouth Bass

YELLOW PERCH

This handsome gold- and black-banded resident of lakes and ponds will readily accept a baited hook, lure, or fly the year around. The combination of great flavor and easy capture makes the Yellow Perch one of the most popular Great Lakes' fish, with an annual catch over 5 million pounds. Omnivorous feeding habits, which include small fish, insects, bottom invertebrates, and fish eggs, have enabled it to be widely transplanted to the West from its original range around the Great Lakes. Each spring the eggs are laid in weedy shallows in long strings. As they absorb water, the egg strings, which may be seven feet long, swell to become wide ribbons, containing over 40,000 eggs and weighing several times more than the parent. After two weeks the eggs hatch, and the fry school in protected shallow water. An average adult is under a pound.

Yellow Perch

Tarpon

Carp

Minnow

TARPON
Acclaimed the most exciting game fish in America, the Tarpon has rightly earned the name Silver King. In spite of its generally inferior taste, Tarpon is the most sought-after game fish on the Atlantic Coast. It is big, up to eight feet and 300 pounds, and filled with fury. The initial reaction of a hooked Tarpon is to leap clear of the water and shake off the hook. It succeeds three out of four times. If the hook holds, a fisherman is in for a long, hard fight filled with spectacular leaps and sudden lunges. Sharks appear to be its main predator and in some areas it is almost impossible to boat a whole Tarpon. It is prolific as it is spectacular. A 200-pound female may lay 15 million eggs a year. Although its early life-history has been followed in laboratories, the place and timing of Tarpon spawning is a mystery. Its center of abundance is the Gulf of Mexico.

CARP
The history of the introduction of Carp from Asia to the U.S. is a frightening lesson in ecological disturbance. Carp, in spite of its large size, up to 70 pounds, is actually a prolific minnow. It is extremely adaptable and can live in crowded and polluted conditions intolerable to most native fish. Carp was introduced by the U.S. Government in 1877 and hailed as the world's greatest food fish. Thanks to this publicity Carp soon spread across the nation. Before long it was found that Carp, by feeding on vegetation, severely disrupted aquatic habitats and ate or smothered the eggs and fry of many game fish. In some areas the game fish were eliminated. We now know that any introduced species can cause severe ecological disruptions and should be prohibited. Carp is now considered a trash fish, and millions of dollars have been spent to control it.

MINNOWS
Minnows comprise a large and distinct Family of over 1500 species. The U.S. has over 200 species of minnows, most of them less than six inches. The well-known group called shiners is found in most fresh-water streams and ponds. There are over a hundred American species of shiners, some of which are raised commercially as bait. Dace, another group, are the beautiful, small, iridescent minnows found in eastern streams. Some species are restricted in distribution and may be eliminated with the destruction of free-flowing streams by pollution and dams. The recently introduced European Bitterling is a most distinctive minnow. A female lays its eggs in the mantle cavities of fresh-water clams where they incubate and hatch. The abundant and diverse clam fauna could assist the rapid distribution of this minnow.

Catfish

CATFISHES

The familiar Brown Bullhead is typical of most North American catfishes. Scaleless skin, four pairs of mouth barbs, and sharp spines in front of the dorsal fins are distinctive characteristics. A Brown Bullhead is small, may reach only ten inches, and weighs less than a pound. Its close relative the Blue Catfish may be five feet long and weigh over a hundred pounds. Many catfishes build nests into which the eggs are deposited and guarded by one or both parents until they hatch and are able to fend for themselves. Catfishes are well-adapted to muddy waters and feed on bottom organisms at night. Farming catfish has recently become big business. They have firm, sweet flesh and are grown extensively in southern farm ponds. The largest natural fishery is in the Great Lakes and Mississippi Valley. Over 40 million pounds are harvested annually.

Common Sucker

SUCKERS

Suckers are the garbage collectors of American lakes and streams, sucking up invertebrates, insects, eggs, and aquatic vegetation. Of the more than a hundred described species, 65 are distributed throughout the U.S. mainland. The protruding, underslung, fleshy mouth distinguishes them from the similar Minnow Family. They are usually indifferent to baited hooks, but the White Sucker of the eastern states and Buffalo Sucker of the Mississippi are readily caught. The Humpback Sucker of the Colorado and Gila River basins is easily distinguished by the large hump behind the head. This hump is thought to create resistance in fast water and force the fish to the bottom where it feeds. In spring mature suckers migrate upstream, where each female lays up to 100,000 sticky eggs. Most suckers are small and average less than two pounds.

Striped Bass

STRIPED BASS

The lure of Striped Bass is a well-known affliction of many surf fishermen. It is big, strong, delicious, and abundant. Each spring it ascends rivers in protected bays to lay 2 to 3 million eggs. The eggs develop and hatch as they float downstream. From these nursery grounds fish scatter up and down the coastline in search of food. Although 125-pound fish have been caught by commercial methods, most taken by rod and reel average about 20 pounds; 50 pounders, however, are not uncommon. Until 1879, when it was released in San Francisco Bay, this great sport fish was confined to the East Coast. Today it is found abundantly from Los Angeles to the Columbia River. While the Striped Bass is reserved as a sport fish on the West Coast, it is still taken commercially on the East Coast. Surf-casting is best between Long Island and Cape Cod.

Killifish

KILLIFISHES

The abundant and adaptable killifishes, also called topminnows, are found in both fresh and salt water, from hot desert-pools to near-freezing Arctic lakes. There are more than 300 species in the Family, with 40 in the U.S. Most are under three inches and play an important role in converting minute crustaceans to a food source for many valuable species. These egg-laying fish, excellent for home aquaria, are extremely adaptable. Unfortunately this very trait has led to the extinction of five of the 13 forms of the Desert Pupfish because isolated populations are dependent on particular waterholes. They can live in water over 110°F., six times more saline than sea water, in mud puddles and, if need be, they can leave the water to cross to a nearby pool. It would indeed be tragic if these amazing fish were lost forever. They belong to the genus **Fundulus.**

Dolphin

Lanternfish

LANTERNFISHES

The name lanternfish is an apt description for this group of small, deep-water fish. The distribution of numerous, small, round photophores along the head and sides enables experts to identify the 150 described species. The photophores are filled with bacteria whose light-producing activity is controlled by the fish themselves. So powerful are these light-making organisms that a single two-inch fish can light a small room. Each night lanternfish swim up from a depth of several thousand feet to the surface for food. One presumed function of the photophores is to attract the minute crustaceans, called copepods, on which lanternfish feed. Lanternfish are attracted by bright ships' lights and may be easily netted. On bright moonlit nights, however, lanternfish stay in dark, protective depths where they cannot be seen by their numerous predators.

DOLPHIN

A Dolphin is probably the fastest fish in the sea. Its lightning dashes in the water exceed 40 miles per hour and enable it to outrun its prey, including unfortunate flyingfish who may reach 35 miles per hour in futile flights for safety. A Dolphin **(Coryphaena hippurus)**, which is a fish and not to be confused with the marine mammal, is readily distinguished by its blunt head, deeply-forked tail, body-length dorsal fin, and its magnificent color. When caught, a Dolphin flashes one glorious color after another before it dies. Large, often solitary fish, a Dolphin may reach 80 pounds and six feet in length before its short three-year life span is ended. A female, half the size of a male, sheds its eggs in open water where both sexes spend their lives. The Dolphin does not appear to be abundant in American waters and is often sought for fine flavor and sport.

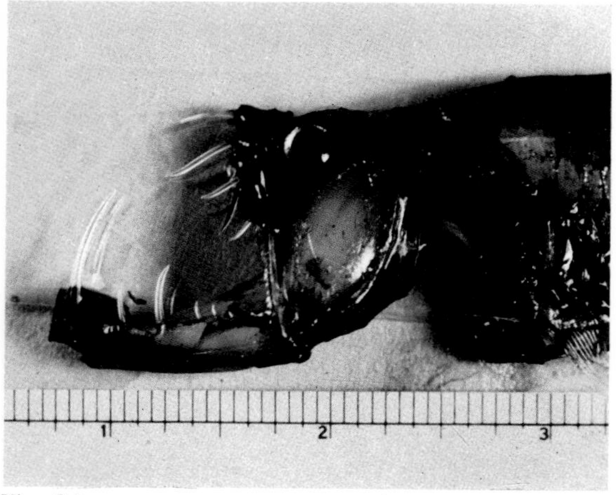

Viperfish

VIPERFISHES

Few more efficient or fearsome-looking predators exist in the sea. Armed with huge mouths filled with sharp fangs and possessing a gaping, distendable stomach, viperfish can and do swallow fish bigger than themselves. Occasionally these greedy fish are trapped by their own gluttony. Unable to free their long fangs, they die with an oversize victim in their mouth. Most viperfishes are about six inches long and live at 500 to 2000 foot depths. Larger specimens, probably able to avoid capture by slow-moving nets, exist. A six-foot viperfish was once seen from a bathysphere. Viperfishes migrate each night with their favorite prey, the lanternfishes. Like them, viperfish have photophores, but in addition, most have a long barbel hanging from the lower jaw. The luminescent barbel may be used to lure unwary fish within reach.

GRUNION

Every summer on the beaches of southern California a remarkable phenomenon occurs—the spawning of the Grunion. At the peak of the tide on the three nights following the highest tide of the lunar month, Grunion come ashore. A female will burrow backward into the sand to lay the eggs which are immediately fertilized by a male. On the next wave both parents return to the sea. When the eggs are freed from the sand by subsequent high tides, either in two weeks or a month, they hatch, and the young return to the sea. Spawning at night protects the seven-inch Grunion and its eggs from predation by gulls and terns. By depositing eggs in sand, the Grunion insures that they will develop in a warm, moist environment free from wave action and hungry fish. Grunion is an excellent food fish and is much sought after during spawning periods.

Grunion

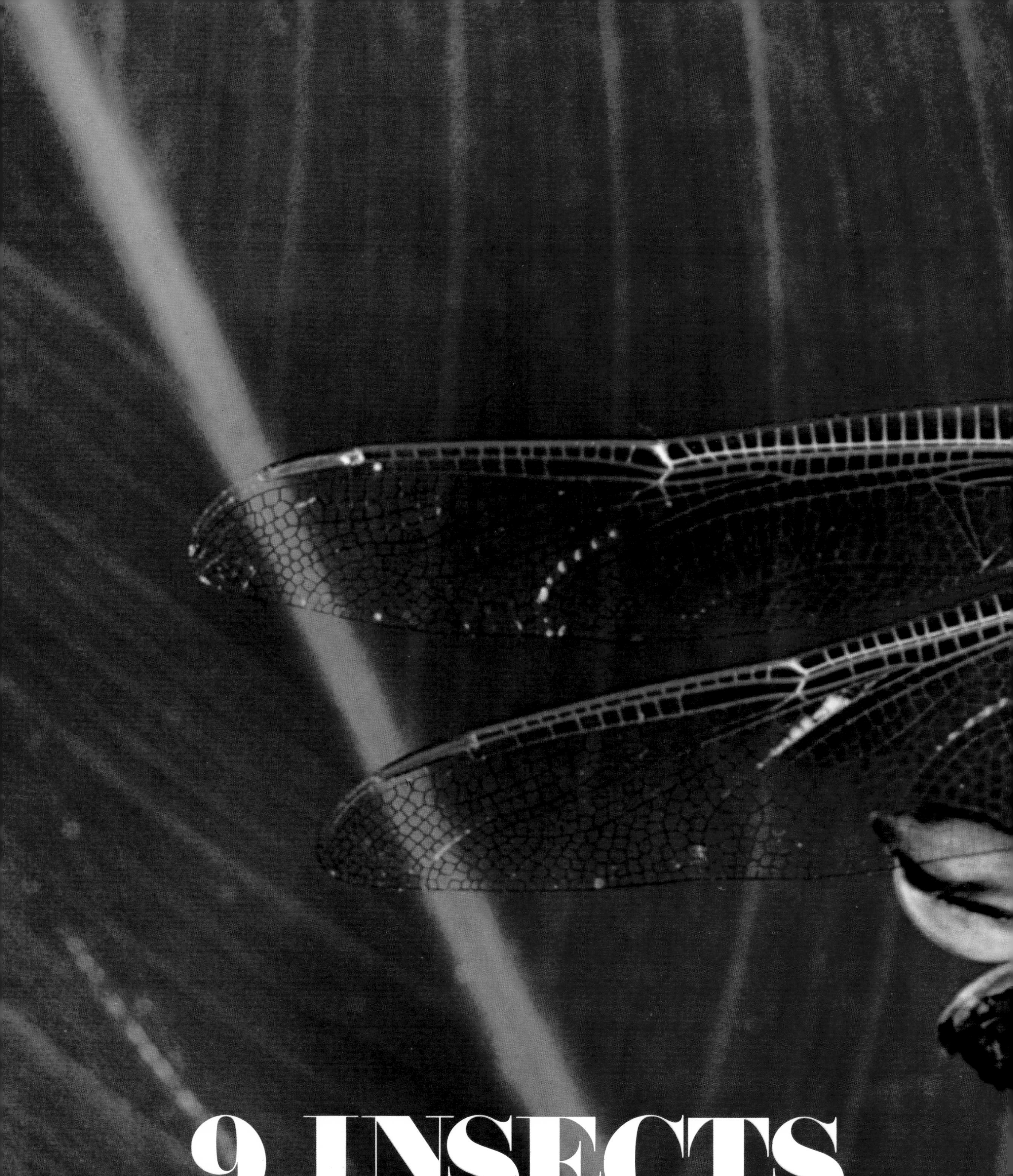

9. INSECTS

INSECTS

More than half the living things on Earth are insects. Their species outnumber all other animals and plants combined. They occur almost everywhere (except perhaps in the ocean), and they play a significant role in the natural world. Most of them are small, and some are very small. North American species vary in length from one hundredth inch to six inches, but most are less than a quarter inch in length. A few acres may contain more kinds of insects than there are birds in the United States, their numbers running as high as several million insects per acre. On the one hand, insects may damage or kill cultivated plants, they may damage or contaminate stored foods and other materials, and they may attack people and animals by biting, stinging, or transmitting disease. On the other hand, insects do a great deal of good. Some are essential agents in the pollination of plants, including many orchard trees, vegetables, and field crops. The pollinating services of insects in the United States alone have been valued at $4.5 billion annually. Some provide such products of commercial value as honey, beeswax, silk, and shellac. Many are important items in the food of birds, fishes, and other animals. Many act as predators or parasites of other insects and help keep undesirable species under control. Many are valuable scavengers. And many are key species in studies of heredity, stream pollution, and other biological problems.

There are fortunately many ways of controlling insects. Some involve the use of poisons. Some involve a modification of the habitat in such a way that the insects cannot complete their life cycle. Others involve agents that result in sterility or interfere with normal growth. And still others involve the use of the insects' natural enemies, such as diseases, parasites, and predators. Poisons are, unfortunately, often hazardous, because they may kill or injure animals or plants. Habitat modification may also affect other animals besides the insects to be controlled. Entomologists are continually trying to find better ways of controlling insects that are effective but have a minimum adverse effect on desirable species.

Insects typically have three pairs of legs, a pair of antennae, and often one or two pairs of wings. Notice that insects are the only invertebrates with wings. The segmented body is made up of three more or less distinct regions: the head, thorax, and abdomen. The head bears the eyes, antennae, and mouth parts. The thorax bears the legs and wings. The abdomen generally bears no appendages except at its posterior end. The antennae and legs, and sometimes also the appendages at the end of the abdomen, are segmented.

The mouth-parts of insects consist of several structures and are arranged somewhat differently in different species. How an insect feeds—and hence the sort of damage it may do—depends on the sort of mouth-parts it has. Many insects chew, which they do by moving their jaws sideways. A chewing insect may eat holes in a leaf, eat pieces out of the edge, or consume the entire leaf. Some insects have mouth parts modified into a proboscis, through which they suck food (animal or plant juices) in liquid form. A sucking insect removes sap when it feeds on a leaf, which results in the spotting or yellowing of the leaf. With continued feeding, the leaf may turn brown, curl up, and fall off. When a chewing insect bites a person (which is seldom), the effect is a pinch. Few insects can bite hard enough to draw blood. When a sucking insect bites a person it pierces the skin with stylet-like structures and injects saliva. The effect, due mostly to the injected saliva, is sometimes a painful inflammation.

The abdomen of an adult insect bears no legs, but may have appendages at its posterior end. These may vary considerably in different insects. Females of some insects have an ovipositor—a structure used for inserting eggs into the soil, or plant or animal tissues. In bees, wasps, and some ants, the ovipositor is modified into a stinger located at the rear of the abdomen. Hence, only females can sting.

Most insects hatch from eggs, but a few are born alive. Insect eggs vary greatly in size, shape, and color, and may be laid singly or in characteristic masses. They are usually laid where the hatched young can find food and other conditions suitable for development. Most insect eggs have to be fertilized before they will hatch, but some hatch without being fertilized. Among bees and wasps, this difference determines sex: fertilized eggs become females, unfertilized eggs become males.

Preceding pages: Dragonfly

The growth of an insect is somewhat different from that of most animals. It is accompanied by a series of molts, during which the body wall is shed and renewed. The number of molts varies in different insects, but is relatively constant for a given insect. Once the adult stage is reached molting ceases.

The stages between molts (called instars) may be either similar or very different, the changes from stage to stage being termed metamorphosis. There are two principal types of metamorphosis in insects, simple and complete. In insects with simple metamorphosis successive stages are very similar. They usually live in the same habitat, and if the adult has wings the wings are present in the early stages as bud-like outgrowths on the thorax which expand to their full size after the last molt. The young of insects with simple metamorphosis are called nymphs.

In insects with complete metamorphosis the early stages are more or less worm-like and are called larvae. They often live in a different habitat from the adult, and the wings (if present in the adult) develop internally. After the molt of the last larval stage an insect changes to a pupa, which is relatively inactive, does not feed, and often looks like a mummified adult. A pupa is sometimes enclosed in a silken cocoon formed by the larva before it pupates. The stage following the pupa is the adult.

The larvae and adults of insects with complete metamorphosis are usually so different that one unfamiliar with their life history would not believe them to be the same insect. They usually live in quite different habitats and feed on different foods. The transformations from larva to adult, which occurs in thousands of insect species every year, are among the most remarkable phenomena in nature. People familiar with these changes may think of them as commonplace—which indeed they are—but if they occurred in a vertebrate animal, it would be like a snake developing into an eagle after an inactive in-between stage during which it hung from a branch, like a ham in a meat shop.

Insects can usually be distinguished from other animals by the presence of one or two pairs of wings (but some insects lack wings), three pairs of legs, and a pair of antennae. The animals most similar to the insects are the myriapods (centipedes and millipedes), arachnids (spiders, mites, ticks, scorpions, daddy long-legs, and others), crustaceans (crayfish, crabs, lobsters, shrimp, sowbugs, and others), and annelid worms (earthworms, leeches, and many marine worms). All of these lack wings. The myriapods differ from insects in having more legs (usually 15 or more pairs); arachnids have four pairs of legs and lack antennae; crustaceans have a variable number of legs (nearly always more than three pairs) and two pairs of antennae (one of which may be small); and annelid worms either lack leg-like appendages, or have them unsegmented.

Since there are so many different kinds of insects (nearly 90,000 species north of Mexico, and several hundred thousand world species), people interested in these animals usually are content to identify most of them only by the major group to which they belong and learn to recognize species in only one or a few groups. Users of this book should become familiar with the general scheme of animal classification, wherein the Animal Kingdom is divided into a number of Phyla, each Phylum into Classes, each Class into Orders, and each Order into Families, Genera, and species. Each group in this scheme has certain characteristics in common, and each has a name. Insecta is the name of one Class of animals, which is divided into more than two dozen Orders. Our concern here will be with the more common Orders.

Insect Orders are based on various structural characters—chiefly of the wings, legs, antennae, and general body form—and on their type of metamorphosis. The wings may vary in number (none, one, or two pairs), size and shape, texture (membranous or thickened), venation (the thickened lines in the wing), and how they are held at rest. Indeed wing venation is used as a key to the identification of many flies and their relatives. The legs, antennae, and body vary in size and shape. The tarsi of the legs—the terminal part or "foot"—and the antennae vary in the number of segments they contain. The information on the following pages should enable readers to recognize most representatives of the more common insect Orders.

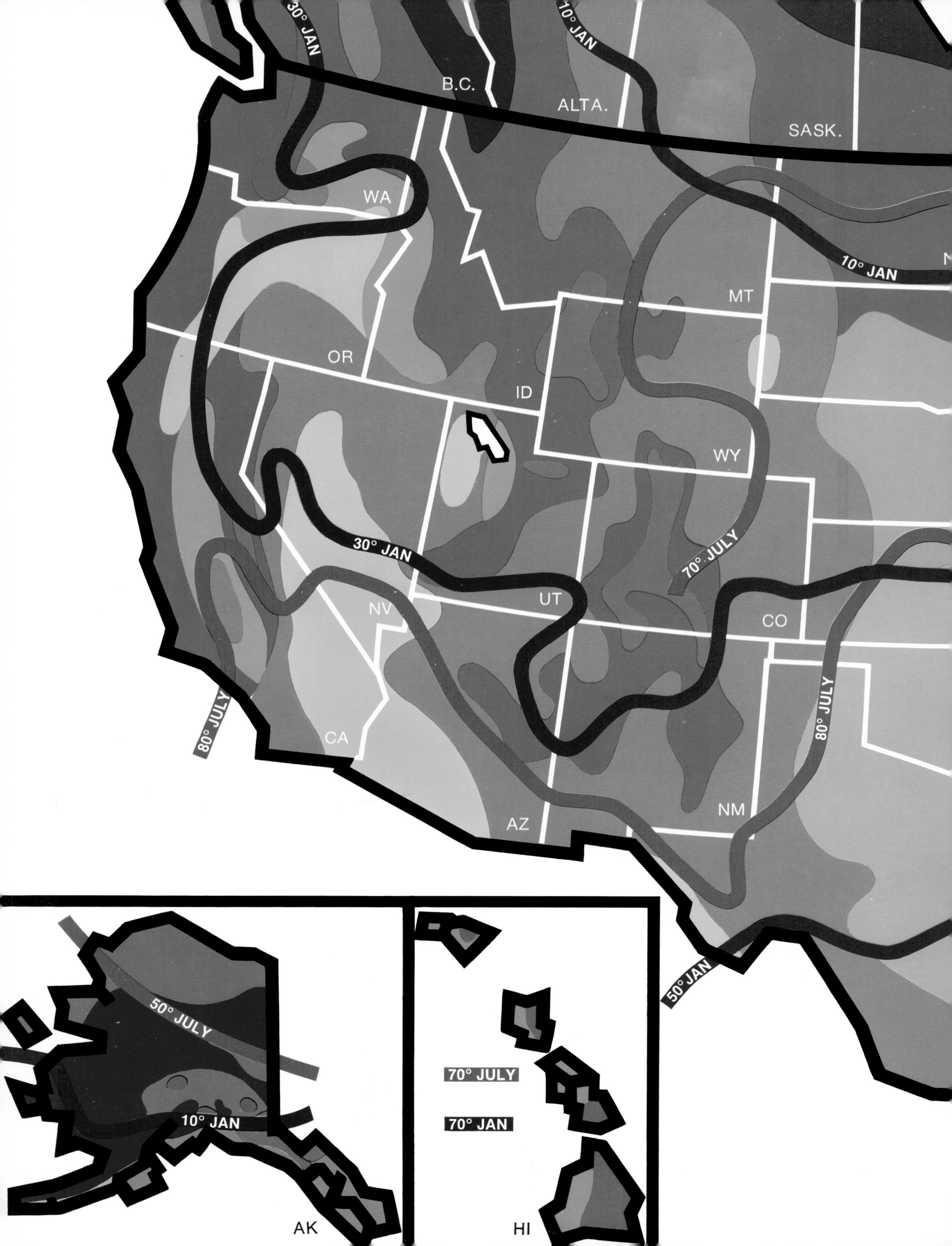
30° JAN
10° JAN
B.C.
ALTA.
SASK.
WA
10° JAN
MT
OR
ID
WY
30° JAN
70° JULY
NV
UT
CO
80° JULY
CA
AZ
NM
80° JULY
50° JAN
50° JULY
10° JAN
AK
70° JULY
70° JAN
HI

CLIMATE & TEMPERATURE

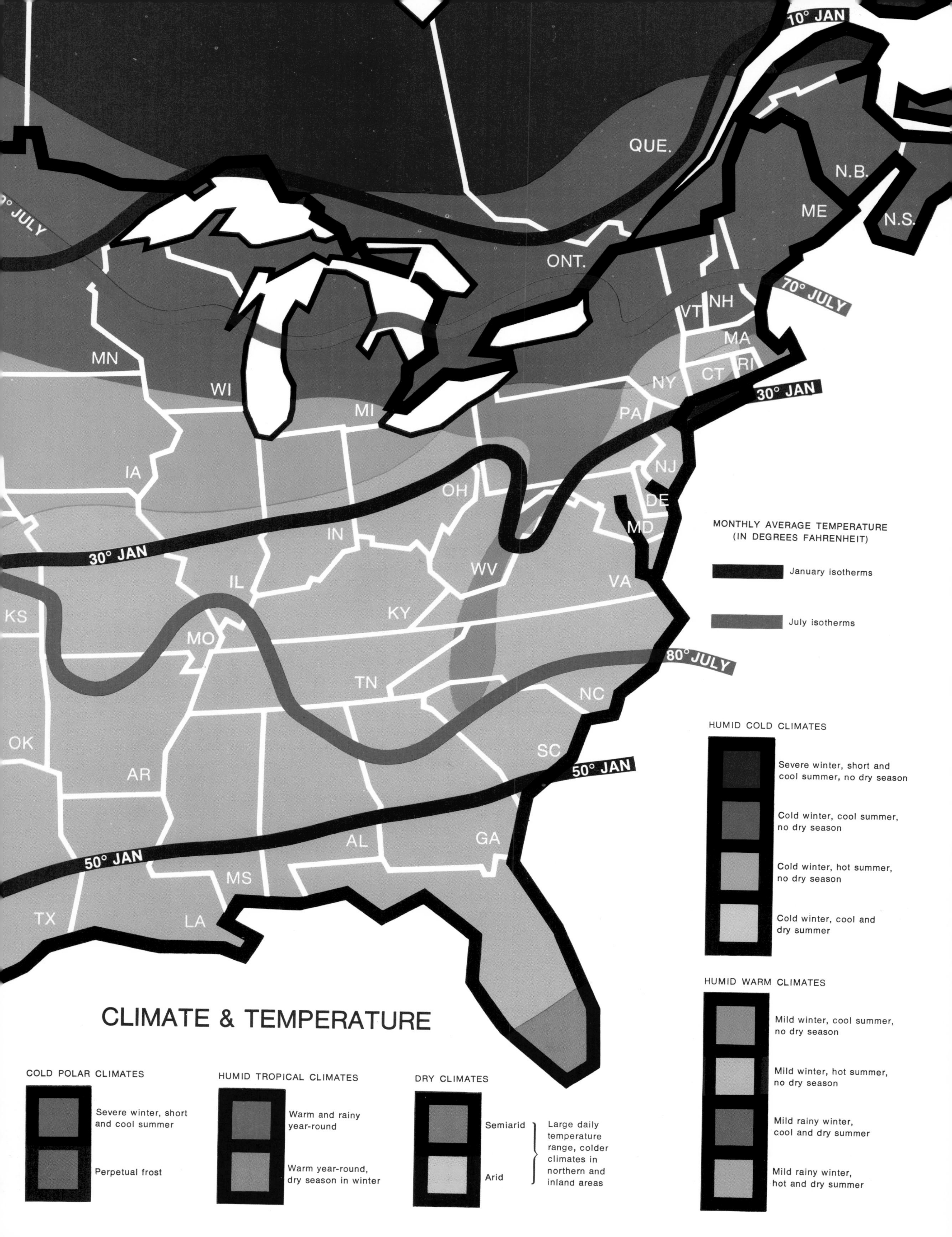

Range Maps of Insects

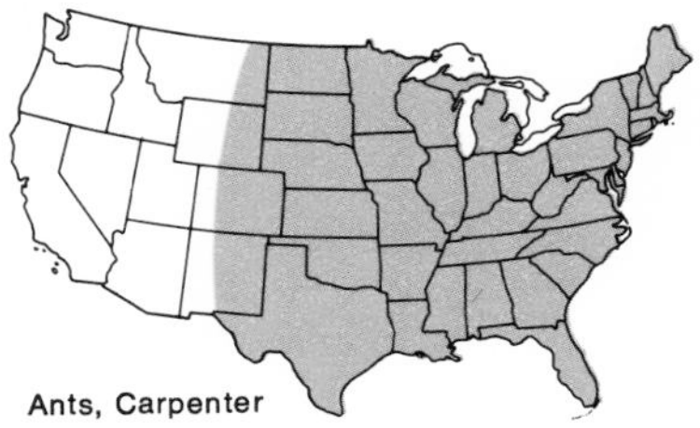
Ants, Carpenter

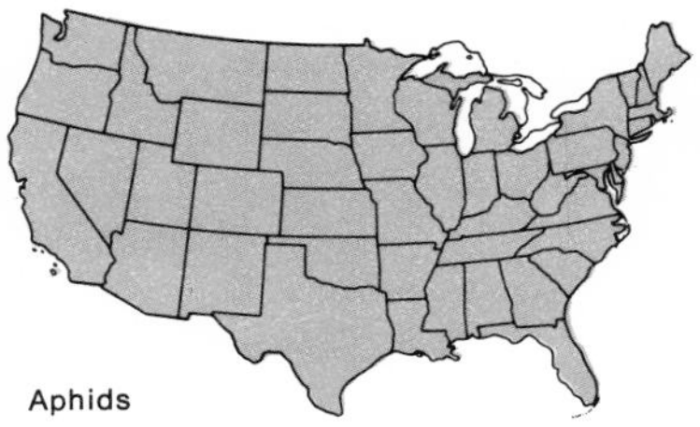
Aphids

Bees, Bumble

Bee, Honey

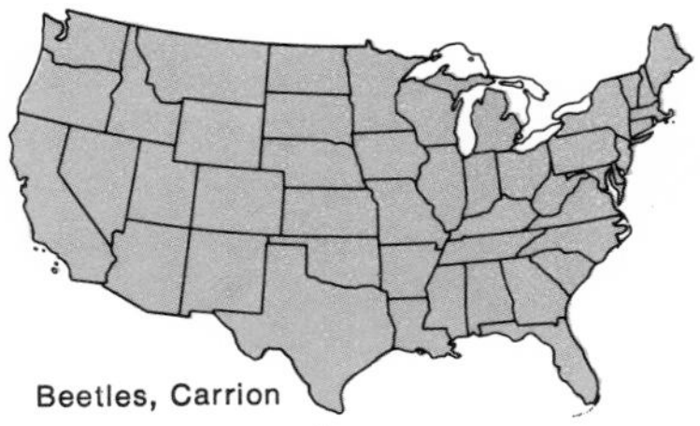
Beetles, Carrion

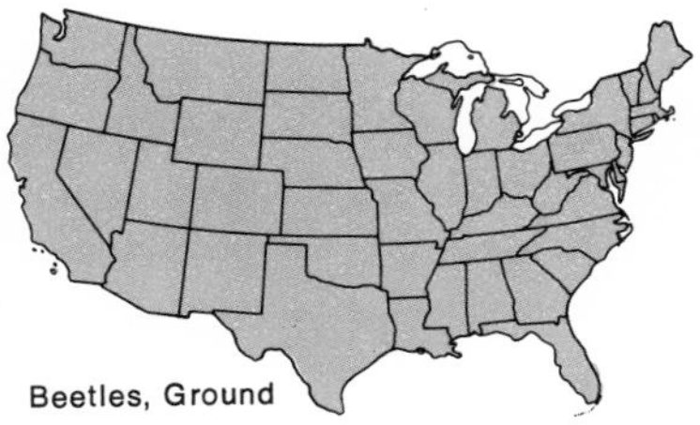
Beetles, Ground

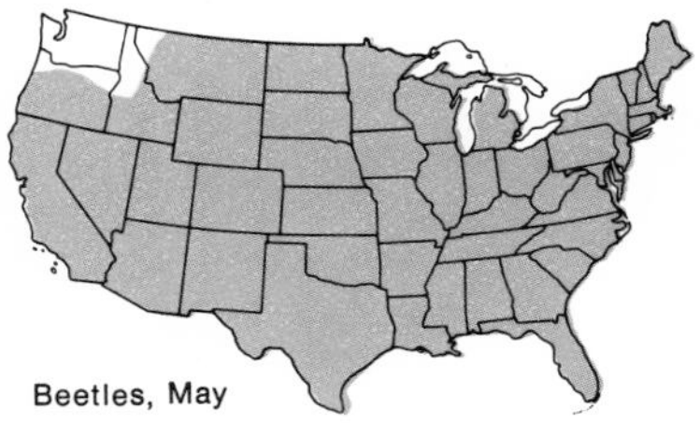
Beetles, May

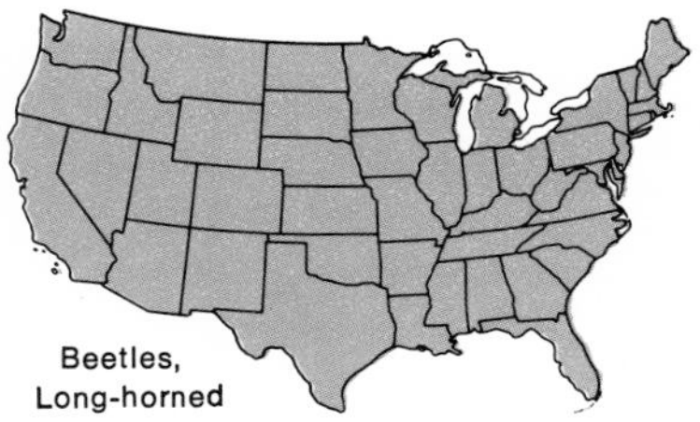
Beetles,
Long-horned

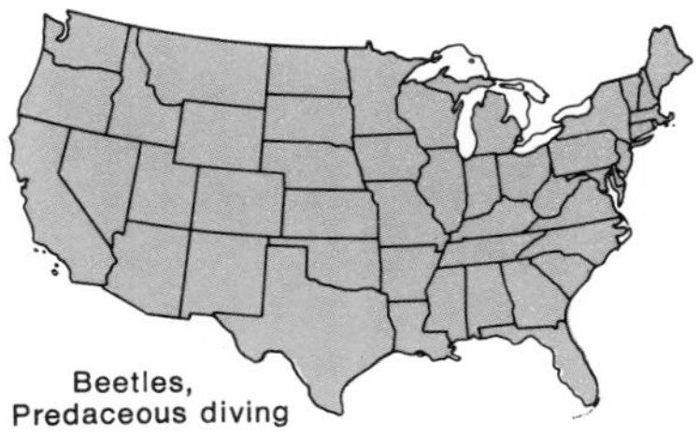
Beetles,
Predaceous diving

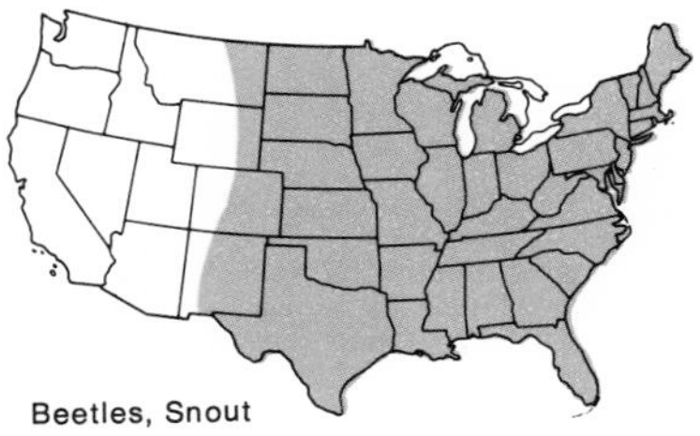
Beetles, Snout

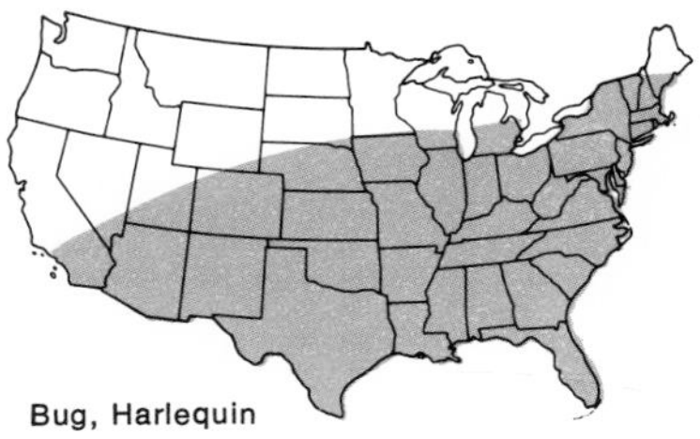
Bug, Harlequin

Bugs, Assassin

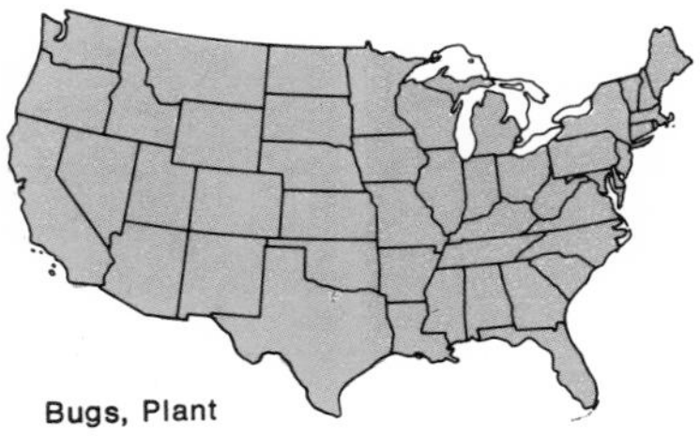
Bugs, Plant

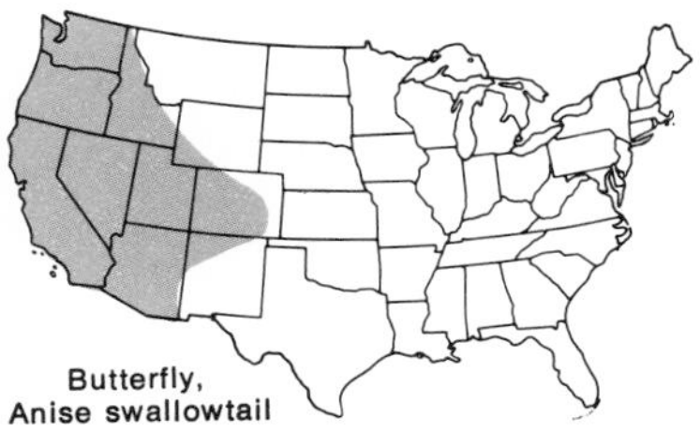
Butterfly,
Anise swallowtail

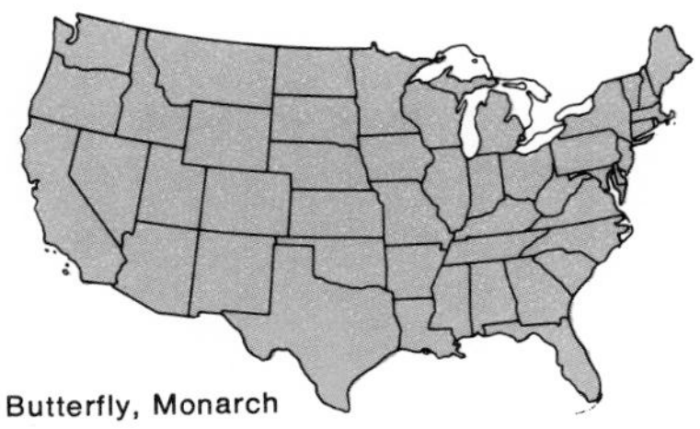
Butterfly, Monarch

Butterfly,
Spicebush swallowtail

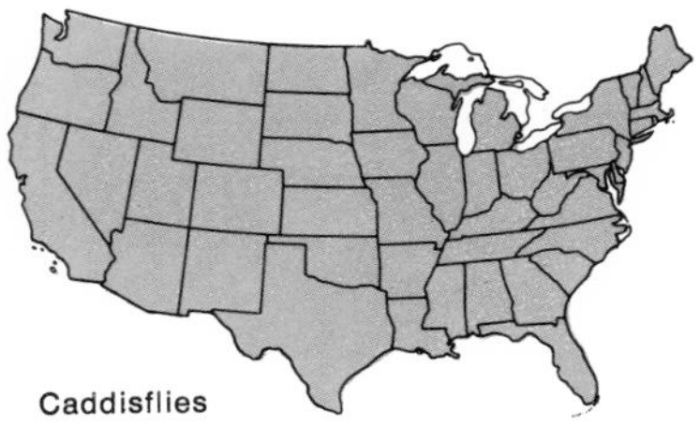
Caddisflies

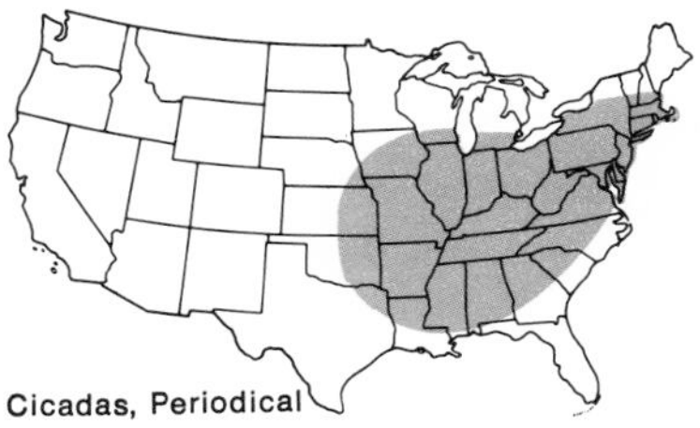
Cicadas, Periodical

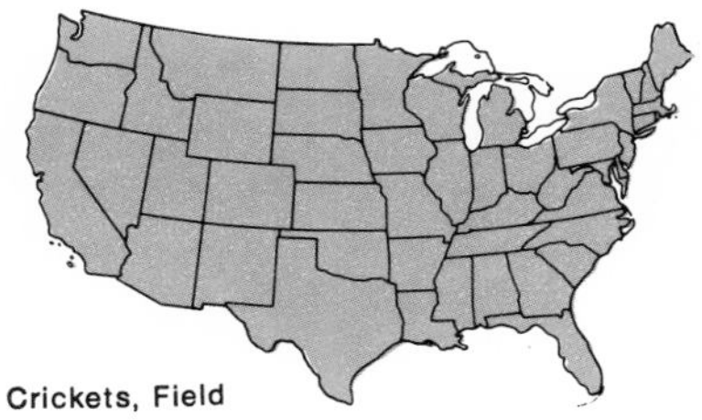
Crickets, Field

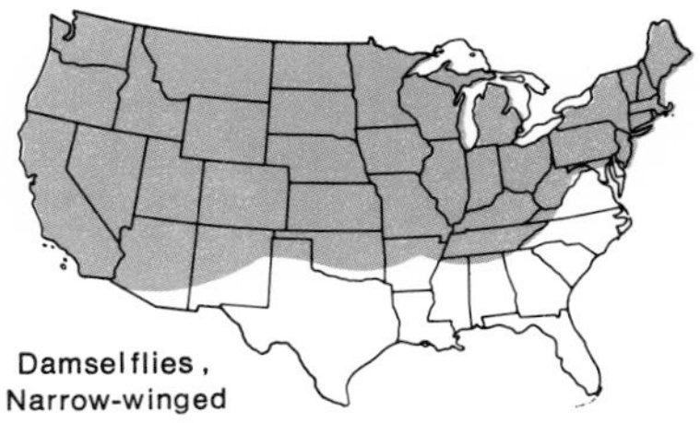
Damselflies,
Narrow-winged

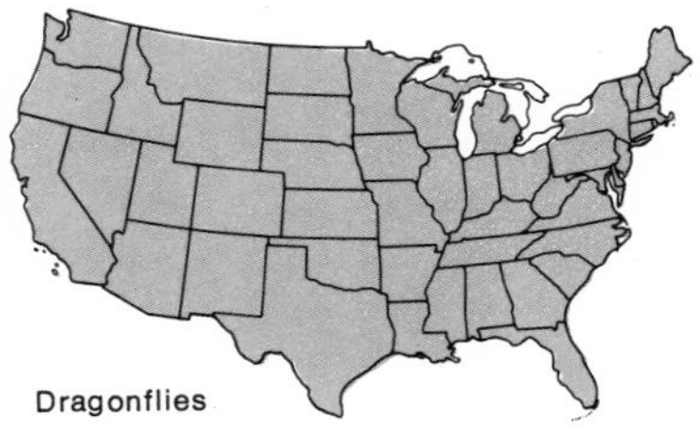
Dragonflies

Earwig, European

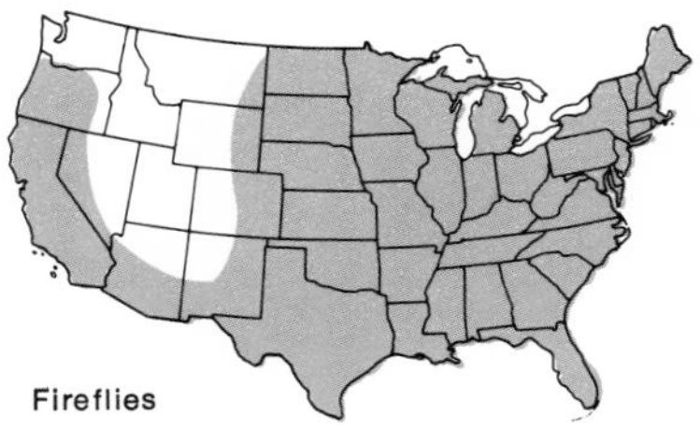
Fireflies

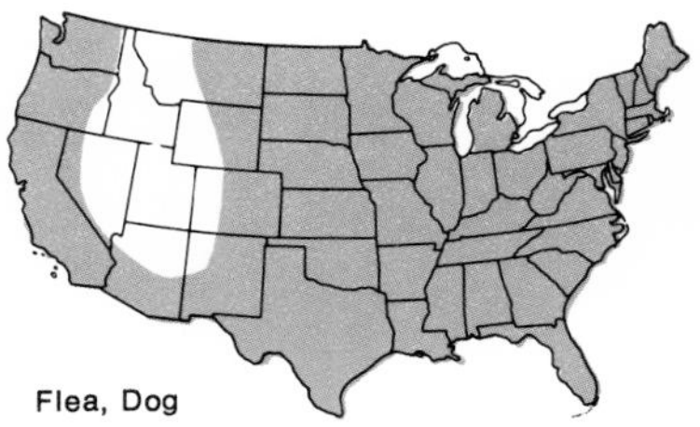
Flea, Dog

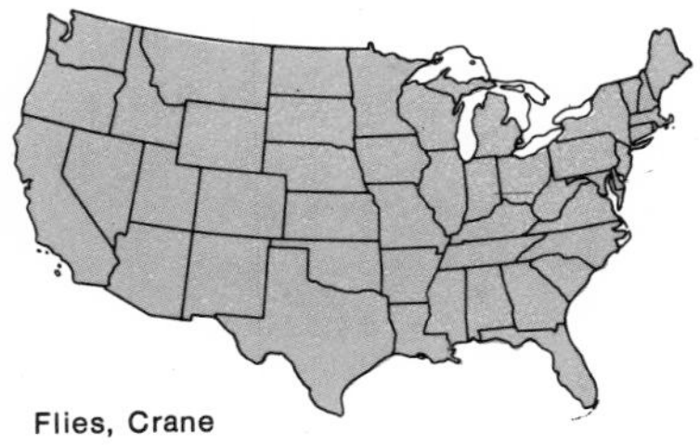
Flies, Crane

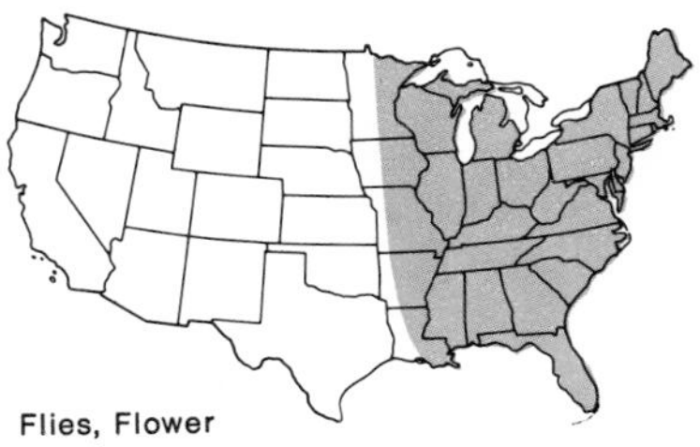
Flies, Flower

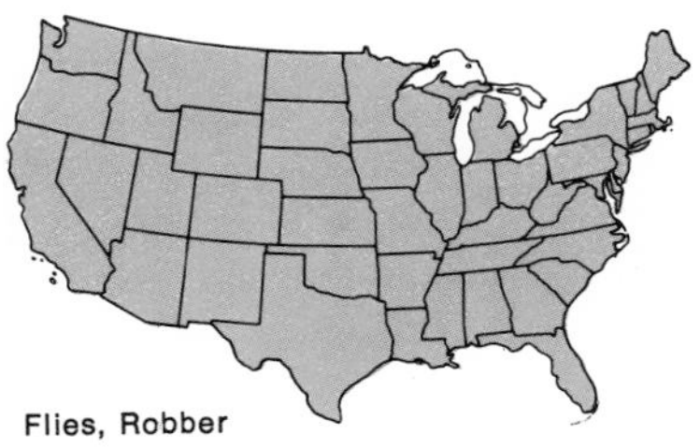
Flies, Robber

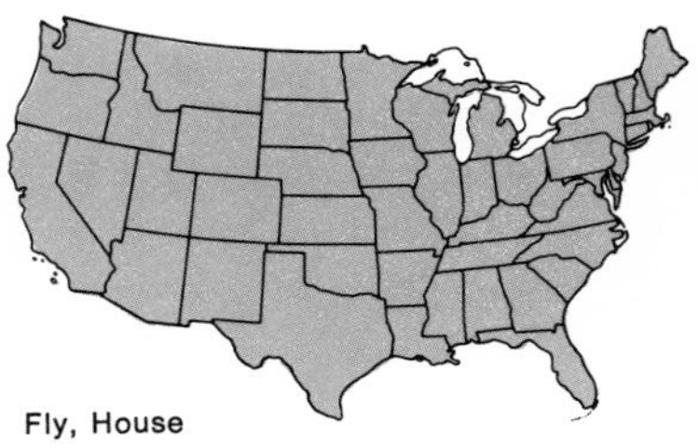
Fly, House

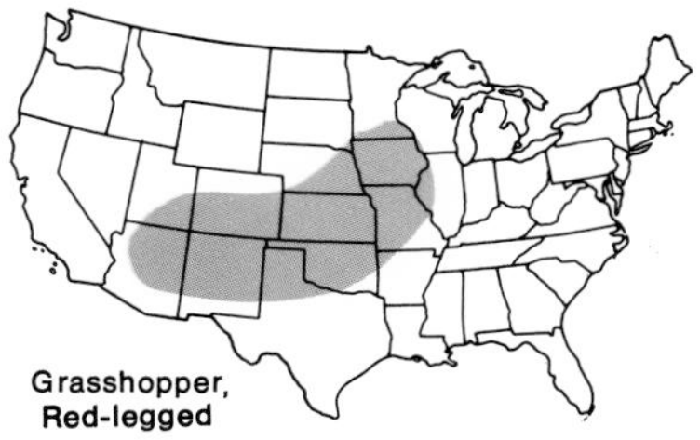
Grasshopper, Red-legged

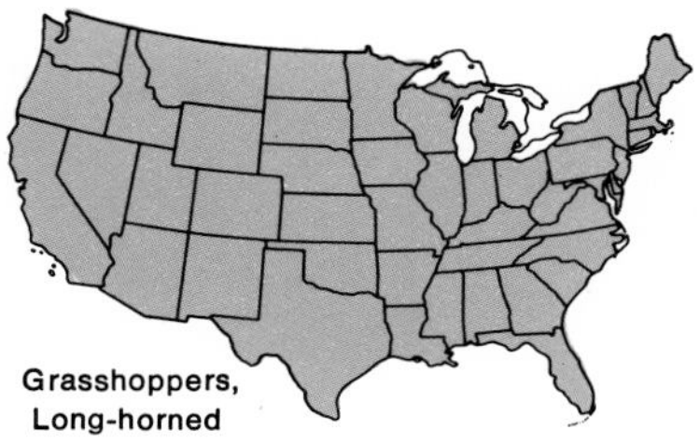
Grasshoppers, Long-horned

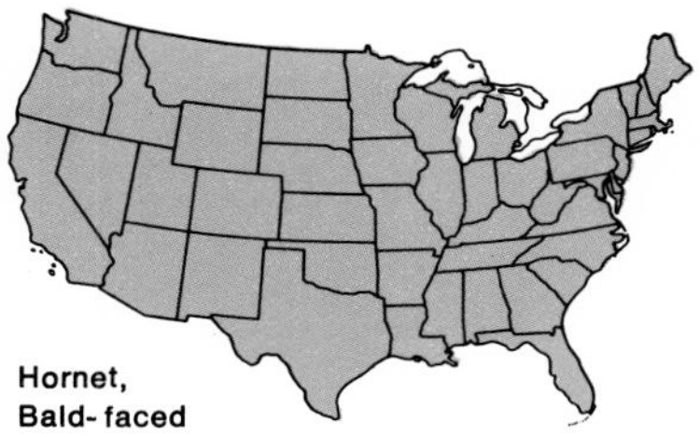
Hornet, Bald-faced

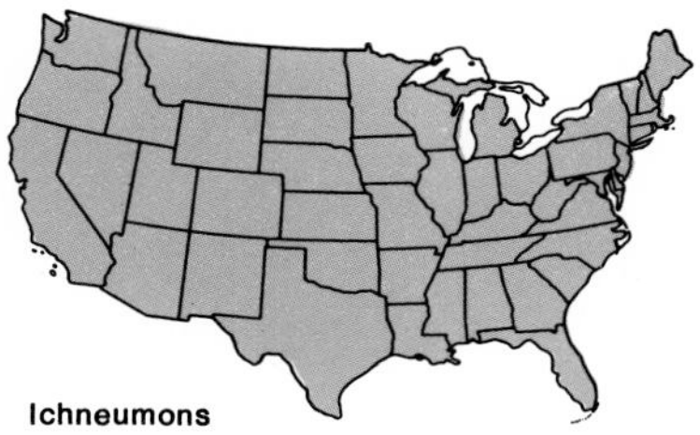
Ichneumons

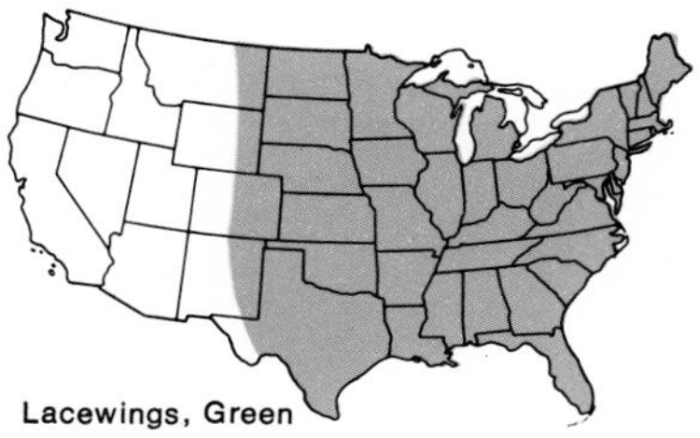
Lacewings, Green

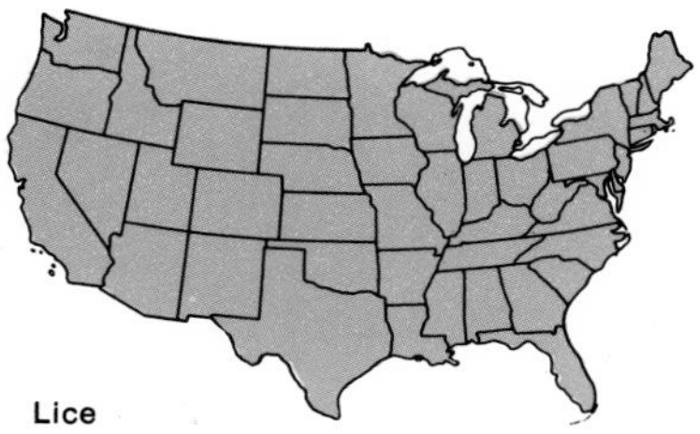
Lice

Mantis, Praying

Mayflies

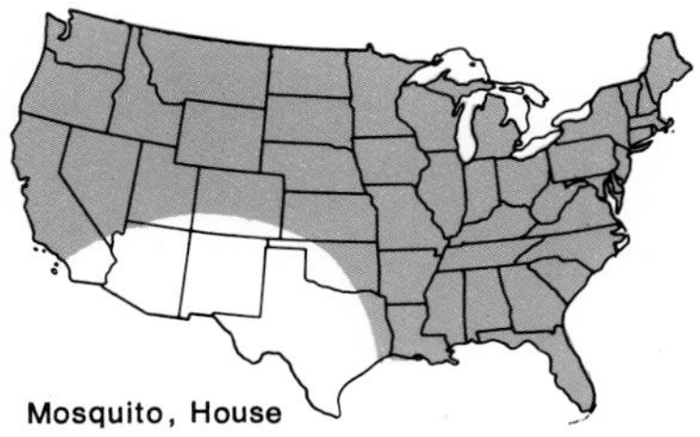
Mosquito, House

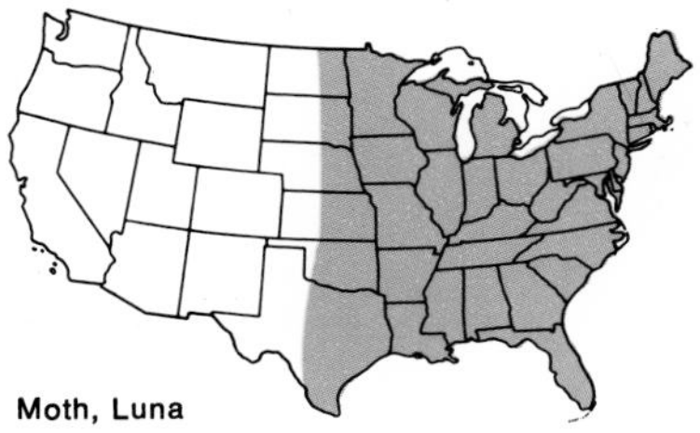
Moth, Luna

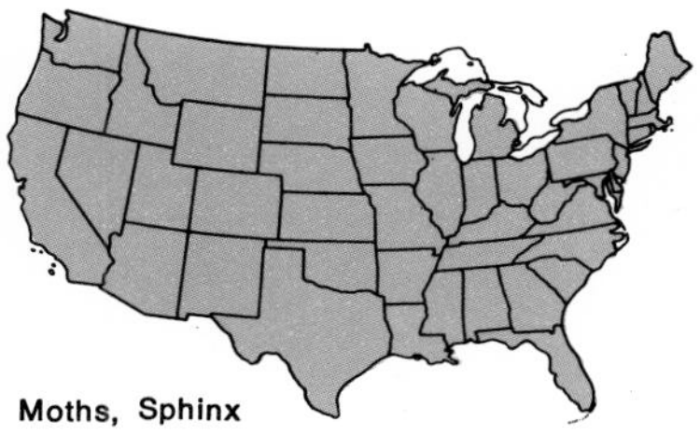
Moths, Sphinx

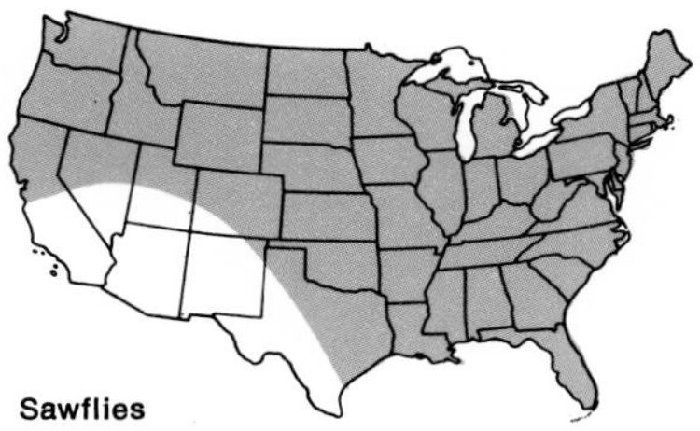
Sawflies

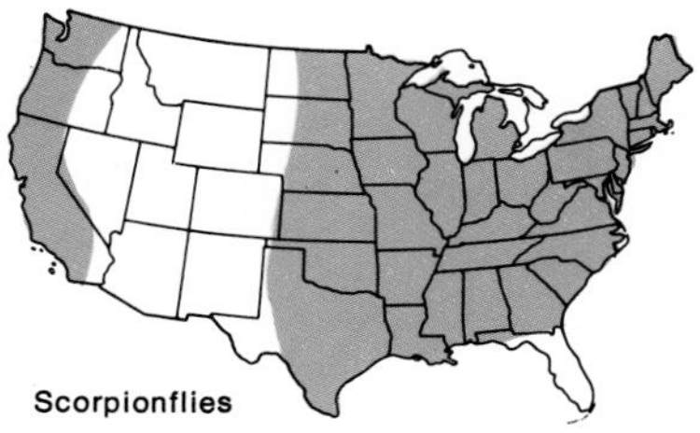
Scorpionflies

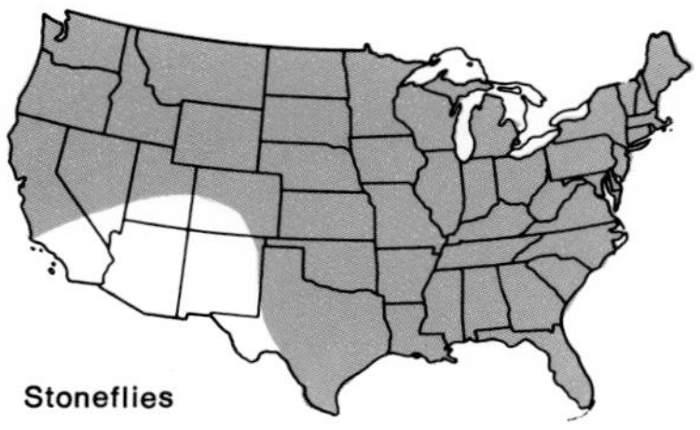
Stoneflies

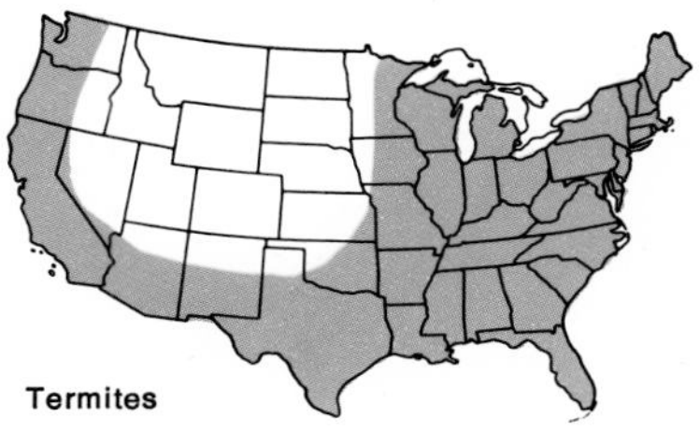
Termites

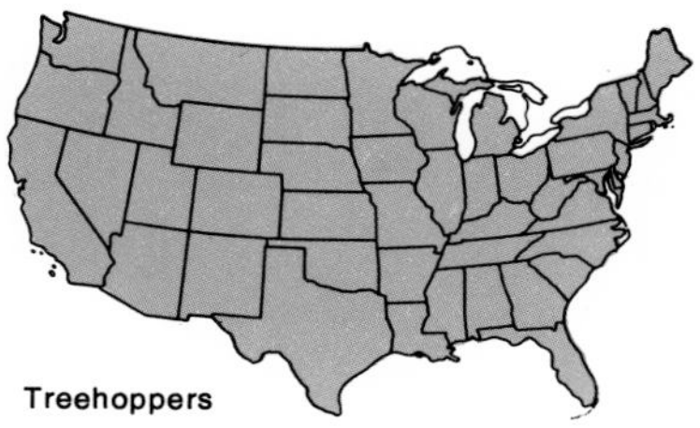
Treehoppers

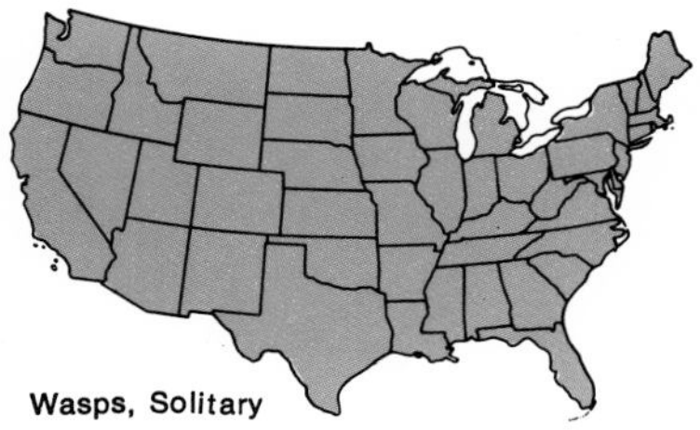
Wasps, Solitary

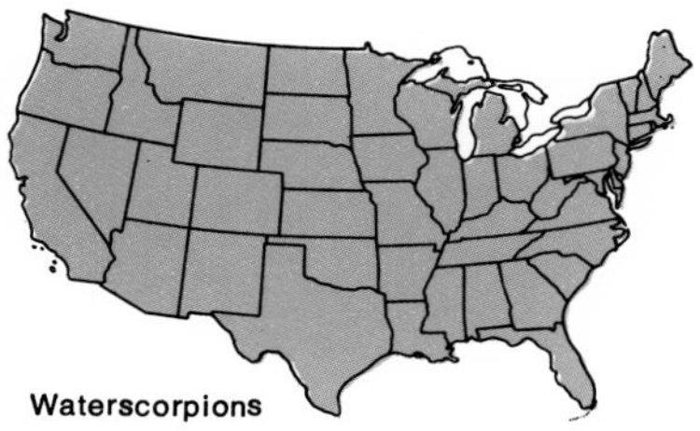
Waterscorpions

PRIMITIVE INSECTS

Bristletails **(Order Thysanura)** are small, wingless, elongate, flattened, often silvery, insects with long antennae and three hair-like tails. The species most often seen is the Silverfish, which is sometimes a pest in houses. Outdoor species live in caves, under stones, or in leaf litter. Some of them are active jumpers. Springtails **(Order Collembola)** are minute, wingless, jumping insects, mostly less than an eighth inch long, that jump with the aid of a tail-like structure which remains folded forward under the abdomen when not in use. Springtails are common and abundant, but seldom are noticed because of their small size and secretive habits. Most of them live under bark, in leaf litter, in the soil, or in fungi. Some live on the surface of fresh-water ponds or in tide pools along the seashore. They feed primarily on decaying material and fungi.

MAYFLIES (Order Ephemeroptera)

Mayflies are small to medium-sized, elongate, soft-bodied insects, with short bristle-like antennae and two or three hair-like tails. Usually they have two pairs of wings that are held together above the body at rest. The front wings are large and triangular, the hind wings are small and rounded, and both pairs usually contain many veins. Metamorphosis is simple. The nymphs are aquatic, and the adults are usually found near water. Nymphs are elongate, with leaf-like gills along the sides of the abdomen and three tails. Some are free-swimming, and others burrow in the bottom of streams and ponds. Nymphs are plant feeders. Unlike other insects, the last nymphal stage molts to a winged stage at the water surface. This stage later molts to the adult. Adults do not feed and, as is literally explained by their Latin name, they live only a few days.

STONEFLIES (Order Plecoptera)

Stoneflies are elongate, flattened, soft-bodied insects usually found near streams. They have four membranous wings. The front pair are long and narrow, and the hind pair are shorter, nearly always with a rounded lobe on the trailing edge. At rest the wings are folded flat over the abdomen. The antennae are fairly long and conspicuous. The tarsi are three-segmented. Metamorphosis is simple, and the nymphs are aquatic, usually living under stones in streams. Nymphs are elongate and flattened, with long antennae and two tails. Some nymphs are plant feeders, others are predaceous. Some have reduced mouth parts and do not feed. Others feed on algae. Most stoneflies are brownish or grayish, and vary in length up to about two inches. Many adults are noctural and are attracted to lights. Some emerge and mate during the fall and winter.

Mayfly

Stonefly (adult)

Dragonfly

Narrow-winged Damselfly

DRAGONFLIES & DAMSELFLIES (Order Odonata)

These are relatively large (up to 3½″) predaceous insects. They have two pairs of elongate and many-veined wings, a long and slender abdomen, short and bristle-like antennae, and three-segmented tarsi. Metamorphosis is simple, and the nymphs are aquatic. Adults are usually found near water, but many are strong fliers and often occur some distance away. Nymphs have a peculiar lower lip, kept folded under the head when not in use, which can be thrust forward quickly to catch prey. Adults usually capture prey on the wing. Adults often fly in tandem, males holding females with the tip of the abdomen by the head or by the back of the neck. Females lay eggs either by washing them off the end of the abdomen at the water surface or by inserting them into aquatic vegetation. Most species require a year to complete their development. Some require two or three. When full-grown-nymphs are ready to molt to adulthood, they climb out of the water onto a stone or other object. Newly emerged adults are pale, soft-bodied, and poor fliers. The body usually hardens in a few hours, but it may be a week or two before the coloration is fully developed. Many adults are brightly colored and beautiful insects. These insects may seem like veritable dragons to small insects, but they are quite harmless to man. They do not sting and, while larger ones may bite if handled, a bite is seldom more than a slight pinch. A dragonfly held by the wings will usually eat small insects offered it. In fact, it will generally chew on anything put in its mouth—even its own abdomen. Dragonflies at rest hold their wings outstretched. The hind wings are wider at the base than the front wings. Many have reddish or blackish markings on the wings. The gills of nymphs are in the rectum, and they breathe by taking water into the rectum through the anus and expelling it. This serves also as a means of locomotion, the insect in effect moving by jet propulsion. Damselflies usually fold their wings together over the body at rest. The front and hind wings are similar in shape and are narrowed at the base. Damselflies are usually very slender, sometimes almost needle-shaped, hence the popular name darning needles. It is not true that they attack people. Most damselflies have clear wings, but a few, which occur along streams, have reddish or black markings on their wings. The gills of nymphs are three leaf-like structures at the end of the abdomen. Nymphs swim by body undulations. All stages of dragonflies and damselflies feed on mosquitoes, midges, and other small insects. They are voracious predators.

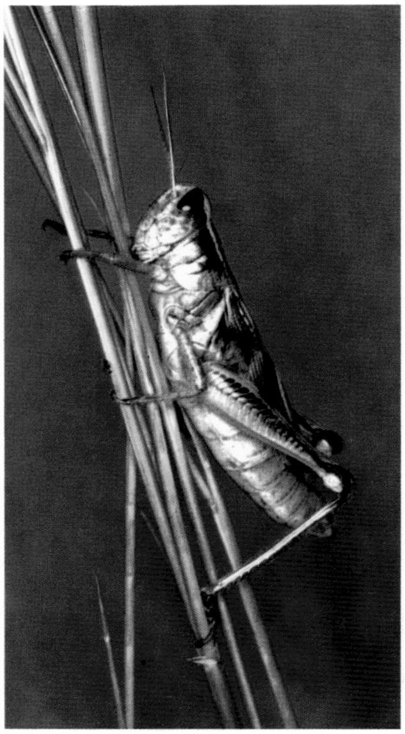
Short-horned Grasshopper

Long-horned Grasshopper

Field Cricket

GRASSHOPPERS & RELATIVES (Order Orthoptera)

The jumping Orthoptera include the grasshoppers and crickets. Their non-jumping relatives include the mantids, walking sticks, and cockroaches. When wings are present, the front wings are elongate and thickened, and the hind wings are membranous and, at rest, are folded fanwise under the front wings. Antennae are long and many-segmented. Jumping Orthoptera have enlarged hind legs and three or four tarsal segments. Non-jumping Orthoptera have slender hind legs, usually with five tarsal segments. Many jumping Orthoptera sing by rubbing the front wings together, as long-horned grasshoppers do, or by rubbing the hind legs over the edges of the front wings, as short-horned grasshoppers do. Each species has its own song, and only males sing. It enables females to recognize males of their species.

Short-horned Grasshoppers have relatively short antennae, three tarsal segments, and an eardrum on each side of the basal abdominal segment. The most common are the spur-throated grasshoppers, which have a tubercle between the base of the front legs and usually have clear hind wings. Many of these are very destructive to crops; the migrating swarms of some western species devastate entire fields. Band-winged grasshoppers lack the tubercle between the base of the front legs and generally have brightly-colored hind wings. They sometimes produce a crackling sound when they fly. Slant-faced grasshoppers have a slanting face and clear hind wings. They are usually found in wet meadows and are seldom numerous enough to do much damage. Pygmy grasshoppers are small and have the pronotum prolonged back over the abdomen and pointed at its tip. Their front wings are very small.

Long-horned Grasshoppers are mostly greenish. Many are called katydids, and nearly all are good singers. They have long hair-like antennae, four tarsal segments, and eardrums located on the front legs. Some of the best known are the true katydids. They live in trees and bushes and sing at night. These insects often sing in unison in two groups that alternate songs—*katy-did* from one group and *katy-didn't* from the other. Other katydids have songs that are high-pitched and lisping. Cone-headed grasshoppers are greenish, about two inches long, and occur in weedy fields and bushes. The songs of most species are high-pitched buzzes. Meadow grasshoppers are greenish and about an inch long. The songs consist of a series of short zips alternating with a prolonged buzz. Shield-backed grasshoppers are dark with short wings; a western species called the Mormon Cricket is a serious crop pest.

Crickets have long hair-like antennae, eardrums on their front legs, and three-segmented tarsi. All are good singers. Their songs are more musical and often lower pitched than the songs of long-horned grasshoppers. Field crickets are dark brown to black, about an inch long, and occur in fields and lawns. Their songs (usually chirps) may be heard day and night. Ground crickets are brownish, about a half inch long, and occur in pastures, woods, and along roadsides. Most of their songs are high-pitched trills. Tree crickets are greenish and an inch long or less. Some occur in trees and bushes, others in weedy fields. The song of most species is a prolonged trill, but one species, the Snowy Tree Cricket, chirps. Its chirping, a common night sound in many parts of the country, varies with temperature. The number of its chirps in 15 seconds, plus 39, gives a figure very close to the temperature.

Non-jumping Orthoptera include mantids, walking sticks, and cockroaches. Mantids are large (2″–3″), brownish or greenish, and very distinctive in appearance. All are predaceous and sit in wait for their prey with front legs bent in a praying position. The prey is captured with a quick movement of the front legs and eaten much as human animals eat corn on the cob. Walking sticks live in foliage and are protected by their resemblance to twigs. Common species are brownish, two to three inches long, and wingless. All are plant feeders. Cockroaches are generally brownish, flattened, and oval, with long hair-like antennae. The species seen by most people are those that inhabit houses, where they are often pests, but there are species that live outdoors. U.S. species reach a length of about one and a half inches, but larger tropical species occasionally come north on fruit shipments.

TERMITES (Order Isoptera)
Termites are small, soft-bodied, usually pale-colored insects that live in colonies and have a caste system. Reproductives (kings and queens) are produced in large numbers at certain seasons. They leave the colony in a swarm, mate, shed their wings, and establish new colonies. The bulk of the colony consists of workers, which are wingless, sterile adults. Most colonies have a soldier caste of individuals with unusually large heads and jaws. Termite colonies of millions of individuals occur in the ground or in wood and may exist for 50 years. Their food consists principally of wood and other vegetable matter. Termites often do great damage feeding on the wood of buildings, utility poles, fence posts, and the like. But they are beneficial in converting dead trees and other plant materials into substances useful to new plants.

Praying Mantis

EARWIGS (Order Dermaptera)
Earwigs are small to medium-sized, elongate, flattened, and usually brownish insects, with a pair of pincer-like structures at the end of the abdomen. The antennae are thread-like and about half as long as the body. The tarsi are three-segmented. Winged earwigs have four wings. The front ones are short and thick, and the hind wings are membranous and folded under the front pair at rest. The pincers are used in defense and may inflict a painful pinch. They differ in shape according to sex, being straight and close together in females and more curved in males. Males can generally inflict a more painful pinch than females. Some earwigs use also a type of chemical warfare in defense. They can squirt a foul-smelling liquid from glands on the upper side of the abdomen. Earwigs are largely nocturnal. Most are scavengers, but some feed on plants.

Termites (immature)

European Earwig

Feather Louse

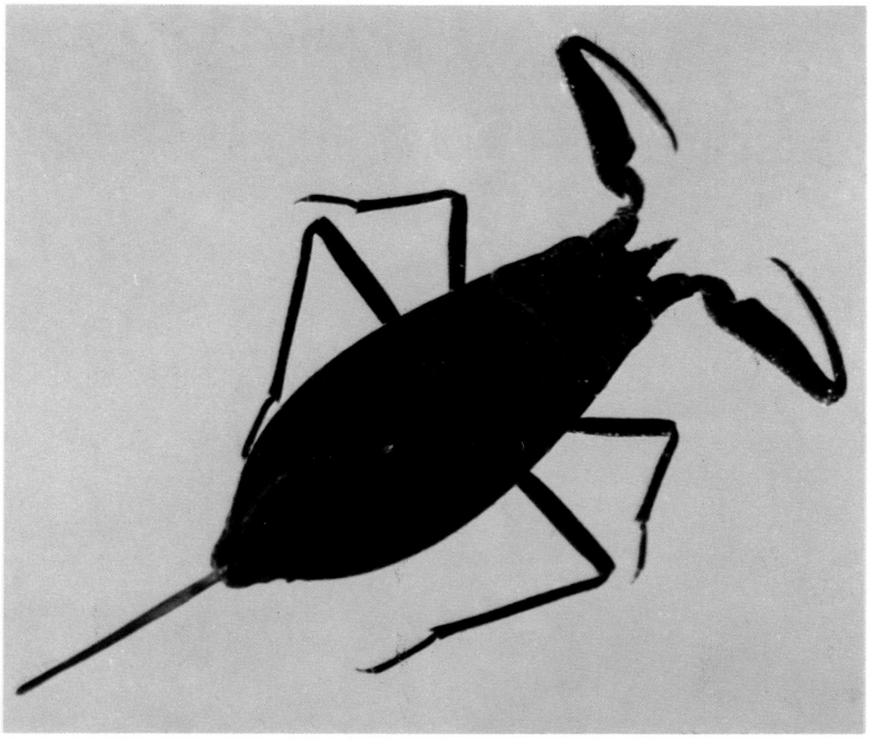

Waterscorpion

LICE
(Orders Mallophaga & Anoplura)
Lice are tiny wingless insects that live as parasites on the bodies of birds and mammals. Chewing lice **(Order Mallophaga)** feed on bits of hair or feathers. Most occur on birds, but some live on mammals other than man. Sucking lice **(Order Anoplura)** live only on mammals, including man, and are blood-sucking. For people, the important species is the Body Louse or "cootie," an irritating pest which may serve as the vector of epidemic typhus and relapsing fever. Many people go through life without ever seeing lice. Those who work with birds or mammals may get lice from these animals, but the infestation is temporary. Body lice are most often encountered where people live in crowded conditions, and seldom bathe or change clothes. Despite their importance to man, many naturalists seldom see them.

BUGS (Order Hemiptera)
To many people almost any small, crawling or flying thing is a bug, but technically a bug is an insect in the Order Hemiptera. Here the bug part of the name is a separate word. In other Orders the syllable bug is combined with the descriptive word (e.g. ladybug, which is a beetle). Winged bugs have their front wings thickened at the base and membranous at the tip. At rest they are held flat over the body with the membranous tips overlapping. The hind wings are membranous. Antennae are usually fairly long, but contain only four or five segments. The tarsi contain three or fewer segments. The mouth parts form a slender, jointed beak that arises from the front of the head. Bugs pierce the tissue they feed on with stylets in the beak and suck out fluid. Metamorphosis is simple. Bugs form a large group and occur in many habitats; some are pests.

Aquatic Bugs include several types of bugs that spend most of their lives in water and get from one aquatic habitat to another by flying. Most of them are predaceous and bite, sometimes severely, when handled. All get air at the water surface. Waterscorpions have a long tail that serves as a breathing tube. Waterboatmen and backswimmers are small (about ½" or less) and have one pair of elongate and oarlike legs. Backswimmers are so-called because they swim upside down. Giant water bugs are brownish, oval, flattened, and one to two inches long. The eggs of some species are laid on the backs of the males who carry them around until they hatch. Most waterscorpions are about one and a half inches long, brownish and slender. They look a little like walking sticks, but have front legs like those of mantids. Water striders run about on the water surface.

Assassin Bug

Plant-feeding Bug

Harlequin Bugs

Predaceous Bugs include assassin bugs, ambush bugs, and several other groups that feed largely on smaller insects. Assassin bugs are brownish, elongate, and vary in length up to about an inch. Many are ornamented with spines, and one species, the black Wheel Bug, has a ridge shaped like a cogwheel in the middle of the pronotum. Most assassin bugs are predaceous on other insects, but a few are blood-sucking. Many will inflict a painful bite if handled carelessly. Ambush bugs are usually found on flowers (often goldenrod), where they lie in wait for prey. They are small (less than ½″) and very inconspicuous because they blend with the flowers. They feed on flies, bees, and other insects that visit flowers, often capturing prey much larger than themselves with their greatly thickened front legs. Ambush bugs do not bite when handled and quickly paralyze any prey they catch.

Plant-feeding Bugs include those that feed on plant leaves, seeds, or tree leaves. The most common are the leaf bugs, which occur on vegetation almost everywhere. They are small (less than ½″), soft-bodied, elongate-oval, and vary greatly in color. They have only one or two closed cells in the membranous part of the front wing. Many are serious pests of cultivated plants. Seed bugs resemble leaf bugs but are hard-bodied and have a few branching veins in the membranous part of the front wings. The most important member of this group is the Chinch Bug, a tiny, slender, black-and-white bug that is a serious pest of wheat and other grains. Lace bugs are mostly whitish or gray, somewhat oblong in shape, and a quarter inch in length or less. The body is covered with a network of ridges. They feed on the foliage of trees and shrubs and, when abundant, they can completely defoliate a tree.

Stink Bugs are broad-shouldered and shield-shaped, with a conspicuous triangular area in the middle of the back. They differ from most other bugs in having five antennal segments. Stink bugs (and many other bugs as well) give off a disagreeable odor when handled. Some stink bugs feed on plants, and others are predaceous. The plant feeders have a slender basal segment at the base of the beak which, when at rest, fits into a groove on the underside of the head. The Harlequin Cabbage Bug (about ½″ and brightly colored with red and black) is a serious pest of cabbage and related plants, especially in the South. Predaceous stink bugs are mostly brownish. The basal segment of the beak is stout and does not fit into a groove on the underside of the head. Stink bugs feed on various small insects. Many stink bugs have a sharp spine on each side of the body behind the head.

CICADAS, HOPPERS, & OTHERS (Order Homoptera)
The major types of insects in this Order are the cicadas, hoppers, aphids, and scale insects. They are similar to the bugs but have the front wings uniform in texture (entirely membranous or thickened). All are plant feeders, and many are important pests, damaging cultivated plants by their feeding or serving as vectors of plant diseases. Cicadas and hoppers have short bristle-like antennae, three tarsal segments, and are active insects. Aphids have long antennae and two tarsal segments. All are relatively inactive, and many are wingless. Most scale insects are uninsect-like in appearance, lacking legs, eyes, and antennae. They spend most of their life under a scaly covering of some sort. Those with legs have only one tarsal segment. Females are wingless, and males have only two wings.

Cicada (emerging)

Aphids

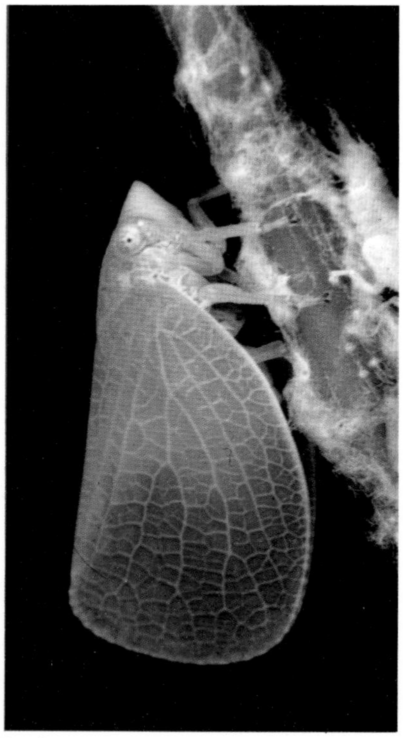
Treehopper

Cicadas are large insects (mostly 1″–2″) with membranous, clear wings and a short head. The males sing, and each species has a distinctive song (usually a loud, pulsating buzz) produced by a pair of membranes near the base of the abdomen on the lower side. This song is a mechanism for bringing the sexes together. Cicadas lay their eggs in twigs, which generally break off. The nymphs live in the ground, feeding on plant roots. Most species require one to a few years to complete their life cycle, and are seldom very abundant, but the periodical cicadas require 13 or 17. Large numbers of periodical cicadas usually appear at the same time, and their emergence is a striking event—cicadas (and their cast skins) everywhere, the air full of their songs, and the birds and other animals that eat cicadas having a field day. Many swarms have been eliminated by development and excessive use of pesticides.

Aphids & Scale Insects are sometimes troublesome both to home gardeners and agriculturists. Aphids are small, soft-bodied, oval or pear-shaped insects that often have a pair of slender finger-like structures near the posterior end of the abdomen. Wings may be present or absent. Most aphids have a rather complex life cycle, with two or more generations per year, some having wings and others lacking them, and with different generations feeding on different food plants. Many aphids are serious plant pests. Scale insects are small, oval, and usually have a waxy or scaly covering. Females are wingless and sometimes lack eyes, legs, and antennae; males are midge-like, with only one pair of wings. Mealybugs are more insect-like than most scale insects and have legs and move around. Most scale insects, once they settle on a food plant, stay there the rest of their lives.

Hoppers are small (½″ or less) jumping insects, elongate to oval, and varying greatly in color. Most common are the leafhoppers, which have one or two rows of small spines on the hind tibiae and, generally, are slender. Froghoppers are similar, but are usually more oval, and their hind tibiae bear only a few large spines. Nymphs of froghoppers live in a mass of spittle-like material and are thus called spittlebugs. Treehoppers have an enlarged and often oddly shaped pronotum which extends back over the body. Some treehoppers look like thorns, other appear humpbacked. Planthoppers have antennae arising on the sides of the head. The front of the head between the antennae bulges forward. They resemble leafhoppers, but lack the rows of small spines on the hind tibiae. Hoppers are common insects, and many are serious pests of cultivated plants. Some transmit plant diseases.

BEETLES (Order Coleoptera)
This is the largest Order of insects. There are nearly 300,000 world species, about 30,000 in North America north of Mexico. Most beetles have four wings, with the front wings (called elytra) thickened, sometimes quite hard, and meeting in a straight line down the back. The hind wings, when present, are membranous, longer than the front wings and, when at rest, are folded under them. The antennae vary in form, but usually contain nine to 11 segments and are fairly conspicuous. The tarsi usually have three to five segments. Metamorphosis is complete, and the larvae vary considerably in form. Many beetles are serious pests of cultivated plants, feeding on foliage or tunneling into parts of the plant. Some damage food, grain, clothing, and other stored materials. Others are valuable predators or scavengers. Many are aquatic.

Predaceous Diving Beetle

Ground Beetle

Firefly

Aquatic Beetles, as the name suggests, live in water. Whirligig beetles are black and oval, a half inch in length or less, with very short, clubbed antennae. They commonly swim on the water surface, sometimes in groups, usually in an erratic fashion. They are very fast swimmers. The larger species give off an odor like pineapples when handled. Predaceous diving beetles and water scavenger beetles are similar in appearance. Both are oval, brown or black, and up to one and a half inches long. The antennae of diving beetles are long and thread-like, while those of water scavenger beetles are short and clubbed. The larvae of both are predaceous and rather ferocious. Larvae of diving beetles are called water tigers. All aquatic beetles get air at the water surface. Some carry a film or bubble of air on their bodies below the surface, from which they breathe while submerged.

Predaceous Beetles play important roles in controlling the populations of other insects. Ground beetles are elongate, oval, and flattened, usually dark colored and often shiny. They are generally found on the ground or under logs and stones. The antennae are thread-like, the legs are long, and the tarsi are five-segmented. The head is nearly always narrower than the pronotum. Many have fine longitudinal grooves on the elytra. They feed on a variety of insects. The form of the antennae and tarsi of tiger beetles resembles that of ground beetles, but the elytra are smooth and often brightly colored. Their head is a little wider than the pronotum. They usually are found in open areas and are good fliers. Ladybug beetles are small, oval, convex beetles that are often brightly colored. Adults and larvae feed chiefly on aphids and are of great value in keeping these pests under control.

Fireflies, or lightningbugs, are well known because of their flashing "taillights." They are elongate and parallel-sided, and the elytra are quite soft. The head is largely concealed by the pronotum. The light-producing organs, when present, are on the terminal segments of the abdomen. They can be recognized when not glowing by their pale color. The light produced by fireflies is cold, i.e., nearly all the energy given off appears as light. In our electric lights only about ten percent of the energy is given off as light; the rest is heat. The flashing of fireflies is a means by which members of a species recognize each other. Each species has a characteristic flash rhythm. During the day fireflies are usually found on vegetation. The larvae prey on smaller insects. The females of some species are wingless. These, as well as firefly larvae, are luminescent and are called glow-worms.

Lined June Beetle

Long-horned Beetle

Scarab Beetles are stout-bodied, oval or elongate, and vary in size and color. Their tarsi are five-segmented, and the antennae end in a lopsided club. Larvae are white grubs. Many scarabs are dung feeders. Some, called tumblebugs, form a ball of manure, roll it along, bury it, and lay their eggs in it. Most dung beetles are black, but some are brightly colored. The most common plant-feeding scarabs are June beetles—stout-bodied, brownish, about one inch long. They are common around lights on late spring and early summer nights. Adults and larvae feed on various cultivated plants. The introduced Japanese Beetle, broadly oval, about three-eighths of an inch long, and dark shiny-green with reddish-brown elytra, can be a very destructive species, feeding on the fruit and foliage of many cultivated plants. Our largest scarabs (some of the rhinoceros beetles) are nearly two inches long.

Plant-feeding Beetles include, among others, leaf beetles and snout beetles. Leaf beetles are mostly small (½″ or less), oval or elongate, with short thread-like antennae and the tarsi appearing four-segmented. Many are brightly colored. Adults and larvae are usually foliage feeders. This group includes such pests as the Potato Beetle (large, oval, convex, with black and yellow stripes), the Cucumber Beetle (yellow with black spots or stripes), and the flea beetles (tiny, blackish, beetles that jump). Snout beetles have the front of the head drawn out into a snout which is sometimes as long as the body. Most snout beetles are small and dull colored, with the antennae elbowed and clubbed. Most larvae burrow into stems or fruits of the host plant. This group includes the Boll Weevil (a pest of cotton), Plum Curculio (a pest of orchard fruits), clover weevils, nut weevils, and grain weevils.

Wood-boring Beetles are important in the conversion of wood into soil. They open up the wood and hasten decay. On the other hand, they reduce the value of logs cut for lumber when they tunnel into them. A few species serve as agents in the transmission of tree diseases. Most wood-boring beetles lay their eggs in crevices in the bark, and the larvae tunnel into the wood, sometimes excavating galleries several inches long. Larvae pupate in these galleries, and the adults leave the log by way of the larval gallery or through an exit tunnel they cut themselves. Adults may be found around freshly cut logs or on flowers. Most wood-boring beetles attack freshly cut logs or blown-down trees; a few attack live trees. While rarely killing one, they may greatly weaken it. The most important beetles of this type are the long-horned and metallic wood-boring beetles.

Carrion Beetles are relatively large (up to 1″ or more), elongate or oval, flattened, with clubbed antennae. Many are marked with yellow or red. Those with short red-marked elytra are able to excavate beneath the body of a small animal, such as a mouse, and bury it. Then they lay their eggs on it; they may even move the body of such an animal several feet before burying it. Rove beetles, which are also common around carrion, are slender and elongate. The antennae are thread-like or only slightly clubbed, and the elytra are short. Most are less than an inch. All are active and fast-running. Many run with the end of the abdomen elevated. Their jaws are long, slender, and sharp. Larger rove beetles can inflict a painful bite when handled. Many rove beetles are probably predaceous, but are generally found around carrion. The sanitary role the carrion beetles play is significant.

Acorn Weevil

Carrion Beetle

SCORPIONFLIES
(Order Mecoptera)
Scorpionflies are medium-sized (mostly less than 1") slender-bodied insects with a long-faced appearance. Most are yellowish or brownish. Males of some species have the end of the abdomen bulbous and recurved, like the stinger of a scorpion (hence the common name), but they do not sting. Most adults have two pairs of membranous wings, but a few are wingless. The front and hind wings are similar in size and shape and are often spotted. Metamorphosis is complete, and the larvae are caterpillar-like. Scorpionflies are usually found in areas of dense vegetation. Common scorpionflies (which give this group its name) feed largely on dead insects and other animal matter. Hanging scorpionflies are predaceous on small insects. They spend most of their time hanging by their front legs from leaves or twigs.

Scorpionfly

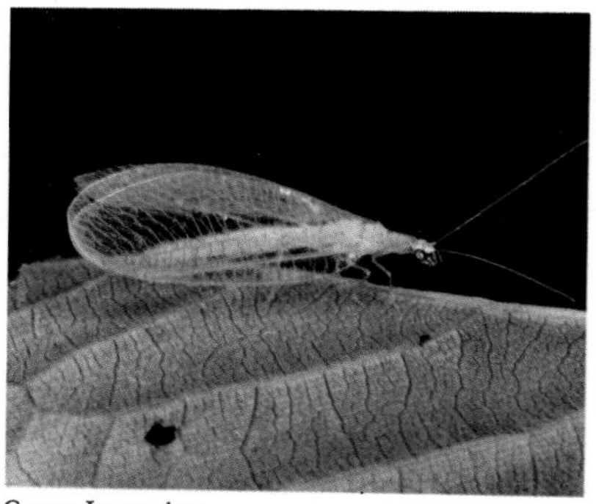
Green Lacewing

Caddisfly Cases

LACEWINGS & RELATIVES
(Order Neuroptera)
Members of this Order are elongate, soft-bodied, with four membranous wings. The front and hind wings are similar in size and shape, and are usually held, roof-like, over the body at rest. The antennae are relatively long. The tarsi are five-segmented. Metamorphosis is complete, and most larvae are predaceous on other insects. The most common neuropterans are green lacewings, which are greenish with coppery eyes and mostly a half to three quarters inch long. Their larvae are important predators of aphids. Green lacewings give off an unpleasant odor when handled. Antlions resemble damselflies, but have the antennae knobbed and relativly long. The larvae, called doodlebugs, live buried in sandy or dusty soil at the bottom of a conical pit, feeding on ants and other insects that fall into it.

CADDISFLIES (Order Trichoptera)
Caddisfles are moth-like insects, generally an inch or less and not brightly colored, with long hair-like antennae. The wings are rather hairy and are held, roof-like, over the body at rest. The tarsi are five-segmented. Metamorphosis is complete, and larvae are aquatic. Adults are usually found near water. Most caddisfly larvae construct tubular cases, but some build nets. The cases are made of bits of leaves, twigs, or pebbles; each species makes a characteristic case. When the larva is full grown it attaches its case to an object in the water, seals it, and pupates inside it. Net-spinning caddisfly larvae generally live in streams. Their nets are cup-shaped or conical and attached to a stone or other object, with the open end facing upstream. The larva spends its time near the net and feeds on the materials caught in the net.

BUTTERFLIES & MOTHS (Order Lepidoptera)
This Order contains many beautiful insects which are to the insect world what the many wildflowers are to the plant world. Their beauty is only on the surface because the wing color comes from a covering of tiny scales that are easily rubbed off—appearing as powder on one's fingers. Butterflies differ from moths in having knobbed antennae; those of moths are usually hair-like or feathery. Butterflies are generally small-bodied, large-winged, and active in the daytime. Moths are usually stouter-bodied and are mostly nocturnal. Adults feed chiefly on nectar (a few do not feed), sucked through a long proboscis, coiled beneath the head when not in use. Metamorphosis is complete, and the larvae (caterpillars) are mostly plant feeders. Many are serious pests of cultivated plants, and some attack stored products.

Caterpillars are usually elongate and cylindrical, with a well-developed head, a pair of short legs on the first three segments, a pair of stout leg-like structures called prolegs on four segments farther back, and another pair of prolegs on the last segment. Some caterpillars, such as inchworms, have fewer prolegs and move by alternately looping and extending the body. Caterpillars vary greatly in size and color. Many look ferocious, but none bites man, although a few have stinging hairs. All spin silk, which is used in making cocoons and shelters. Many live in shelters made by tying leaves together with silk—sometimes just a single leaf rolled up, sometimes just a few leaves, and sometimes almost entire branches. Many moth larvae spin cocoons and pupate inside. Most butterfly larvae do not spin cocoons; their pupae (chrysalids) are often brightly colored or ornamental.

Large & Small Butterflies is obviously a catchall category. Our largest butterflies are the swallowtails, so called because of the tail-like prolongations on the hind wings. Their larvae are smooth-skinned and have an eversible scent gland—a forked structure that is everted (turned out) from the upper surface of the body just behind the head. It not only emits a disagreeable odor, but gives the caterpillar a ferocious appearance. The most common swallowtails in the U.S. are the Tiger Swallowtail (larva feeds on various trees), the Black Swallowtail (larva feeds on carrots, parsley, and related plants), and the Spicebush Swallowtail (larva feeds on spicebush and sassafras). Our smallest butterflies (most with a wingspread of less than 1") include the blues, coppers, and hairstreaks. Many are beautifully colored. The larvae of some blues excrete honeydew, to which ants are attracted.

Brush-footed Butterflies have greatly reduced front legs not used in walking. These species may seem to have only two pairs of legs. Their chrysalids are hung by the tail from leaves, twigs, or other objects. The North American Monarch is common and widely distributed. Its larvae feed on milkweed. It is one of the few insects that migrate. Marked individuals have been known to travel in the fall from Canada to Mexico. Monarchs are rarely eaten by other animals; evidently their body fluids are distasteful. The Viceroy, which resembles the Monarch (a little smaller, with a black line across the hind wing) is afforded some protection from predators by this resemblance. The Mourning Cloak is a common species whose larvae feed on elm and willow. It is blackish, and the wings are bordered with yellow. It overwinters as an adult and may fly about on warm winter days.

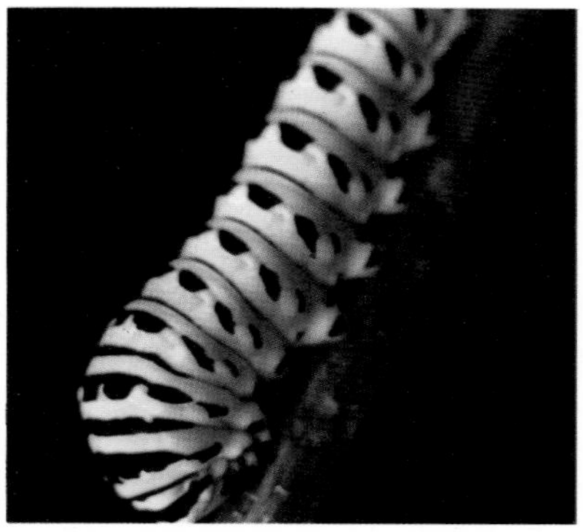
Anise Swallowtail Larva

North American Monarch

Spicebush Swallowtail (emerging)

Luna Moth

Sphinx Moths

Moths comprise more than 90 percent of Lepidoptera and vary greatly in size and color. About half of them have a wingspread of one inch or less. The largest moths are the giant silkworm moths, some of which have a wingspread of about six inches. They have feathery antennae and eye spots on their wings. The larvae feed on various trees and pupate in silken cocoons. This group includes the Cecropia, Luna, Polyphemus, and other large moths. Hawk moths are heavy-bodied, with rather narrow wings; in flight they may resemble hummingbirds. The larvae usually have a spine at the rear end of the body and are called hornworms. Some are pests of tomatoes and tobacco. Tiger moths are small to medium-sized, usually light colored, and often brightly patterned or striped. Most larvae are quite hairy and are sometimes called woollybears. The noctuid moths comprise the largest Family in the Order, with some 3000 North American species. Mostly they are small to medium-sized, dark colored, and with hair-like antennae. The most strikingly colored noctuids are the underwings, whose hind wings are usually banded with pink and black. This group includes the Armyworm, the cutworms, and other important pests. Tent caterpillars are best known from the activities of the larvae, which attack wild cherry and various orchard trees. They construct a silken tent in a fork, foraging out from it and feeding on foliage. When abundant they can defoliate a tree. The larvae are active in late spring and early summer. The adults (brownish with a 1″ wingspread) appear in midsummer. Tussock moths are rather plainly colored, about one inch in wingspread (some females are wingless), and have feathery antennae. The larvae are rather striking in appearance, with four toothbrush-like tufts of hair on the back, two slender tufts of long hair at the front end, and a similar hair tuft at the rear. These larvae feed on orchard and shade trees, and sometimes do a great deal of damage. The Gypsy Moth (an introduced species, with both sexes winged) is a serious pest of shade and forest trees in the East. About half of the moths are grouped in a subdivision of the Order called the **Microlepidoptera.** They are mostly small to very small, and many have narrow and pointed wings. The larvae vary in habits. Many are leaf rollers, leaf tyers, or leaf miners. Some important pests are the European Corn Borer (a serious pest of corn), the Meal Moth (which attacks cereals, flour, and meal), the Codling Moth (a pest of apples and other fruits), the Peach Tree Borer (of which the adult resembles a wasp), the Pink Bollworm (a pest of cotton), the bagworm moths, and the clothes moths.

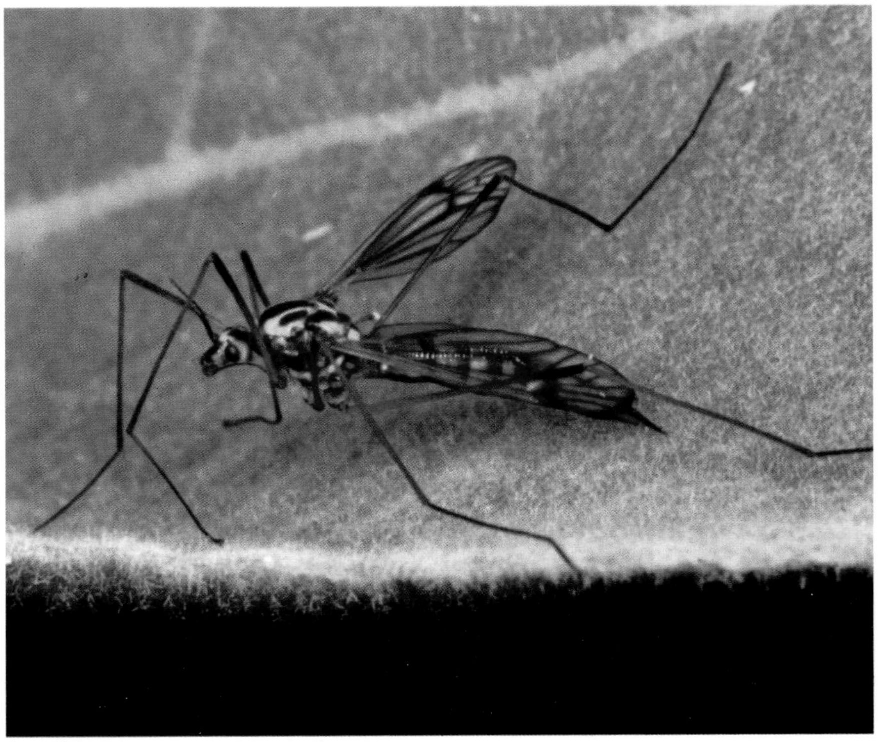

Cranefly

FLIES (Order Diptera)

This is a large Order (some 16,000 North American species) whose members occur almost everywhere. Diptera differ from other fly-like insects in having only one pair of wings. The mouth parts are in the form of a sucking beak on the lower side of the head. Flies that bite do so by piercing the skin and sucking blood. Most flies are small (1″ or less) and soft-bodied. Their wings are membranous and may be clear or variously patterned. Metamorphosis is complete. The larvae, usually called maggots, live in water, soil, decaying materials, or in plant or animal tissues. Most adults feed on plant juices, but some are predaceous on other insects. Some are blood-sucking pests of man and other vertebrates, often serving as disease vectors. Many flies are useful scavengers. Others help to keep pest species under control. A few are themselves plant pests.

Long-horned Flies differ from other Diptera in having relatively long, many-segmented antennae. Most are slender and mosquito-like, and the wing venation is variable. They, along with mosquitoes, make up the **Suborder Nematocera.** Crane flies (nearly 1500 North American species) look like overgrown mosquitoes with very long legs. They do not bite and generally occur near water or in areas of dense vegetation. Midges resemble mosquitoes, but have a short proboscis and lack scales along the wing veins. They occur nearly everywhere, but are most common near lakes and ponds, sometimes occurring in enormous swarms. The larvae are aquatic, and many live in tubes constructed of debris. Biting midges, or punkies, are very tiny. Many bite and are very annoying. Black flies are small, dark-colored, stocky in build, and vicious biters. The larvae live in swift streams.

Mosquitoes differ from other long-horned flies in having a long slender proboscis and tiny scales on the wing veins. Males differ from females in having whorls of long hair on the antennae. In addition, only females bite. Mosquito larvae are aquatic and usually breathe at the surface through a tube at the rear end of the body. They live in many aquatic habitats, even in tin cans that get filled with water. The pupae also are aquatic and quite active. Adult mosquitoes feed on vertebrate blood and on nectar. Only females are blood-sucking, and some must have a blood meal before they can lay eggs. Mosquitoes are important not only as biting pests but because they may serve as vectors of malaria, yellow fever, dengue, and encephalitis. Malaria is transmitted by a species of **Anopheles,** which has patches of dark scales on the wings and alights with the body and beak in a straight line.

Mosquito

Robber Fly

Short-horned Flies have relatively short, three- or four-segmented antennae and usually eight or ten veins reaching the wing margin. They are generally rather stout-bodied. They make up the **Suborder Brachycera.** Horse flies (½″–1″) are commonly found near water; their larvae are aquatic. Females are blood-sucking and often serious pests. The head is often somewhat concave behind. The eyes usually are brightly colored. Most horse flies are gray or blackish with clear wings. Smaller ones, usually brownish with dark spots on the wings, are called deer flies. Robber flies are of moderate to large size. The thorax is stout, and the abdomen is usually tapered. The top of the head is hollowed out between the eyes. Robber flies are predaceous on other insects. Some of the larger ones will inflict a painful bite if handled carelessly. Long-legged flies are small and generally metallic green.

House Fly

Flower Fly

Muscoid Flies differ from other flies in having a U-shaped suture on the face and arching over the bases of the antennae. The head and body are rather bristly, and most are shaped like the House Fly. Many muscoids (house flies, blow flies, flesh flies, and others) are scavengers, their larvae feeding in decaying materials. They perform a valuable service in removing these materials. Some are annoying pests, and a few serve as vectors of typhoid fever and dysentery. Other muscoids, especially tachinids, are parasites of other insects and serve as an important natural control of many pest species. Tachinids resemble the House Fly, but usually the large bristle on the third antennal segment is bare. Because they are bristly, they are often good pollinators. Other muscoids, such as fruit flies, are pests of orchards and field crops. A few muscoids, such as stable flies, are biting pests.

Circular-seamed Flies have only six or seven veins reaching the wing margin. The antennae are three-segmented, with the third segment larger than the others and bearing a large bristle. Syrphid flies are usually brightly colored, and many resemble bees or wasps. Although they do not bite or sting some buzz quite loudly. Nearly all have a spurious vein in the wing—a thickening extending lengthwise through the middle. The bodies are not bristly but may be hairy. These flies feed on nectar and are common around flowers. They frequently hover, and their wings are often iridescent. The larvae of many syrphids are important predators of aphids. Other larvae are scavengers, occurring in various decaying materials. Thick-headed flies usually resemble wasps, but do not sting. Their larvae live as parasites in bees and other insects. The syrphid flies comprise one of the largest Families of flies.

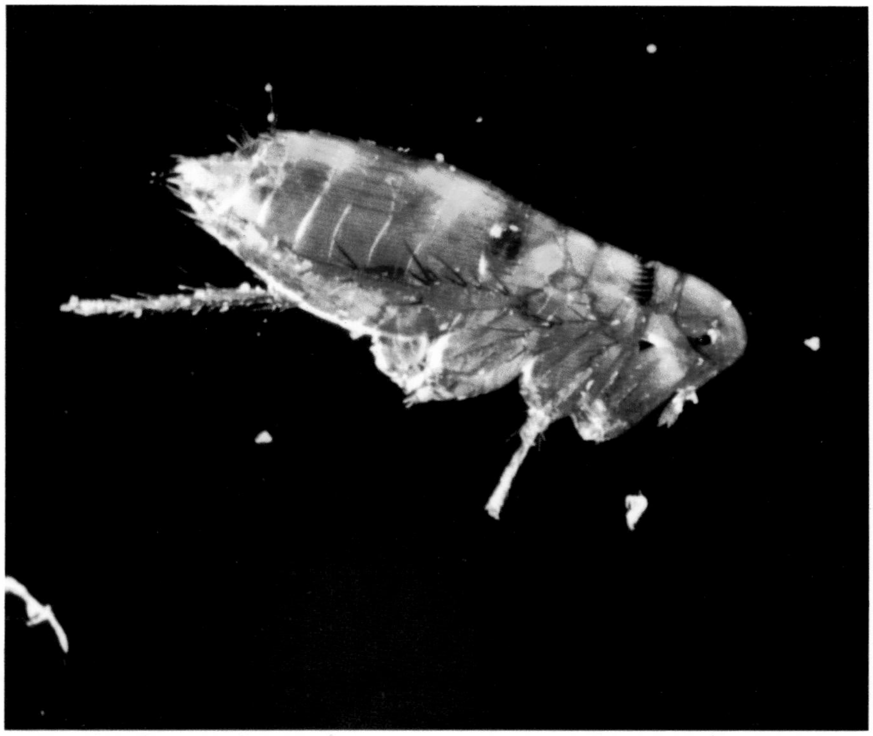

Dog Flea

FLEAS (Order Siphonaptera)
Fleas are small (less than ¼″), wingless, laterally flattened insects that are ectoparasites of birds and mammals. They are blood-sucking and often very irritating. Fleas are active, long-legged, jumping insects that spend most of their time on their host, but some may spend considerable time off as well. Metamorphosis is complete. Some maggot-like larvae live in the dirt and debris of birds' nests and are legless. The fleas most often encountered are those that attack cats and dogs. People with such pets often are bitten as readily as their pets. Fleas are important not only as biting pests, but also as disease vectors. They transmit a type of plague in rodents called sylvatic plague, and certain species transmit the plague from rats to man (at which point it is called bubonic plague). Fleas, along with body lice, serve also as vectors of endemic typhus.

WASPS, ANTS, & BEES (Order Hymenoptera)
Hymenoptera are wasp-like insects, usually with two pairs of membranous wings (some are wingless) that contain relatively few veins. The antennae generally contain ten or more segments, and the tarsi are five-segmented. Metamorphosis is complete. Hymenoptera vary in length from a hundredth inch to two and a half inches. This is a large and important group. Many species are very valuable, others are harmful. Many are parasites of other insects and serve as a natural control of undesirable species. Bees provide valuable pollinating services, and one species (the Honey Bee) is our source of honey and beeswax. Some Hymenoptera are pests of various crop plants and forest trees. Most bees and wasps, and some ants, sting. The stinger, a modified ovipositor, is at the rear of the abdomen. Only females sting.

Sawfly

Sawflies and their relatives **(Suborder Symphyta)** differ from other Hymenoptera **(Suborder Apocrita)** in having the abdomen broadly joined to the thorax. Apocrita have the abdomen constricted at the base. Many Symphyta resemble wasps, but do not sting. The larvae are nearly all plant feeders, and many are pests of cultivated plants. The most common symphytans are the sawflies. Most are three-quarters inch or less and many are brightly colored. Their larvae, frequently mistaken for caterpillars, feed on foliage, sometimes doing considerable damage to the host plant. A few are leaf miners, and some are gall makers. Horntails are large insects (1″–1½″) and brownish to black. Some have blackish wings. Their name derives from the fact that they have a sharp spine at the end of the abdomen. Females have a long ovipositor in addition to this spine.

Ichneumon Wasp

Ichneumons are the most common of the parasitic Hymenoptera, and about half of the Hymenoptera are parasitic, living as larvae in the bodies of other insects. They serve as natural controls of other insects. Many have a long ovipositor with which they reach hosts in cocoons, burrows, or other seemingly protected places. Ichneumons resemble slender wasps. They do not sting (with rare exceptions) and differ from wasps that do in having more antennal segments (16 or more). Wasps that sting have 13. Females have the ovipositor extruded, sometimes as long as the body or longer. Such an ovipositor looks like three hair-like tails. Some long-tailed ichneumons, which parasitize wood-boring larvae, are able to insert their ovipositor through a half inch or more of wood to get their eggs into the tunnels of their hosts. There are more than 5000 species of ichneumons in the U.S.

Carpenter Ants

Ants live in colonies that vary in size from a few dozen to many thousands of individuals. Most nest in the ground, but some nest in various natural cavities. Colonies usually contain one or more queens (larger individuals which lay all the eggs), workers (wingless females, sometimes of two or more sizes), and males. Males and queens are produced at certain seasons, and mating occurs in mating flight. After mating, the males die, and the queen sheds her wings and starts a new colony. A queen may lay eggs for as many as 17 years. Ants feed on a variety of foods. Some, such as leaf-cutting ants, feed on a fungus that they cultivate in the nest (on the leaves they bring in). Some ants feed on honeydew (an excretion of aphids) and treat the aphids much like we treat our livestock—moving them from one host plant to another and bringing them into their nest in the winter.

Bald-faced Hornet

Wasps are insects that feed as adults on nectar and fruit juice but capture other insects or spiders as food for their young. The females sting. Some are social, living in colonies consisting of queens, workers, which are sterile females, and males, while others are solitary. Most build a nest of some sort in which the young develop. A few do not build a nest but lay their eggs in nests of other species. Social wasps (yellow jackets and hornets) build a nest of a papery material (mostly chewed-up wood), either in the ground or above ground. Some hornet nests may be a foot in diameter. The larger nests contain several layers of cells surrounded by a strong, water proof, papery envelope. Some consist of a single layer of cells without a surrounding envelope. Social wasps feed their young as they grow largely on insects and spiders which they have first captured and chewed up.

Solitary Wasps nest in the ground, construct nests of mud above ground, or nest in some natural cavity, such as a hollow stem. After constructing a nest, the females go out and capture other insects or spiders (the prey varying with the type of wasp), bring them back to the nest, lay an egg in the nest cell with the food, seal up the cell, and then repeat the process to construct a number of cells. When the wasp larva hatches it feeds on the food provided by the adult. The food has been stung and paralyzed, and usually remains as fresh food in good condition. Many solitary wasps nest in the ground and provision it with other insects or spiders. The prey is sometimes as big as or bigger than the wasp, and consequently there is often quite a battle before the wasp subdues its prey. Mud daubers make nests of mud and provision them with spiders. Aphid wasps use only aphids.

Solitary Wasp

Bees are among our most valuable insects. Without them many garden and orchard crops would not be pollinated and would produce no fruit or seeds. Bees are flower feeders. When they visit a blossom, pollen sticks to their body hairs and is later rubbed off onto the stigma of another flower—more or less by accident as far as the bee is concerned. A bee periodically combs this pollen out of its body hairs, transfers it to a "pollen basket" (usually on the hind legs), and carries it to its nest, where it serves as food for larvae. Bees resemble wasps in their nesting habits but they feed the larvae with pollen and honey instead of insects and spiders. Most are solitary, but a few, such as the bumble bees and the Honey Bee, are social. Social bees feed their young as they grow. Solitary bees construct cells that they provision with nectar and pollen on which the larvae, on hatching, feed.

Honey Bee is one of the few insects man has "domesticated." It was brought to this country by the early settlers and is now widely distributed and very common. Most colonies are in man-made hives. Those that are not are usually built in such sheltered places as a hollow tree or under eaves. The Honey Bee is a very valuable insect, not only because of the honey and wax it produces but because of its pollinating services. It is often possible to increase the yields of such crops as orchard fruits and clover seed by introducing hives of Honey Bees when the crops are in bloom. The Honey Bee has an interesting "language." A foraging bee that discovers a source of nectar comes back to the hive and tells the other bees about it—which direction it is from the hive and how far — by means of a special dance. The kind of flower is communicated by its odor on the bee or in its honey.

Bumble Bee

Honey Bees

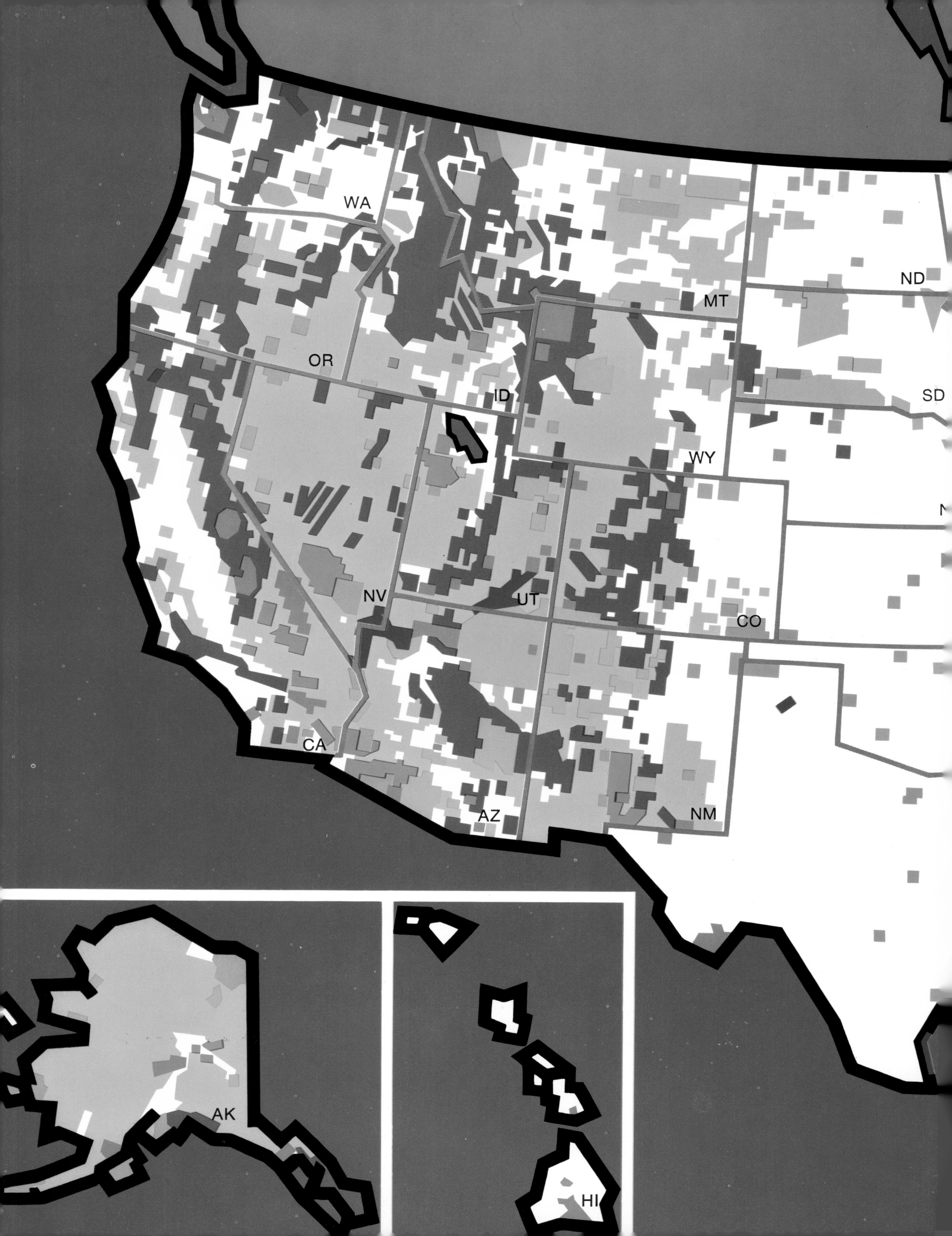
WA
ND
MT
OR
SD
ID
WY
NV
UT
CO
CA
AZ
NM
AK
HI

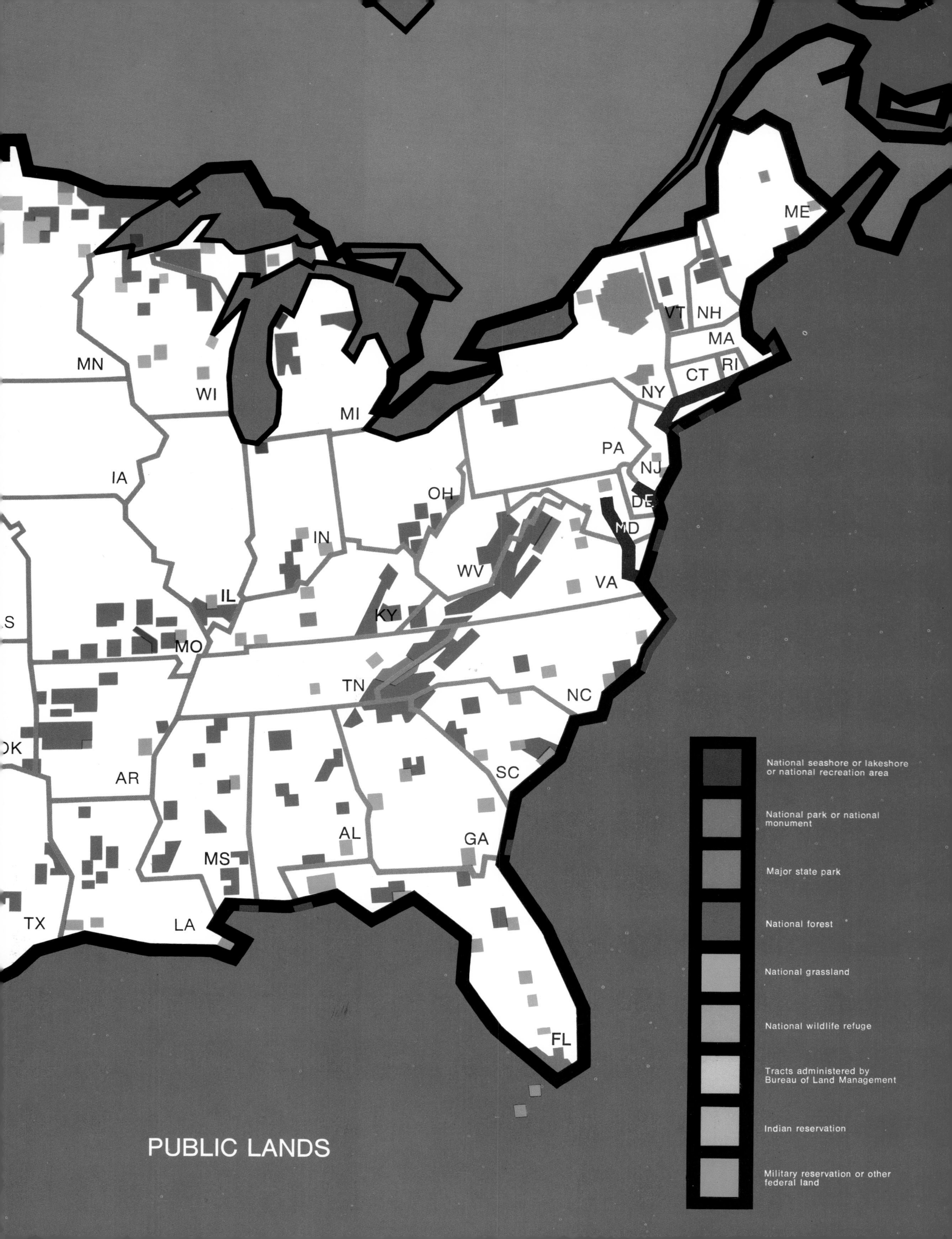

PUBLIC LANDS

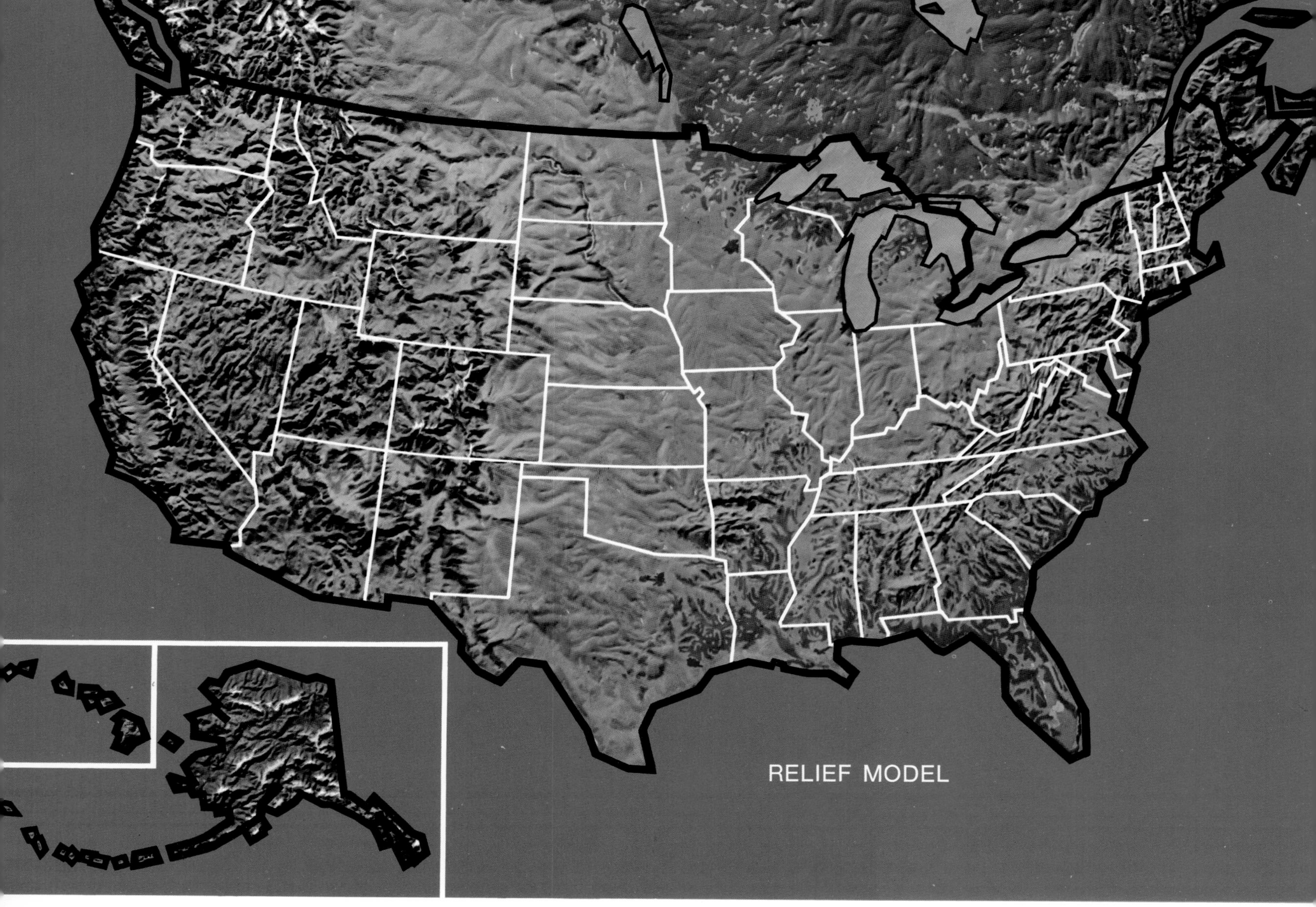
RELIEF MODEL

GLOSSARY

ALPINE the region above the timber line on mountains.
ANTICYCLONE an atmospheric disturbance of high pressure and clockwise (in the Northern Hemisphere) winds.
ATMOSPHERE the thin envelope (about 18 miles deep) of air which surrounds Earth and imposes a pressure of 14.5 pounds per square inch at sea level.
BENTHOS bottom-dwelling, marine organisms.
BIOSPHERE the thin zone of life which surrounds Earth.
BIOTA the flora and fauna of a region.
BLIZZARD a wind storm that swirls up snow.
BOG a wet area dominated by Sphagnum Moss, grass-like plants, and shrubs of the Heath Family. It is usually acid, decomposes slowly, and forms peat.
BUSH a word misapplied to a shrub; it also refers to uncultivated brushlands and wild places.
CALDERA the collapsed summit of a volcanic cone.
CHAPARRAL dense shrub vegetation in a Mediterranean climate, especially in California.
CHRYSALIS (plural, chrysalids) a butterfly pupa.
CONIFER a cone-bearing tree, usually evergreen.
CONGLOMERATE rock made of pebbles and gravel.
CORDILLERA the mountains of western North and South America.
COROLLA the crown of a flower, made up of petals.
COXA (plural, coxae) the basal segment of an insect leg.
CYCLONE a low-pressure atmospheric disturbance, or storm, with anti-clockwise winds in the Northern Hemisphere. Hurricanes are violent tropical cyclones.
DECIDUOUS shedding leaves (or other parts) seasonally.
DIKE molten igneous rock intruded as a vertical slab into other rock and solidified in place.
ECOLOGY the study of the interrelationships of living things and their environment; now often used as a substitute for environment or nature.
ELYTRON (plural, elytra) a thickened wing-cover in such insects as beetles and earwigs.
ESTUARY the mixing zone where salt water and fresh water come together at river mouths, usually behind a barrier island.
FAMILY a category of related living things between Order and Genus. Family names of animals end in *-idae*, those of plants in *-aceae*.
FEMUR the thigh bone of a vertebrate; the first long segment of an insect's leg.
GENUS (plural, genera) a category between Family and species in the classification of animals and plants.
GLACIER accumulated snow that forms ice under pressure and usually flows down its valley.
INVERSION a reversal of the usual atmospheric conditions, wherein a layer of cool air underlies the warmer air (see Lapse Rate). It is most common where clear nights cause rapid radiation and entrapment of cool air in a valley. In calm weather, it may occur anywhere at night. Inversions trap air pollutants and lead to smog formation.
LAPSE RATE the normal decrease of temperature with height, about 3°F. per thousand feet.
LARVA (plural, larvae) the immature, worm-like stage, between the egg and pupa of an insect having complete metamorphosis.
LEVEE a natural river bank caused by overflow and silt deposition. Artificial levees are built atop these.
MARSH a wetland dominated by grass-like plants.
MESOTHORAX the middle segment of the insect thorax, which bears the front wings (if any) and middle legs.
METAMORPHOSIS a change in form during development.
MORAINE unsorted glacial deposits, deposited either as ground moraine, and frontal or lateral moraine, the latter associated with valley glaciers.
NYMPH the immature stage of an insect that does not have a pupal stage but does have simple metamorphosis.
ORDER a large category between Phyllum and Family.
PALP segmented, feeler-like mouth parts of some insects.
PELAGIC living at sea, away from shore.
PHYLLUM (plural, Phylla) the broadest classificatory category within the Plant and Animal Kingdoms.
PLANKTON minute, unicellular or multicellular organisms (plant and animal) that drift in oceans and lakes.
PROLEG a fleshy abdominal leg of a caterpillar.
PRONOTUM the upper surface of the prothorax.
PUPA (plural, pupae) a usually inactive stage, sometimes enclosed in a cocoon, occurring between the larval and adult stages in insects with complete metamorphosis.
SANTA ANA winds of southern California, which, coming off desert plateaus, descend to the coast, dry out everything, and make chaparral fires very dangerous.
SPECIES (plural, species) the basic plant-animal category, i.e., a population of interbreeding individuals.
STALACTITE recrystallized calcium carbonate which forms an "icicle," the result of constant dripping through a limestone cave.
STALAGMITE a column of similar material erected by drip accumulations on a cave floor. Sometimes stalactites and stalagmites meet and form a solid column.
TAXONOMY the science of classifying plants and animals according to their relationships.
TECTONIC the forces which warp the crust of the Earth.
THORAX the middle of the three parts of the body of an insect.
TUNDRA the treeless plains of the Arctic.

PICTURE CREDITS

1. Our American Land
8 Shelly Grossman, Woodfin Camp, Assoc.

2. Rocks & Minerals
20 Shelly Grossman, Woodfin Camp, Assoc.
27 Ed Cooper
28 John H. Gerard
29 John H. Gerard
30 John H. Gerard
Joel E. Arem
31 John H. Gerard
Ed Cooper
32 John H. Gerard (both)
33 John H. Gerard
Shelly Grossman, Woodfin Camp, Assoc.
34 Shelly Grossman, Woodfin Camp, Assoc.
36 John H. Gerard
John H. Gerard
Joel E. Arem
37 Jeff Himmelstein for
Environmental Education Assoc.
John H. Gerard
38 Ed Cooper (Both)
39 Ed Cooper

3. Trees
40 Ed Cooper
48 Albert Squillace
Bill Browning
49 Thase Daniel
Joy Spurr, Bruce Coleman, Inc.
Robert Zappalorti
50 Thase Daniel
Roland C. Clement
Richard B. Fischer
51 Josephine von Miklos
Bill Browning
Richard B. Fischer
52 Ed Cooper
53 Norman Myers, Bruce Coleman, Inc.
54 Thase Daniel (all)
55 Harry Engels
Roland C. Clement
56 Byron Dalrymple
Leonard Lee Rue III
57 John Borneman
Albert Squillace
58 Roland C. Clement
Richard B. Fischer
59 Richard B. Fischer
60 Roland C. Clement
Gene Ahrens, Bruce Coleman, Inc.
61 Richard B. Fischer
62 Thase Daniel
63 Josephine von Miklos
Albert Squillace
64 Albert Squillace
Thase Daniel
Josephine von Miklos
65 Stephen Collins
66 Josephine von Miklos
67 Richard B. Fischer
Albert Squillace
68 Josephine von Miklos
69 Leonard Lee Rue III
Thase Daniel

4. Wildflowers
70 Ed Cooper
79 Thase Daniel
Jeff Himmelstein for
Environmental Education Assoc.
Thase Daniel
80 Roland C. Clement
Paul Schwartz
Ed Cooper
81 Thase Daniel (both)
82 Josephine von Miklos (both)
83 Josephine von Miklos
Richard B. Fischer
84 Thase Daniel (both)
85 Thase Daniel (both)
86 Norman Owen Tomalin,
Bruce Coleman, Inc.
Richard B. Fischer
Josephine von Miklos
87 Richard B. Fischer
Bob Hagel
Josephine von Miklos
88 Josephine von Miklos
89 Harry Engels
Thase Daniel
90 Ed Cooper
91 Ed Cooper
Bill Browning
92 Bill Browning
Richard B. Fischer
Josephine von Miklos
94 Thase Daniel (both)
95 Bill Browning
Thase Daniel
96 Byron Dalrymple
Thase Daniel
97 Josephine von Miklos
Thase Daniel
98 Thase Daniel
99 Harry Engels
Thase Daniel
100 Erwin A. Bauer
Leonard Lee Rue III
101 Thase Daniel (both)
102 Thase Daniel
Josephine von Miklos
103 Thase Daniel
104 James Simon, Bruce Coleman, Inc.
105 Thase Daniel
106 Josephine von Miklos (both)
107 Richard B. Fischer
Thase Daniel
108 Thase Daniel
109 Wendy Watriss, Woodfin Camp, Assoc.
Josephine von Miklos
110 Thase Daniel
Josephine von Miklos
111 Erwin A. Bauer

5. Mammals
112 Harry Engels
120 Leonard Lee Rue III (all)
121 Leonard Lee Rue III
Leonard Lee Rue III
John H. Gerard
122 John H. Gerard
Joe Van Wormer
123 Bill Browning
Bryan Films
124 Leonard Lee Rue III
125 Leonard Lee Rue III
126 Leonard Lee Rue III
Erwin A. Bauer
Joe Van Wormer
Bill Browning
128 Erwin A. Bauer
Dick Rowan
129 Leonard Lee Rue III
Joe Van Wormer
Harry Engels
130 John H. Gerard
Leonard Lee Rue III
Leonard Lee Rue III
131 John H. Gerard
Leonard Lee Rue III
John H. Gerard
133 Stephen Collins
Robert Leatherman
John H. Gerard
Leonard Lee Rue III
Leonard Lee Rue III
Erwin A. Bauer
134 Leonard Lee Rue III
Joe Van Wormer
135 Harry Engels
Bill Browning
Harry Engels
136 Erwin A. Bauer
137 Harry Engels
Leonard Lee Rue III
Bill Browning
138 Bill Browning
Harry Engels
Leonard Lee Rue III
139 Jen & Des Bartlett,
Bruce Coleman, Inc.
Paul D. McLain

6. Birds
140 Bill Browning
145 Alexander Sprunt IV,
National Audubon Society
148 Erwin A. Bauer
Erwin A. Bauer
David Hughes, Bruce Coleman, Inc.
149 Bob Hagel
Joe Van Wormer
150 Erwin A. Bauer
151 Joe Van Wormer
152 Walter D. Osborne
Tony Florio
Harry Engels
Bill Browning
Bill Browning
Erwin A. Bauer
154 Thase Daniel
155 Leonard Lee Rue III
156 Joe Van Wormer
Joe Van Wormer
Jeff Himmelstein for
Environmental Education Assoc.
157 Harry Engels
158 Harry Engels (both)
159 Walter D. Osborne
Harry Engels
160 Bruce Coleman
Erwin A. Bauer
161 Erwin A. Bauer
Bill Browning
Joe Van Wormer
162 Tony Florio
163 Joe Van Wormer
Ron Austing, Bruce Coleman, Inc.
164 Ed Caesar, National Audubon Society
Harry Engels
165 Erwin A. Bauer
Leonard Lee Rue III
166 Joe Van Wormer
Joe Van Wormer
Thase Daniel
167 Leonard Lee Rue III
Byron Dalrymple
168 Leonard Lee Rue III
Bill Browning
Erwin A. Bauer
169 Leonard Lee Rue III
Joe Van Wormer
Harry Engels
170 Jen & Des Bartlett, Bruce Coleman, Inc.
Joe Van Wormer
171 Thase Daniel
Harry Engels
172 Thase Daniel
Robert Leatherman
173 Ron Austing, Bruce Coleman, Inc.
174 Leonard Lee Rue III
Thase Daniel
175 Erwin A. Bauer (both)

7. Reptiles & Amphibians
176 Robert Zappalorti
183 Thase Daniel
184 Shelly Grossman, Woodfin Camp, Assoc.

185 Jeff Himmelstein for Environmental Education Assoc.
Robert Zappalorti
Ed Cooper
186 Robert Zappalorti
Ernest G. Hofmann
Ernest G. Hofmann
187 Robert Zappalorti
Thase Daniel
Ernest G. Hofmann
188 Robert Zappalorti (all)
189 Robert Zappalorti (both)
190 Leonard Lee Rue III, Bruce Coleman, Inc.
Ernest G. Hofmann
191 Robert Zappalorti
Thase Daniel
192 Robert Zappalorti
Jeff Himmelstein for Environmental Education Assoc.
Manuel V. Rubio
193 George Porter
Thase Daniel
George Porter

8. Fishes
194 C. A. Spinage, Bruce Coleman, Inc.
202 Kenneth R. H. Read
S. C. Bisserat, Bruce Coleman, Inc.
203 Karl Maslowski
Allan Power, Bruce Coleman, Inc.
204 Charles F. Waterman
W. T. Davidson, Bruce Coleman, Inc. (left)
Jerry Hout
205 Karl Maslowski
A. J. McClane
206 Erwin A. Bauer
William N. Watkins
207 Marineland, Inc.
J. S. Becket, Fisheries Research Board of Canada (right)
William N. Watkins
208 Milt Rosko
Karl Maslowski
George Lower, National Audubon Society
209 Marineland, Inc.
George Lower, National Audubon Society
Kenneth R. H. Read, Tom Stack & Associates
210 Ed Cooper
211 Jane Burton, Bruce Coleman, Inc.
Al Gidding, Bruce Coleman, Inc.
Thase Daniel
212 Russ Kinne, Photo Researchers, Inc.
A. J. McClane
Jane Burton, Bruce Coleman, Inc.
213 Charles F. Waterman
William Hassler, American Museum of Natural History
214 Karl Maslowski
215 S. C. Bisserot, Bruce Coleman, Inc.
B. E. Johnson, National Audubon Society
216 Ron Austing, Bruce Coleman, Inc.
William Hassler, American Museum of Natural History
217 Frank Puza, American Museum of Natural History
H. W. Kitchen, National Audubon Society
218 Marineland, Inc.
David Stein
219 David Stein
Cy La Tour

9. Insects
220 Robert Leatherman
228 Stephen Collins (both)
229 Walter J. Kenner
Jack W. Wilburn
230 Stephen Collins
Walter J. Kenner
Jack W. Wilburn
231 Jack W. Wilburn (all)
232 Stephen Collins
233 Walter J. Kenner
Jack W. Wilburn
Jack W. Wilburn
234 Stephen Collins
Stephen Collins
Richard B. Fischer
235 Stephen Collins
Walter J. Kenner
A. J. Dignan, Bruce Coleman, Inc.
236 Jack W. Wilburn (both)
Stephen Collins (both)
237 Stephen Collins
Stephen Collins
Richard B. Fischer
238 Walter J. Kenner
Walter J. Kenner (right)
Jack W. Wilburn
239 Walter J. Kenner
Thase Daniel
240 Stephen Collins
Robert Leatherman
241 Stephen Collins
A. J. Dignan, Bruce Coleman, Inc.
Richard B. Fischer
242 J. A. L. Cooke, Bruce Coleman, Inc.
A. J. Dignan, Bruce Coleman, Inc.
243 Stephen Collins (both)
244 Richard B. Fischer
Alexander Klots
245 Richard B. Fischer
Stephen Collins

SUGGESTED READING

Anthony, H. E., **Field Book of North American Mammals.** *New York, G. P. Putnam's Sons, 1928.*

Borror, Donald J., **Introduction to the Study of Insects.** *New York, Holt, Rinehart & Winston, Inc., 1969.*

Butcher, Devereaux, **Exploring Our National Parks & Monuments.** *Boston, Houghton Mifflin Co., 1969.*

Butcher, Devereux, **Exploring Our Natural Wildlife Refuges.** *Boston, Houghton Mifflin Co., 1963.*

Clark, Kenneth M., **Landscape Into Art.** *Boston, Beacon Press, Inc., 1961.*

Clement, Roland C., **American Birds.** *New York, The Ridge Press, Bantam Books, Inc., 1973.*

Collingwood, G. H., and Warren D. Brush, **Knowing Your Trees.** *Washington, D.C., American Forestry Association, 1955.*

Darling, Lois and Louis, **Place in the Sun, Ecology & the Living World.** *New York, William Morrow & Company, 1698.*

Golden Nature Guides, Golden Science Guides, Golden Field Guides, Golden Regional Guides, and Golden Handbook Guides. New York, Western Publishing Company, Inc.

Kenfield, Warren G., **Wild Gardener in the Wild Landscape.** *New York, Hafner Publishing Company, Inc. 1966.*

Laycock, George, **Sign of the Flying Goose.** *New York, Doubleday & Company, Inc., 1965.*

Martin, Alexander C., et al., **American Wildlife and Plants: A Guide for Wildlife Food Habits.** *New York, Dover Publications, Inc., 1961.*

Matthews, William H., III, **Guide to the National Parks, Their Landscape & Geology.** *Garden City, Doubleday & Company, Inc., 1973, 2 vols.*

Peterson, Roger Tory, editor, **The Peterson Guild Guide Series.** *Boston, Houghton Mifflin Co.*

Pettingill, Olin S., Jr., **Guide to Bird Finding East of the Mississippi.** *New York, Oxford University Press, Inc., 1951.*

Pettingill, Olin S., Jr., **Guide to Bird Finding West of the Mississippi.** *New York, Oxford University Press, Inc., 1953.*

Porter, George, **World of the Frog and the Toad.** *New York, J. B. Lippincott Company, 1967.*

Pough, Richard H., **Audubon Bird Guide.** *New York, Doubleday & Company, Inc., 1951, 2 vols.*

Shimer, John A., **Field Guide to Landforms of the United States.** *New York, Macmillan Company, 1972.*

Watts, May T., **Reading The Landscape.** *New York, Macmillan Company, 1957.*

INDEX